TO CLEAR

£1-00 /JS

# With Those in Peril

# With Those in Peril

## A Chaplain's Life in The Royal Navy

*[signature: F Lovell Pocock]*

### Rev. Lovell Pocock
OBE MA RN (Retd)

First published in 1986
© Rev. Frank Lovell Pocock
This edition published in 1989 by
Rev. Frank Lovell Pocock
in association with
The Self Publishing Association Ltd
Lloyds Bank Chamber, Upton-upon-Severn,
Worcs.

A MEMBER OF

© Rev. Frank Lovell Pocock 1989

British Library Cataloguing in Publication Data

Pocock, Frank Lovell, 1908–
With Those in Peril:  The Journal of a Royal Naval Chaplain
during and after the Second World War
1. Great Britain. Royal Navy. Pocock, Frank Lovell, 1908
I. Title
359.3'47

ISBN 1-85421-047-5

Designed and Produced by The Self Publishing Association Ltd
Printed and Bound by Billing & Sons Ltd. Worcester

# CONTENTS

*To my wife Mary*
*and our children*
*who seemed to be constantly*
*in transit*

Eternal Father, strong to save,
Whose arm hath bound the restless wave,
Who bidd'st the mighty ocean deep
Its own appointed limits keep:
O hear us when we cry to Thee
For those in peril on the sea.

# FOREWORD

Foreword to the first edition by
  The Right Reverend S. W. Betts, CBE, MA,
  Bishop to the Forces 1956-1966

The author has been a personal friend for more than 50 years. This diary of a Royal Naval Chaplain's war and peace experiences will appeal not only to his friends, but also to a wider readership; since in addition to accounts of service in the North Atlantic, the escape from Singapore and the Sicily landings, he tells of unusual exploits such as the patrols up the rivers into the deep jungle of the East Coast of Malaya.

Read as a spiritual saga, it encourages one to 'stay the course' as we see how spiritual resources can be mobilised in very adverse circumstances.

As Bishop to the Forces, I found on visiting his stations in peace time the same single-mindedness and effectiveness.

Since leaving the Royal Navy, he has helped country parishes in Hampshire and Kent. Although most of his time in the Service was spent with the Royal Navy, the Fleet Air Arm and the Royal Marines, it is no surprise that he now lives in Deal, the former site of the Royal Marine Depot, where he served three times.

The present micro-chip computer world is very different from that of the time when he was ordained in 1933, by Lord William Cecil, beloved Bishop of Exeter. Now, the same Faith, though more mature, continues to inform his life as he continues to serve Him, Who is the same today and for ever.

Stanley W. Betts.
Bishop.

1985

Foreword to the new edition by
Major General Sir Jeremy Moore, KCB, OBE, MC, Royal Marines

Rev. Lovell Pocock was on his second appointment as Chaplain to our Depot in Deal, Kent when I joined the Royal Marines just after the War. He is a gentle and modest, though active and energetic man and a fine priest. This journal of his service in peace and war reflects that. It also gives some fascinating insights into the turmoil and terror, the dedication and hard work as well as the long periods of inactivity and apparent aimlessness of so many wartime lives. It also illuminates the humanity and faith which Mr Pocock brought to so many of those lives.

1989

Jeremy Moore

# INTRODUCTION

These chapters came to be written practically by accident. My wife and I had been invited out to supper in Deal by some friends. There were two other guests, a man and his wife, both of whom, unknown to us, had been journalists in the House of Commons for thirty years.

During the evening I told them two or three incidents to do with my Naval career.

The man said, "Have you ever put these down on paper?"

I said, "No."

He turned to my wife and said, "He ought to write down accounts of some of his Service Commissions, covering both war and peace. It will take him two or three years. Do you think he can stick it for that length of time?"

She replied, "Yes, I think he can and will."

What follows gives a brief outline of how one Naval Chaplain set about his job and also how the Church functions or doesn't function at sea and ashore, both in war and peace.

The chapters are, of course, personal. Other Chaplains could have made a far better job of the subject. However, they may give the landsman some idea of Church Life in the Royal Navy, the Fleet Air Arm, the Royal Marines and the Royal Marines Band Service. Perhaps I should say that the earlier chapters deal with the war years and the others cover Commissions after the Second World War.

Before I proceed, perhaps I had better state how I came to be a Naval Chaplain. I had been ordained as Deacon into the Ministry of the Church of England in Exeter Cathedral in December 1933 and had my first job in Newton Abbott. I decided after two years there that I would serve the Church in some capacity overseas. I looked at two or three jobs in Australia and Kenya on a Mission Station but they did not materialize.

I was invited to supper in Devonport by the Rev. Percy Dodwell, the Chaplain of HMS *Furious*, an aircraft carrier. I had lived in Devonport and so it was like going home.

After supper the Chaplain took me on a tour of the ship before returning to the Wardroom. There a surprise awaited me. He had arranged for me to meet a party of Officers. They wanted to know why I wouldn't join the Royal Navy as a Chaplain. I really had no reason or reasons for not joining so I said I would volunteer. It meant that I had been press-ganged. The Chaplain told me his Mess Mates were highly delighted that their recruiting methods had borne fruit. Later, in 1985 I heard from a Cambridge friend of mine with whom I had not corresponded for over 50 years. In his letter, he said he had heard that I had been a Naval Chaplain. He went on, 'So you fulfilled your Cambridge ambition to be a Naval Chaplain.' I had completely forgotten this at the time I was being press-ganged in HMS *Furious*.

I joined at Devonport in January 1936 and after two months was appointed Chaplain of HMS *Woolwich*, the Destroyer Depot ship in the Mediterranean. Two and a half years later I was appointed to the Depot, Royal Marines, Deal, in October 1938 where I served as Junior Chaplain and Chaplain to the RN School of Music. I left Deal in July 1939 for the 11th Cruiser Squadron living in HMS *Ceres* and our war station was the Northern Patrol. Then five years later, I returned to Deal; this time as the Chaplain.

During those five years, 1939 to 1944, I had travelled in the four countries of the United Kingdom, including the Isles of Orkney and Shetland. On land, I had visited West Africa twice, South Africa twice, Aden, Ceylon, Malaya, Penang, Singapore, Indonesia, Egypt, Malta, Gibraltar and Sicily during the Sicily Landings of July 1943. At sea, besides being in the Arctic Ocean, I had sailed in the North Atlantic, the Western Approaches, the South Atlantic, the Indian and Southern Oceans, the Arabian, the China, the Java and the Mediterranean Seas. I had come through five years of war without a day's sickness or a single scratch. Three of the ships I had sailed in had been sunk and I had lost my gear three times. So it was with a very grateful and thankful heart that in July 1944 I found myself appointed once again to Deal.

The aim of the Chaplain will be to plant the message and Way of the Cross in the hearts of all those with whom he is serving and to build up the Faith of the faithful into the life of the Church. He probably has about two and a half years with his flock so there is no time to waste or lose.

This particular Chaplain wishes to place on record the tremendous help, support, encouragement and kindness he has received over the years from both Officers and Ratings of the Royal Navy and the Fleet Air Arm, from the Officers and Other Ranks of the Royal Marines and the Royal Marines Band Service, from the WRNS and the Civilian members of Admiralty in the Dockyards and the Naval Bases. Added to this he has had the comradeship, advice and prayers of his brother Chaplains. What more can any man wish for?

*In 1939 the Reverend Lovell Pocock was a very young Chaplain on board HMS Ceres at Scapa Flow.*

CHAPTER I

# The Chaplain's Role

*Part of the diary of the Rev. F.L. Pocock, during his Commission as Chaplain of the 11th Cruiser Squadron, from July 1939 to February 1940. The Squadron consisted of HMS **Colombo** the Flagship, HMS **Capetown**, HMS **Caradoc** and HMS **Ceres**, where he was accommodated.*

It was about 10.30 am on 19th July 1939, stand-easy time, and I was having a cup of coffee with a number of the School of Music Staff in East Barracks, RN School of Music, Deal when the Church Verger, Mr Lyall, arrived.

He said to me, "Mr Ryan (the Senior Chaplain) wants to see you at once". Mr Lyall was a good friend of mine. Since the previous October I had been playing rugger for the Depot Team and Mr Lyall was our touch judge, so he always travelled with us when we had away matches and we got to know each other well. We walked over to South Barracks.

I said to him, "What's it all about? Has my draft come through?"

He said, "I think so, but he didn't say much. Just said I was to get you from East Barracks immediately".

11

*Reserve Fleet Royal Review in Weymouth Bay in August 1939. HM King George VI passes HMS Ceres in his Royal Barge. The ship's company were Pensioners and Reservists and the Chaplain, the Reverend Lovell Pocock, was youngest but one on board!*
*(Copyright - The Associated Press of Great Britain Ltd.- 20 Tudor Street, London EC4)*

On arrival, Mr Ryan handed me the letter he had received from the Chaplain of the Fleet (Venerable Thomas Crick). The letter read, "Regretfully, I am taking Pocock away from you and from the Depot and am appointing him to the 11th Cruiser Squadron. He will join HMS *Ceres* on 27th July". So that was that and I was off again.

I had been sailing on the Norfolk Broads at Easter on a Boys' Cruise and I must have returned to Deal full of it. As a result one of the Company Commanders of the Band Boys in East Barracks, Captain Claude Aylwin and I decided to take six Band Boys on the Broads during the summer leave in August. I had booked the yacht *Ripple Three* for a week through Powells of Wroxham. Then in June Claude Aylwin was drafted to HMS *Penelope* in the Mediterranean, so he arranged for his Company Sergeant Major Carter to take his place. Also we had the six boys chosen and we had the agreement of their parents. Now I had received a draft so I had to cancel the whole thing. It took Claude, myself and Powells about six months to sort out the business side.

About 12.30 pm I went over to the Mess and as I entered someone called out,

"Has the Parson got a draft?"

I said, "Yes".

Another voice said, "Where?"

I said, "The *Ceres* for the 11th CS".

A very old Royal Marine Officer called out, "That means the Northern Patrol in the Arctic; I was there last war".

Everybody laughed except me. I had been at the RN School of Music for nine months and they had been very happy months indeed. Now with war coming over the horizon and getting closer, the Reserve Fleet was being commissioned and all of us young ones in Barracks were being sent off to sea. The day I left, Mr Ryan gave me a little book, called 'My Prayer Book', for men and boys. It was a book we gave to all those who were confirmed at the Depot. In it are written these words. '23rd July, 1939 . . . date of leaving the Depot for the 11th Cruiser Squadron'. During the war, I lost everything twice and nearly everthing three times, including my Bibles and Prayer Books but somehow I managed to keep this little book and I still use it.

When I went to say goodbye to the 2nd I/C, Col. Sturdee, he said, "Cheer up. We all hope that it will only be six weeks boating for the Reserve Fleet and then we shall all be back".

I said that I would like to think so, but I felt we were going to war with Nazi Germany.

The spring and summer of 1939 were anxious times for the nation. Germany seemed to be swallowing up most of Europe while Britain and France did nothing.

When the King and Queen sailed for Canada in the *Empress of Australia* the thoughts and hearts of our people went with them as they began their tour of that great Dominion. They received a tremendous welcome as they journeyed from east to west, but we were anxious to have them back in Britain.

However, before they returned to England, the King and Queen visited the USA at the invitation of the American President, Mr Franklin D. Roosevelt. During their stay, a musical evening was arranged for them by the Department for Indian Affairs. The Department asked Chief Whitefeather to sing a group of songs. He finished by singing, 'I'd rather have Jesus', with words by Rhea Miller and the music by George Beverley Shea. He said the song was his personal declaration of faith in Christ. The last verse was as follows:-

> 'I'd rather have Jesus than silver or gold;
> I'd rather have Jesus than riches untold;
> I'd rather have Jesus than this world's fame,
> I'd rather have Jesus and bear His shame.'

The Queen thanked him and said that the words expressed her own thoughts and that they were the King's too.

Their simple Christian testimony became world news and did us all a power of good.

I spent a night or so with my parents at Teston, Maidstone and then drove down to Devonport with my gear and joined *Ceres* on the evening of 26th July. I had left most of it at Deal, in the hope that we might after all not be going to war. The *Ceres* with the rest of the other Cruisers in the Squadron was lying out in the Hamoaze on the Cornish side. They turned out to be practically empty hulks so the storing in every department had to commence from scratch.

So, here I was! In an HM Ship again off to sea. My Commission in HMS *Woolwich* had seen the confrontation with Italy over Abyssinia at Alexandria, followed by the Spanish Civil War. For the *Woolwich* this meant eighteen months spent either on the east Spanish coast or in Oran, North Africa. Then came the delightful nine months at Deal with the Royal Naval School of Music, when I served under the splendid Senior Chaplain Mr Ryan. Now we were all asking what the future would hold for us as individuals, families, Ships' Companies and a nation.

Nazi Germany was a different cup of tea to Mussolini's Italy. Mussolini himself was known as 'Saw-dust Caesar'. I am sure that the fear of war was greater than the hope of peace. There was no joy whatsoever at the prospect of war. I think there was great sadness. I sensed during my first few days in the ship that although the majority of the men were leaving families behind, there was no flinching from the dreadful prospect and no ducking of the issue. To me, a young Chaplain, it was an impressive, startling and steadying experience to be living and moving amongst these four to five hundred men. They seemed to go about their work and business with confidence and determination, without whining or moaning. Within a few days the Ship's Company were a tower of strength to me and I earnestly hoped that their Chaplain could be the same to them.

Let me describe the Ship's Company. Although I was Chaplain of the 11th Cruiser Squadron of four Cruisers we were so rarely together that, in fact, I became Chaplain of HMS *Ceres* and a visiting Chaplain to the others.

**The Ship's Company** consisted of Officers and Ratings.

**The Officers** included the Captain, the First Lieutenant (there was no Commander in these cruisers), the Gunnery Officer, the Navigating Officer, the Royal Marines Officer, the Doctor, the Chaplain, the Schoolmaster and the Paymaster Midshipman, who were all Royal Navy. The rest were RN Retired, or RNR, or RNVR.

The Paymaster Commander (RNVR) was manager of the Westminster Bank, Liverpool, aged 50, the Engineer was a retired officer, aged 56.

There were stockbrokers, business executives, managers and so on.

The Warrant Officers were RN and retired. A splendid lot!

There was a certain number of RN key Ratings. The majority of the rest

14

were Pensioners, with some RNR and RNVR. The latter included some Newfoundland seamen who could neither read nor write.

The Royal Marines detachment, except for three or four including the Sergeant Major, were all retired. Three older Pensioners in the detachment were commonly called 'The Three Musketeers'. They could often be found when not on duty, sitting together on the deck, quietly smoking and using the bulkhead as a backrest.

Except for the Paymaster Midshipman, who was the Captain's Secretary, I was the youngest man in the ship.

There was no Chapel in the 'C' and 'D' Class Cruisers. We had no ship's Bible, no ship's Prayer-book, no RN ship's store Prayer and Hymn-books, no Hymn cards. Nothing. From the Dockyard I obtained a ship's Bible and Prayer-book, both large, and a number of 'RN Ship's Store' combined Hymn and Prayer-books. I informed the Paymasters of the other Cruisers what they could get and where.

The RN Barracks had no Hymn cards to spare so I went on the scrounge. The Chaplain of the Royal Marines Barracks, Stonehouse let me have two hundred Hymn cards and the same number with nothing but carols on them. These dated back to Queen Victoria's reign, and they were to prove invaluable.

About the third morning, we had the Commissioning Ceremony and I conducted the Service. Later I took the Service in HMS *Colombo*. It consisted of a reading of Scripture and the prayers. We sang 'Eternal Father', followed by the National Anthem, and ended with the Grace.

When possible, weekend leave was granted. For those on board we had a Sunday Service on one of the Mess Decks. Also I arranged Communion on Sundays in some corner of the ship, and in the other Cruisers when possible.

By arrangement with the First Lieutenant we had prayers for the Ship's Company once or twice a week. I seemed to have an appreciative and attentive congregation.

The First Lieutenant had no writer to type out the ship's orders, Daily Orders, Fire Orders, Watch-keeping lists and so on. I heard him discussing his problem in the Wardroom so I volunteered to give him two to three hours each day doing his typing for him in the Commander's Office. I said I would type anything he wanted and we would review my position after a month. We managed to get a ship's typewriter, but until it arrived I used my own. So every day after my own hour for Morning Prayer and Meditation in my cabin, and my daily visit to a different part of the ship, I repaired to the Commander's Office to carry out the First Lieutenant's typing instructions until lunch time. My time there produced unexpected results . . . for me!

My offer of help was much appreciated by the Upper Deck Officers and the Chief and Petty Officers. It meant that a good relationship was struck up straight away between all these people and myself.

I learned the names of nearly all the Seamen Pensioners very quickly and

I also gave some simple reading and writing lessons to the Newfoundlanders, though I never heard whether the Schoolmaster thought I was doing him out of a job!

As the 'Commander's Office' was also the Mail Office, I came into contact with men from every Mess in the ship.

I didn't go ashore often so I spent most of the Dog watches either on the Upper Deck in the Messes or in the Commander's Office. All sorts of people dropped in for a chat. Some of those who came in were ancient seamen who wanted to change their watches for going ashore with other seamen. I used to swop the names around to help them. They never let me down, but it was probably most improper for a Chaplain to do this sort of thing. The Commander's Office was really more use to me than my cabin as it was more or less amid ships, whereas my cabin was aft where men would be less likely to seek me out.

Having joined the ship from Deal, I was always welcome in the Royal Marines Mess. One of their number I knew pretty well. He had recently, until his retirement a few weeks before, been serving at Deal. He had finished his time there, twenty-two years in all. During his last few months at Deal he had the job of marching new Recruits around the Depot for the first week or so, to the Doctor, the Clothing Store, the Church, the Gym, the School and so on. He proudly told the new Recruits that he was finished with it all, that he had a civvy job on Birmingham's buses and that they, the Recruits, were prize fools for joining this outfit. He was only on his buses a fortnight before he was recalled and found himself part of the *Ceres* detachment. As he came aboard the others noticed he had quietened down a bit since Deal. He had spoken too soon!

Within a few days we were at sea, exercising by ourselves and with the Squadron. The Pensioners knew their jobs alright but needed time to adjust themselves to the equipment and to see how everything worked, including the guns and torpedoes.

Early in August the Reserve Fleet anchored in Weymouth Bay. The Fleet included the old battleship *Revenge* and the Aircraft Carrier *Courageous*. It was the last time I saw the *Courageous*. She was sunk a few weeks later. I took a photograph of her while she lay at anchor in Weymouth Bay.

It was August the 9th, I think, that George VI reviewed the Fleet. As he passed up and down the lines of ships in his barge he received a tumultuous welcome from the Ships' Companies. It was a most inspiring and historic occasion. After the review we were out in the Channel, day after day, for the rest of August, exercising with the rest of the Reserve Fleet.

Weymouth itself was a disappointment to the Ships' Companies of the Fleet owing to the enormous crowds ashore. I well remember the weekends. Whether the public realised that this was the last month before war, I don't know, but whenever we went ashore, after a long trip from the ship to the jetty and then a long walk into the town itself, we found it absolutely packed with people. It was almost impossible to obtain even a cup of tea and we often returned to the ship hungry and tired.

# CHAPTER II

# War with Nazi Germany
# September 1939

*The Squadron anchored in Portland Harbour on Saturday 2nd September. On Sunday 3rd September, all Ships' Companies assembled on their Quarter Decks to listen to the Prime Minister's address to the Nation at 11 am. Mr Neville Chamberlain informed us that as the German army had not withdrawn from Poland and in spite of all his efforts we were now at war with Nazi Germany and that we would be fighting evil things.*

We in *Ceres* followed this address with 'Stand-up Church'. For me, a young Naval Chaplain, this Service was to be one of the most moving occasions of my life. We sang the hymns, 'O God, our Help in ages past', 'Eternal Father, strong to save' and finally:

> 'Holy Father, in Thy mercy, hear our anxious prayer;
> Keep our loved ones, now far distant 'neath Thy care.
>
> Father, Son and Holy Spirit, God the One in Three,
> Bless them, guide them, save them, keep them, near to Thee.'

The words were on the hymn cards I had obtained. We had no organ or anything else but it made no difference to the singing. I read a passage of Scripture and then used the Naval Prayers, a Prayer for the Royal Family, the Nation and for our Families. The Lord's Prayer we said together before the Grace. The singing of *Ceres'* Ship's Company echoed back and forth across the harbour that morning. I have never heard the word *'Amen'* uttered from the hearts and throats of five hundred men with such meaning. It was a thrilling experience and quite overwhelming.

After we had finally concluded the Service with the singing of the first verse of the National Anthem nobody moved. No one wanted to. Time seemed literally to stand still. Finally, the Captain looked at me and I left the Quarter Deck. Then came the Order, "Officers fall out. Ship's Company dismiss".

I then went over to *Colombo* in the ship's motor boat, and took their Service, In the other two ships, *Calypso* and *Capetown*, the Captains officiated.

Probably as a result of this Service, I decided to go ashore alone for a long walk so that I could try to think the whole business through. The ship was under sailing orders at four hours notice so going ashore in the 2 pm boat meant that one would return at 6 pm from the jetty at Bencleves.

That afternoon I made my way to the path, inland from Chesil Beach, which has been described as one of the Wonders of the World.

As I walked along, I asked myself questions about The Chaplain, The Parson. What was his place in the ship? When he is suddenly jolted out of the normal routine, 'the daily round and common task', into a national crisis, a personal crisis, in such unexpected circumstances, how is he to react? Here I was, pitchforked with millions of others into a gigantic European war! Here I was, the Chaplain of a ship of the Royal Navy with the possibility of engaging the enemy at any time. What was my job? How was I to function?

The Navigating Officer, the Engineer, the Royal Marines Officer, the Doctor, the Paymaster, the Gunnery Officer, the Chief Petty Officer Bosun, the Captain of the Foc'scle, the Mess Deck Sweeper, the Wardroom Mess-Man, the Corporal of the Gangway, the Ship's Baker, the Shipwright, they all had definite and recognised jobs. The Chaplain doesn't seem to fit in with any of this and seemed to have no recognised place of duty, In this situation, therefore, he has to create the need for himself to be wanted.

I reminded myself that there would be no time, place or respect for the Chaplain if he tried to hide himself behind privilege, dog-collar or rank, even though a Naval Chaplain has no rank. I realised that I had to be natural, sure of my calling and hopeful in outlook. It has long been my custom to read and re-read Chapter 12 of the King's Regulations and Admiralty Instructions which deals with Discipline, Sunday Work and the Chaplain. In fact I knew it by heart. I have no idea who wrote it but he must have been a man of great understanding. How strange that The Chaplain is the first person to be mentioned in this Chapter headed Discipline! Probably the vast majority of the ship's company would put the Chaplain last not first when Discipline is dealt with, if they ever think of him at all! Also, the Chaplain's duties are dealt with in a negative way . . . possibly to help him. Briefly, those in authority are informed or reminded that nothing must be put in the way of the Chaplain fulfilling his Duty to God . . . Praying . . . and his Duty to Man . . . Visiting. He is given no guidance as to how he should fulfil his task, but has to work it out for himself. There is no mention either of Christian Vocation as set out in the Ordination Service, but perhaps this is taken for granted.

The second passage which I also knew by heart is also worth quoting.

'Ye are called to be Messengers, Watchmen and Stewards of the Lord; to teach and premonish, to feed and provide for the Lord's family; to seek for Christ's sheep that they might be saved through Christ for ever.'

Chaplains are sometimes told that they are dealing mostly with agnostic ships' companies. It may be true that there are few thorough Christian believers practising their faith. My short time in *Ceres* led me to believe that if many of them were agnostic in outlook, they were extremely tolerant towards their Chaplain. Far more likely, the vast majority were God-fearing without being committed to Christian practice. The remarkable Service on the Quarter Deck, a few hours earlier bore testimony to that.

So I returned to my ship . . . my parish! In the words of Georges Bernanos in his Diary of a Country Priest . . . "to my dear parish; perhaps my last parish. My parish! The words cannot be spoken without a kind of soaring love . . . I know my parish is a reality and that we belong to each other for all eternity . . . Our Lord saw us all from His Cross." It occurred to me that I might make use of this passage in my next Sunday's sermon. But the eyes of my parish provoked a general smile, and I stopped short in the middle of a sentence with a definite feeling of play-acting! As I climbed the gangway to the ship, I had learned the lesson imparted to me by Georges Bernanos. I would not take myself too seriously, like a keen and earnest young curate who had just been hatched out of the proverbial egg.

As I entered the Wardroom, someone called out, "Here's the Priest; I wonder what he has been up to, ashore and alone for four hours"! Before I had time to answer, one of the older Officers, just back from the East Indies Station, said that before he left, their Parson had put on a Sunday Spectacular. He described this event as follows.

> "There were two Cruisers in the bay, and being Sunday morning both ships had Divine Service at 10.30 am on the Quarter Deck. The weather was perfect, and with the Royal Marines Band playing the hymns, we had a good Service. We finished by singing the first verse of the National Anthem. Then, the Chaplain stepped down from his box, was at the top of the Captain's Gangway and was about to descend. The fans in the aft part of the ship had been turned off during the Service to spare us the continual hum and noise. When the duty Electrician, down below somewhere, heard the singing of the National Anthem he knew that the Service was over. He waited a few seconds and then switched on the fans. The result was a great rush of air up the Captain's Gangway, just as the Chaplain, standing on the top step, was about to descend; this rush of air got under his cassock and surplice and blew them right over his head. To the great astonishment and amusement of the assembled Ship's Company, he had absolutely nothing on underneath! A tremendous cheer rent the air; the poor fellow couldn't see of course, and was in danger of falling headlong down the gangway. He stepped back on to the Quarter Deck, still in

his unique attire. After a good deal of fumbling, he managed to get his cassock and surplice in their proper places once more. He turned to the Captain, bowed and apologised for this extraordinary happening; he then turned to the Ship's company, bowed and apologised to them. This provoked Cheer No. 2. Finally, he went down the gangway, and just before his head disappeared, a very, very red faced Chaplain smiled at the Captain, and then the Ship's Company. This brought forth Cheer No. 3. 'Church' was the main talking point during the following week.

To cap it all, a signal came from the Admiral in the other Cruiser, "Explain intermittent cheering during Divine Service." The Captain sent the following reply, "St Mark's Gospel; Chapter 14; 2nd half of verse 52. "For 'young man' read 'Chaplain' (It reads, "The young man fled from them naked.")

On Monday 4th September in the Commander's Office, I told the First Lieutenant that I felt I should give up being his writer now. By this time he had discovered one, so I turned the job over to the newcomer. Doing this work for the past month had been worth its weight in gold to me, in the way I was accepted by the Upper Deck. The First Lieutenant told me that it looked as if I was going out of the frying pan into the fire as the Captain wondered whether I would be willing to join the Cypher team. I agreed. The Cypher Team consisted of the Paymaster Commander, a Paymaster Lieutenant, the Schoolmaster, the Paymaster Midshipman and the Chaplain. We worked in eight hour watches and so it wasn't too arduous and gave me plenty of time around the ship. Also it was good for me to be part of a team.

In the afternoon, the ship was still at 4 hours notice, so a few of us went ashore to see how the land-lubbers were facing up to war. We were surprised to find a number of shops in Weymouth boarded up, against possible bomb blast. My only purchase was one gramophone record. When ashore in Devonport at the end of July, I had bought a gramophone for 10/-, having already a number of records. When at sea during August and when it wasn't too rough I went for'ard with the gramophone and played the thing either on the Upper Deck or on the Mess decks. I used to be asked for and often the Messes had their own records. There was no piped music around the ships in those days.

The Athenia, about 100 miles west of Ireland, was on her way to Canada. She was carrying children and civilian passengers when she was torpedoed and sunk by a German U Boat. 118 children and adults were lost, including 23 Americans. The children were the first evacuees on their way to Canada and safety! This torpedoing did the Germans no good. A wave of hatred swept the Royal Navy, the country and the world. It woke the Navy up with a start. Now we knew what we were up against and what to expect.

"Children ran screaming for their mothers. Women raced for their children. We saw the bodies of children on the deck and in the water. Other little ones had lost their parents and ran around screaming . The terror increased as shells hit the ship," wrote William Dawson of Glasgow. Two of our destroyers plus the US City of Flint and the motor yacht Southern Cross saved 1300 survivors.

The Squadron was not left in peace long at Portland after the outbreak of war. The first week of September 1939 found *Colombo* and *Ceres* providing cover for convoys from Bristol to Brest, ships were transporting the BEF to France. I think the other two Cruisers, *Calypso* and *Capetown* were doing the same thing, although we did not see them. The next week, *Ceres* covered a convoy to Gibraltar and then returned with another one. The warmer weather made one almost oblivious of the war. However the constant zig-zagging of the convoy and the many German submarine alerts, which meant endless 'Action Stations' kept the whole ship's company awake! It was Sunday 17th September, when we were back in the Western approaches and off the Lizard, that we had our first real excitement. But first of all a word about 'Action Stations' from the Chaplain's point of view.

The normal place for the Chaplain at 'Action Stations' is the Sick Bay. In time of war most ships have two Sick Bays when in action, one for'ard in the proper Sick Bay and the other in the Wardroom, the improvised Sick Bay. The senior Medical Officer is in the For'ard Sick Bay and the junior Doctor and his team in the Wardroom. The very first time we had 'Action Stations', which was soon after we left Portland, the first Lieutenant invited me to join him in visiting every part of the ship. He commenced with the guns' crews on the upper deck and then proceeded to work right through the ship from the bows to the stern, deck by deck, through endless bulk-heads and watertight doors. There were the ammo' parties, the W/T section, various Damage Control parties, Sick Bay parties, ERA,'s Stokers and so on. As I went with him, I had the feeling that the Ship's Company was glad to see the Chaplain going along with him, From my point of view, it meant that I was in touch even in a slender way with the majority of the men on board. Also while the First Lieutenant was talking to the Officer or Rating in charge of the particular party, it gave me time to have a chat with one of the others there. I got into the habit of going with him every time 'Action Stations' was sounded. They were always sounded just before dawn and just before sundown every day and of course when anything suspicious was sighted.

I never overcame the mental shock of the ship's buzzers going off in the middle of the night, when one was in a deep sleep, calling us to 'Action Stations'. It was quite impossible to know whether a German warship or submarine or anything else was being engaged. As most of us slept fully dressed, it was only a matter of tumbling out of one's bunk, half-dazed and imagining all sorts of things, slipping on shoes, and then rushing off to one's Action Station, passing dozens of others probably running the other way.

Another terrifying experience was to be woken up for the Cypher Watch, for the 'Middle' from 12 midnight to 4 am or the 'First' from 4 to 8 am, by the Royal Marines sentry. He wore a thin moustache like a Chinaman trailing down both sides of his mouth to his jaw. He banged loudly on the cabin door, put his head in, shone his torch on his face yelling, "Middle or Morning Cypher Watch Sir. Wakie-wakie" and he was gone. He was commonly known as "Who Flung". The thought of the Buzzers and Who Flung's face still sends a shudder down my back whenever I think of it all, 40 years on!

Security increased at the outbreak of war. Peace time routine died hard and at the beginning, so long as one had a Ship's Pass to get in and out of the Dockyard, no one seemed to bother very much.

Suddenly everything changed. It was while we were in and out of Devonport during the latter part of September and before we proceeded on the Northern Patrol that Security became alive.

One evening I had gone ashore with one of the Warrant Officers to visit a cinema which was showing the film 'Blossom Time', the film version of the play 'Lilac Time'. When we reached the cinema, there were Army Red Caps and Naval Patrols all over the place. A member of a Naval Patrol asked us for our Ship's Passes, which we fortunately had. The Passes were closely inspected before being handed back. In those days, Naval Chaplains had no uniform. The 'dog collar' was his uniform. I also used to wear a trilby. Having a Naval Pass and not being in uniform, caused some further questions, but I was able to instruct them on a Naval Chaplain's rig! Later we found out the reason for the increased security.

We were told that during September, a German submarine had been sunk in Whitsand Bay, just west of Plymouth Sound. The submarine was salvaged, and in the breast pockets of some of the Officers were found ticket stubs of a Plymouth cinema dated September; also one or two railway tickets from Looe to Plymouth. It would seem that some of the German Officers had gone ashore in a dinghy from the submarine, landed near Looe, and then proceeded to Plymouth by train. There they had visited a cinema and later returned the same way. Whether this was true, we never found out, but it made a good story and provided a good excuse to tighten security.

The second possible reason was told to me by a young man who had just passed out as a Royal Marine in August, 1939 after his nine months training.

When war broke out, he joined a party of Royal Marines, who had to keep guard at an ammunition store or dump the other side of Saltash. I think he said there was a Sergeant, two Corporals, and 12 Marines. They were divided into three watches with the Sergeant in charge of one and the Corporals in charge of the others. The sentries did an hour at a time but when they were on at the entrance of the dump or store they were not in touch with the Guard Room.

One morning, while he was on sentry duty, a car arrived with two Officers. One, a Captain, said, "Sentry, I am going to show this Colonel the store". When the sentry asked for their passes, they had none, but the Captain said, "You know me; I have been here many times before". The lad informed the Officers that no one was allowed in without a Pass. It just happened he had not got his whistle and so he was unable to get in touch with the Guard Room. He repeated his instructions and added that if they went on, he would fire. The Officers went back. The sentry rushed to the Guard Room, told the Corporal what had happened, got a blast for not having his whistle and ran back to his post. The Corporal reported the incident to Plymouth at once and the story went round that these people were a couple of spies. The young Marine said that he was very frightened when he stopped these two Officers, but still more frightened when he realised he might have let a couple of spies through. This tale made another very good story, and certainly security was tightened up.

It was during the first dog watch, on 17th September, that I was sitting in my cabin decoding a cypher which had just arrived. I remember so distinctly writing, "*Courageous* torpedoed 100 miles west of Ireland. *Colombo* and *Ceres* proceed immediately to pick up survivors. *Kelly* to take command". I could hardly believe what I had written. I called across to the Paymaster who had the cabin opposite, "Pay, please come quickly and check this cypher; it's urgent." He came at once, checked it and said, "You are right". So we rushed off to the Captain who was on the bridge. There were no telephones in those old cruisers! *Ceres* at once altered course and, in company with *Colombo*, sped off at full speed into the Western Ocean. The dear old ship simply rattled along. It was a perfect evening, warm and still with a gentle swell. We arrived in the area of the sinking about 11 pm, reduced speed and trailed lines over the side for the benefit of any survivors in the water.

There was a merchant ship, stationary and lit up in this area. *Ceres* was following *Kelly* and *Colombo* in a wide circle around this ship. Suddenly it was reported that a torpedo had passed between *Colombo* and *Ceres*. None of us who was on the upper deck saw it but it was a very dark night. A signal came from *Kelly*. "The two very old ladies (i.e. *Ceres* and *Colombo*, both 1917 vintage!) get to blazes out of it and go home." So we set course for Plymouth. Later it was thought that this ship, which turned out to be Dutch, was sheltering a German submarine and had been press-ganged into this business. As neither *Ceres* nor *Colombo* had asdics or life-belts, we were more of a liability than an asset. On the way back *Ceres*, the junior ship of the two, was detailed to stand-by two destroyers which had collided. We had to stand-by until two tugs arrived to take the destroyers in tow. *Ceres'* Ship's Company were not impressed by the seamanship of the destroyers. As they were within hailing distance they were able to tell them what they thought of them. They had the whole ocean to fool around in, and still there wasn't enough room! To say that we were pleased to see first the Eddystone, then Plymouth Sound and finally Devonport Dockyard was putting it mildly.

After our arrival, the Captain put in vigorously for life-belts. 518 Officers and Ratings had been lost when the 22,000 ton carrier was sunk. The majority of *Courageous'* Ship's Company were Pensioners and many were non-swimmers and there were few life-belts. There was considerable disquiet about this. The years before the war had been lean ones for the Royal Navy thanks to the politicians. But time passes, the guilty men are forgotten and Jolly Jack pays the price.

On arrival in Devonport there was 48 hours Leave to each Watch. I went on the first and can remember the day and a half at home at Teston Rectory, Maidstone, after the hectic weeks at sea. I arrived about 5 pm. At 5.30 pm my parents went across the road to the church for Evening Prayer and I went with them. There were a few others present. To me this simple act of Worship, of reading the Psalms for the day, of hearing the Lessons read from the Old and New Testament and then joining in the ancient Collects, was quite overwhelming. It was satisfying and strengthening. I was able to join them again the next evening before returning to Devonport on the overnight train. There was only one person in the compartment at Paddington and he was the Surgeon Lieutenant from the *Ceres* which we joined together the next morning.

The Eleventh Cruiser Squadron's Northern Patrol commenced in September 1939. We left Devonport during the last days of the month when both Watches had returned from leave, after storing and fuelling the ship and taking on board clothing for a winter in the Arctic. I have a vivid memory of the Ship's Company of a Polish destroyer which had escaped and lay alongside us. They were in great spirits and very keen to get into action.

I had returned to the ship after my 36 hours leave, encouraged and strengthened by the spiritual experience I had been through at Teston. Also I was heartened by the knowledge that all over the country, men and women were gathering in countless Parish Churches, Rectories or Vicarages to join in Evening Prayer and to pray for the Nation and the world. This side of the battle went completely unnoticed by the country at large. I was determined to join with this countrywide fellowship, day by day, during the coming months in the Arctic. My parents had told me that they would think of me and pray for me every night at 9 o'clock when Big Ben struck.

The forenoon we sailed from the Haomaze, Devonport, we had prayers on the Quarter Deck and then proceeded through the Sound with the other Cruisers and turned westward for Scapa Flow. We passed Penlee Point, the Eddystone, Land's End, St George's Channel, the Irish Sea, the North Channel, the Minches, Pentland Firth, and then went through the Boom into the Scapa anchorage.

Scapa Flow at this time was not a safe anchorage. A German Submarine (Captain Preen) had managed to enter the Flow, sailing round the north of the Block Ships. She had sunk the Battleship HMS *Royal Oak*, with the loss of about 800 lives. More Block Ships were being brought up to Scapa and placed in position to prevent any further entry by submarines and this operation was still going on when we arrived.

The patrols lasted 6½ days. We went out in the afternoon on the first day and returned during the morning on the seventh day. The 36 hours in harbour proved a welcome break, but there was little anyone could do. The ship took on fuel and stores as necessary. There was a short afternoon leave to each Watch, which at Scapa meant we could pay a brief visit to Kirkwall or play football ashore.

All outgoing mail had to be censored and this was the task of the Wardroom Officers. It had to be handed in the night before the Patrol ended. Even Wardroom Officers put their mail in the Ship's Company post boxes so no one was exempt. Incoming mail was avidly received and read and the Navy at all times made strenuous efforts to see that ships received their mail regularly.

There were of course, no Ship's Laundries in those days and those who didn't do their washing by hand sent off a parcel each week. Many men sent their dirty washing home. Some sent a weekly parcel to Millbay Laundry, Plymouth who had as their motto, 'Don't kill your wives. Let us do the dirty work!' I found them a splendid firm and they never let us down.

It was the custom of *Ceres* to have Prayers on the Quarter Deck immediately we returned to harbour after the Patrol. On Sundays I tried to have Holy Communion somewhere in the ship when we were at sea if it wasn't too rough. We had church either on a Mess Deck or Stand-up Prayers on the Quarter Deck, dependent on the weather.

A large number of the Ship's Company suffered from sea-sickness including myself, and it was some time before any of us got over it. For me, the first three Patrols were very trying and a great test. I began to wonder whether I would ever get over it and be able to stick it. At the beginning of the fourth Patrol we went out from Sollum Voe into a tremendous sea and I was on the Quarter Deck with the Paymaster Commander.

As the ship made her way north, rolling and pitching I said to the Pay, "Pay, I have been ill for three weeks, but I have a feeling that I am cured."

He said, "I too have had a miserable three weeks, but like you I think it is now all over."

It was, for both of us!

Besides the Dawn and Dusk Action Stations, there were the ever constant calls during the day. Numerous ships were sighted, stopped and boarded. The Duty Boat's crew went away in one of the ship's whalers carrying the Duty Officer and an armed boarding party. While this was taking place, *Ceres* kept her distance, with all guns and torpedos trained on the particular

26

ship. This business went on in all weathers. Wireless silence was maintained throughout the patrol and we were blacked out at night. Having no asdics, we were handicapped in locating submarines and all hands were ordered to wear life-belts all the time. By now I knew my way all around the ship and the thing which impressed me was the great bond of friendship which had developed throughout the ship. The Stokers and the Royal Marines spent a lot of time in each others' messes.

I think we did two Patrols from Scapa and after the third one returned to Sollum Voe instead. That was about the 15th October which I think was a Saturday forenoon. Peace-time routine dies hard and being Saturday forenoon, when we returned guns were stripped and cleaned at 11 am. It was a pleasant morning for weather and everybody relaxed after the Patrol and took life in a rather leisurely fashion. Suddenly 'Action Stations' sounded but it was too late! A German aeroplane came over the southern hills, dropped its bombs, which all missed us and *Colombo* anchored close by, and disappeared over the northern hill without a gun being fired. At 2 pm that afternoon Flag Officer Shetland, an Admiral, came over the southern hills in a flying boat. Every gun in the ship and every gun in *Colombo* opened up on the poor fellow! Numerous flares were dropped signifying 'friend'. His aircraft wasn't hit! I heard that the Admiral was deeply impressed by the instant readiness of the two Cruisers!

On the fourth Patrol, our 'beat' was just south of Iceland. We sailed east to west and west to east, for about 200 miles. While on our western beat the seas became so enormous that the Captain decided not to turn the ship round in case she overturned as we went about. So we sailed on and on westwards. Wireless silence was maintained so no one at the Admiralty knew where we were. How far we went I never heard, but we couldn't have been far from Cape Farewell; 'From Greenland's icy mountains'. It was on this patrol that one member of the ship's company was reported missing. It was thought the whole business was too much for him and that he had thrown himself over the side. Another story circulating at the time concerned HMS *Newcastle*, which was somewhere near us. Her Captain had forbidden anyone to go on the fo'c's'le owing to the danger of being caught by the huge seas sweeping on board. A Boy Seaman disobeyed and strayed for'ard. He was swept off the ship, but the lucky young monkey was fortunate enough to be swept back on board and on to the Quarter Deck, where someone was able to grab him before he deserted the ship again for good!

For several reasons Sollum Voe was not considered a safe anchorage and so 'there being no peace for the wicked', we were moved away. After the next Patrol we returned to Loch Ewe, on the west coast of Scotland. This was a magnificent anchorage and could take the whole of the Fleet from Battleships to Destroyers. We entered Loch Ewe for the first time at the beginning of November. Again, we came in on a Saturday forenoon and so remained there until Sunday pm. The weather was fine and warm. We had

Divine Service on the Sunday forenoon on the upper deck and I can still remember the sound of the hymns being sung by the many ships in the Loch echoing round the hills which surrounded us. I think we were all deeply moved by the singing.

It was here that a German submarine laid one of the first nests of magnetic mines. The smaller ships, Destroyers and Cruisers, swept out of the entrance and then came HMS *Nelson* with her deep draught. She touched off this nest of mines and blew up. At least, they made a tremendous hole under her bows. However, the Ship's Captain got her back into the Loch. About 120 sailors had been injured by the explosion. They patched her up and then the dear old Nellie as she was known made 12 knots to Southampton. Her escort was a single Sunderland flying boat as there was such a shortage. She was repaired without the Huns knowing what had happened.

We heard that the aim of Board of Admiralty was to replace the "C" Class Cruisers, which had a very low free board, with liners. Armed Merchant Cruisers had a very high free board. This was because of the enormous seas which swept acrosss the north west Atlantic Ocean.

At about the same time as this transition was to take place, Admiral Raeder, the Commander-in-Chief of the German Navy, ordered the *Scharnhorst* and the *Gneisenau* to 'roll up the enemy control of the sea passage between Iceland and the Faroes.'

*Ceres* had left the Patrol Line just south of Iceland on 20th November and our place was taken by the Armed Merchant Cruiser *Rawalpindi*. The Armed Merchant Cruiser *Chitral* another P & O Liner had also just arrived and was patrolling the west coast of Iceland. *Ceres* proceeded to Sollum Voe to refuel and then returned to the Patrol Line south of *Rawalpindi*. The weather was very bad indeed. On 23rd November, the two German Battle Cruisers *Scharnhorst* and *Gneisenau* had almost broken out into the Atlantic when they came face to face with *Rawalpindi* just south of Iceland. In the dusk, Captain Kennedy of the *Rawalpindi* had time to send the signal "Enemy Battleships sighted" before he was smothered with shells from the two German ships. Although she only had six inch shells *Rawalpindi* sailed away from her mighty opponents firing all the time. She was soon ablaze from bow to stern and after a quarter of an hour of brief, heroic action she sank. *Ceres* was ordered to carry out a Night Torpedo Attack on the German ships but the seas were so great that we made little headway towards them. Newcastle then sighted them and alerted Admiralty.

Then followed a three days 'sweep' by the Home Fleet, Destroyers, Cruisers and Battlecruisers. The French Battlecruiser *Dunkerque* joined in this operation. In this sweep to the Arctic I remember seeing the hills of Norway for the first time and I was instantly reminded of a hymn we used to sing at school, 'Hills of the north, rejoice'. But the only people rejoicing were the Germans, who had slipped through the net and returned safely home.

As a result of the last patrol in tempestuous seas and the ship's efforts to carry out Admiralty orders to close on the two enemy Battle Cruisers, we suffered considerable damage to the upper deck. The three days sweep up and into the Arctic took place in calm seas and icy cold air. Admiralty instructions were that *Ceres* should proceed to Glasgow for repairs and to 'have her boats replaced. They had been swept away in the storms. This news was received with general relief and great satisfaction by the Ship's Company. It meant that we would be in Glasgow for a few days with the opportunity for shore leave.

Our journey south took us through the Little Minches, south-eastwards through the Sound of Mull and Loch Linnhe, southwards through the Sound of Jura, past the Mull of Kintyre and so to the Clyde. It was the nearness of the islands and the narrowness of the Sounds which impressed us. It was late autumn and the hillsides were purple with heather. We all felt that the Navigating Officer did a good job in taking this 5,000 ton Ship at high speed, safely through the Sounds, which to us seemed almost like rapids.

Our first stop in the Clyde was Greenock, where we spent a night alongside. We were allowed ashore to use the telephone with strict instructions *not* to mention the name of the ship or where we were. When my turn came to use the telephone, I rang my parents at Teston Rectory, Maidstone. The lady operator put this call through and my Father answered it.

I heard her say, "Trunk call for you from Greenock, Scotland".

He answered, "Good gracious; he is up there, is he? We thought he was in the South Atlantic and you say he is calling us from Scotland; I can't believe it".

The operator said, "Well, here he is".

Having heard all this I said, "I'm not allowed to tell you where I am. I can't tell you the name of the ship." I went on, "There is little I can tell you. You know now that we are still afloat and you have some idea of our whereabouts".

My Mother came on then and said, "When we think and pray for you at nine o'clock tonight, for the first time for months, we shall know where you are; these few minutes have been the best present and the best moments we have had for weeks and weeks".

We moved to Glasgow the next day and then it was forenoon, afternoon and evening leave for all who could be spared. Two of us went to Edinburgh by train the next day, had a meal, looked round and returned. A lot of telephoning went on from Glasgow and a lot of mail was posted ashore. However, nothing very vital could have been disclosed, and anyway it was all past history. I was continually impressed by the spirit of cheerfulness, comradeship and determination which pervaded the ship when there was so little to look forward to. After four days in Glasgow we set off for the Northern Patrol again, with several cold, dark and bleak months ahead.

The days were very short now, with daylight of a sort, lasting only for the four hours between 10 am and 2 pm. For most of the time we lived in the twilight, in semi-darkness or in the dark. To me it was surprising that there was so little depression in the ship, with nothing but these endless Patrols and what we all realised was to be a long war. It was rather like entering a dark tunnel with no end in sight. Regarding the war itself, which the whole ship's company discussed, we all knew that we were up against 'evil things' and we were determined not only to stick it out, but see the whole business through to a successful conclusion and victory. When we had Ship's Company prayers, I often used the words of Sir Francis Drake's famous prayer.

> 'It is not the beginning, but the continuing of the same until it
> be thoroughly finished which yieldeth the true glory.'

I had come to realise slowly that war between nations, war within nations, whether riots, lock-outs or strikes, fights and feuds between families or individuals, were in every case a hindrance to the establishment of God's Kingdom in the hearts of men. But that must be no reason for not persevering in the Christian Way. So in the midst of international war and with the human problems of the 500 men in this ship living under the most unnatural conditions, my daily prayer must be, 'Thy Kingdom come'; for myself, for the Ship's Company, for the Nation and for the whole world.

The name Aurora Borealis or 'The Northern Lights' comes from Aurora meaning a luminous atmospheric phenomenon, and Borealis meaning Northern. During October, November and December, on clear nights, we were privileged to witness this wonder of nature, this miracle. The whole sky seemed to be aglow and we were told that the lights were due to the electricity originating at the North and in the Antarctic, the South pole. The whole Ship's Company seemed to be mesmerised by this phenomenon and we spent hours on the upper deck getting very cold, watching and gazing at this wonderful sight.

A radio programme which enlivened the Ship's Company came nightly from Hamburg, Germany. This particular programme was put on by an English traitor, William Joyce who was executed in 1945. He broadcast with such an appalling Oxford accent, that he was known nationally as Lord Haw-Haw. His claims of German victories, night after night, were so absurd that there was nearly a sweepstake on what he would claim next. As no one believed a word of what he said there was no need to jam Radio Hamburg.

The Wardroom tables had been fitted with fiddles, wooden frames to take cups, plates, jugs and so on. As a result it meant that in a bad sea, when the ship was pitching or rolling or both, the crockery remained more or less in position. I can still remember the evening of 2nd December.

We were seated both sides of the table and the Senior Engineer, a peace-time Stockbroker, was at the end of the table and back to the door. Suddenly an enormous sea must have hit the ship and sent her into a steep pitch and roll. The crockery was lifted out of the fiddles and landed with the food and drink on the deck. Those of us sitting on either side of the table were thrown into two heaps, with the chairs on top of us. While this was happening the Senior Engineer disappeared backwards, out of the door. He was flung across the flat, smashing the door of the cabin opposite and ended up inside it sitting on the floor.

The occupant of the cabin, a watch-keeper who was asleep, woke up and heard the Senior Engineer say, "I do apologise for barging in"! In the Wardroom the food, the soup, and the tea were slopping about on the floor and remained there for some hours. The same sort of thing happened right through the ship. As all deadlights were closed on leaving harbour at the commencement of a Patrol and remained so until we returned, the stench of stale food, wet clothes, unwashed bodies and stale air filled the ship from end to end.

Our ship's bakery was on the upper deck. As this was awash for several days, the only way out for the bakers and the bread was through a hatch in the roof. Both the bakers were Pensioners so getting them in and out four times a day was a major operation, but they never failed us with their baking. I spent several hours with them while they were incarcerated in the bakery.

It was on this Patrol that a depth charge broke loose and rolled off the stern of one of the other "C" Class cruisers. It went without permission and without anyone knowing! The thing blew up in the wake of the ship and smashed most of the crockery on board. They received an aldis lamp signal from *Ceres*.

"Naughty! naughty! We are anxious to help you, but have no crockery to spare. Feed well."

After lunch one day while on this Patrol 'Action Stations' sounded and news spread that we were under attack from a German Zeppelin which was approaching fast. The Zeppelin came quite close and caused considerable excitement. A vast amount of ammunition was expended by the ackack teams, trying to hit the thing, but without success. The Zeppelin, we heard later, turned out to be a German Barrage balloon which had broken loose from Hamburg. High winds had brought it our way and it was finally brought down in Iceland!

I think it was about 13th December, that in spite of the general gloom and darkness of the days and weeks, the Ship's Company were electrified to hear news of a sea engagement between three of our cruisers, the *Exeter*, the *Ajax*, the *Achilles* (New Zealand) and the German Pocket Battleship, *Graf Spee*, in the South Atlantic. The general excitement, anxiety and suspense continued until the 16th, when we heard that the *Graf Spee* had blown herself up. This victory at the Battle of the River Plate did the ships in the Arctic a lot of good and came at the right time.

31

# CHAPTER III

## Christmas 1939

*Our third Patrol ended early in the morning of 25th December, Christmas Day, and we returned to Scapa Flow once more. This anchorage was now considered safe. Prior to entry the Captain had sent for me at 4 am and said, "It's Christmas Day and we ought to have a Carol Service. Have you any Carol Sheets?" I told him that I had 200 Hymn Cards with nothing but carols on, a relic of Queen Victoria's Navy. They were the ones I had been given by the Chaplain of the Royal Marines Barracks, Stonehouse, Plymouth. The Captain called a meeting of all Heads of Departments and myself on the bridge.*

*There was a blizzard blowing at the time and he said that we would have a Carol Service for the whole of the Ship's Company as soon as possible after our arrival, blizzard or no blizzard, snow or no snow.*

Once the ship was secured, Lower Deck was cleared and the whole Ship's Company mustered on the Quarter Deck. They wore oil-skins in the blizzard while I wore cassock, surplice and scarf. The Service consisted of a Carol; the Prayers, a Carol, the Blessing and the National Anthem. It was a most inspiring occasion and I don't think that anyone present would have missed it. I arranged through the Captain and the First Lieutenant to have the Christmas Communion in the evening. More of that later. But first, there can be no surprises on Christmas Day, even in Scapa Flow.

After lunch our Doctor, the senior Roman Catholic on board, came to me and said, "Padre, I'm drunk! I can't take the RCs at 5 pm. Will you take them for me?"

I said, "Give me the book and I will do my very best for you".

At 5 pm, the RCs mustered in a corner of the ship. I told them that the Doctor was unwell and that he had asked me to conduct their prayers. In those days, the RCs stood very much apart. They were very much Non-Conformists and the Church of England Chaplain was looked upon with a certain amount of suspicion. These *Ceres* RCs were surprised to find me standing in front of them, but they accepted the situation. They had to. It was me or nothing. We all went right through the book and sang 'O come all ye faithful' in Latin! It was a good Service and they all left smiling and the anomaly of the Chaplain taking a Christmas Service for the RCs was not lost on the Ship's Company or the Wardroom.

Later that night, when I entered the Wardroom, the RC's Service was under discussion. One Officer said, "Why can't the Chaplain take them again at say, Easter?"

Some wag replied, "Well, of course he can. All we have to do is get the Doctor drunk again!"

The Doctor who was a dear friend of mine said to me later, "Padre, promise me two things. First, don't tell my Priest that I was drunk, and secondly don't tell him that you took my Service. If you do I doubt if he will ever absolve me".

I told him that there was a move afoot to get him drunk again at Easter so it was beginning to look as if he would be losing his job again. On my side, I dared not tell the Chaplain of the Fleet what I had done.

I was forty years ahead of the times and had managed integration without all the hugging and kissing by the Archbishops, Popes and all the rest of them. A side effect of this RC's Service is worth mentioning. As I have already said they were very much apart from the other denominations in those days. As a result of the Christmas Day Service in *Ceres* any thought of suspicion towards me had vanished and the RCs became some of my greatest allies in the ship.

After lunch, the weather cleared and I took a photo which I still have of all the Officers who had grown a 'set' or beard whilst at sea.

The day was rounded off with fifty or sixty of the Ship's Company attending the Communion Service. It was a deeply moving experience for me. Here I was, except for the Pay-Midshipman, the youngest man in the ship, administering the Sacrament to so many of my dear flock. As I went round the ship after the Service, I found them noticeably quiet, with the majority, I suspect, locked in their own thoughts and with their own families.

> 'O perfect Love, outpassing sight, O light beyond our ken,
> Come down through all the world tonight and heal the
> hearts of men.'

It was nearly the end of Christmas Day at Scapa Flow in the Orkney Isles. When I finally returned to my cabin to turn in it was with a thankful heart, first for Christmas Day itself, second for our preservation as a ship and Ship's Company over the past months, third for the opportunity and privilege of ministering to these fine men and fourth for the love, constant care and affection with which we were surrounded, as shown by the enormous mail which arrived. I have to admit that I felt homesick as I went through all my mail in that tiny cabin. All day long I had had the tune and words of a carol which I had learned as a child on my mind and perhaps they make a suitable ending to this particular Christmas Day in Scapa Flow.

> 'Carol, carol, gaily, carol all the way;
> Christ our loving Saviour, born on Christmas Day.'

Next day in the first Dog Watch, *Ceres* sailed out of the Flow and once more we headed north. There was general satisfaction throughout the ship that we had been in Scapa for Christmas Day. The Carol Service in a blizzard on the Quarter Deck, the evening Communion for nearly 60 of us, the RC's Service, the Christmas mail and the Paymaster's Staff's efforts to give us all a worthy Christmas dinner; all had helped to make the day worthwhile although we were hundreds of miles from home.

This Patrol was little different from the others. Winter gales, short days, everlasting Action Stations at every sunrise and sunset and several times in between. As we headed north past the Faroes, a group of storm-beaten Islands midway between the Shetlands and Iceland, I was reminded of a short poem I had come across, written in these Islands and entitled 'The Church'.

'A band of faithful men, Met for God's worship in some humble room,
Or screened from foes by mid-night's star-lit gloom;
To hear the counsels of His Holy Word, Pledged to each other & their common Lord.
These . . . few as they may be, Compose the Church, such as in pristine age,
Defied the tyrant's steel, the bigot's rage; For where but two or three,
Whate'er the place, in faith's communion met, There with Christ present is a complete Church.'

Pounding north past these desolate islands on our starboard beam I was conscious that the message of the poem applied to *Ceres* too.

This time we were the third ship in the Line south of Iceland. First there was an Armed Merchant Cruiser which had taken the place of the *Rawalpindi*. Second was another "C" Class Cruiser, poor things, and then ourselves. The Patrol passed off uneventfully except for two or three unconnected incidents.

There were two submarine scares. As we had no asdics there was little the Captain could do except have a few depth charges rolled over the stern from time to time to scare the subs away. The other feature of this particular Patrol was a change in the wind from the prevailing south-west to north-east. This north-easter seemed determined to let the rest of the winds know that he was a real Champ! So on the westward beat of the Patrol, instead of having a head-on sea, we had a more or less following one from the north east which kept slewing the ship round. This movement of the ship was very tiring for everyone. But in spite of this movement, the semi-darkness, the stale air, the smell of human bodies, and the same old faces, there was great tolerance, generous friendship and a continual sense of humour.

We returned to Sollum Voe on New Year's Day. There was absolutely nothing except the hillsides and a tanker. As usual we had Ship's Company

34

Prayers on arrival. Also it was New Year's Day so we had a hymn. The Prayers consisted of the hymn, 'O God our help in ages past', a reading from Joshua Chapter one, the Naval Prayer, the Naval Collect, the Lord's Prayer, the Fifth Flotilla Prayer and the Grace.

I very rarely said anything besides the Prayers and reading from the Bible, but on this occasion I passed on to them some words I had learned years earlier.

'Look back with thankfulness; look to the present with cheerfulness and look to the future with hope.'

The spirit in the ship had deeply impressed me during this last Patrol and that is why I included the Fifth Flotilla Prayer.

"Most merciful God, grant, we pray Thee, that we may never forget that as followers of Christ, we are the observed of all men, and that our failures may cause others to stumble, that in a measure God places his honour in our hands.

Help us that we may be true to the best and highest that we know, and that we show forth this truth and loyalty in every activity of our common life.

Grant us the royal gift of courage, that we may do each disagreeable duty at once.

Grant us a keen sense of honour, that we may never give ourselves to the benefit of the doubt, and that we may be specially just to those we find it hard to like.

And finally, we pray for a true sense of humour; may its kindly light and its healing power relax life's tension.

All this, O God, we ask in the *Name of Jesus Christ, Thy Son, Our Lord. Amen.'*

The end of the *Ceres* . . . for me. The next day we were off again and it was while we were on this Patrol receiving the same mixture and medicine from the elements and the sea as before, that we heard *Ceres* was to go to Belfast for a refit. Afterwards *Ceres* and *Colombo* were to proceed to New Zealand for some centenary celebrations. Leave was promised to the Ship's Company on arrival at Belfast and I suppose it could be looked upon as belated Christmas Leave. We felt that after these strenuous months at sea the Leave was well deserved.

As soon as we had docked and then turned over to the Dockyard, most of the Ship's Company proceeded on Leave. It was a long journey for most of us. First a sea passage to Stranraer, followed by the long haul by rail to London. I then went on to Teston, Maidstone. A day or so later I went to London to call on the Chaplain of the Fleet. He informed me that I would be leaving the 11th Cruiser Squadron, and that he was appointing me as the first Chaplain of HM Naval Base, Singapore.

This news was a great blow to me. I had only been nine months with the RN School of Music at Deal from where I was sent off to the 11th Cruiser Squadron. This I could understand, as it was owing to the war. Now after another seven months, I was to be moved again. I protested that he wasn't giving me a chance to do my job properly, and that I considered this second change unreasonable, unsatisfactory and unfair. He was very understanding, took my tirade pretty well and said that he had his problems too. He was a fine Chaplain of the Fleet, and I was very fond of him. We were to meet again, nine years later, when he was Dean of Rochester and when he was staying at Horsey Hall, near Horsey Mere, where we spend our summer holidays.

He said that he had to fill the vacancies and he had to place the RN Chaplains in the key positions. He went on to say that the Singapore Naval Base had expanded very rapidly and he must have an RN Chaplain there and possibly an RNVR Chaplain in addition later. He also told me that the 11th Cruiser Squadron was being disbanded and that he could not afford a Chaplain for the two Cruisers, *Colombo* and *Ceres*, which were going to New Zealand. In fact, they never reached New Zealand. By the time the re-fit was completed and they had reached Singapore, Italy had entered the war and so they were brought back to the 'safe' East African Station, with other "C" and "D" Class Cruisers.

I did meet the *Ceres* Ship's Company again when they called at Singapore, and again in 1942 after the fall of Singapore, when I called on the ship at Capetown on the way home. But that is another story.

The "D" class cruisers were also put on safe stations. However, the *Durban* and *Dragon* came into Singapore in January, 1942 and so became caught up in the real thing. Dragon will always have a secure place in my heart for she took me from Singapore to Indonesia just before Singapore fell to the Japs. So she was my Saviour Ship but that is another story too.

Finally he told me to return to Belfast, collect my gear and get it on board the *Andes,* at Greenock. After that I could continue my leave for a few days and then pick up the *Andes* at Marseilles after crossing France, not yet fallen, by train. So that was that. I left his office very angry and very confused. Naturally, I was disappointed to be leaving my present love, *Ceres.* Possibly it was because we as a Ship's Company had been through so much together and had become so closely knit that I felt almost heartbroken. The plain fact was that I would not be meeting them again. At that moment I didn't know that I would be welcomed on board at Singapore and again at Capetown, two years later.

When I arrived home my parents could see that I was rather down so I told them that I was leaving *Ceres* and being sent to Singapore. We had all heard so much about this impregnable Naval Base, that it immediately began to fill our conversation. They helped me to get a balanced view of things. The immediate problem was to get to Belfast, collect my gear, say

Cheerio to the few of the Ship's Company still on board and move on to Greenock. It was now Tuesday and I decided to leave on Thursday.

During the few days I was at home, and before I went off to the Far East, I looked once again at some notes I had left at home on 'The role of Chaplain'. I suppose the subject has been discussed by successive generations of Chaplains. He has to be, or try to be the 'Man of God' and also 'The friend and adviser of all on board'. This seems positive enough, but does not seem to produce the same results as the Navigating Officer who gets us to the right place at the right time, the Engineer who drives the ship, the Paymaster who produces the food, or the Doctor who heals his patients. In a few words, the Chaplain has to Pray and he has to visit. These I had attempted to do in *Ceres*. The easiest thing for the Chaplain is not to pray. What with Action Stations, rough seas and unpleasant weather, this duty can easily go by the board. I had tried to discipline myself using Morning and Evening prayer as a framework to build on. Even this had been a great struggle at times. Whether I had carried out the Ship's Company Prayer and Services thoughtfully and zealously I cannot say. I hope so. Although there were a number of regular Communicants in the ship and they remained faithful and regular, I didn't manage to build up a 'Church' Fellowship. In this I failed.

In 'the duty to man' being the friend and adviser of all on board, visiting came easier than the Praying, and thanks to the First Lieutenant I literally visited the ship's company at Action Stations, twice a day. This gave me the privilege and opportunity of knowing large numbers of men fairly well. Regarding the Chaplain's task as stated in the Ordination Service in the Prayer Book, 'Ye are called to be Messengers, Watchmen, Stewards, to teach, premonish, feed and provide for the Lord's sheep and to seek out the lost', I fear I failed. Long afterwards, I felt that *had* I been more conscientious, I should have seen something of the fruits of my labours. But in matters of faith and in the things of the Spirit, who is to judge? In wartime it is so easy for the Message and the Person of the Crucified to be pushed into the background. And so possibly the Chaplain's chief task is to keep the Message of God's Love before his flock.

My time in *Ceres* was now behind me, but I had been greatly enriched by living with her Ship's Company under adverse conditions. This experience was indelibly imprinted on my mind. I had learned to value the thoughts and experiences of so many men, who came from a variety of professions and occupations. It had been a humbling experience and an education for a young Chaplain. What the vast number of married men, leaving wives and families, must have suffered is beyond calculation. The separation for most of them was to last for between three and four years.

It was only natural that after these months with my dear Shipmates I could not keep the experience out of my mind, although I had plenty to get on with regarding my next appointment.

I often found myself in mind, standing in front of the Ship's Company on the Quarter Deck at Prayers, watching their faces as either the Captain or one of the Officers read a passage from the Bible. The words of J. E. Rankin's famous hymn, which I learned as a youth were continually on my lips for the Ship's Company.

> 'God be with you till we met again; By His Counsels guide, uphold you,
> With His love securely hold you; be with you till we meet again.'

*Later on in the summer of 1940, HMS Ceres steamed up the Straits of Johore and came alongside one of the docks in the Naval Base. During her time there I was able to arrange outings for members of the Ship's Company to Singapore and also up country in Malaya, where they were entertained by many of the Planters. Many of the Ship's Company I was able to entertain in my small bungalow. They all wanted to come.*

Forms of Prayer to be used at sea are found after the Psalms in the Book of Common Prayer and they seem to breathe a spirit of humility, tolerance and mercy.

In *Ceres* and other Ships of the Squadron in which I conducted Prayers, it was my custom to use the Naval Prayer and the Naval Collect regularly. 'The Prayer during a storm' 'The Prayer before a fight', and 'The Hymn of Thanksgiving' were used as the occasion demanded.

A unique feature of 'Forms of Prayer to be used at sea' is that nowhere else in the Prayer Book is there found 'Prayers for single persons' who cannot join in prayers with others by reason of the fight.

'Sir Francis Drake's Prayer' I made this my own for the future whatever it should hold in store.

> Oh Lord God, when Thou givest to Thy servants to endeavour any great matter, grant us also to know that it is not the beginning, but the continuing of the same until it be thoroughly finished, which yieldeth the true glory; through Him, Who for the finishing of Thy work, laid down His Life, even Our Redeemer, Jesus Christ Our Lord. Amen.

### A Chaplain's Prayer for old Shipmates

> O Eternal God and Everlasting Father, Whose never failing providence watcheth over all from the beginning to the end; keep under Thy protection all those who at any time have been committed to my care; and grant, I beseech Thee, that the ties which may have been formed between us may neither through sin be broken, nor through multiplicity of cares be forgotten; and that whatsoever good I may have

been permitted to communicate to them from Thy Holy Word, may by Thy power bring forth the fruit of Christian living, and in the end Everlasting Life; through our Lord and Saviour Jesus Christ. Amen.

Most of the "C" and "D" class cruisers of World War I vintage went to the breakers yards towards the end of the 1940s.

In the 1950s, the Supply Branch of the Royal Navy moved to Wetherby in Yorkshire and was named HMS *Ceres*. This branch moved to HMS *Pembroke*, RN Barracks, Chatham in the 1960s and later the name *Ceres* was dropped.

During 1984 Admiralty decided to give all the RNR establishments around the country Ships names.

The RNR Communications Centre at Yeadon, Leeds was given the name of *Ceres*. As I had been the last Chaplain to serve in a ship bearing the names of *Ceres* my wife and I were invited to the Commissioning Ceremony and I took most of the Service. I had taken the Commissioning Service 45 years previously in 1939. I felt very honoured to be asked to officiate and to be involved with *Ceres* again. It was a most moving experience.

After the Service, one Rating introduced himself to me and said, "You served with my Grandfather in the *Ceres* in 1939." I said, "Your Father?" He said, "No, my GRANDfather."

I said, "Oh dear" and everybody laughed!

CHAPTER IV

# England to Singapore
# February to April 1940

*My first war-time 'Locum'. 2 Cor. 11.26: 'In journeys often.' France was still with us. Italy had not yet come into the war. The Mediterranean was still open.*
*The Chaplain of the Fleet had informed me of my new appointment as Chaplain of HM Naval Base, Singapore, on the Monday and I had to sail from Southampton the following Saturday week.*
*My problem was how to return to Belfast, Northern Ireland, pack my gear, then get it to Greenock on the Clyde and place it on board the Andes; this done, return to Teston for a few days leave before departing via Southampton and Le Havre for Marseilles where I was to join the Andes for Singapore.*

**Day One. Thursday.**

I left Teston Crossing Halt at 4 pm, on the Thursday in thick snow. My Father saw me off. The whole business was depressing in the extreme. There was 'General Blackout' ruling the nation. The whole country was in the grip of snow and ice while the railway carriages were illuminated with dim blue lights. I caught my connection at Euston and reached Carlisle about 10.00 pm. There should have been a train going west to Stranraer but nothing arrived. Owing to a blizzard no trains came in or went out of Carlisle that night. The Waiting Room was shut at 11.30 pm, so another unfortunate and I spent the night huddled together covered with what clothing we had, sitting on a seat on Carlisle station until 6 am the next morning.

**Day Two. Friday**

At 6 am the Waiting Room opened and we were able to sit out of the wind! Later we managed to get a hot drink and some breakfast. *No trains at all* came through Carlisle either way all day. I was not to know this and so I could not and did not leave the platform just in case a train came in. During the day we saw the Station Master and he arranged to have the Waiting Room left open and to have a coal fire lit for us. During the day I managed, with great difficulty owing to security, to telphone *Ceres* at Belfast and to speak to the Commander. I explained the position and gave him the news that I was unfortunately leaving the ship, that I had to get my gear to Greenock, and that I was stuck at Carlisle.

He was kind enough to have all my gear in my cabin packed and crated. Then he had it all taken to Larne and put on a boat for Stranraer. All this meant considerable work for him and his staff and I was deeply grateful to him for his kindness. He followed all this up with a very moving letter in which he expressed his disappointment at my sudden draft and offering his best wishes for the future. I still have his letter which he needn't of course have written at all and his action was so typical of so many men in the RN with whom I was to serve.

### Day Three. Saturday.

On Saturday morning, wonder of wonders, a train arrived from the south and, as the railway line to Glasgow was still blocked, the driver decided to go to Stranraer. He had no wish to be stranded at Carlisle Station. All this suited me so I hopped in and received a rousing send-off from the Station Staff. By this time I had become one of the family, but homeless! Arriving at Stranraer I found the Larne to Stranraer boat alongside with my gear on board covered with snow. I humped it all ashore myself as there were no porters and put it into the train. Back we went to Carlisle where I now unloaded everything. In fact the Station Staff were most amused to see me return and they did most of the humping for me. It seemed that they now had a Parson permanently on the Staff and I was promoted to their small canteen! There were still *no trains* to Glasgow and so I spent my third night on Carlisle Station, by now well established in the Waiting Room.

### Day Four. Sunday

By this time, I had fallen into a regular routine. After washing and shaving I had breakfast which really set me up for the day. I usually sat by the fire and waited for something to happen. As it was Sunday, I did my best to 'Keep' the day by reading through and meditating over the Collect, Epistle and Gospel for the day from the small Prayer Book I carried with me. This spiritual exercise proved a great help to me. It did much to calm my impatient and frustrated spirit. I realised also that thousands of others, not only in the United Kingdom but across the world, would be reading and thinking over the same passages of Scripture.

Finally, during the forenoon another train arrived from the south and as the main line to Glasgow was still blocked we went via Dumfries reaching Glasgow in the afternoon.

On arrival I took a taxi with all my gear to the Naval Headquarters and unloaded it into the hall. The Duty Commander that Sunday afternoon had known me when we lived in Devonport years earlier, when I was a boy. My Father in those days was the Vicar of St Paul's, Devonport. This Naval Officer had been a member of his Sunday evening congregation and often stayed to supper with us after the Service. I told him what had happened and I asked him how I could get my gear to the Andes at Greenock.

41

He said, "Leave it all to me and I will see that all your stuff is put on board the *Andes*, before she sails. Off you go for your last few days leave. Give my kind regards to your Mother and Father and thank them for everything in years gone by."

I hardly knew what to say. his generous help was quite overhwhelming. First it was the commander of the *Ceres* and now it was the Commander of the Naval Headquarters. What remarkable people I was serving with.

At Glasgow Station, I learned that *no trains* were entering or leaving Glasgow Station that night! So I spent night number four sitting on Glasgow Station. I sat on a seat with others. We had no Waiting Room and no fire! I missed my railway friends from Carlisle.

## Day Five. Monday.

It was Monday forenoon. There were no trains going south and I was getting desperate. I happened to see a train marked 'Edinburgh' and it was beginning to move, so I took a chance and jumped in. At Edinburgh my luck still held! As we pulled into the Station platform the London train was beginning to move out. I jumped out of one moving train, rushed across the platform, jumped into the next and I was on my way to London! Except for waking up occasionally and going along to the restaurant to get something to eat, I slept all the way. Whether the other passengers in the compartment thought I had sleeping sickness, or whether they thought that I was just a lazy Parson who slept all the time, I didn't know, neither did I care.

Fortunately, I was fit and well and didn't even have a headache. It didn't take long to get from King's Cross to Charing Cross. I phoned home to Teston and said that I hoped to be at the Crossing Halt at 2.15 am.

## Day Six. Tuesday

My father was there to meet me, bless him. I can still see him waiting on the platform in cap, mufflers, wellingtons and torch, in the deep snow. We were at home at 2.30 am. I had no heavy luggage, only a little case. Then after a chat with my mother and father, I went to bed to sleep and sleep and sleep. I hadn't been to bed since the previous Wednesday night and it was now Tuesday morning. I asked them to wake me on Thursday morning. That gave me Thursday and Friday, two whole days before I departed on the Saturday for London, Southampton, Marseilles and Singapore.

## Day Ten. Saturday

I suppose that I must have been in touch with Mary's brother, David Cummin, because he came to meet me at Waterloo Junction and see me off. We had a meal together in the Station Restaurant at about 3.30 pm. Rationing was just coming in. When we met after the war he told me that when the waitress came round with the cheese, I said, "Dig in David. No rationing yet. It's on the house."

He came to the train and saw me depart. I thought it was so good of him to come all the way from Norfolk where he was stationed with the RAF just to speed me on my way. We weren't to meet again until 1945 although the ships we were travelling in passed each other at the Cape in 1942. I was on the way home from Singapore and he was on the way to India. When we met in 1945 I was his brother-in-law. Mary and I had married in 1942.

I spent the Saturday night in a 'One Star' Hotel in Southampton. I was thankful and lucky to find somewhere near both the station and the harbour. I had supper in the Hotel restaurant alone and then turned in early. During my Biblical mediation that night I went back in mind to the previous Saturday night which I had spent on Carlisle Station. I also looked ahead to the coming Sunday which I presumed would be spent crossing the Channel and France by ship and trian. We are creatures of habit and I had come to appreciate Sunday and all it stood for. During the past months in the Arctic in *Ceres*. in spite of the enemy, the tempestuous weather and the dark days, we had always kept Sunday. Now I seemed to be all adrift and hoped it would not be long before, in Naval language, Sunday routine would be restored.

After supper I had rung up my parents at Teston, for the last time before leaving England. My days at Teston had been a tonic and I knew that they supported me in their prayers, day by day, as I set off for the Far East and the unknown.

## Sunday February 1940 Southampton to Le Havre in the Amsterdam. Le Havre to Marseilles by train.

I woke early for my journey from Southampton to Le Havre in the *Amsterdam* and on to Marseilles by train. After dressing and getting ready, I decided to mark the day by reading the Collect, Epistle and Gospel for the Sunday and also a verse of Scripture my father had given me on leaving Teston. It was Isaiah Ch. 43; V 2 and the first part of verse 3. It reads thus.

> "When thou passest through the waters, I will be with thee; when thou walkest through the fire thou shalt not be burned; for I am the Lord thy God, the Holy One of Israel, thy Saviour."

We had a very rough crossing and from the state of the ship on arrival at Le Havre it was obvious that the majority of the two thousand men had not only had a very good breakfast, but had brought it all up again! On landing we were herded into three special trains which crossed to the south of France and Marseilles, stopping here and there on the way. Ratings and Other Ranks had strict instructons not to leave the train but of course it was hopeless. I was on the first train and we lost 24 ratings on the journey. I can't speak for the other Services. Most of the 24 joined the other trains which were following. However at the full muster at Marseilles, the RN contingent were seven Ratings short, lost somewhere in France and for all I know they are still there to this day.

During the train journey across France I found myself sitting next to Sub Lieutenant Woolfe. As I had remembered to bring a pocket Chess set with me we spent several hours playing chess. More about him later.

On board the Royal Mail Steam Packet Liner *Andes* the voyage which had commenced at Greenock, now continued from Marseilles to Port Said, Aden, Colombo and finally to Singapore. These ports of call could not of course be mentioned in our mail, owing to censorship. One's mail home was therefore terribly dull. This journey was *Andes'* first as a Trooper and she was still extravagantly fitted out as a luxury liner with coloured menu cards at every meal and special names for the various saloons and bars.

"This ship is the most luxurious affair I have seen in my life and at first I was simply appalled by the sheer extravagance of the whole thing. I hear that there is keen competition on her route and you will know that she plies between England and South America. I am living with another Chaplain, in a £36 a day suite. The large sitting room we have turned into a Chapel. We live in the rest of the suite which has thick carpets, tables, armchairs and book cases. It also has luxurious bedrooms, private bathrooms, three wash basins which we use in turn and there is a Hall of Mirrors. Every now and then I get a fright when I see someone move and discover it is myself. However it is all very delightful. Everybody, including the Ratings and Other Ranks, is astonished at the accommodation, the amenities and the space and so we are all going to make the most if it."

Although the Army usually ran the Troopers, the RN were in charge in this one, possibly because there were so many Naval personnel. After Boat Drill, which took place fairly frequently so that everyone got used to his Boat Station and was able to get there quickly, there was a general meeting of Officers, when we were all allocated our jobs. Besides the Duty Officers, RN and Army, Divisional Officers, Baggage Officers and PT Officers, there were those appointed for Church affairs, Censoring, School, Indoor Games, Upper Deck Games, Swimming, Concerts, Choirs, Debates and so on. There were over two thousand men to be kept occupied. The two Chaplains were asked to take charge of all the censoring of mail and we were given a team to help us. Also we were asked to be responsible for all Church affairs.

While we found the BBC News both dull and boring it was Lord Haw-Haw broadcasting from Hamburg who set the whole ship cheering. Twice we heard the dogmatic announcement that a brave submarine of the German Reich had sunk the Troopship *Andes* with heavy loss of life. Heil Hitler!

Boat Drill took place four times a day and occasionally without warning. Daily inspection of the RN Army and RAF Messes became a routine with prizes for the best.

There were inter-Service competitions for tug-of-war, swimming, running races, obstacle races, table tennis, ludo, deck quoits, chess, draughts and so on. There were also concerts put on by some of the Messes, and some musical evenings. There was a swimming pool which was always well patronised. I don't know whether the water was ever changed but by the end of each day it seemed to have changed colour!

I was appointed the Chaplain for this voyage and my assistant was an RNVR Chaplain, a member of the Australian Bush Brotherhood, Bob Bonsey. He had joined the *Andes* at Greenock and was due to leave us somewhere on route to join his ship, HMS *Gloucester*. He was a simply charming man, so willing and helpful.

We arranged to have Holy Communion in our Chapel twice a week. We said Morning and Evening Prayer daily and for the latter a number of men joined us every evening. Sundays gave us the opportunity of having big Services on the Upper Deck or in one of the many saloons, or both.

We also advertised classes for Christian Instruction, questions, debates on topical religious subjects and so on. We were both surprised at the general interest shown in nearly everything we put on. Jumping the gun a little, much to my regret, Bonsey left us at Colombo and joined the *Gloucester*. She was sunk off Crete and Bonsey was one of those missing. I couldn't have had a finer companion and after he had gone I missed him enormously. Morning Prayer we had usually said alone. We had had long conversations on how we should face our task as Naval Chaplains. In the end, we went back to the King's Regulations and Admiralty Instructions which clearly state that the Chaplain is to be given no executive duty which will interfere with his duty to God, Praying and Preaching and his duty to man, Visiting. What *really* mattered was *how* we carried out these duties. We were to persevere and to persevere more!

I decided to go ashore at Port Said with the chess companion mentioned previously, to go riding. I had told him that when my Father was on the way home from India in 1900, he had ridden a donkey on the sands at Port Said.

He said, "It is now 40 years on, 1940, So let's improve his donkey by getting hold of either horses or camels." We did.

I might add that he and his Father were Directors of a small firm which made small electric organs for Churches and Chapels. With the coming of war, they made mines instead of organs and they were informed that the mines were being sown in and around Jerry's harbours and rivers and that there had been encouraging results!

We managed to hire one horse and one camel; Sub Lieutenant Woolfe took the horse to my great relief, and I mounted the camel. Both animals were led about two miles along the beach by two Arabs who also towed a couple of donkeys. The animals were then turned round and faced home. There was no stopping them. The Sub on his horse hung on for dear life, as the thing galloped beside my camel which loped along at a rare old pace. I managed to keep my hold and was easily first back to the starting line. Although the horse arrived galloping, he was simply no match for my camel. The Arabs returned at a leisurely pace on the donkeys. It was good fun and something to write home about. Letters home were naturally terribly boring because we were not allowed to say where we were, merely that it was getting hotter and hotter.

About six days later, having left Egypt and the Suez Canal well behind, we anchored off Aden. A few hours leave was given. This time I went ashore with my colleague, Bonsey. We hired a taxi and went for a two hour drive into the hinterland. There was little to see except mountains and sand, but we were glad of the break from the daily routine and also to have seen the place.

Leaving Aden, Service Personnel were informed that inoculations would be taking place for one and all, with no exceptions, over the next day or so. We were told that the inoculations were against typhoid and malaria and that our arms would be sore. They were. The ship moved along so quietly and smoothly that I kept forgetting we were moving at all. The whole trip was a great improvement after my Northern Patrol experience. The food was excellent. I understood that there were no complaints from any of the two thousand men aboard.

I never quite became used to my 'suite' or cabin being surrounded by mirrors. All too often I walked across to fetch something and found I had bumped into a mirror. We became used to hearing no news and what little there was concerned the war at sea.

The Naval First Lieutenant invited me to join him on Rounds soon after we left Marseilles and I did so. It became a very useful way of gradually getting to know the hundreds of Ratings on board. The majority of them were bound for Singapore and so I should be seeing most of them again.

At Colombo we were pleased to see several HM Ships in the harbour on our arrival. Most of them sent a small calling party and I discovered one of the visitors had served with me in HMS *Woolwich*. It really was good to meet an old shipmate and he stayed to lunch with me.

My colleague Bonsey left us to join HMS *Gloucester*. She was in harbour and left for the Mediterranean. Sub Lieutenant Woolfe also left us to join his ship, HMS *Mauritius* and she escorted us on the last leg of our voyage to Singapore.

In the Indian Ocean with my colleague gone, I was very much on my own as regards church affairs. This part of the journey was memorable for two days in the Church Calendar.

**Good Friday**

The numbers attending the morning Service on the Upper Deck at the aft end of the ship were simply astounding. Of course there was nothing else to do, but that so many were prepared to attend a Church Service surprised me. The Colonel in charge of the 1250 Other Ranks of the Army told me that he wasn't a great church-goer, but that this particular Service had deeply affected him and, he added, many others too.

## Easter Day

Thanks to the ship's Chief Steward I was able to prepare for the Services in good time.

For the Communion at 7 am and 8 am we had cut up two or three loaves for the bread and he gave me several bottles of his own for the wine. There were I think, about 120 Officers, Ratings and Other Ranks at these two Services.

The main morning Service, which took the form of a shortened Matins with plenty of Easter Hymns, drew several hundred men. I hope that many of them found it a time for commitment and decision as they all commenced their new jobs in Singapore and Malaya. The day was rounded off with large numbers crowding on to the upper deck after dark to gaze at the stars. They seemed so near and that wonderful and remarkable constellation, the Southern Cross, twinkled away into eternity. It seemed to underline all that I had attempted to do that day.

We entered Singapore Roads after dark and the ship dropped anchor at once. There we waited patiently for the next day.

I think we all felt the excitement of arriving at this wonderful city sometimes called The City of Light or The Gateway to the East.

The island had come under British Administration in the 1820s through Sir Stamford Raffles. Today, the most famous hotel in the island is called The Raffles Hotel. The population of Singapore City grew rapidly during the 19th century and by 1940 it had between one and a half and two million inhabitants. The value and importance of the island grew with the building, during the 1920's of the so-called impregnable Naval Base on the north side of the island. With the coming of World War Two the Base now assumed new importance for the whole of the British Empire, especially Australia and New Zealand. *Andes* had brought reinforcements for all of the three Services. My own humble job was to be the first RN Chaplain of HM Naval Base so I was starting from scratch. That night before turning in we went round thanking both officers and crew for bringing us safely to Singapore and for their continual kindness, care and interest in us. It had been a great privilege to have taken passage in this wonderful ship, The Royal Mail Liner *Andes*.

Steaming into Singapore is a memory to be treasured for ever. To me it was one of the most beautiful sights of the beautiful East. As the Straits narrowed the *Andes* passed between the mainland; green with mangrove swamps creeping out into the water; and the islands which seemed to be clad with the rich vegetation of the jungle. As the channel grew narrower and narrower we saw peeping out from the islands, the barrels of the guns,

47

which, we had been informed, would guard this 'Gibraltar' of the East.

Suddenly to those of us on board there seemed to be literally nowhere to go. Then the ship took a sharp turn with trees almost touching her side. We went through into a large bay with wharfs lining one side of the harbour. There were ships of every nation flying every known flag except German. On the other side appeared a long chain of islands.

I think that the hundreds of us lining the upper decks, who had been held spell-bound by this unexpected vision of luxurious vegetation after our weeks and weeks at sea, were surprised to discover that the ship had stopped and was alongside one of the wharfs. It was 9.30 am. Whatever the future held in store for us the experience of the past two and a half hours coming through Singapore Roads into the Harbour, with the beauty of the islands and their green trees and plants, was something which would never fade away. But now it was back to reality, to routine and disembarkation.

CHAPTER V

# HM Naval Base, Singapore
## April to December 1940

*Having disembarked from the Andes, four of us piled into a 15 cwt truck and were driven to the Naval Base at the north side of the island. We travelled the famous 25 miles long Thompson Road round each of its fifty-nine bends. We passed through green, green jungle, such a pleasant change from the English winter we had left behind.*

*When we reported at the Dockyard we were informed that we were not expected and no one knew what to do with us! It was very disheartening and deflating.*

*We were finally allocated a four-roomed bungalow on stilts and I sat down to work out my plan of campaign. Wherever did I begin?*

*The first afternoon I returned to the Main Office and commenced calling straight away.*

The Rear Admiral is in charge of the Base. I introduced myself and he then made two or three suggestions to me. First, he said I should inform the Singapore Cathedral authorities that I had arrived and that from now on I would be responsible for all church matters on the Base. Second, he suggested that I should see the Civil Secretary about the Chaplain's accommodation.

Next, I called on the Captain of the Dockyard. He, I think, was pleased that I had arrived, although he thought that the way I was sent out without anyone being informed was most unsatisfactory. I told him that I was not to blame for that. He asked me to return to see him in about a week to discuss Church Services in the Naval Base Chapel, in the RN Barracks and the one or two Outstations. He wished to discuss arrangements for Divine Service for visiting Ships without Chaplains and finally the opening of a Dockyard School for the children of the Base.

My third call was on the Civil Secretary. Whereas the Captain of the Dockyard is responsible for all naval affairs and personnel under the Rear Admiral, the Civil Secretary is responsible through the Heads of Departments for all the civilian side. I told him what the Admiral had said about accommodation and he said he would do all he could to see that I had a place of my own. However small, I could eat and sleep there, use it as an office and I could invite people to visit me. He added that as my arrival was unexpected it might take a few weeks to get something done.

Before leaving his office, he suggested that I go to the stores and draw a Service bicycle. I did so straight away and rode this contraption back to our communal bungalow. I was greeted by my Messmates with hoots of laughter. They were astonished that I had been able to acquire this machine so quickly. Later, they were only too thankful to have the red bicycle on the premises. It served us well.

When I returned to the bungalow, there was a pile of luggage dumped at the bottom of the steps. I should have had seven trunks, suitcases and boxes, but only four were there.

The Chinese man who was looking after us said, "Driver gone; no more luggage; finish."

I had no idea where the rest might be or who might have it, so I decided to leave it for now. Fortunately, the case containing my books had arrived, so I took out my Bible and Prayer Book and read Evening Prayer, at the same time telling my Chinese servant to make me some tea. The tea and the reading of the Evening Office helped to quieten my restless spirit.

The excitement of arriving in Singapore had evaporated as I realised the extraordinary and pathetic position in which I found myself. I was literally on my own. I knew nobody and it had not occurred to me that a Chaplain was the last person in the world the authorities expected to have on their hands.

*We passed through green, green, jungle, such a pleasant change from the English winter we had left behind.*

There was a telephone in the bungalow so I decided to make two calls.

As it was about 4 pm, I presumed that the Main Offices were still open. I rang the Admiral's Secretary and told him who was speaking. Before I had time to say anything, he told me that the Admiral had discussed my arrival with him and he had decided to send out a General Signal about me. He read it out.

"A Naval Chaplain has now arrived at the Base. From today, he is responsible for all Church affairs and he will be responsible for next Sunday's Church Services. Over the next few days, he will be calling on all

Heads of Departments, Service and Civilian. Departments are requested to give him every assistance as he commences his work as Chaplain. He, the Rev. F. L. Pocock, can be contacted through the Fleet Mail Office. Thank You."

I asked the Secretary to thank the Admiral for helping me to get off to a good start and he told me to let him know how I got on and to drop in to see him if I wanted help or advice as he was on my side. I felt that things were beginning to look up!

The Staff of St Andrew's Cathedral, Singapore, consisted of the Bishop, the Archdeacon, the Dean, and two or three Canons. I explained that I had just arrived at the Naval Base and was the Chaplain.

"Fancy coming at such short notice," he said.

I told him that my appointment had been made over two months ago but if the letter had come by sea mail it might not have arrived yet.

It was quite obvious that the Cathedral enjoyed their visits to the Base so I must see to it that they were invited out occasionally.

Jumping the gun a bit, it didn't take me long to realise that my unexpected arrival had put several people's noses out of joint. Very few people indeed attended the Base Church and its Services and without a Resident Chaplain those who did attend ran the show. So gradually and gently I had to let them know that a Chaplain was in charge.

I thought that I had done enough for one day and as my cabin mates had asked me to join them for tea I accepted thankfully. A small Mess had been opened for us near by with a couple of Chinese to look after us. They congratulated me about the General Signal and we commiserated with each other over our lost luggage. We had all lost some. They offered to find out where it had gone and bring it home. After a lazy evening we all turned in early to the sound of crickets.

To misquote the Scripture concerning our arrival, Genesis Chapter One. verse five.

*"And the morning and the evening were the first day."*

I had already decided that the whole Base should know what the Chaplain did. And when and where. So I let the Main Offices know that I would be at the Base Chapel every morning from 8.30 am-9.30 am - for Morning Prayer and meditation. After that I would be round and about.

I spent most of the time at the Base Hospital with the Medical Staff. They only kept in the Hospital those who were likely to be sick for a day or so. Anyone who was seriously ill was sent to Barhu Hospital just over the causeway in Johore, Malaya, the Singapore General Hospital or the Alexandra Military Hospital in Singapore. Johore was seven miles away, the other two about 18 miles. Also at the Base there was an independent anti-malaria unit composed of a Surgeon Captain and a team of six Naval Ratings who spent their time tracking down mosquitoes. The northern part of Singapore Island was at one time an enormous swamp and a breeding ground for these insects. Malaria had been eliminated and the task of the anti-malaria unit was to keep it that way. They did, and very successfully too.

The Captain of the Dockyard had kindly had an official RN car put at my disposal for paying my calls in Singapore and elsewhere outside the Base.

My first stop was at the Cathedral and I was fortunate to find everybody at home. I met the Bishop, the Archdeacon, the Dean and the Canons. I explained my unexpected arrival and said that although I had now taken over as Chaplain at the Base, I hoped that they would like to come out now and then.

Next I called to meet the Presbyterian Minister, who was the official Free Church and Church of Scotland Officiating Minister for the Base. He visited on the fourth Sunday of each month when I went to an out-station ten miles away, so his routine continued as usual. On Sunday afternoons the Malays and Tamils used the Base Church, so it was in use practically all day.

As I was very short of tropical clothing, the outfitters shop was my next stop. I purchased eight white shirts, two pairs of white shorts, white stockings and shoes. Another six pairs of shorts I intended to have made by a Chinese tailor who lived near the Base. I gave him a pattern and he copied it. Instead of paying £3 in the shops he charged 2/6. I gave him a new pair to copy. A Naval Officer who advised me to do this told me what happened when he had some shorts made by this man. He ordered a dozen pairs and gave him as a pattern an old pair. When he went to collect them he discovered that they had been copied perfectly, including a large square patch on the behind.

I was advised when purchasing a car, to get a saloon and not an open one or a tourer. This was because of the very heavy rain which Singapore experiences for a short time daily. Against the general advice I purchased a tourer and never regretted it. It is hard to describe the feeling of driving at night in an open car in the warm air and under the wonderful tropical skies. I purchased a 9HP Ford Tourer that afternoon. I sent my syce, or Malay driver, back in my official car, and eventually returned to the Base in my own.

I still had a little time left, so I thought I would call on the Resident Medical Officer at the Singapore General Hospital. As I walked down a long, long passage I passed a man very like someone with whom I had sailed the Norfolk Broads in 1939 and with whom I had been at Emmanuel College, Cambridge. I went a few yards, stopped and turned round to have another look. He had done the same. It was him, Dr David Molesworth, now the Resident Medical Officer of the Hospital. We had a brief chat and as he was on an errand he sent me up to his quarters to wait for him.

"I was married just before we came out here. My wife will be back soon for tea. Ask my Malay servant to show you my honeymoon photos," he said.

As I went through the pictures I thought the background seemed familiar but I couldn't place it. When he came up he told me that they had had their honeymoon in Shetland, one of the places I had just come from. For me it was a Godsend meeting the Molesworths and they often came out to see me at the Base. Their flat in the Hospital became a home frome home for me.

During my time at the Base, the Molesworths went up to Kota Baharu, north-east Malaya, to take charge of a Leper Colony. He was taken prisoner by the Japs, and survived. After the Far East War, wonderful to relate, he went back to the Leper Colony and remained there for some years. They now live in Devonshire where I saw them recently. David Molesworth is a UN expert on Leprosy and travels for them, literally all over the world.

The average temperature was about 80° F and the humidity was about the same. It was very hot and extremely sticky. There was about an hour's heavy rain every day which kept everything green with a cool breeze usually following the rain.

By the evening of my first Sunday, I was exhausted, due to the weather, the number of Services and the newness of the whole business. I had an 8 am Holy Communion at the base Church, 9.30 am Morning Service at the Fleet Shore Accommodation, the RN Barracks, a 10.30 am Morning Service at the Base Church and at 6.30 pm Evensong there too.

On Monday evening, we had our first committee meeting. I took the chair. The Captain of the Dockyard came along and several men and women from the Civilian side of the Base.

We arranged Wardens, Sidesmen, Organist, Choir Practice on Fridays, and Sunday School teachers for the children who we hoped might come! A Secretary, Treasurer, Flower arrangers and so on. It all seemed to go off very happily. It was really my honeymoon period.

There is an old saying amongst the Clergy that when one goes to a new job, "The first year you can do no wrong. The second year you can do nothing right, and the third year you can do as you like."

We agreed that on weekdays I should have one Service of Holy Communion and that I should fix the time for early morning, mid-day or evening. Also that whereas I said Morning and Evening Prayer in the Church daily, one evening a week church members should try to join me. Then we could pray for the needs of the world, the Base and our church.

Next day I visited the W/T Station at Kranji, ten miles away and to the south-west of the Base, half way to Singapore. The Commanding Officer there, a Lieutenant Commander, took me round the Station and introduced me to the Officers and Ratings. I met one of his senior Ratings who had caught a number of snakes which he preserved in a bottle of meths. Kranji seemed to abound with these creatures and occasionally the deadly cobras appeared. As the next Sunday was the fourth Sunday in the month, when I was due to come, I arranged the service then and there. I also suggested to the Commanding Officer the day and times I should visit Kranji pastorally.

On Wednesday the Captain of the Dockyard asked me to meet him to discuss the formation and building up of a Dockyard School. First of all we appointed ourselves as the Governors and then set out a few general principles.

I told him that I would like to start it as a Church School with Assembly every morning and regular Christian Instruction given by the Chaplain. There should be regular visits to the Church at the Festivals, the beginning and end of term and on particular Saints' Days. When the time came for us to hand it over to the Service Educational Authorities we would be handing over a Church School with strong Christian traditions. He told me that he had only thought of the present not of the future. He agreed that he would wholeheartedly support me in this idea and it would be a joint effort by both of us. We had two lady teachers in the School already and we were looking for a permanent room.

Commencing this first Thursday, I spent the whole day with the Matelots. We had Prayers at about 7.30 am. I returned to the Base Chapel for an hour and then went back to the Barracks for the rest of the day. I visited the Messes, took lunch and tea with the Officers had a Celebration of Holy Communion about noon, watched or played games after lunch and then swam in the Pool before I returned home.

I decided, for my own benefit, to read again some of the words of Commission to Clergy given in the Ordination Service. The paragraph contained these words.

> "Ye are called to be Messengers, Watchmen, and Stewards of the Lord. To seek for Christ's sheep in this naughty world, that they might be saved through Christ for ever." This means Duty to God, Praying; and Duty to man, Preaching and visiting.

By this time, I had worked out and was following a weekly routine which I tried on the whole to stick to. As I have already stated I was at the Base Church daily from 8.30 am until 9.30 am.

My routine which I had circulated covered the Base, Hospitals and Outstations for the whole week.

The advantage for me in this programme meant that I had something definite to work on. Also the various people knew where I was, or at least where I should be!

Added to my normal duties I was responsible for censoring all the mail from Kranji W/T Station. I did some each day. One of the Main Office Messengers brought the mail up every day and took away all that was ready for posting.

At the beginning of June, I saw the Admiral again, and told him that it was imperative I had a bungalow and office. I had now done between 60 and 70 visits and had nowhere to return any hospitality.

I also saw the Admiral's Civil Secretary and told him the same thing. He was due to return to the UK and I wanted, if possible, to have the matter settled before he went. He was most sympathetic and told me he was determined to get my accommodation fixed. The result of all this was that I was allocated a small bungalow by the end of June, at the east end of the Base near the Mata Gate.

Moving meant an immediate improvement in my life and work. It had been a long wearisome struggle, but now it paid handsome dividends. Others cast envious eyes at my home and wondered why the Chaplain should have a place to himself!

At the rear of my bungalow was accommodation for my Chinese boy, his wife and child. His name was Jock Seng and I couldn't have wished for a better or more loyal servant.

Whenever I had guests he always saw to it that I was well turned out in a white suit his wife had washed. He also made sure that the bungalow was swept and dusted. He appeared clean and smart, and was ultra polite. He waited at table, cooked well and did his best to make the evening a success.

On one occasion he came to me and said, "Master let Jock Seng go to Singapore, three o'clock for wedding."

I said, "Yes."

I discovered that all the boys had asked their masters at our end of the Base if they might go to Singapore for a wedding. The result was that they were quite stupid for about three days!

As I had most of my meals alone I used the time to learn a little Malay. I had a simple book of words and phrases beside me on the table and I tried to learn two fresh words a day. Jock Seng always spoke to me in Malay, except when he wanted something and I tried to answer him in his own language. The result was that before long I could chatter in Malay with the local traders in the village shops in Singapore. The Chinese or Malays then realised at once that I wasn't a Tourist to be fleeced; not that there were many tourists in those days.

I was now living in a small bungalow which was surrounded by a wire fence about three and a half feet high, so I purchased a dog , a wire-haired terrier who became a good companion. She came with me on my parochial visiting. As the Base was five miles long and about a mile wide, with bungalows scattered over the whole area, I started by car and then, having parked it, I did my calling on foot. I took my dog with me and tied her up at the entrance of the bungalow I was visiting. She was a great asset in breaking down barriers for me.

We received about an hour's heavy rain daily and during the monsoon two or three hours, often with thunder and lightning. Afterwards the place was like a Turkish bath and mosquitoes popped up in droves and enjoyed some juicy meals off most of us, I found the climate delightful, especially the evenings which were cool and breezy.

Now that I had my own place, I purchased a secondhand radio which, on the short wave, kept one in touch with world and war news from both sides! I could tune in to London, Berlin, Calcutta, Rangooon, Singapore, Manila, Western Australia, Tokyo, San Francisco, Hong Kong, Colombo, Delhi, Mombassa and so on.

I tried to call on the many ships which came into the Base and I let them have a list of Church Services. In the HM Ships I tried to meet the Chaplain and invite him to my bungalow. I told those who wanted to come ashore that they were welcome whether I was there or not and that they could rest, eat and sleep there if they wanted to. I had rigged up a camp bed in my office. One Chaplain I called on was a bundle of nerves. He seemed thankful to come and told me that he smoked 70 cigarettes a day and couldn't stop. I hope he returned to his ship rested in mind, body and spirit.

As the Chaplain I was put in touch with various Planters up country who welcomed parties of sailors to visit them. These visits were appreciated by both sides, by the Planters and the Matelots.

During May, to my great surprise, *Ceres* arrived in the Base, in company with the *Colombo*. They didn't stay long and soon set sail for New Zealand where they were to represent the UK at their centenary celebrations. Then, with the Italians coming into the war, the celebrations were cancelled and the two ships returned to Singapore Naval Base for two or three weeks.

I can't describe the joy of going on board or the kind of welcome I received. I was able to have several little parties for Officers, for Warrant Officers and for Ratings. Through my contacts a number of the Ship's Company went up country and stayed with Planters for two or three days. *Ceres, Colombo* and some of the other Cruisers which came in, arranged for quite large parties of sailors to spend a few days in Frazer's Hill, the highlands of Southern Malaya.

During their stay I took prayers on board for *Ceres* Ship's Company and for *Colombo* too. I found it a very moving experience being with them again but all too soon they left us for the East African Station.

"We have all been watching the war in Europe closely and anxiously," I wrote in a letter to my parents. "Also we have been stirred by the magnificent efforts of the RAF and the RN to save our soldiers and bring them back home from Dunkirk."

Good old Shakespeare was right when he wrote, "This precious stone set in a silver sea, which serves it in the office of a wall, or a moat defensive to a house against the envy of less happier lands."

"I suppose it is rather a relief to have Sawdust Caesar, Mussolini, and his clowns in the war. These Italians are certainly a nuisance to our

Mediterranean Fleet and they will provide the Nazis with some useful bases. It is generally thought that, nuisance as they are, they provide the comic turn to relieve the strain. We are told that the Italians have fast ships which look nice but that they are, nevertheless, a Fair Weather Navy and "don't put to sea in rough weather"!

We kept the Day of Prayer called by the King in May. It would seem that 'The Miracle of Dunkirk' was God's answer to us. Humanly speaking the Army should never have got away. I took as a text 2 Chronicles, Chapter 7 verse 14; and as a thought, "Prayer moves the power that moves the world." I exhorted our large congregation to join in faith with the whole Empire, in imploring God's mercy and help for the salvation of the British Army. "God moves in a mysterious way His wonders to perform," and he makes us sweat for our victories. The result was "The Miracle of Dunkirk". One outcome of this particular Service was that a number of Dockyard folk, men and women, now came to church regularly.

As a result of the Italians entering the war, we received no more mail via the Mediterranean. Sea mail came via Capetown while an air mail route was being developed East about. This involved a Flying Boat to Hong Kong. From there it went by 'Pacific Clipper', Flying Boat to Vancouver or San Francisco, aeroplane to Halifax or New York, and finally 'Atlantic Clipper' to England.

By August, 1940 we were receiving our first sea mail via Capetown and it seemd to come in batches. We had been reading the end of May and early June copies of the London Times. They included long long lists of the Dunkirk losses, under the headings 'On Active Service' lists. It all made terrifying reading.

Someone arrived who survived 'Dunkirk'. He said the organisation for evacuating the beaches was first class and that once inside the steel boxes, the destroyers, they all felt as safe as houses. He added that the German infantry were, soldier for soldier, no match for ours and that they were 'mostly undersized'.

Johore was just across the Causeway and the State was ruled by a Sultan, who was really a dictator. While there I purchased a few low valued stamps, to send home. The 8 cent one was issued in honour of the Sultan's visit to Europe. Incidentally, while there he 'picked up' a new wife, a Roumanian young lady whom he met in an air raid shelter during an air raid. The rumour had it that she was his one great love. We were also informed that he had a French actress amongst his collection. I suppose they all enjoyed the delights of the romantic East! Many Service personnel, went to Johore for a hair-cut. After the Japanese war had commenced, it was discovered that the barber was a Japanese Colonel. By the time he was rounded up, it was too late. The damage was done and all kinds of Service information had been passed on unsuspectingly in this barber's shop.

During the first month or so, I had signed a number of Visitors' Books.

They included the Governor's, Sir Shelton Thomas; the GOC Singapore, General Bond, who both lived in Singapore: The RN Commander in Chief, Admiral Layton and the Admiral of the Base, Rear Admiral Drew. They both lived on the Base, Admiral Layton in a pleasant house on the Straits of Johore and Rear Admiral Drew further inland. Sir Geoffrey and Lady Layton were regular and faithful members of our Sunday morning Service. These calls had interesting results. The Governor held a Cocktail Party at his Residence on 24th May, Empire Day, with crowds of Singaporeans present who looked down on Service men. They not only enjoyed the party to the full, but sang the National Anthem at the tops of their voices, while at the same time howling about the UK Income Tax, which only applied to the highest incomes. Their social clubs were exclusive and because Service Officers were not often in port, they were given honorary membership. With the coming of war, it was proposed to stop this and make the Service Officers pay in full with an entrance fee too.

There was hardly anything in Singapore for Ratings other than the Missions to Seamen's Hostel. Then there was the expense of getting there. Mrs Drew, the Rear Admiral's wife organised a number of coffee mornings and from the profits bought a bus. As a result any sailor or Royal Marine could get into Singapore for a very reasonable fare.

The General Officer Commanding, General Bond and Mrs Bond had some very interesting people to dinner the night I was invited. I felt I was on show, being the only one present who had been in the war in Europe and at sea on the Northern Patrol.

Sir George and Lady Layton entertained a number of us at a tennis party. They had a couple of pleasant courts right by the water's edge. Some of us were invited regularly to join their tennis parties, which made a nice change for us.

Rear Admiral and Mrs Drew asked some of us to a very early supper party, before taking us off to see the film, 'Gone with the Wind'. It lasted four hours! Several of the Principal Officers on the Base used to have regular tiffin, the local word for lunch, or supper parties and were kind enough to invite me, many of them more than once.

One dinner or supper party remains in my mind. We arrived at 7.45 pm for 8.15 pm. There were eight guests plus the host and hostess.

While the Chinese boy was serving the drinks I heard him say to our hostess, "Missy say, 'dinner for eight' now Missy have ten."

Hostess, "I say eight guests."

Chinese boy. "No plenty chicken for ten."

Hostess. "What can you do?"

Chinese boy, "Boy kill more chicken and cook chicken, quickly, quickly."

Chinese boy looked at the guests and said to our hostess, "Boy give guests plenty, plenty drink."

Hostess, "Boy cook more chicken plenty, plenty quick."

We all had chicken for supper at 10 pm.

One of the things which saddened me was to see Ratings either from the Fleet Shore Accommodation in the Barracks, or the ships in harbour, just wandering around the Base.

One afternoon, I was driving through when it began to rain heavily. I offered a lift to a Petty Officer who was going my way. As he was going nowhere in particular he came to my bungalow to tea with me. As he left afterwards he thanked me and said that he had been in the Base for months and months but this was the first time he had been offered a lift and the first time since leaving the UK that he had been in a private house.

Soon after this we were able, with the help of Dockyard civilans, to form and open a Social Club for both Dockyard personnel and Ratings. This proved to be a real blessing to the Ratings, because they met many Dockyard Officers and their wives at the Club. As a result numbers of Ratings were invited into private homes.

The funeral of a sailor who died in the Alexandra Hospital, Singapore in August 1940 was the subject of a letter I wrote home to my parents. It read "A naval Rating died in the Military Hospital, Singapore, and I was asked to conduct the funeral the next day at 4.45 pm at the Military Cemetery. I arranged for a Royal Navy car to pick me up at 4 pm to take me to the cemetery. The Malay driver took me to the wrong one and at 4.40 pm I was miles away from my appointment. I brow beat this Malay to drive at great speed through the streets of Singapore. He did this most reluctantly. On the way we overtook a Chinese funeral and another hearse travelling alone. I hoped that it was mine! On reaching the cemetery at 4.45 pm exactly, I was met by a Lieutenant who was in charge of the whole funeral, the bearers, mourners and firing squad.

He greeted me with the words, "Where's the body? Haven't you brought it with you?"

I said that I had passed one on the way and that I hoped it was ours.

By the time I had changed and emerged from the vestry the hearse I had passed arrived and we all prepared to process to the graveside where the Service was to take place. I told the bearers, sailors of unequal height; two very tall; two very short, to follow me. We proceeded about 200 yards along the path. Every now and then I turned round to encourage the bearers with not much further, for they were literally floundering along. Their faces dripped with sweat and their uniforms were soggy in a temperature of about 90°F. Then to my horror the undertaker turned left and proceeded for about a 150 yards up a steep incline to the grave. The pace became slower and slower but all the bearers arrived, shouldering their coffin, under their own steam. At the graveside the mourners and the firing party sorted themselves out and we went thrugh the Burial Service. The whole thing went off in good Service fashion and we had all tried to do our best.

When the Service was over the bearers told me that the coffin was very, very heavy indeed and that they were most surprised that one man could be such a weight. On arrival back at the Base, I met a Naval Officer. I was all dressed up in my best white suit and he asked me what I had been doing to be dressed up like this. I told him that I had been taking a sailor's funeral and that all had gone off satisfactorily. I added that the pall bearers had complained about the weight of the coffin and that they couldn't understand how a sailor could be so heavy.

He said, "Did you open the coffin and have a look at the sailor?"

I said, "Of course not".

He was silent for a few seconds and then said slowly, "You are new to all of this aren't you? But you will learn in time. Bodies have been surrounded with loot you know which has been removed later. However, you seem to have had a warm job and besides, "Alls well that ends well'."

What he had said was news to me and I had no misgivings about the whole business. I liked the undertaker who had gone the extra mile to help us. We had all done our best for this matelot especially the bearers under quite difficult cirucmstances. As ever, sailors are very generous to their messmates. The dead sailor's gear was auctioned again and again and the proceeds sent to his next of kin at home. Letters also went from the Ship and from myself. These were followed by a photograph of the headstone and the grave. There was no more we could do.

I read a book called 'Scapa Flow, an account of the greatest scuttling of all time' by Admiral Von Rutter. The scuttling of the German Fleet in Scapa Flow, took place after the end of the First World War in 1919. I never hear the word 'Scapa' or 'Scapa Flow' mentioned without thinking of my Commission in HMS *Ceres* in the winter of 1939/40. The returning from patrol to the Flow, the frost and the ice, the early yet wonderful sunsets, the tramps in the snow, the visit to Kirkwall and its red stone Cathedral, the air raids, the excitement of the arrival of the mail, the Christmas Services with the Carols in a Blizzard on the Quarter Deck and the moving Communion Service on Christmas evening, the Royal Oak buoys, the fisherman's tales and rumours, the barrenness of the Orkneys, the Northern Lights and above all the great friendship and comradeship around the ship all remain fresh in my mind.

This German Admiral, who wrote the book and who detests the English, nevertheless strikes a common cord and puts it far better than I am able to write it down. He writes: "The internment weighed on us all, and what comradely friendship could not give us, and what the hate of the enemy could not rob us of, was the wonder of nature at Scapa Flow. The scenery around us was really harsh and desolate. There was water, mountains, and otherwise nothing. And yet this forgotten corner of the earth had its attractions, its beauty – not by day during glaring sunlight or when rain clouds painted everything grey on grey, but in the evening or by night.

Then it was that the Northern Lights would cast their rays like searchlights over the clouds, and light them to a yellow hue; then again pour themselves over the whole firmament in a single sea of fire. And there were the sunsets, wonderful in their coloured splendour!

It was during a May evening, the sun sank to the horizon at a late hour and all the colour of which it seemed possessed, was poured over the evening sky; the spectacle was overpowering and enchanting. And then, as though this were not of sufficient splendour, the Northern Lights flung their fiery streams into the blaze - the clouds were fired and in their flaming fire rose the dark naked cliffs of the mountains of Orkney. There is yet a God!"

As I read this nostalgic book I was transported back to the tremendous days, nights, weeks and months, when struggling against the enemy, seen and unseen, on the sea, under the sea and in the air: against the gigantic forces of nature, sea, sleet, wind, snow and rain. Against our unnatural living conditions. We were lifted up as by an unseen hand to view the wonders of nature, and they kept us spell bound and sane.

I was reminded of Worsley's remark to Sir Ernest Shackleton after he, with Shackleton and Crean, had marched across and climbed the icy mountains of South Georgia in 1916.

"Skipper," Worsley said as they marched along together. "I was conscious of the footfall of a fourth."

As Nebuchadezzar looked into the burning fiery furnace, he said, "Did we not cast three men into the midst of the Fire?"

They said, "True, O King."

He said, "Lo, I see four and the form of the fourth is like the Son of God."

Sir Ernest Shackleton's experience was the same.

As Henry Lyte wrote, "In life, in death, O Lord, abide with me." This experience of 'The footfall of a fourth' was also ours.

Towards the end of July, David and Rosemary Molesworth asked me whether I would baptise their baby daughter Jennifer. I felt very honoured to be asked, especially as they were well known at St Andrew's Anglican Cathedral in Singapore. They told me that if I was willing, they would make all the arrangements with the Cathedral authorities.

It was a great occasion for the parents and for me too. David and I had overlapped at Emmanuel College, Cambridge in the early thirties, and we had both been sailing on the Norfolk Broads during the Easter vacations. And it was so unexpected to be baptising their baby, Jennifer, in the font of St Andrew's Cathedral. I was a comparative newcomer to Singapore, but the Cathedral clergy were most co-operative. David, Rosemary and Jennifer had a large number of supporters. From my point of view, the baby was perfect. No crying or yelling and there were no hitches. Archdeacon Graham White attended the Service as a guest and he said he had no wish to officiate. We thought it was a generous gesture on his part. When the

Japs took Singapore in 1942, he was interned and died in captivity. After the Service at the Cathedral we all returned to the General Hospital for the Christening tea. During the Service I went back in mind to some of our Emmanuel friends. They included Dr Oliver Bark, Rev. Aidan Chapman, Rev. Lawrence Wright, Dr Jim Scorer and many others. Perhaps I shouldn't have let my mind wander in this way, but I had the feeling that they would have been delighted to have seen David and Rosemary with their baby, and myself performing the Service.

During these months some quite extraordinary events took place in the Base. It was all hush-hush, but quite impossible to camouflage. Some of the world's largest liners slowly steamed up the Straits of Johore and took their places, one at a time, in the huge graving dock. Once there, they were converted from passenger liners, carrying two to three thousand passengers, into troopers which carried about 15,000 troops. No one could fail to see these huge ships steaming up the Straits. They dwarfed the trees and jungle on either side. Unfortunately, I was not allowed to name the ships when I wrote home but can now say that they included the *Queen Mary*, the *Queen Elizabeth*, the *Ile de France*, and the four funnelled *Aquitania*.

Merchant Ships came into the Base regularly, bringing Naval stores of various kinds. Once a week I used to call on them and made many friends. There were always some of their crew at our Church Services and I think they enjoyed this haven of peace. My job was so vast that I never gave them the time or the attention I would like to have done. I am all the better for having met them.

In August another Church of England Chaplain arrived and he told me at once that his appointment was to the Royal Naval Barracks and the Cruisers. He didn't wish to be involved with the Base Church and its routine. I was disappointed at the time as I should have enjoyed his co-operation, especially on Sunday evenings. So we worked as two distinct Parishes and he certainly had plenty to do in the Barracks.

The arrangement worked quite well until he suddenly went off to sea for one, two or three weeks in one of the Cruisers. Then the Commander would get in touch with me saying that the Chaplain had gone and what were the arrangements for Sunday Services and pastoral visiting! So I tried to fill the gap and quite enjoyed a day or so with the Matelots again. I had no ill feelings about the set-up, as I knew he was very much an individualist.

After the Japanese war had started and the Royal Navy was evacuating the Base, he joined a ship. I saw him briefly in Jakarta before he left for Australia. From there he returned to the UK east-about and I lost touch with him. He did a good job in the Barracks and was much liked by the Matelots.

In 196. when in Somerset I called on him. He had a parish a few miles away from Yeovilton, where I was at the time. Later in 1980 I called on him again after his retirement to Dorset.

The Roman Catholic Chaplain for the Base and Barracks arrived at the same time as our RNVR Church of England Chaplain. He asked me if he might come and spend a day or so with me in my bungalow while he had a look round. I provided him with a camp bed in my office and with meals for two or three days. I also took him round and introduced him to the Heads of Departments. He decided to live in Barracks where the Commander fitted him up with a chapel and cabin-cum-office.

After three or four weeks he asked if he could come to supper and spend the evening with me discussing his work. I felt rather sorry for him. He said he had about half a dozen enthusiastic families in the Dockyard and a number of Ratings in the Barracks and the Ships which come and go. He said that he couldn't go calling on them all the time. I suggested that he went off to sea in a Cruiser for a week or so now and then, which he did. I also told him that he was appointed to look after his flock, whether many or few, and that when living in the FSA his Christian influence was all to the good. Regarding visiting. I said to him, "I am still calling and am not halfway round for the first time yet!"

# CHAPTER VI

## Extracts from letters home to my parents

*I wrote a great many letters home during the time I spent in Singapore. They all had to be censored of course but at least they were able to give my parents some impression of the kind of life we led. It was a great comfort to be able to talk to someone not involved with our war and the letters were to prove a great aid to my memory in later years as they were all waiting for me to read again when I finally returned home.*

**September 2nd 1940**

(My sister) Polly has arrived from Shanghai and started work at the Army's Alexandra Hospital in Singapore. She has come down with several other army nursing sisters and I think they are all glad to be here as Shanghai has become rather cut off. I went into town to see her and took her to the Singapore Swimming Club where we had tea with Dr David and Rosemary Molesworth. They invited her to their flat in the General Hospital so she now has one contact outside her job. She is on a two-year commission so should return home in early 1942. I hope to see her every couple of weeks till then.

**September 9th 1940**

The Molesworths came to supper with me and brought Polly. She was astonished at the length of the Base and the General layout of the place. She liked my bungalow although she found it rather spartan and masculine but was impressed by its neatness. I was quite flattered. Jock Seng provided his usual splendid meal and was all attention to my guests. They left at about 10.30 pm and returned via the Thompson Road and all its fifty-nine bends. Polly phoned to thank me for the evening and said that Rosemary had offered to take her shopping. I can't think why she wants to go out shopping when she has full board and lodging and 'all in' accommodation. They have offered to bring her to church sometimes too, and can all stay to lunch afterwards.

**September 16th 1940**

All your sea mail letters, which I notice you have numbered, have arrived safely. At least no numbers are missing so far. As they all come via the Cape, it speaks well for our command of the seas and oceans.

## September 20th 1940

We in the Royal Navy had our first rugger match last week against the RAF Command. Our pitch is delightfully situated just by the straits of Johore. Nearby are the tennis courts and open-air swimming pool. As it rains every day the green pitch is in splended condition. Thanks to the practice we have had over the past two or three weeks, the RN team were in splendid condition physically, with the result that we thrashed our opponents through sheer speed and fitness. I am playing on the wing for the RN at the moment. The match produced tremendous excitement and practically the whole Barracks turned out to cheer us on. I suppose a rugger match is a change from the everlasting sameness of the life here. After the match we had to shower to remove the mud before a dip in the swimming pool. It all seems too good to be true.

## September 28th 1940

The RN Rugger Team is now know as 'Royal Navy, Malaya'. It sounds rather grand but it is the same team.

Our next opponents were the Sappers of Singapore Island. They came with a great reputation and rather fancied themselves but once again our training and speed meant that they were soundly thrashed. There were crowds of supporters for both teams and with tumultuous cheering there was a real 'Cup-Tie' atmosphere.

*During my time as a member (and sometimes as Captain) of the rugger team, called 'Royal Navy Malaya', we had as members Lt.Cdr, (S) Harry Lehmann of HMS Sultan and Lt.Cdr Wallace Kemp of HMS Stronghold. The latter was a survivor of a ship sunk by the Japanese. He spent 3½ years as a Japanese POW in Sumatra . . . and survived.*

*Today, Harry Lehmann is a Lay Reader at a church in Denmead, and Wallace Kemp is a Churchwarden at Lustleigh in Devonshire. Well done, Sirs.*

I love the continual warm weather. It is so easy to get up in the morning. The rig is shorts and open neck shirts all day. No frosts and no chilblains although I have to admit that I miss the nip in the air which we get in September and October at home.

We have about 12 hours of darkness out here, approximately from 6 pm until 6 am. At night the sky is very clear. The stars appear to be white and very near. I usually spend some time gazing at them before I turn in. The Plough appears upside down. Orion is well up while the Southern Cross stands out clearly. The Monsoon broke in July which means more rain than usual, occasional storms and great humidity. During these weeks it is just as if someone had taken out the plug 'upstairs' as the water seems to come down in a solid mass or lump.

## October 2nd 1940

On Sunday, we had our Harvest Festival and Thanksgiving. It is difficult when there are no seasons and when everything remains much the same all the year round.

However, it is one of the occasions when quite a number of people come to the Services who rarely, if ever, come at other times. I suppose people come for all sorts of reasons. Some obviously come for Thanksgiving for the Harvest. Some because the Service reminds them of England. Some possibly to give the parson a helping hand, and a few to do God a good turn. Which ever it was we had a first class turn out and it proved to be a very moving and inspiring occasion.

The sameness of the climate gets on folks' nerves. The continual heat produces the Malayan outlook on life. 'Tid'apa'. Never mind. 'Don't do today what you can do tomorrow.' I find it is an easy philosophy to fall into so I still try to do today what should be done today. I hear that in the pre-war days Colonial Servants were granted nine months leave every two years to recover. They needed it!

I am quite sure that this year at any rate, 'Harvest Festival and Thanksgiving' had us all thinking of all good gifts around us sent from heaven above. It proved a good antidote to the 'Tid'apa' everyday spirit.

## October 6th 1940

Soon after my arrival here in April I sent home to Admiralty a claim for my travelling expenses involved in my varous journeys about the country before I left. Teston to Stranraer. Stranraer to Glasgow, to London to Teston. I spent three days stranded on Carlisle Station during a blizzard! They wanted receipts for my meals and another for the taxi I took from Glasgow Railway Station to the RN Headquarters. They also asked what had happened to my luggage after I reached the RN Headquarters.

Can you imagine the mentality of the kind of person who writes this rubbish? What a contribution to the war effort! I have written a reply, not very friendly I'm ashamed to say. Now I suppose I shall have to wait for about six months for an answer.

## October 8th 1940

We are continually concerned at the merciless bombing and the endless destruction and also at the change of the way of life, especially in the south east of England. The problem of evacuating thousands and thousands of people must be enormous. The papers now arriving tell us what is happening. London and the south coast seem to be the areas most affected. Deal, I see from a local paper, has only 8,000 left out of a normal population of 24,000, and Deal is only one small town. The bewilderment, heart-ache and misery of moving so many old people, besides all the women and children, more often than not to unfamiliar surroundings, passes comprehension. It amazes me that, with all these Germans, Italians and Japanese hordes filling the world with warlike cries, we had peace in the thirties for so long.

This week we are having a Flag Day, which is called, 'Wear a smile for England' and 'Wear a smile for Britain.' The papers arriving from the UK still have 'Invasion' as a top priority, but the general feeling out here is that the Krauts have missed the bus, and we doubt if they will risk it now.

July and August offered them their great opportunity, but nothing happened.

The way the small RAF managed to keep the Nazi Bomber Fleets at bay simply staggers us, as does the cheeky way the RN escorts convoys up and down the Channel under their very noses.

You must be aware that the behaviour of the civilian population is an example to the whole world. We continually discuss all those who travel to London daily and those who live and work there: Doctors, Nurses, Police, those engaged in banks, business, factories and so on. It is not only the British who are impressed by the wonderful example of Britain but also the native population. Together with this goes the magnificent example and cheerfulness of the King and Queen who seem to be here, there and everywhere. And beyond this there are the stirring speeches of Winston Churchill, so uplifting, comforting and challenging. We love the way in which he taunts the Nazis, "Those wicked men, who live in the abodes of the guilty!"

At the same time we are constantly looking over our shoulders at the Sons of Nippon who are creeping nearer and nearer. What about the Americans? Will they ever come in and join us? Or, will they wait until they are attacked? In the first war, they were 3½ years late! How late will they be this time?

Some American ships and sailors have been in Singapore recently. I heard one American sailor say, "Your British Government tells you nothing. You are all under a strict censorship and no better than the Germans. How many of you know that your Battleship, the *Nelson*, had a hole blown in her bottom big enough to drive a train in?" I personally knew as I was fairly near when it happened.

### October 10th 1940

We had our third meeting of the Parochial Church Council. The Captain of the Dockyard, my Vice-Chairman, was full of encouragement and commented on the steady growth of the congregations over the past months. Also he backed up any suggestions which I put forward.

We went through the Church business fairly successfully and I managed to persuade the PCC to give away one collection a month. I tried to impress on them that the priorities were first the quality of the Services and second bringing in the outsiders. Everything else took second place. I told them that I was doing my part in visiting the people and also that I was at the Chapel every morning and for Evening Prayer once a week on Wednesdays and that I hoped that they would join me, though there was nothing dogmatic about this. In fact several do join me for this weekday worship and intercession. I was encouraged by the happy and united spirit that prevailed.

### October 12th 1940

A civilian friend of mine, employed at the Base phoned me from up-country the other day and asked me to take a day or two off and meet him in Malacca. He is an engineer employed by Railton, Tophams and Jones who are building the Base. They have been building it for years!

I obtained the necessary permission to be away and set off north for Malacca, which is about 150 miles away on the west coast of Malaya. By arrangement we both arrived at 4 pm at the Government Rest House, a very decent hotel, and booked in. After some tea we spent a pleasant and leisurely hour wandering round the place before sundown.

In front of the hotel there is a pleasant green and below the cliffs, the sea. So we sat on the green and watched the sun set over the Straits. It was a great relief to be away from the Naval Base if only for a few hours.

Malacca was founded by the Dutch in the 16th Century and has their picturesque architecture. In the 1930s it became a favourite retiring place for rich Chinese from Singapore. The next forenoon we again strolled round the town and I sent off about a dozen postcards to relatives and friends, including the Cummins. If these are not lost at sea they should arrive about December. After lunch, we made our way back to Singapore, travelling in convoy, in our two cars.

My dog, Small, is a great asset to me on my parochial visiting, which I am determined to stick to. I usually wear a dog-collar in spite of the heat so that my victim will know who is arriving. Small has several puppy friends but her great pal is a monkey who lives near us. It is owned by one of the Dockyard Officers and lives in a box by a pole. When he is not in his box he sits on a little platform on top about seven feet above the ground.

Small sits at the bottom of the pole, while the monkey sits on his platform, literally for hours. Every now and then the monkey races down the pole, jumps on Small's back, makes circles round her and then is back again on the top of the pole before she knows what is happening. This sort of routine goes on every day.

The Roman Catholic Chaplain and I have joined the Cypher Watch. It is night work. We man the Cypher Office from 12 midnight to 4 am on Sunday and Wednesday nights. All the other Watches are done by Paymasters.

My little vicarage garden is surrounded by a four foot high wire fence but the problem is getting anything to grow as the soil is so sandy. My Tamil gardener, had put in numerous shoots. A couple of creepers have found their way along the fence. They have a white flower which blossoms at night. Also a honeysuckle has taken root, while two banana plants are showing signs of producing bananas. The spinach is growing too well!

Many of my visitors tell me how different my little bungalow looks since the time it was an office to the Base builders, Topham, Railton and Jones. With its garden and creepers it looks like a corner of old England. Also they tell me that I am the only person on the Base to have a garden gate, which opens and shuts. I have to have one, because of the dog.

### Sunday October 20th 1940

The Bishop of Singapore came to preach at our Matins today for the last time. He is leaving for the UK shortly. It was a good morning for the congregation, for the Bishop and for me. After the Service we met for coffee and he was able to speak to a number of the congregation.

He told me that he was most impressed by the size of the numbers and the spirit of the Service. He preached with conviction and with power. I told him that many had come because the Bishop of Singapore was preaching and for the last time. I added that there had been a slow steady increase in the number attending all the Services on a Sunday. I put this down to there being a Chaplain living on the Base and to my constant visiting, although I had not got round all the houses once so far. I pointed out that the Choir, in spite of many tribulations, had improved enormously which meant better quality Services.

He told me that he left the Base greatly encouraged at what he had seen. I replied in the words of Scripture, "That there remaineth very much land to be possessed."

At the Coffee Party after the Service, he told us a joke about a Bishop. An English Bishop who fasts twice a week still puts on weight, and becomes enormous. After six months he decides to weigh himself on a speaking machine. When he steps on, the Weighing Machine, says, "One at a time please."

### All Saints' Day, November 1st 1940

There was a good muster of the faithful at 7.30 am for Communion. Then at 9 am the Dockyard School came in for a Service. I have now been here about seven months and seem to be getting the School into a good Church routine. Both Staff and Scholars seem to like coming. Even on the lowest level it makes a change from their daily routine.

In the evening we enjoyed Choir practice. With it I included Evening Prayer. I have a very keen organist who has an enthusiastic and vocal band of supporters. But he can hardly read music although he is a great trier. On the other hand I have another very good organist who is considered a usurper by the choir who do not co-operate. As this fellow is absolutely humourless and rarely speaks, just plays, I really don't know what to do. The miracle is that somehow we put on a reasonable show!

### Saturday 2nd November 1940

I understand that we are having our winter now although it is very hot. Storms have been arriving from the north-east about 1 pm every day. They are preceded by violent gusts of wind, which remove photo frames from the tables and shelves and blow the curtains at right angles. We have no glass windows but chocks which work like a blind and unroll.

Now and then Jock Seng and I have been caught by the storm while lowering the chocks and trying to fix them, with blinding rain coming into our faces and simply drenching us, although we are indoors. However, it is so warm we soon seem to dry and are none the worse. Electric fuses are constantly blowing so I keep literally dozens at the ready. The Electricity Department have taken to turning off the mains lately as soon as the storm commences. One one occasion recently they had over one hundred fuses to renew.

My Tamil gardener has produced a load of soil from somewhere which he says should encourage the plants to grow. He is a delightful man and appears to love his work. He is a very good advertisement for the Tamils. They will always have a warm place in my heart because of him. It is quite moving to watch his enthusiasm when he inspects the honeysuckle and when he points to the bananas which are coming on apace.

I have spent about two hours today, writing and addressing Christmas cards and I am sending you four Chinese calendars. They are rather unusual and quite attractive. Please do what you like with them. Keep them or send them away.

I am also sending you some butter. If it arrives in good shape I will send more, but if it is rancid I won't bother. We have masses of tea out here, but we are not allowed to send that.

This afternoon at 4 pm I had tea with the Commander-in-Chief, Admiral Layton, and his wife. Afterwards his Flag Lieutenant, two others and I, had some very good sets of tennis. His house and the tennis courts are on the Straits of Johore which makes the whole setting quite delightful.

### Sunday 3rd November 1940

This evening I took Evensong at the Church Missionary Society Church of St Hilda in Singapore. There was a young congregation, mostly Eurasians. I thought that the Eurasian men were very handsome and their women quite beautiful.

Afterwards we met for coffee and biscuits. I found it most refreshing to meet a completely new set of people who have their own ideas of life, the world, the British, the war and the future. They were very friendly and said they hoped I would come again. They have a straightforward, happy and simple evangelical Faith. I hope they will ask me again soon.

### November 11th 1940

This Monday evening after dark I decided to run round the world's Wireless Stations. Most of them talk to the world in English for the benefit of British listeners.

Tokyo broadcasts in English telling us all of 'Smashing successes against China.' Delhi hardly mentions the war but concentrates on 'Hindu soccer victories.' Sydney, giving Australian news, always refers to the English as 'Limeys.' They say that the English in the Western Desert would be in a poor way if it weren't for the ANZAC Divisions.

All the rest, Berlin, Rome, Saigon and so on pour out 'loaded' news which is boring to the extreme, to put it mildly.

Last Saturday I played rugger for RN Malaya at a place called Regnam, 60 miles up in Johore. I took two of our team with me in my car and we travelled through torrential rain all the way. The match was at 4.15 pm by which time the rain had stopped. Regnam is a place where large numbers of Planters gather and they have a good Rugger team.

The pitch was in a native village and the club had a huge crowd of Malays, Chinese and Europeans to cheer their team on. We had a fine game but again, the fitness of the RN players meant that we ran out easy winners. Afterwards we met the Europeans in a fine Club House for drinks and tea. It did us a power of good to meet all these fresh faces. I have a great admiration and respect for the planters who seem to have a happy approach to life in general.

After tea some of us left for Singapore. Some remained for supper while a few stayed on and spent the week-end with the planters and their families.

### November 12th 1940

I forgot to tell you that about a week ago Rosemary Molesworth rang me up and told me that her husband David had dengue fever and had asked to see me. I felt very flattered! I went along and found him very weak after his attack. I told him that a few days would see him fit and well again, and am thankful to say that I was correct. While he was sick Rosemary and the baby went to stay with friends near by.

Then on November 8th the Molesworths asked me if I could meet them and Polly at the Singapore Swimming Club for tea and a swim. I went. They looked a little bewildered when I arrived and this was their story.

I have already told you that Dr David had volunteered to take over the post of Medical Officer at a Leper Colony in Kedah, North Malaya. He was to change places with the Medical Officer up there and be in sole charge of the Colony. The actual move was postponed owing to his sickness. Now he was better they had said all their Goodbyes and were waiting for the Doctor from Kedah to arrive. They suddenly heard that he had

71

changed his mind and would not be coming after all.

It was all very embarrassing for them. They had had farewell dinners with all sorts of people. Rosemary had been given a beautiful handbag with her initials on it. She said that if the letters hadn't been there she would have given it back. So for the Molesworths it is 'business as usual' at the Singapore General Hospital and they have the same flat. They have decided to move round all the furniture just to make it look different.

We all managed to have a good laugh over the sorry business and they have taken their disappointment extremely well.

**November 16th 1940**

These National Sundays bring all sorts of people into the church. To me, the huge congregation at the Remembrance Service seemed anxious, sincere and single-minded. Large numbers of folk stood outside the open doors of the church and sat on the ground for the lessons and sermon. It was a very moving occasion and we all felt that we were identifying with millions not only in Britain, but all round the world. Not only remembering the fallen of the First War, with pride and thanksgiving, but seeking victory in the present desperate struggle. Although there is no feeling of boastfulness the news of the Fleet Air Arm attack and victory at Taranto, together with the courage of our pilots who appeared to have been stretched to the limit, has been most heartening to us here and to the whole world. It seems that this victory came just at the right moment for Britain to help sustain and steady her under severe night bombing attacks. After this Service I am convinced that if we as a nation are found on our knees regularly before Almighty God, there can be no doubt whatsoever about the final outcome. That is my reading of Scripture. At the end of the Service and just before we sang the National Anthem, we all joined in the General Thanksgiving for the miracle of Taranto.

**November 17th 1940**

On Friday, when in the Hospital at Johore, I invited an RAF Officer back to lunch. He comes from an RAF Station up country and knows no one down here. He is recovering from a badly poisoned leg and although he is not allowed to return to his Station yet, he can be taken out locally. When he goes back north he told me that he intends to invite me to stay in his Mess for a day or so which will make a pleasant change.

We were amused to hear on the the news that a German ship in the Gulf of Mexico had scuttled itself while two others surrendered. They thought they saw two of our warships but they turned out to be Americans who obligingly told the RN that they could have them if they wanted them.

There is tremendous admiration for the King and Queen as they tour the country, especially the bombed cities and we hear that they spent five hours in Coventry. God save the King.

Recently, I received a letter from Evan Mortimore. It had been forwarded from my last ship which I left nine months ago. He is a Schoolmaster and was evacuated to a village near Oxford. He has just got married. His parents still live at Seaford. Evan is still 'reserved' but attends the Home Guard several times a week. He says that he can now hit an elephant at 20 yards and is becoming quite an expert at lobbing hand grenades, thanks to his prowess at cricket.

Thank you for your mail which arrives regularly. I usually pass your letters on to Polly when I go into her Hospital in Singapore. The sea mail arrives in bundles which include letters, papers and magazines. The last were posted in England on October 3rd. I have some interesting UK Magazines lent to me. One about 'This England' is full of coloured prints of all parts of the country; Kent, the Norfolk Broads, Wales, and the West Country. They are such a treat to look at after the endless green of the rubber trees and the jungle.

### November 25th 1940

Recently while in Singapore I bought some Carol Books with music; and Carol Sheets with just the words, for the Christmas festivities. The Choir and organists are keen to put up a good show both at the Carol Service in the Church and at a Carol Party round the Base.

The Base is an extraordinarily difficult place to live and work in. We at the church have discovered that another Carol Party has been organised by the non-church goers, led by some of the senior Dockyard Officers. They have recruited my opposite number in the RN Barracks although he has not mentioned it to me. My choir and carol party are very fed up. In fact they are furious that we have not been informed about it all. However, I have pacified them and told them that there is plenty of room for two parties to be singing around the Base and the ships. I added that it is up to us to put up a really good show and I am producing a programme stating when we shall be singing and where.

### November 26th 1940

I am very upset to learn that you have 40 soldiers billeted on you and that they are actually living in the Rectory. I sincerely hope that they have some good Officers who are able to exercise some discipline and good behaviour. Perhaps they will find the Rectory draughty and will be anxious to move on. It may be that their stay is only temporary and that with the threat of Invasion passing they will return to Barracks. I hope so.

### November 28th 1940

Yesterday, I took the day off. A party of five of us, including Polly, the RAF Officer in Johore Hospital I have come to know, and two Royal Marines Officers from a Cruiser, left the Base in my car for Mersing on the east coast, 87 miles away. It was a more or less straight road through the rubber trees and the jungle and we arrived well before lunch. We reached a fine sandy beach and after a swim in the shallows – we didn't venture out further because of the danger of sharks – we had our picnic lunch. We spent a pleasant lazy afternoon on the beach before going over to the Government Rest House for tea and we left for Singapore about 6.15 pm.

It was dark by 6.45 pm and about 7 o'clock, as it looked like rain, we stopped to put up the hood. We all got out to help fix it but before we had time to secure it we heard a great roar; we had visions of a hyena or a tiger jumping on us from out of the jungle so we scrambled back into the car and raced off. Within a few minutes the rain was torrential so we just had to stop. We kept the engine running, left the headlights full on, tied the electric horn down to keep it on. All this was to keep any beasties away. We buttoned on the hood as quickly as possible for we were all very frightened. Although we were soaked to the skin we were thankful to be on our way once more. Gradually, with the engine spluttering, we ground to a halt and decided that there was water in the carburettor. As it was my car and I knew something about the engine I got out, raised the bonnet, cleaned out the carburettor and filled it with petrol. Just as I lowered the bonnet a laughing hyena or a tiger let out a piercing roar and yelp just nearby. I was nearly too scared to get back into the driver's seat! It seemed to take me an age to cover the few steps to the car door. If there was a hyena near by the language which the RM Officers directed at me in their effort to make me move on must have frightened the animal back into the jungle. Mercifully the car's engine started and we were gone with the wind.

We were back about 9 pm after a pleasant day at Mersing and more thrills than we had bargained for, having done nearly 180 miles. Had we had a puncture it would have seemed like Doomsday, but we were spared that and only imagined it in our dreams.

**November 30th 1940**

As yesterday was Polly's Birthday, I took her out to supper at 'The Gap', a pleasant open air café. We were joined by Rosemary and David Molesworth and had a leisurely evening and meal to the music of a Hawaian Orchestra. I had been introduced to this place by the Royal Marines Officers who had taken me out to dinner. I hope Polly enjoyed the outing.

There are endless 'Funds for Britain' out here, run by the ladies of Singapore: 'The Malayan Patriotic Fund,' 'The War Fund,' 'The Lord Mayor's Air Raid Fund,' 'The Buy a Bomber Fund.' They provide an excuse for endless and enormous parties which take place all the time. However, they bring in the cash so everybody is happy.

At Kranji, there is the RN W/T Station. It is situated about halfway to Singapore on high ground in the west of the island. I was out there last Sunday for my monthly visit for a Church Service. Then half way through the month I visit them pastorally, spending several hours on the Station. I have made a number of friends among both the Officers and Ratings and they are all so kind to me. The Services seem to be much appreciated and I suppose they help to keep the Church Flag and its Message flying in this rather out of the way place.

### December 1st 1940

As I have already told you, I try to get the children into the Church on special days and St Andrew's Day is certainly one of them. So we had the children from the Dockyard School in church for a quarter of an hour.

On Sundays after the Morning Service at the church, two ladies well versed in church matters take the children for a class and they do a fine job. Their two cars collect the children from all over the Base. The parents of the children won't bring them in and so we do. After the Sunday School I usually take them back, except for the 4th Sunday when I am at Kranji. Then the two ladies do the return journey too.

### December 12th 1940

From time to time when ships have been at the Base I have had a few of the Officers to supper, I think they have appreciated being invited into a house even though it is only a bachelor's bungalow. Possibly to return this small act of hospitality, some of them took me out to supper in Singapore. We went to 'The Gap' by arrangement, we all went in my car. After supper, we went to a cinema which was air-cooled. We saw News Reels of London and English towns which had suffered severe bomb damage. These were followed by Service News Reels showing the RAF in action and the Royal Navy bombarding Italian ports. finally, there was a News Flash stating that 20,000 Italians had been captured in the Western Desert. How they must regret allowing Mussolini to drag them into this war. The performance ended with the film 'Charlie's Aunt'. As we were about to leave the cinema, there was a final News Flash, 'Large sea mail from England.'

Many thanks for letters, papers and magazines.

### December 22nd 1940

I was with my friends at Kranji for the monthly Service and then in the evening we had our Carol Service at the Base Church which is dedicated to St Peter! We had a full house and the choir were splendid. Monday and Tuesday evenings, 23rd and 24th December, the Church Carol Party were out carolling round the Base. There were numerous parties going on in private houses wherever we went and received a happy welcome. Both nights we ended up on the Dockyard jetty and sang to the HM Ships and the Merchant Ships. Christmas Eve ended or Christmas began with a midnight Communion Service and Carols. Once more we had a full house with numbers coming from the Merchant Ships.

We had Communion at 8 am and the main Service at 9.30 am, when Rear Admiral Drew read the Lesson. I find it quite extraordinary the way people crowd into these Services. Twice more the church has been full. It may be that Services remind them of home, or that they like a church service occasionally, especially if it is a Festival. Anyway they came during the past week. When I look back to last April, with the congregation in single figures and compare it with the large numbers we get now, I hope that the church and its Message are making themselves felt right across the Base.

Immediately after the Morning service I sped away to Kranji. I really do enjoy my visits there. Both Officers and Ratings put themselves out to help me with the result that we had an inspiring Service. I gave them Communion afterwards. I came away thinking it is quite wonderful that, with a world at war, everything seems to sink into insignificance compared with the Birth of the Holy Child on Christmas Day.

About 7 pm the Molesworths brought Polly out and we had our Christmas dinner together. Jock Seng did us proud. Fish, Turkey and Christmas Pudding. By that time we didn't want fruit and nuts so we just had coffee and they left about 9.45 pm.

Last year I was in Scapa Flow; this year in Singapore, while 1942 and 1943 are in the future and unknown. However, the Message is the same as we sang at Scapa.

> 'Carol, carol gaily, Carol all the way;
> Christ our Loving Savour, born on Christmas Day.

# CHAPTER VII

## A New Year and More Letters Home

*A safe New Year to you all at home. It can't be happy while we are at war and I don't think it's going to stop this year or next. However the Huns seem to have stopped in their tracks. At this side of the world the Japanese are moving steadily south and staring with greedy eyes at Malaya and the whole of the East Indies. I don't like it. Looking back over the year and at the world, what a mess we are in. We must be thankful for mercies granted so far to the British Empire. We have not gone under and it seems to me that we are slowly gathering our strength. It is very hard indeed for the Kingdom of God to become established in men's hearts when their minds are so taken up with the things of this world, with the war, with eating and drinking, with existing and above all, with hating. At the end of my time in the Ceres I felt that my priority was to maintain the Worship of God, show forth the Gospel Message and to help individuals spiritually. Whether I did so or not, and whether I have done so here, I don't know. But that is my ideal.*

**January 3rd 1941**

On New Year's Eve I went to bed at 8 pm and managed to get up at 11 o'clock for our Watchnight Service at 11.30 pm. Although most of Singapore Island seems to be given over to drinking and dancing, we had another full house at church. The theme of the Service was 'O God our help in ages past, our Hope for years to come'. We ended with the hymn 'Father, let me dedicate this year to Thee' and this seemed to express the mood of all those present.

At five minutes past midnight I hurried back to my bungalow, changed into shirt and shorts, before carrying out my cypher watch at the Main Office until 4 am. Was I glad to get back to my bed and sleep!

My opposite number in the RN Barracks has informed me that he is going off to sea in a Cruiser for a month and that the Barracks will be my responsiblity. The Captain of the Dockyard is furious with him for his off-hand way of carrying on. He had suggested to me that I ought to take a week or two's leave soon and he had suggested January. Obviously this cannot be so I shall try to get away in February.

Life out here is very pleasant in many ways. Far too pleasant for many who become affected, cynical and supercilious. In a ship one gets to know people but not here, unless one joins one of the many sets, cliques or 'circuses' as they are called. I find that I have a large number of acquaintances and very pleasant ones too. Having said that, I find it wise to lead a rather detached life.

Some of the senior Dockyard Officers have been extraordinarily kind to me. Three of them live together in Johore. They have had me over there to dine with them and they insisted that I attend their quarterly Cocktail Parties. I am the only RN present. One of them is my partner in the Men's Doubles Tennis Tournament at the Naval Base. We reached the final a few weeks ago and won our match in the final, so they are quite pleased with me!

## January 24th 1941

Some weeks ago I was approached by the Manager of the Singapore Radio Station and invited to take the Sunday night broadcast Service. Having consulted the various authorities and found out when a Royal Marines' orchestra would be available, we fixed for the Sunday evening of January 16th.

It needed considerable organisation on my part, first to arrange the practices for our Choir and the orchestra; second, transport on the night to get the Choir, the Bandsmen and their instruments to the Singapore Studio, and third to have the Royal Marines invited out to supper on the Base afterwards.

Fifteen cars took us to Singapore. There were some faces I had never seen before. It is quite extraordinary how something of this kind attracts people.

We received precious little help at the Studio. When the Bandmaster asked for a room to have a final practice he was told it was quite unnecessary, which meant that they were too lazy.

All the Studio Manager said was, "When the red light comes on you are on." So that was that. I took the Service which meant saying a little about ourselves, who we were and where we came from. I announced the hymns, a Dockyard Officer read one Lesson and a Rating the other. I led the prayers and gave the address. The orchestra were simply first class and gave an inspiring and leading performance.

The next day, Monday, I was rung up by a civilian friend of mine in Singapore.

He said, "I listened to your Broadcast Service last night and if it is any encouragement to you, it was the best service I have listened to for a long time". He went on, "Did you have a gramophone for the hymns?"

I said, "No; why?"

He said, "The singing was actually in time and in tune with the music. I really thought it was a record."

I said, "Good heavens, no. It was the Church Choir and a Ship's Orchestra."

"Regarding your address," he said, "In the words of Scripture, 'Almost thou persuadest me to be a Christian'."

I said, "Next time, if you repeat the Scripture, I trust you will be able to omit the word 'Almost'." He was an unbeliever.

Later on the same day, Monday, I was rung up by the Manager of the Singapore Broadcasting Company offering me another Sunday as he was so pleased with our effort. I had to refuse as I knew the cruisers would be at sea. He told me that the Senior Army Chaplain had been in to see him and asked what we did in the Service. Apparently, the GOC, Malaya had listened to our broadcast and he told his Senior Chaplain that it was of a completely different class and standard to the one the Army had put on. The Naval Service left them standing and he was told to buck up!

I informed the Admiral of the Base what had been said. As a result he sent out a signal congratulating the Church Choir and the Orchestra on their splendid performance. This was a great morale booster for us all, although we felt that the Army Chaplain's morale must have sagged a bit. In my heart I hope that God received some of the glory. As the hymn states, 'To God be the Glory great things He hath done,' not what we have done.

The RM Bandsmen much appreciated being taken out to supper after the broadcast by our supporters, who entertained them royally. Apparently, the Bandsmen were full of praise for the way their hosts had looked after them and many were invited to go again some time. I heard all this when I went on board on the following Tuesday. . . I heard it from the ship's Doctor, Dr Petro, he and I had been at Emmanuel College, Cambridge together in the early 1930s.

I have been asked to go and crew for a man who lives in Johore and who keeps his yacht at the Naval Base Sailing Club. We discovered that we were both up at Cambridge at about the same time. He was at Queens when I was at Emma. We met at a party in Johore and when he invited me to crew for him I jumped at the idea. There are weekly races on the Straits of Johore so if I come up to scratch the first time I hope that I will be going out regularly. He is searching for a church to attend so I hope that he will be joining us at the Base Church.

During these weeks while I have been at the RN Barracks I have been watching the cricket matches. As a result I have allowed myself to be talked into taking on the job of cricket secretary for HMS Sultan. It involves arranging matches, pitches, transport, gear and so on. It will keep me in touch with Officers and Ratings, so I think it will be worthwhile. Otherwise I seem to spend my time with Dockyard personnel for the Base outside the Barracks and I think they will enjoy it.

The Rear Admiral knew I was about to go on leave and asked to see me before I departed, which I did.

He said that he had been pleasantly surprised at the upsurge of church life over the past nine months and its influence on the whole Base. The 'National Days of Prayer', the Bishop of Singapore's final visit, Remembrance Sunday, the Christmas Services and finally the Broadcast Service had all made their impact, especially the latter and he hoped that I was encouraged so far, but that in the words of Admiral Sir Francis Drake, "It is not the beginning, but the continuing of the same until it be thoroughly finished which yieldeth the true glory".

I feel that I am most fortunate to be supported by those in authority, who have helped me throughout the time I have been here.

Next, it was the turn of the Captain of the Dockyard. He told me that as my Churchwarden, he felt that the church and church life were on a sound footing; that the Ships and Outstations were being visited and provided for spirtually and that the Dockyard School had taken root as a church school. He impressed on me the importance and duty of taking leave; of getting away from the Base and making the most of the opportunity of exploring this wonderful country, Malaya. He pointed out that this opportunity might never recur so I had better make the most of it.

I told him that I was planning to go away on Tuesday 15th February for about two weeks and that the Cathedral would be taking care of the Morning Services and the Senior Chaplain of the Army would be coming out for Evensong. I added that the Cathedral were delighted to be invited, while the Army Senior Chaplain rather wanted to see what we got up to after the blast he had received from his GOC!

## February 11th 1941

As a result of the Captain of the Dockyard's remarks, I intend to see as much as possible on what may be my only opportunity to tour Malaya during my stay in this part of the world. I want you to have some idea of this peninsular in its present peaceful existence, although how long we shall be left to enjoy it, none can say. The little yellow men are coming nearer and nearer.

First there is the Crown Colony known as The Straits Settlements which include Singapore, Malacca, Penang and Port Wellesley.

Secondly there are The Federated Malay States which take in Perak, Selangor, Negri, Sambilain and Pahang.

Thirdly there are The Unfederated Malay States including Johore, Redah, Perlis, Kelantan and Treggain which, I gather from the book *Lights of Singapore*, have no wish whatsoever to become Federated.

I have 14 days leave and intend to spend about a week travelling and a week in the Cameron Highlands.

I left the Base early on Tuesday, the first day of my leave, in perfect weather. I had the car's hood down and she ran beautifully. My first stop was to be Malacca. After covering 50 miles running north through rubber plantations, I turned west. I crossed a couple of rivers in funny little ferries which could only take two cars at a time. Progress was slow as there were geese, goats, donkeys and bullocks, all moving in a leisurely fashion with hardly any one in charge. I had no idea where they all came from or where they were going.

Everything is green, all the way and all the time. However, it is very restful and better than desert. Later on I passed women and children who were all dressed up and in very attractive colours and their costumes showed up well against their dark skins.

It seemed to be the time for cutting the grass on both sides of the road. This is done by squads of Malays who brandish scythes round their heads in a sweep of the arm and they cut the grass in this way. As you pass you hope they won't let go their scythes or that the ends won't fly off.

One passes through numerous little villages. The bungalows are built off the ground and are reached by about half a dozen steps. They are chiefly built of wood and roofed with thatch. The inhabitants are Chinese and Malays. The Chinese have their temple and the Malays have their mosque. Occasionally there was a Christian building but nothing to show to what branch of the church it belonged.

After a brief stop at Malacca I pressed on to Seremban, another 50 miles, where I had lunch at the Government Rest House. Off again and I reached Kuala Lumpur, the Federal Capital at 3.30 pm, having covered 240 miles. I booked into the Hotel Majestic and ordered tea. My room is on the top floor and I have a wizard view from my window. I look past some minarets which form part of the railway station to the mountains beyond.

A couple I had met in Singapore had invited me to call on them if ever I came here so I rang them and after wandering through this most attractive city called on them for an hour. I returned to the hotel for supper and turned in early after a very good first day.

I left Kuala Lumpur early on Wednesday and made for Ipoh, the centre of the Mining Industry, 140 miles to the north. As I entered Ipoh after a good run, a peculiar noise developed in the engine so I stopped at a garage. It was a broken axle! While it was being repaired I wandered round the town and decided to stay the night, with the intention of a quick get-away in the morning.

Thursday was another simply wonderful morning. My journey took me north again through Taipah, an attractive little town, and on to Butterworth. There I made the half-hour ferry trip by sea to Penang. In true tourist style I did the island and had lunch at an hotel run by a firm called Whiteway, Lairdlow & Co, a firm you, Dad, used to say you knew in India in the 1890s!

Returning to the mainland I journeyed south again via Taiping. About ten miles from Taiping whilst travelling at about 50 mph there was a sudden bang. One of my back tyres had burst. I pulled up quickly and safely and changed the wheel. I had hardly started again when there was another bang as the spare burst. So there I was miles from anywhere with two burst tyres.

I jacked up the open car, locked it as best I could and waited by the side of the road, I was lucky. A taxi came past overflowing with natives, but the driver stopped. With the opportunity of an extra fare he put me inside while one of the other passengers had to sit on the bonnet. The Malay driver took me to a garage and said that he would take me back when the tyres were repaired.

After about half an hour he came to the garage and said, "Go now; hurry, hurry."

The repairs were out of my hands so I could not 'Hurry, hurry'. Then he wanted more money.

I said, "No more money," so he succumbed.

On the way back he stopped the taxi and said he was going into a house to pick up another passenger.

He said to me, "Master wait," and he disappeared inside a house.

I waited and waited and at last went to the house where someone said, "Man upstairs with wife; you wait, wait."

I said that was just what I had been doing and I added, "Tuan Besar". That means Big Master "Go. Tuan Besar finish. Goodbye. No money." That did it and he came rushing down and with a sullen face took me on my way again. By the time I had got the tyres on again and reached Ipoh I had had my fill for one day so I put up at a pleasant little hotel.

Any depression one has is swept away by the wonder of the early mornings and this particular Friday had its own magic as I set out for my destination, the Cameron Highlands. The ascent to 5,000 feet with non-stop twists and turns took me about an hour and a half. On the way I passed deep ravines, steep hill sides, dense jungle and the everlasting green. The various sorts of butterflies and birds were amazing. I saw numerous birds as large as small crows, but with white tips to their wings and tails. There were numbers of small yellow birds rather like wagtails. I booked into a room at the top of the Cameron Highlands Hotel facing east-south-east. The surroundings were spacious. In front of the building was the Golf Course while at the sides and rear were numerous footpaths leading up and down the hillsides.

Among the people I have met here are a naval couple who live and work in Singapore City. They have a son at one of the two boarding schools up here. As there is no resident Chaplain, I took the Sunday Services there today for the Church of England pupils. It was a nice change and I found it a refreshing experience.

It is only five days since I left the Base but it seems years ago. I suppose that is because I have visited so many places. I have travelled 750 miles to get here but it will be a mere 450 miles to return to Singapore. The mornings are beautifully fresh. The sun rises in the south-east at this time of year immediately opposite my room and I watch it climb over the hills. As the mist rises the sun sparkles on the grass and hillside, while the birds sing as if they are enjoying the morning too.

The Naval folk have invited me to join them for meals at their table with another man, a mining engineer from Ipoh. During the day, the four of us proceed casually round the golf course accompanied by an army of Malay caddies. I am able to keep up my kitchen Malay by chatting to these boys. As ever there are caddies and caddies. Being out of doors most of the day we have all caught the sun and will be returning to Singapore looking like bronze statues.

There has apparently been a Far East crisis although the local papers are less than illuminating. My own feeling is that there is a Far East crisis all the time and those three words are getting larger and larger. It is not whether the Sons of Nippon will spring, but when. It can't be long delayed. When the Japs do strike it will mean that the British Empire will be taking on the three axis powers alone and we keep wondering about the Americans.

This place has reminded me so often of North Wales; hills on all sides; occasional rain and mist sweeping across with low lying clouds clinging to the mountains. The sun is much stronger than in Wales of course but we are used to it.

On Tuesday my tooth began to ache. So on Wednesday I left the hotel for Ipoh, 80 miles away, where the nearest dentist lives. He dealt with me at 9 o'clock and I was back at the hotel by 12 noon. I travelled 160 miles to have a tooth stopped but it was worth it!

The evenings have given me time and opportunity for some serious reading and study. Having to prepare addresess for two Sundays at the school has been good for me.

We had some interesting and open discussions on the subject of religion in Malaya. We accepted the fact that about 50% of the population are Moslem; 10% Hindu; 25% atheist and animist and about 10% Christian. Of these 5% are Roman Catholic 5% non-Romans divided between the Anglicans, the Methodists, and the Presbyterians. They asked me what are the chances of a Christian Malaya.

I said, "Very little at present and more especially with a war on," and continued that I thought the churches were a help to the expatriates and enabled them to hold on to Christian Faith or in the words of Scripture," to stand fast in the Faith."'

I told them that I considered my own task at present was to care for the spiritual welfare of the men of the Merchant Service whose ships frequented the Base, and the Service and Civilian folk at the Base. This means preaching the Gospel and building them up in the Christian Faith and in the life of the Church.

To my surprise mail has been forwarded from the Base. Two of your letters dated 12th and 15th December and several from other folk. All of it was quite unexpected so this has been a real red letter day! I am reminded of the sentence in the Book of Proverbs. 'As cold water to a thirsty soul, so is good news from a far country;' Proverbs 25:25.

It is Saturday evening. I have packed my gear and am ready to go. This has been a wonderful week, spent with delightful people and amidst lovely surroundings. I have been out on the golf course and on the hillsides every day with them and then in the evenings there has been time for chatting, reading and thinking over my own job.

Tomorrow is Sunday and I am taking the Morning Service at the school before leaving for Kuala Lumpur, where I will attend Evensong at the English church and will spend the night before starting for Singapore and home.

**February 27th 1941**

Thursday and I'm back at the Base once more, feeling somewhat depressed.

Besides your welcome letters, I received a card from The Rev. Peter Brook with whom I was at Emmanuel College, Cambridge. He is Chaplain of Clifton College and they have been evacuated to Carbis Bay, Cornwall. Another was from Captain Claude Aylwin a friend from my School of Music days who informed me of his new appointment to HMS *Prince of Wales*, a very fine job. The other was Major Bobby Lang, a *Woolwich* shipmate who is the RM Officer in the *Repulse*.

Bundles of English Daily Papers have also arrived, for which many thanks. They describe the terrible bombing not only of London but also Coventry, Liverpool, Birmingham, Southampton, Glasgow, Belfast and finally Dublin which was by mistake! We all hope that you can all hold out until our defences catch up with their attacks and we can wear them down. What a titanic struggle it is.

As you will appreciate, it is very difficult to have a black-out in these parts where we have no proper blinds or windows, so the authorities switch everything off from the mains. This includes refrigerators! I was in the bath tonight when the electricians struck! I dressed quickly and rushed off to the air raid shelter which was absolutely crammed full of every kind of Asiatic and European. The smell of hot sweating bodies has to be experienced to be believed. I now go armed with a mouthful of garlic to dilute the odour.

On the way back from leave, I stopped for tea at Seremban and met the Australians. They really are a magnificent set of men and I quickly acquired a great respect for them. The majority are simply huge, well over six feet. They are all volunteers and many have given up good jobs as solicitors, bankers, seamen, businessmen, farmers and so on. They are very keen and longing to get into the fight and to get the war won and behind them. They are so proud of the way the Australian Imperial Force chased and cleaned up the Italians in the Western Desert. I really felt sorry for the Italians having to face men with such enthusiasm and spirit. We hear that the Malays and Chinese in these parts are frightened of them as lurid stories of what they did in Egypt and the Desert filter through. They are also delighted to find the Royal Australian Air Force living near them. I am very glad they are all on our side!

Our bad news is that Petrol Rationing commences on 1st March in two days time, so we are all filling up our tanks for the last time. However, the East being the East, I don't suppose there will be any real shortage. I shall be using my bike to go to the Church every morning instead of the car.

I have decided to step up my visiting as a Lenten task. With over 600 houses and bungalows to get round, the job is endless. It must be like painting the Forth Bridge. Before you are half-way through the job, it is time to start again. I find it a great education and it produces all sorts of surprises connected with people. For many of these folk it is the first time they have ever had a chat with a Parson. I am determined to get round the whole place so that one and all will know that there is a Chaplain on the Base.

### March 3rd 1941

Recently, I met an old UK friend of mine with Polly at the Singapore Swimming Club. Duncan Hearle and I used to camp together with dozens of others in North Wales in the pre-war days and he supports me well. He tells me that he is always struggling to keep out of debt which is a problem many expatriates have out here. I have told him that he is an idiot to let others lead him astray. If he overspends it serves him right and he must take the consequences. I think his firm expect him to do a considerable amount of entertaining. He told me that I was lucky to be living 20 miles away from the temptations and delights of Singapore. I replied that those of us living in the Base have to think twice before making the 40 miles round trip and now with petrol rationing we think three times!

### March 16th 1941

It seems that the whole Empire is relieved that the Lease and Lend Bill has passed safely through the American Congress and we are indebted to President Roosevelt for this fine gesture. The American Radio declares that the Americans have no intention of letting the stuff they give us be sent to the bottom of the sea by German submarines so they are going to escort it all the way. What a tremendous help this is going to be to the Navy as they struggle to keep the sea lanes open. All we want now is for the Americans to take the plunge and come in with us.

### March 20th 1941

We have a large insect world out here which comes to life at sunset. We have mosquitoes, moths of all sizes, some with a wing span of 18 inches, bats, spiders, and crickets which make an eternal noise. In the end one doesn't hear them. I might add that the cockroaches increase and multiply rapidly not to mention the lizards, ants, mice, rats and snakes.

## March 24th 1941

Yesterday we kept the Day of Prayer. I can never understand why so many folk support these occasions. It must be a gross lack of faith and understanding on my part. Is it the cry of the human heart to 'Our Father which art in heaven'? Is it personal faith rekindled in God as Saviour and guide? Is it an appeal to a far off being who might hear? Do they believe that God answers prayer? Does Patriotism draw them?

I feel that my business is not to go into the whys and wherefores but to guide, lead, encourage and inspire them in the Christian Way by preaching and teaching the Everlasting Gospel. This I have tried to do all along. Whether I succeed or fail is not for me to judge. I am to persevere. Dr and Mrs David Molesworth came to our Evensong and brought Polly with them. They all remained for supper and left at 9.45 pm as I was on cypher watch at midnight.

One problem many of us suffer from out here is other people's blaring radios.

As our windows have no glass the noise carries far and wide. Some of us ring up the culprit politely and sweetly and ask them to turn their radio down. At other times we are so angry, we ring them up and deliver a blast.

## March 27th 1941

I want to add a few further lines about my Chinese Boy, Jock Seng. I find him so sensible, helpful and thoughtful in so many ways. I keep my car under a bungalow about 30 yards away from mine. Recently I returned in my car as a tropical storm was raging. Jock Seng arrived under his umbrella and bringing mine with him, so that I could cover the 30 yards home without getting soaked. He is first class at cooking meals, cleaning the car, putting out the right suits on the right day and so on. But he doesn't seem to be able to sweep the rooms! I have to tell him, "sapu, sapu, sweep, sweep! This room today, that room tomorrow."

When I tell him I am going to the office at midnight he leaves my gear ready with a thermos flask full of Ovaltine which I drink as the hours pass. When I had bad toothache for a week he left another thermos, full of boiling water, ready for me to use. He dotes on Small, my little dog; takes her for walks and hunts for ticks! He gives her an egg a day. Eggs are small and plentiful out here. He says to me, "Dog muchy like egg."

## March 29th 1941

There have been suggestions and rumours going around the Base that we ought to have some form of Base magazine, to give general information about the goings on and the various organisations. The Captain of the dockyard asked me to discuss the matter with him and to let him have my ideas. I told him that if there was to be a Base Magazine, it would be a good move if the Church offered to produce it as a kind of Parish Magazine.

I said that it might help to make the Church the centre of the Base which it wasn't at present and that it should be a force for spreading the Gospel and church news. He asked me if I had any further comments. I said that it would mean considerable work and that to start with about three issues a year would be sufficient. We discussed cost, distribution and sales. I told him that I was convinced that there would be enormous sales as everybody would want to send home a copy of our own magazine, good, bad or indifferent. He told me to go ahead. I started at once.

## March 31st 1941

The Civil Engineers offered to produce several designs for the cover for me to choose from.

Individuals from most of the Dockyard Departments offered to write articles on all sorts of subjects.

Shops and Bazaars on the Base, near by and in Singapore were keen to advertise to boost their trade, so it looked as if the cost would be no problem. I took adverts for a year to cover 'Summer,' 'Christmas' and 'Spring' numbers. Perhaps I shouldn't include the following jokes I heard on the Base in our Parish Magazine!

1. Hitler phoned Mussolini and said, "What's up with you? You are messing everything up. You have failed in Africa. You have been chased out of Greece and now your fleet has taken a hiding at Taranto."

"Tell me, Adolph," Musso replied, "Where you speaka from, London?"

2. A choirboy asked his Vicar who was wearing a gold watch, if he believed in prayer.

"Yes, of course," said the Vicar. "Especially if you have as much faith as I have."

"Well," said the choirboy after thinking for a moment, "you give me your gold watch and as you have great faith you pray for another."

3. What's in a name?

Patient in doctor's waiting room, "I'm aching from neuritis."

Second patient, "Pleased to meet you. I'm Mendleson from Chicago."

4. A little man was sitting in a London Underground Train with his gasmask on the seat beside him. A woman weighing about 17 stone plopped down breathlessly smashing the mask, cardboard box and all. She apologised but the little man was very angry.

Then a voice behind him said, "Cheer up, mate. It could have been worse. Your face might have been inside your mask."

## April 13th 1941

It has been a perfect day for weather and from my point of view a splendid Easter Day. The church had been decorated tastefully and the Easter hymns are always inspiring. Your son has been busy all day. I had Communion at 7 am and 8 am, Matins at 9.30 am, Matins and Communion at

11 am, and Evensong tonight. The Molesworths came out to the 8 o'clock Communion and stayed for breakfast. It was a 40 mile journey for them, there and back.

After the Service, he said, "That Service was the next best thing to being in Martham Parish Church on Easter Day."

We had both been there at Easter 1939, when we were sailing on the Norfolk Broads.

### April 16th 1941

I attended a top-level Cocktail Party on Easter Monday evening. Among those present were the Commander-in-Chief and Lady Layton, Rear Admiral and Mrs Drew and Captain and Mrs 'Hooky' Bell.

During the evening one lady told me, "There is one thing I would like to say to you and I hope you won't mind. Every time I see you in that suit I think what a magnificent cut it is. You are the best dressed gentleman here. My husband, whose suit is all wrinkles and folds, thinks so too."

I was very surprised and very flattered. In fact it is a tropical suit which I had made by a Chinese, who merely copied it from one of my UK suits, before I put the latter into cold storage.

Last month the Captain of the Dockyard received another letter sent by some Admiralty civilian clerk asking, "Why was this Officer, [me], travelling about the country in this way and why was he spending so much time in doing it?"

My reply to the Captain of the Dockyard was, "Why hasn't this civilian clerk been called up?"

There are several clubs in Singapore, the Tanglin Club, the Singapore Cricket Club and various private clubs; all very expensive and only open to Officers. The Singapore Swimming Club we can enter on a communal ticket, which makes it reasonable for us to join financially.

For Ratings and other ranks there are the Missions to Seamen Hostel and the Salvation Army. They both do a magnificent job and meet a great need. However as there are literally thousands of Service men in and around Singapore, they are only a drop in a bucket.

There are three 'Worlds', the Great, the New and the Happy, each a kind of huge fun fair with sideshows, boxing booths, plays and dancing run by the Asiatics. Crowds of Sailors, Soldiers and Airmen go to them.

The dance floors provide hostesses who sit at tables nearby. If a man wants to dance he buys a book of tickets, four for a dollar, and gets four dances. These are very short and he hands over a ticket for each one. The hostesses are, of course, Asiatics. One night I walked round the 'Worlds' to see what went on and once was enough. The stench and the dirt were just too much for me. However crowds seem to enjoy them, including Europeans, Asiatics and Africans.

The other places of entertainment for one and all are the clean and air-conditioned cinemas. The air is dried so it makes a visit comfortable. One does not sweat all the time. Coming out afterwards is like walking into a steam bath or an oven.

## May 4th 1941

At our 9.30 am Matins today I noticed some strangers in the congregation and had a word with them afterwards. One of the men was a London Missionary Society missionary and the other a Religious Tract Society missionary returning to Shanghai. They were also four lady missionaries returning to Shanghai but they had left the church before I had time to speak to them. They all enjoyed the Service and wished their stay could be longer. I told them that only a day or so ago I had read their magazine giving an account of their valedictory meeting in London in September 1940. In it were photos of the two men going to Shanghai. Strange to say I knew both these two, who are in another ship in Singapore and I hope to see them tomorrow. The two men I spoke to in church came back to lunch with me and spent the afternoon there while I was out at Kranji. I returned for tea and then we all went to Evensong. Afterwards I took them back to their ship and remained for supper. It made a pleasant change for me and I hope, for them.

## May 12th 1941

Father Cunningham, the RC Priest who lives in a small Mess about 30 yards away, came in at lunch time and stayed on for a chat. He often drops in to discuss his work and flock. He is efficient and gives a lot of time to his sailors.

We were talking about the wealth of the Chinese and he described to me a lunch party he had been to on a Church Feast day. When they had finished, they went off to another Chinese house and had 22 courses, with champagne flowing like water. They don't seem to live too badly under British rule.

At the School's Ascension Day Service we had a number of parents. They would like a regular monthly service. So our School-Church connection still grows.

I gave a lift to an Australian Officer who was down from his unit in Malaya. After lunch I took him to Singapore to the Swimming Club. I discovered that he was a keen Presbyterian and he was glad of a chat, the little hospitality at lunch and the Club and the encouragement I was able to give him to continue in the Christian Faith. While we were sitting at the Swimming Club we were able to watch the Pacific Clipper arrive and touch down in the harbour. She had flown in from Manila with mail for us on board I trust.

## May 24th 1941

I am reading a fascinating book called *Chorus to Adventurers*, being the later life of Roger Pocock a frontiersman. The writer of the foreword says, "Captain Roger Pocock has been a vagrant adventurer for 50 years. His old book, *A Frontiersman* told us how he had been labourer, painter, missionary, mounted policeman, seaman, cowboy, arctic explorer, miner, pedlar and the like. The peculiar charm of this writing is that his readers are in the company of a geologist and anthropologist who can read the relics of the Stone Age with an eye accustomed to peoples and regions where metal tools are scarce; a mystic who has lived with robbers, desperados and murderers; a despiser of the stay-at-home and city-bent gent, yet fanatically in love with his own England."

What a remarkable person he must have been. I wonder whether he is connected with the Pococks of India or a relation of Lovell Pocock of Burma, I would like to think so.

The Molesworths are coming to tea tomorrow, Sunday. Then he is going to speak at Evensong on Grenfell of Labrador. During the Long Vacations while he was at Emmanual College, Cambridge, David went out to Labrador to help in the Mission Hospitals. The next Saturday, David and Rosemary both leave for the Leper Colony in north Malaya. I am really going to miss them as persons, not to mention their hospitality and their Christian encouragement. It has been a great experience having them in Singapore.

**June 6th 1941**

I ordered 300 copies of the first edition of our News Bulletin and they have all been sold. It is impossible to please everybody and the questions and comments are endless.

If it is produced by the Church, why isn't it all about the Church? The anchor on the cover is upside down. Why? Is it superstitious? Why doesn't it come out once a month? Who chose the title? Why is it 50 cents and not 25 cents? How much does it cost to produce? What will the Chaplain do with all the money he gets and the profits?

The Captain of the Dockyard, who encouraged me to produce it, considers that we have made a good start and that it has put the Church on the map.

**June 20th 1941**

A number of New Zealanders have arrived at the Base to man the Patrol Boats. They have been in harbour for a few days. When I called on them, each boat insisted that I spend some time with each of them and they have made me an Honorary Member of every boat's Mess. They are a very close community so I feel very honoured to be accepted by them so soon.

One boat in particular hopes that I will be able to go on one of their patrols with them and in return they want to come to my bungalow and sleep ashore when they return to harbour!

## June 23rd 1941

We can hardly believe the news of Germany's attack on Russia. It seems to be a case of 'When thieves fall out.' So now we have a gang of two-faced, double-dealing atheists as our allies.

We feel that it is a feather in your caps. They couldn't subdue England so they have turned east. In doing so they have sealed their doom. I wonder if the German nation realises this fact.

The Dockyard have made us a most attractive little Lectern for the church and also some rails for the choirboys to kneel against. Until now they have knelt against nothing! Over the past month or so I have managed to recruit six. They are still keen and I want to keep them that way.

I was invited to have supper at the Naval Club in the Base by the two Officers of the New Zealand ship *Hung Joa*, Lieutenant Bill Mellor and Sub Lieutenant Tony Clarke. Afterwards they came back to my bungalow and spent the night there. As I have two camp beds rigged for this sort of occasion it was quite easy to put them up. Last Sunday night about a dozen of them turned up at Evensong. I think the Service reminds them of home. They have informed me that a good dozen will be coming next Sunday night a..d afterwards they all want to return to my bungalow for supper. They have promised to bring plenty of food.

I have been receiving mail from Hong Kong, Japan, the Philippines, Australia and New Zealand; from men and women who heard our Broadcast Service and they wanted to know when we will be on the air again. All this is most encouraging for the Choir and the Band as well as for the Base generally, who like to share the credit! We have been invited by Singapore Radio to take another Service and we have provisionally fixed Sunday, 17th August as the date.

## July 23rd 1941

I have received a number of letters from the wives of the New Zealanders based here, thanking me for having them along to my bungalow and for looking after them. They have sent several parcels of cakes, biscuits, soups and so on to help stock my larder. These men are so keen on their boats and work and are quite unsophisticated. My bungalow is very small and sparse but if they look upon it as home from home it is doing its job. Some of the wives' letters state that the whole life of their men here in Singapore seems to have changed for the better now that they have somewhere to go! Sometimes when I return to my bungalow a number of them are already there.

They say, "We have seen Jock Seng and told him that there will be eight of us to supper tonight and we have given him armfuls of food!"

Evan Mortimore is still at Oxford and has put in for the Headmastership of Ashford Grammar School. I think that he will get the job. The age limit for schoolmasters has been raised to 35 and he is due to be called up in July of this year. He has put his name down for the RAF but now wishes that he had asked for the Navy. So do I. I wonder if you would mind sending him a postcard saying, "Lovell says offer for the RN even now. You will get a Commission as a schoolmaster. Do it now as the RN is by far the best Service to join and the White Ensign the best flag to fly under. All this, of course, if you are not appointed to Ashford."

## August 5th 1941

Another batch of WRNS have arrived at Kranji. While visiting there a day or so ago, one of them said, "Are you the Rev. Lovell Pocock?"

I said, "That's me."

She said, "You were at Cambridge with my brother. He said that you were both at one of the North Wales Camps and that while you were at the School of Music at Deal, he visited you from Broadstairs, where he was teaching."

Yesterday we kept the Queen's birthday with flags and toasts. God save and bless the King and Queen.

All new arrivals speak so highly of Durban, South Africa. They say that every time a ship comes into harbour from England, the whole population appears to come down to greet the passesngers and offer them hospitality.

Yesterday I came across two Royal Marines walking through the Base. They were out for a stroll from their ship. I gave them a lift back to my bungalow and they stayed to tea. One of them had been my servant at Deal! It was a great pleasure to see them and they seemed to appreciate their visit. They said they felt sure that more of the detachment would like to find their way to my small abode if asked. I must see what I can do.

The Base amenities for the Sailors have improved enormously over the past year. There is a fine swimming pool, excellent sports fields for rugger and soccer and good tennis courts and a large well run canteen. The great thing lacking is any kind of home life. What I can do in having a few Ratings and Royal Marines in now and then is hardly a drop in a bucket.

While I walked around the Base the other day, an Officer on one of the latest patrol boats to arrive called out, "Are you the Rev. Lovell Pocock?"

I said, "Yes."

He said, "Welcome aboard; I understand that our first batch claim you as their Chaplain. All of us arriving want you to be ours too." So I now belong to these people too. Soon after returning home, the phone rang. It was Bill Mellor and Tony Clarke of the *Hung Joa*. They had returned to the Base a day early. They asked me to take my car down to their ship as they wanted a bath and would bring their supper. I went down and as we loaded their gear into the car they handed me a crate full of live hens.

I said, "What's this?"

They said, "As we have come to stay for a day or so, we are bringing our food and Jock Seng can cook one or two of these each day."

They really came to invite me to go with them on their next cruise. It needed a little organising but no one seemed to have any objections and it now depends on the little yellow men who are becoming increasingly menacing and unpleasant.

**August 21st 1941**

I knew the routine for the Broadcast this time and we all seemed to know our parts, the choir, the Royal Marines Orchestra, the cars for transport and supper afterwards. Everything seemed to go satisfactorily at the Studio, but we won't know how the Service went over until we receive the fan mail afterwards. I have turned in all the proofs for our second number of the Base Bulletin and the Magazines should be ready for distribution and sale by the time I get back from my cruise in the *Hung Joa*.

**August 23rd 1941**

First of all, before I tell you about this Patrol, I want to give you Polly's news. I have delayed writing about it until I was certain that her letter was on the way to you. Mike Halliday of the East Surreys has asked her to marry him. They are very happy and everybody is delighted. I have only met him a couple of times but was very impressed by his easy and happy spirit and his confidence.

HMS *Hung Joa* is an RN Patrol vessel carrying a 3" gun on her fo'c's'le. She has a ship's company of 16, made up of the Skipper, Lieutenant Bill Mellor; a First Lieutenant, Sub Lieutenant Tony Clarke; an ERA from the RN barracks whom we called 'The Chief', a Malay crew of 12 and a Chinese cook and steward.

Thursday afternoon we provisioned the ship with food from the local shops inside and outside the Base. About 7 pm we returned to my bungalow for a meal and then joined *Hung Joa* about 10 pm.

Bill Mellor, the Skipper, slept in his own cabin on the upper deck. Tony Clarke and I shared Tony's cabin under the fo'c's'le. The ERA also had a small cabin under the fo'c's'le while the Malay crew and the Chinese cook slept aft. In fact Tony Clarke and I slept on mattresses on the fo'c's'le, either side of the 3" gun. After being ashore in my bungalow it was beautifully fresh on the deck and we didn't need a mosquito net.

**August 24th 1941**

We were up by 5 am and steamed eastwards down the Straits of Johore. Then we turned north into the China Sea and along the east coast of Malaya. It was a wonderful day with a pleasant breeze and a quite heavy swell. Most of the Malay crew were seasick but by the end of the Patrol they should be cured. The rig of the day is just shorts and gym shoes. The ship's company is engaged in daily routine and my two hosts insist that I stick to mine, allowing me an hour in the forenoon and an hour in the evening for my prayers, meditation and reading. They have passed the word that I am not to be disturbed or spoken to during these sessions. It is really quite amusing.

We met our other ship about 6 pm and paid them a call, returning for supper about 7 pm before a final hour's sailing. We anchored at 9.30 pm in a quiet little bay off Mersing. There was no wind or swell. We turned in about 11 pm under these wonderful skies with their brilliant white stars and dropped off to sleep with the sea lapping gently against the side of the ship.

## August 25th 1941

Today, Sunday, has been rather an unorthodox one for me. The *Hung Joa* has to be at certain places at certain times so we keep to a strict schedule. Today we are steaming west again, to the mouth of the Romplin, then north until we reach the mouth of the river Pahang.

As we steamed east we occasionally passed a couple of Saki, sailing a very primitive boat. The Saki are the uncivilised natives of Malaya, who are unfortunately dying out. Also we passed enormous canoes covered with thatch. We presume they are houseboats because they appear to be crammed with people, who carry on their business in the villages. This is the way trade is carried on out here. We try to slow down when passing these craft but the current is so strong that Bill Mellor has his work cut out to keep the ship on a steady course. We seem to be racing along though the engines are full astern, twisting and turning, with the jungle occasionally coming on board and threatening the wireless aerial.

There is hardly time to take in the beauty of the bird life. The monkeys appear to be having the time of their lives. They swing from branch to branch, staying with us and chattering away non-stop all the time.

We were at the mouth of the Romplin by 12 noon. Bill Mellor thought the boys could do with some exercise so we went for a march ashore, passing through the village of Romplin on the way to some waste land where he gave them some drill. Around us were goats and water buffaloes with their huge horns.

At 2 pm we set off north again making for the River Pahang but within an hour we had run into a sharp tropical storm. The sky went jet black and then the heavens opened. The wind whipped the water of the sea and the rain was icy. Even hail came down. We changed quickly into bathing costumes, produced some soap and had a good wash in the rain on the upper deck. These two men are first class yachtsmen and handled the ship extremely well.

At the height of the storm, when visibility was very poor, we sighted a Chinese sampan struggling along in the big seas and the rain. We worked round them and gave them a tow to their fishing kampong or village. They spent the time  during the tow baling water out of their craft. Even in time of war His Majesty's Navy still manages to carry out small acts of mercy!

They yelled out, "Trima cassi, berjenji ikan kendian hari" which means, "Thank you. We promise fish next day!"

Then the black sky, the wind and the rain disappeared as quickly as they had come. We continued our journey north and anchored at the mouth of the Pahang River. The Skipper decided to call it a day so, after supper, we did some reading and writing. They made sure that I did my Parson's reading as they call it. Later the four of us, Bill Mellor, Tony Clarke, the ERA and I sat on the fo'c's'le drinking coffee and watching the new moon, with Venus about two feet below, endeavouring to catch up the moon and sit in her lap, but in vain.

### August 26th 1941

We were up by six o'clock and I took the dinghy away to the shore while the usual ship's duties were being carried out. Bill and Tony told me to return for breakfast about 7.30 am which should, they said, give me time not only to pray for the Naval Base but our enemies too! Having beached the dinghy I had a quick bathe by myself, keeping a sharp lookout for sharks on one side of me in the water, and tigers on the other side on the land. After breakfast we sailed north, passing some pretty little islands, until we reached the mouth of the Romplin. Here Tony Clarke took me ashore with him to search for ice. At present the ship has no refrigerator so we have to hope that we can obtain some in the villages we visit. We were fortunate to purchase the ice in a completely native village. It will keep the ice-box going for a day or so.

After lunch we steamed slowly up the river for 22 miles and then dropped anchor for the night. The purpose of these Patrols is to show the flag; visit the scattered villages in the rivers; ascertain how far the rivers are navigable for this kind of craft; and finally to look out for any of our little yellow friends who may be snooping around these parts.

The 22 miles provided a fascinating experience. The Romplin is a long, winding river with magnificent reaches and thick tropical jungle on both sides. We had tea sitting on the fo'c's'le and watching bits of wood drifting down stream. Suddenly one of the pieces of wood turned out to be a crocodile! By the time Bill Mellor fetched his rifle the crocodile must have been laughing at us.

'The Chief' of this ship lives in the Isle of Orkney. That takes me back in mind to the winter of 1939/40 when Scapa Flow in the Orkneys and Sollum Voe in Shetland provided some of the bases from which we used to work.

### August 27th 1941

Another wonderful Monday morning. Bill, Tony and I took a plunge over the side to wake ourselves up. We didn't remain in the water long for fear of sharks. Our day's sailing took us up to the Pahang about 15 miles then down again where we visited the village and managed to replace the ice. As the Skipper was anxious to reach the mouth of the River Endau by sundown we were off soon after lunch and had an uneventful afternoon at sea, arriving at about 6 pm. This Patrol is passing all too quickly.

### August 28th 1941

At 8.30 this morning we were visited by an Army Captain who was doing a recce of these parts. He had a Sergeant and two Privates with him. They hailed us from the shore and came out in a local sampan. While we chatted we served them all with coffee. They seemed fascinated and delighted to discover that the Navy were up here. It seemed to me as an outsider that there is precious little cooperation between the Services.

After their departure a Mr Mavor, the District Customs Officer, came aboard by arrangement to spend two days with us. Although dutywise the purpose of this visit was to travel by river over his vast parish, the private purpose of his visit was to discuss with me the Baptism of his infant son who was four months old. He came to inquire whether the Baptism could take place on board HMS *Hung Joa*.

We steamed west along the Endau for some miles with the State of Johore on the south bank and the State of Pahang on the other. Then the Endau turned north but we continued west along the River Sembarong.

Mr Mavor seemed to be a man of strong Christian principles who was anxious to give his baby a good Christian start in life. Aged about 32, he lived at Mersing, 30 miles south of Endau, with his wife and baby. The Mavors being strict Presbyterians from the very north of Scotland wanted their baby brought up in the Protestant Succession. After a chat with Bill Mellor he decided that both the Church of England and I would pass the test.

We went through the Baptism Service in the Prayer Book and he was pleasantly surprised to discover that it contained Scripture. We made one or two alterations and he asked me to add some prayers which I felt would satisfy all Courts of Law.

He said how thrilled he was to be on this trip and he thought that very few white men, if any, had explored this river before.

Our previous experience of the jungle was child's play compared with this journey. The current of the river was so strong that as we rounded the bends, in spite of both engines endeavouring to pull the ship round, she would be swept to the other bank. At times the whole ship was literally lost in branches of trees which came on board! Most of us were employed with boat hooks trying to push the ship out, or with huge knives cutting off branches which literally wrapped themselves round the foremast and mainmast.

The Malay crew seemed terrified and did nothing. Apparently the

Malays are scared by the jungle, especially of snakes and tigers. One bend is very much like the next so one can only generalise. The jungle is so dense that we just peered hurriedly at the huge black monkeys which swung back and forth. We passed a couple of turtles either fighting or making love. Bill Mellor had a hurried shot at them with a rifle but missed so we did not have turtle soup for supper.

I couldn't help comparing my patrol here with that of two years ago in the Arctic. On the latter we had ploughed along in the icy, stormy seas, day after day, week after week, month after month. We were never without a lifebelt, thankful to have greatcoat, mittens and balaclava. On this patrol, clad only in shorts and gym shoes, sailing on glassy tropical rivers amidst dense jungle and with a burning sun above; occasionally the bows became lost in passing branches and the masts were in danger of snapping.

On arrival we tied up to some rasau palms, one of the 132 brands of palm in Malaya. They are like huge reeds growing out of the water. We took the foremast down in preparation for the return journey the next day. From the jungle came the sound of crashing branches and the trampling of twigs which meant that some of the big chaps, tigers and elephants were on the move.

### August 29th 1941

At about 8.30 am we commenced our perilous journey back to the sea. Coming up the river facing the current was difficult, but now having the current going our way made the journey a nightmare. We literally raced along and although both engines were in reverse we couldn't slow the ship down on the bends. Bill Mellor had us all equipped with ropes and large knives. The ropes were used to throw around passing trees to slow us down and the knives to cut off the branches of trees which came on board. While under way we lowered the main mast. It was as well we did otherwise it might have snapped under the weight of branches and the speed at which we were travelling. Some of the ropes snapped and some held. The ones which held we retrieved. Someone was sent back in the dinghy to collect them! One rope which snapped, wrapped itself round the propellor. Bill Mellor bravely dived over the side with a long knife, freed the propellor and then returned on board without having been bitten by a crocodile.

At about 1 pm to our relief we entered the wider reaches of the river and anchored at Endau at 6 pm. Mr Mavor left us and we collected another 30 lbs of ice. So after this exciting day, with no mishaps or accidents, we had an early meal and read until we all turned in at 10 o'clock.

We were under way by 7 am on Thursday morning and made for a beautiful little bay with a curving shore on one side and a small island on the other. Around us were other little islands, all wooded, rising straight out of the glassy blue seas. The air was fresh and we watched the sun rise to commence its daily routine.

After breakfast, while the Ship's Company were engaged in their daily round and common task, I was left alone on the fo'c's'le with my Bible and Prayer Book amidst these heavenly surroundings.

While we were on our hair-raising dash down the River Sembarong the previous day, we took on board hundreds of red ants; huge brutes with a nasty nip. In spite of hosing the decks and killing all we could see there must have still been a large number on the loose. During the night I woke up several times scratching, and in the morning I was told that my back was one mass of bites. Tony Clarke was the same. We covered our backs with iodine, which stopped the itching. As we were already sunburned to mahogany, the iodine didn't make any difference to our colour!

During the forenoon the sailors, Bill Mellor and Tony Clarke, painted the ship while I typed out several copies of the Baptism Service for the coming Christening.

About 3 o'clock we all went ashore in the dinghy, the crew following in relays. We had a wash and a bath in a fresh water well and then spent a couple of hours in and around a very quaint Chinese-Malay settlement. It was too small to be called a village and consisted of about a dozen native bungalows. There was a small shop which sold cigarettes, drinks of sorts, biscuits and coconut oil. The headman was very friendly and insisted on presenting us with fish.

Fishing is their trade and they catch them in varying sizes from sharks to eels or shrimps. The fish are dried on mats and the children sort them into various sizes and put them in baskets. The children also make the nets and lines with 80 hooks and prepare them for the next trip to sea.

Back on board, sitting on the fo'c's'le, doing my evening reading and meditation, I couldn't help thinking how strange life is. Most of the world is engaged in a savage, bitter war, while we, here in the China Seas, are literally lost amidst the wonders of nature. The foliage, the jungle, the palms, the numerous lovely birds, the peacocks, the cheeky monkeys, swinging about in the trees, always chattering, travelling along with us up and down the rivers, and the animals, friendly and unfriendly, the interesting people and even the insects! I found myself turning to Psalm 104.

## August 31st 1941

Sailing south, we anchored off Mersing at 1.30 pm and after lunch prepared our little fo'c's'le for our Christening party. We fixed a white sheet over a tall box for the Font, and placed a basin surrounded by flowers and leaves on the top. It looked quite nice. Service commenced at 4.45 pm.

I had typed out five or six copies of the Service which extended to two pages. I stuck the two pages back to back with a piece of cardboard between, so it seemed more than just a piece of paper.

The little chap, Ian was as good as gold and never murmured the whole time. The parents appeared to be very moved by this little Service and took with them two copies. Tony Clarke told me later that it was by far the most lovely service he had attended for a long time. Later he told me that as we said prayers for the tiny baby, he was thinking of his own little daughter in New Zealand and that, for the first time since he had left home in New Zealand, he had a good weep.

After the Service we all had tea on the fo'c's'le and an interesting and open discussion about the Christian Faith. I hope that I was able to present our precious Gospel to them all in a way which they could understand. Somehow the Service seemed to be much more than a Christening. It was a Service which touched us all.

The Mavors asked me why we make the sign of the Cross on the baby's forehead. I pointed out that the death of the Son of God on a Roman Cross, which we commemorate on Good Friday, was the climax of God's Love for the whole human race and for every individual on earth. So all who took a Christian name also took His Sign on the forehead to remind us that in the words of St Paul, "He loved me and gave Himself for me".

The Mavor family then left *Hung Joa* and I went with them to ring up Jock Seng and let him know that we would be back on Saturday afternoon. This telephone call really brought me back to earth.

Mr and Mrs Mavor and I returned to the ship for dinner. She had brought with her heaps of what we call Keti Makan, little eats, eggs, peanuts, fishpaste, potato crisps and so on, which we ate straight away and then we had dinner. Afterwards a number of Military people arrived from somewhere and we all sat around and drank coffee. We sailed in the early hours as Bill Mellor wanted to catch the tide.

**September 1st 1941**

HMS *Hung Joa* sailed into her berth in the Naval Base at 2 pm on Saturday. While the 'entering harbour and securing' duties were being carried out, I walked back through the Dockyard and Naval Base to my bungalow to fetch the car.

Jock Seng, his wife and child and Small gave me a rapturous welcome which was very heartening. I told Jock Seng that there would be three of us to supper and breakfast. Then I returned to *Hung Joa* with Small and brought the sailors back to the bungalow. But first we took our ERA to the Barracks with his gear.

**September 2nd 1941**

While Bill and Tony slept on and on, I had to be up in good time for the 8 o'clock Holy Communion. This was followed by Matins at 9.30. Next I visited Kranji at 11 am. I usually go there on the last Sunday of the month but to suit me they altered it to the first Sunday.

A whole crowd of New Zealanders joined the usual Evensong congregation which meant a really inspiring Service. There hadn't been a moment for me to think all day but at supper that night I felt I could relax at last.

I wanted to thank these two for having me on board and for giving me such a wonderful week, the journey of a lifetime. They wouldn't hear of my paying a Mess bill, saying that the debt of all the New Zealanders in Singapore could never be repaid for my giving them a home from home.

Isn't it strange how things work out. As you know I had no end of bother getting this little place to myself. Now that I have it, men who I have never heard of, and didn't know existed, have benefited from the place being mine. As they sit around they are always talking about New Zealand and they hope that one day, when this frightful business is over, I will go there to visit them. They tell me that I will love their country and the people. They also say their wives depend on me more than I realise. I find this hard to believe but I really will try to meet them all one day.

The other day the Commander-in-Chief, Admiral Sir Geoffrey Layton, met me and said, "You don't seem to be short of friends these days. Might I drop in and meet some of them? I won't fix a day I will just come."

### September 3rd 1941

Monday forenoon was indeed business as usual. After an hour at the Church and an hour's censoring, I called on a few senior Officers to let them know that the wanderer had returned. Some of them were curious and envious and would like to be invited to go on one of these Patrols. I spent the whole afternoon visiting and then relaxed for the evening. I rang Polly. I think she and Mike Halliday hope to get married in October and they have asked me to be available. It is so pleasant to be able to read through one's mail slowly. I am so thankful that all is well your end and that our atheist allies are holding on. There was mail from all sorts of people but nothing from the Cummin family. I have sent them several postcards.

It is the anniversary of the outbreak of war and I can't close this letter to you without mentioning it. What a lot has happened to the world, to our country and to us as individuals in two years. However, thanks to the help of God and his standards which we fight for, not to mention the steadfastness of all you at home, we are still in the fight, against evil powers and evil things which Mr Neville Chamberlain spoke about in his address to the nation on Sunday 3rd September 1939.

From here it doesn't seem that the end will come before 1944 or 1945. I believe the Nips will come in soon and then things will get worse before they get better. When will America take the plunge? Perhaps, if she is attacked, she will have to come in. Then victory will come sooner. Until America joins us we just keep Tennyson's words before us, "To strive, to seek, to find and not to yield."

## September 6th 1941

The sailors from the *Hung Joa* have had supper here tonight. They returned on board early as they are off on their next Patrol early Friday morning. They have warned me to expect an invasion from the next batch of New Zealanders who are coming back to the Base tomorrow.

## September 12th 1941

In spite of my being away for some days we had two full houses at church last Sunday, including a number from the first New Zealand batch. I hope to be able to persuade the new Bishop of Singapore, Bishop Wilson who had been the Dean of Hong Kong Cathedral, to come out to a Confirmation. I only have three candidates at present but the visit would give him an opportunity to meet the folk here. My candidates are two boys, one lady and perhaps Tony Clarke. Bill Mellor is not certain whether he has been baptised so he has written to New Zealand to find out. If he hasn't I hope to get him thrown in for good measure.

I had lunch in the destroyer *Stronghold* yesterday. It is always such a pleasure for me to go on board. They have a good Captain and are a very happy ship. (*Later . . . 1984. This wonderful little ship was sunk in the aftermath of Singapore. The* Daily Telegraph *wrote In memoriam 'Their name liveth for evermore'.* HMS Stronghold. *Remember with pride this little ship. Timor Sea, 2nd March, 1942.*")

I have the first wedding at the Naval Base Church on September 30th and another one on October 1st. Then Polly and Mike's will be at Tanglin, Singapore on October 9th. Also I have a crop of Baptisms. It never rains, but it pours!

I have collected and sold 300 copies of the second edition of our News Bulletin. There are very few comments this time. The thing seems to be established and taken for granted. When I collected them from the printers the manager told me that, owing to paper rationing, the size of the magazine would be cut by half. I told him that as we only had three copies a year, his suggestion was not on, so he agreed to leave them at their present size.

## September 15th 1941

A young Sub-Lieutenant arrived from England as the Bomb Disposal Officer for the Naval Base. He was accommodated in the next block of bungalows to me, with several Paymasters.

I invited him over to tea and said to him, "I think we have met somewhere before." So we did some research into the past.

I think that it was in 1934, when on my way back to Newton Abbot after spending a few days in Peckham, that I stayed with the Rev. Peter Brook at Canford School, Wimborne, where he was the Chaplain. On the Sunday afternoon we were walking through the school grounds when we passed a boy walking on his own. Peter asked him his name.

He replied, "Lilburn, Sir."

Peter said, "Where do you live?"

The boy replied, "At Coull, Deeside in Scotland."

Peter asked, "Why ever does your Father send you all the way down to Dorset to school?"

He said, "I don't know, Sir."

I had met him before and now he was to be our Bomb Disposal Officer, Sub-Lieutenant Alistair Lilburn. He got hold of a big car, which meant that his petrol ration was quite large. So we were able to use one of the smaller cars with his petrol. This meant that we could go a little further. In fact, he often used my car to save petrol and he proved not only a good Messmate but a valuable member of our church congregation.

*I heard later that Alistair was captured by the Japanese in Sumatra while trying to escape. During the three and half years he was in captivity, he organised and led the Church Services in his camp and he learnt two or three languages. After his return to England at the end of the war he was very ill for many months in Aberdeen, where I was able to visit him. He recovered and became a Professor in Electrical Science. He is a Godfather to our son Andrew and later emigrated to New Zealand where I lost touch with him until his return to Scotland.*

The China Clipper and a large sea mail have arrived. The great news really is that you all seem to be in good heart. In your sea mail there was a long letter from Mrs Cummin. I was glad to have news of all the Cummin family, especially of those who are in London. When you next write to her please thank her for her letter.

## September 18th 1941

Thank you for my birthday letter and card which arrived unexpectedly. The Clippers have been very irregular recently. I think I have already told you that the Mail from here goes by Flying Boat to Manila; Flying Boat to Hong Kong; Flying Boat to Hawaii; Flying Boat to San Francisco or Vancouver; aeroplane across America or Canada and then Flying boat to England! It is known as the Pacific Clipper and the Atlantic Clipper.

I have had a letter from Mr and Mrs Mavor thanking me for taking the Baptism of their son Ian and inviting me to spend Christmas with them at Mersing.

The Happy Couple, Polly and Mike, came out to the bungalow for a Birthday Supper. Also present were the two sailors from the *Hung Joa*, Alistair Lilburn and three others. Jock Seng was in splendid form, serving a first class meal and putting on his best behaviour. It was a good evening.

The seasons come and go but are always the same. It is always green. We have just had Harvest, my second here. I had two big Services at the Base Church, St Peter's, and then another at Kranji, the outstation. I have no complaints about numbers attending but I am afraid that some of the devotion is only skin deep. I am amazed at the amount of overtime being worked on the Base in the Offices, including a good many wives. The great majority would not think of giving up time on a Sunday for God and His Worship. "Ye cannot serve God and mammon" the majority agree, and stick to mammon. The two weddings were happy occasions, not to speak of several Baptisms which besides being happy were also noisy.

Owing to the monsoon and typhoons, the mail and especially the flying boats between Singapore, Manila and Hong Kong have been delayed. The humidity has to be experienced to be believed. We have literally been walking about in a steam bath. Hence, the Malay expression 'Tidapa', meaning 'never mind'!

### October 10th 1941

On October 8th, the day before their wedding, I went to Tanglin Church in Singapore to sign the many forms required for a wedding. There are literally dozens needed in this cosmopolitan city. The forms and registers completed, Polly, Mike and I went through the Service in the Church.

From my point of view it went off very smoothly and with no hitches. The Bride looked most attractive while Mike was confident and clear in his answers. The church looked simply lovely with masses of flowers of every description and an abundance of gardenias and orchids.

The reception was well organised and there were no long, tedious speeches.

I heard one woman say, "I enjoyed this wedding much more than my own."

A man was heard to remark, "Hearing that Service made me want to be married again."

I didn't like to ask him, "With the same wife?"

The whole thing was a simply delightful occasion and I am only sorry that you could not be present. To me, the one disappointing thing about weddings is that they are over so quickly. I am sure they will be writing to you both about the day's events.

### October 11th 1941

After the reception Polly and Mike were driven away in his car. About a mile away from Tanglin I met them and they changed to mine while Mike's car was driven back to Changi by his syce.

I brought them out to my bungalow at the Base for the evening. After supper, a splendid meal produced by Jock Seng with great pride, I drove them over to the Railway Station at Johore Barhu where they boarded the train for the north and their honeymoon.

I met a man in Singapore recently who told me that he was a millionaire. He didn't say whether it was pounds sterling or American dollars. Whichever it is, money is certainly no object and he goes out of his way to help the Services which is very refreshing.

He takes in about ten Naval Ratings at a time, puts them up and feeds them for four days, and then has the next batch. It makes such a pleasant change for the Matelots who do long periods at sea in battened-down ships.

## October 21st 1941 (Trafalgar Day)

The Royal Navy out here have been toasting 'The Immortal Memory' of Lord Nelson and the Royal Navy. How splendid they have been over the past two years in keeping the oceans of the world open for our ships to travel hither and thither. Out here, besides our Trafalgar Day, there is a Hindu Festival and also a Malay one. This means that there is even less work than usual being done. The Dockyard is very quiet.

Some of the New Zealanders have heard that their Patrol boats are being taken away from the east coast of Malaya so I am glad I managed to get my trip in.

In the congregation last Sunday night, besides the New Zealanders, there was a Lieutenant David Fiennes who has a patrol boat similar to those of the New Zealanders, but he is English and comes from Yalding in Kent.

My car is at present in Johore Barhu having the brakes relined. However I am not without transport. Alistair Lilburn has gone to Hong Kong for a week or so and has lent me his, a huge 25 horse power giant!

## November 11th 1941 (Armistice Day 1918) A Gift for the Garden.

Today is the anniversary of Armistice Day, 1918 and I was visited by a civilian member of the Base.

He said, "As you know, I am about to return home. I have had a good look round the Base at the houses, the bungalows and the people, and I have decided on you."

I wondered whatever was coming.

He went on, "If you will accept them, I would like to make you a gift of these flowering plants and this tiny mulberry tree. I ordered and paid for the tree about three months ago; it has only just arrived. I want a good home for them and I think you will fit the bill."

I thanked him for his generous gift and also for doing me the honour of choosing me. I told him that my delightful Tamil gardener would be charmed with all these plants and, even though I am not much of a gardener, they would be in good hands, in good Tamil hands. I must add that when he said he wanted a 'good home for the mulberry tree' he might have been giving me a dog!

I hardly knew this man but I suppose I had called on him when engaged in my parochial visiting. As there are scores of these people, even hundreds of them, it is quite impossible to remember all their faces.

The married men get a house for husband, wife and children while the bachelors and the unaccompanied married men live four to a house.

Anyway, my garden is now looking quite well stocked with creepers, spinach, bananas and now these flowers, plants and a mulberry tree.

## November 14th 1941

Last night I played rugger again for the RN side. In fact I captained the team. We were far too good for our opponents and gave them a merciless hiding.

The Commander-in-Chief and Lady Layton came along to the match. They were supported by a number of Naval Brass Hats. As usual most of the sailors in the Barracks turned up and we were thrashing these people; all the time the cheering was tremendous. Also present were about a dozen New Zealanders who said that they had come to see their Parson play. The Admiral and Lady Layton quickly spotted them and seemed to spend most of their time with them, telling them how much they enjoyed meeting them all at my bungalow. The Laytons, they told me afterwards, have invited several of them to their house on the Straits of Johore.

I was glad to receive such wholehearted support from the RN Officers and Ratings and it did the Church no harm to have the Chaplain of the Naval Base leading the team to victory.

## December 2nd 1941

Last night I went down to the Dockyard to watch the arrival of HMS *Prince of Wales* and HMS *Repluse* at the Base, Singapore.

As I stood on the jetty I heard a voice from somewhere up in the *Prince of Wales* call out, "I spy with my little eye, a turbulent Priest from the Royal Naval School of Music at Deal. How some of us get around in quiet shore numbers too."

It was Captain Claude Alywin with whom I had served at Deal. You may remember that we were both going to take a party of Band Boys on the Broads but as we both picked up ships we never got there. When she had tied up, I went aboard the *Prince of Wales* and he kindly invited me to remain to supper.

As I left I happened to see Major Bobby Lang on the upper deck of the *Repluse*. We had a brief chat and I am going to lunch with him in a couple of days. As you will remember he and I were shipmates in the *Woolwich* in the Mediterranean in 1936/38.

Last week Polly and Mike invited me over to supper and asked me to bring Bill Mellor and Tony Clarke as well. This trip to Changi made a pleasant change for us. After supper they showed us their wedding presents with which they are adorning their most attractive Married Quarter. While we were looking at the presents I think we were wondering what would happen if the Japs attack Malaya.

The general feeling is that the attack from these treacherous Japs can't be long delayed now. By propaganda, they are encouraging the subject people of the British Empire to rebel and get rid of their oppressors. Instead they are invited to join the Japanese and their 'Co-prosperity Sphere of East Asia!' The question we are asking is: "Will they attack America at the same time as they attack the British Empire?" If they do, then in spite of some early successes they will finally be doomed as Germany is after her attack on Russia.

I have collected, and distributed 300 copies of the third edition of the Base News Bulletin and the Magazine is solvent. (*After the war in the Far East had ended in 1945, the Naval Base News Bulletin Account in the Bank in Singapore showed a credit balance of 70 dollars! From the Editor*).

### December 6th 1941

On Saturday December 6th all sports matches were cancelled, and a 'state of emergency' was proclaimed throughout Singapore and Malaya. There was little anyone could do and Sunday passed off quite pleasantly. In fact it was the last day of peace. Although we didn't know it, the little yellow men were already on their way here.

### December 10th 1941

Although it is like preaching to the converted, I thought that you might like to know the lines on which I am thinking and what I try to teach my flock out here.

In November I began to impress on them the importance of keeping the four Sundays of Advent as a time of preparation for the Coming of the Lord; not only looking back to His Birth at Bethlehem, but also looking forward to His Coming again in Judgement. I have been spelling out to them the four-fold message of Advent; 'Wake up'; 'Stand fast'; 'Repent' and 'Be Ready'. How much a Sermon goes across or sinks in, one never knows. Perhaps that is just as well. Usually it is one or two who get the message and often that is enough.

I have tried to teach them that the individual Christian believer and the congregation always face the world; materialism, the flesh; ourselves and the devil; evil, hatred and the war. I warn them that any or all of these could take priority in the believer's heart instead of the Person of Our Lord.

With the coming of war out here, the need for vigilance regarding the soul is even greater and more urgent. What the future holds in store for us as individual believers, as a Christian congregation and as a British Colony is impossible to say.

Yesterday's Message for the second Sunday in Advent; 'Hold fast', seems to have come just in time. This was my Message last Sunday at Matins in the Base Church, at Kranji and at Evensong at the Base. In view of what happened during the following night, Japan's declaration of war, I hope this Advent Message was a help to many.

**December 11th 1941**

During the night of December 7th/8th we were woken up at about 4 am by the sound of air raid sirens, aircraft engines and a few loud crumps. I remember saying to myself, "So they have commenced their campaign of conquest and hatred". However we were back from the shelters by 6 am and were soon asleep again.

That day our two large ships *The Prince of Wales* and *Repluse* left the Base escorted by four Destroyers, the *Express*, the *Echo*, the *Vampire* and the little *Tenedos*. Starting on December 8th the daily bombing of the six targets by the huge Japanese bomber armadas began in earnest and was to continue until the fall of Singapore in February. The six targets were the Naval Base, the four aerodromes and Singapore town and docks.

While we were in the shelters yesterday we heard, from a radio someone had brought in, the terrible news of the sinking of our two great ships *The Prince of Wales* and *Repulse* by Japanese torpedo bombers and that our destroyers were picking up survivors. We were filled with despair, these two ships had sailed from the Naval Base so recently and now they had gone; lying at the bottom of the China Seas.

During the night of December 10th/11th the destroyers returned to the Base carrying about 2,000 survivors. This meant that hundreds and hundreds were lost.

About 9.30 am next morning I was rung up by Claude Alywin. He told me that the Dockyard Clothing Department could not meet the huge demands for clothing for so many survivors. He wanted to know whether I could suggest a clothing shop in Singapore who might be able to fit out the 60 Royal Marines of his detachment. I took him into town and we returned with masses of shorts, shirts and trousers, and a Chinese fitter. I did the same for Major Bobby Lang of the *Repulse*. He told me that he left the *Repulse* by jumping over the side. Then he swam, using a very slow breast stroke, towards the *Express* about a quarter of a mile away. I asked him about sharks.

He replied, "Sharks! I was frightened enough as it was. If I had thought about sharks, I should have had a heart attack and died!"

A large number of men who had been badly burnt or wounded as a result of the numerous Japanese aerial torpedo attacks were taken to various Singapore Hospitals.

The Royal Marines Detachment from the *Prince of Wales* moved to Kranji and took over the defence of the Station.

The *Repulse* Detachment became a roving mobile force about the Base at night, to try to catch those 5th Columnists sending up rockets and flares to guide the Jap Bombers in.

The Officers and Ratings, besides providing extra sentries within the Base, were mannig the RN launches on the west coast of Malaya. The Japs had crossed over the east coast and were now coming down the west coast in small boats. This particular RN party was based on Batu Bahat, south of Malacca.

The Chaplain of HMS *Prince of Wales*, Rev. W. G. Parker, went down with the ship. He was in the Wardroom, which was the Number Two Sick Bay, at 'Action Stations'.

The Chaplain of the *Repulse*, Canon J. S. Bessant, survived but took a considerable amount of oil into his lungs. This was to affect him throughout his career. I understand that he left for Colombo with other wounded fairly soon after the disaster. Some time after the war he became Dean of St John's College, Cambridge.

## December 16th 1941

After tremendous activity by the Naval Base wives to get the Red Cross started and under way, we now hear that all women and children in Malaya and Singapore are to be evacuated in January 1942. Now the Red Cross effort has closed down.

On the Naval Base there are six enormous oil tanks. They were soon set alight by Japanese bombs and they all blazed for weeks.

One evening Polly rang me up from Changi, ten miles away as the crow flies, to enquire whether anything was being done or could be done to control the blazing oil tanks because they had turned night into day.

I said, "Nothing is being done and nothing can be done; they will have to burn out."

## December 26th 1941

Because the Nips work, fly or bomb to a strict timetable, we were able to arrange our Christmas Church Services at times when we knew there would be no heavy raids.

At the Base churches we had our Carol Service, Sermon and Communion on Christmas Eve and Holy Communion and Matins on Christmas Day. Then I moved on to Kranji, ten miles away. This was a most unusual and worthwhile occasion.

We started with carols. Then followed the Baptism of a baby; more carols; a short address and finally the Christmas Communion. The whole Station attended and entered into the Service with heart and soul. A large number of those present took the Sacrament, including my Royal Marine friend Claude Alywin. I found it all most moving and inspiring. The new Christian baby left for Colombo a week later.

Here is a summary of the sermon I preached at the Christmas Eve Service in the Naval Base church.

"My subject tonight is 'Why Christmas?' It is a subject which must be in all our minds. Does Christmas have any meaning when we think through the situation in which we find ourselves here in Singapore? We all know that the Japanese are closing in on us, and that the burning oil tanks have turned night into day. We who meet in this church tonight are a cross section of the Naval Base; men and women; Service and Civilian.

"I must preach what I believe and believe what I preach.

"I believe that Jesus of Nazareth; the Babe of Bethlehem; the Child of Eternity; came to this earth and began life in a manger of wood.

"I believe that until He was aged 30, he lived in a village called Nazareth and was the village carpenter, always dealing with wood.

"I believe that He left his village and became a Wandering Preacher.

"He spoke to men of God and the world, about nature, about flowers and about people.

"He told men and women how they should live, behave and believe.

"Some accepted what he taught while others rejected both Him and His teaching.

"In the end it was too much for some and they managed to get rid of Him by having Him killed in the Roman way, on a Cross.

"He began life in a manger of wood and He ended life on a Cross of wood.

"Now in a wonderful way which I don't understand and can't explain, God used His death to forgive us our sins and the evil in our hearts. 'God so loved that He gave.'

"Tonight I put it to myself and I put it to you that our first priority is not the Japanese closing in, or the blazing oil tanks, or even our own lives. The first priority is that Jesus the Christ should be born and installed and established and enthroned in every heart here.

"I have no other message for you. 'He loved you and gave Himself for you.'

"Receive His word and receive Him in the Sacrament. Receive His Forgiveness and receive His Presence. God be with you all, Amen."

### January 16th 1942

By now, all my neighbours have gone. The wives have left by transport for Colombo. Their husbands have moved to a Mess near the centre of the Base. The Naval Officers Mess, which included the Paymasters, Bomb Disposal and a few others have all moved up to the Fleet Shore Accommodation so I am left in solitary state; nearly solitary confinement! It is certainly rather lonely down at this corner of the Base, especially at night. During the hours of darkness, gun and rifle shots ring out and rockets and flares ascend skywards to guide the bombers in.

Twice this month my Royal Marines friends Claude Aylwin and Bobby Lang have been in for an evening meal. Afterwards Claude returns to Kranji where his detachment are guarding the Station. I have twice been out with Bobby Lang and his detachment. These Marines make a good deal of noise as they move around to scare off the fifth columnists. There was a bit of shooting the other night but all the Marines found in the morning were a few fingers!

With the departure of the women we now have an eight to one majority of men in the congregation.

Last Sunday no organist arrived to play and so we said Morning prayer which made a pleasant change. I think the congregation really enjoyed it. I played at Evensong, including the hymn *A Few More Years Shall Roll*. It is a good old hardy annual and I like it so long as not too many of them roll at the Naval Base!

Last Saturday I had a telephone call from a man living on the west coast of Singapore Island. He had a Mr Laird staying with him; a mining engineer from Ipoh whom I had got to know when I was on leave in the Cameron Highlands. They invited me to tea that afternoon. I said that I had a Royal Marine Officer staying with me and asked if I might bring him along too. Claude Alywin had come from Kranji for lunch and was delighted to have the opportunity of seeing more of the islands. It was new territory for me too. Our hosts were fascinated to meet a survivor of the *Prince of Wales* and we had a most enjoyable time there. Mr Laird had left Ipoh with a high fever, had lost his home and all his possessions, but was thankful to be alive. He was to leave for Australia in a day or so.

### January 17th 1942

We had a long wait for the Japs to unload their explosives on us this morning. As I returned to my bungalow to do some censoring I saw an English woman pass by. Why she was still here, I don't know. I told her to get in the shelter at once. She did! Two or three minutes later I heard the sound of masses of Jap bombers. I knew the sound of their engines by now and I fled to the shelter myself. As I reached the top of the shelter steps I invited a Tamil workman to join us but he declined. I jumped down the 14 steps in one and landed flat on my face. This position saved me. At that moment the bombs arrived and our shelter took a direct hit. I was still on my face. The flash passed over me.

I was the first to leave the shelter and found the Tamil badly wounded. I rushed to my bungalow to get him a drink but by the time I returned he was dead. I too had had a close shave!

The blast of the bombs removed the side of my bungalow and some of the ceilings. As I set about putting out several fires and began to clear up the mess the phone rang. It was the Rev. Cyril Tucker who had just arrived as the RAF Chaplain at Tengah airfield. We had been at Ridley Hall, Cambridge, together.

He said, "I arrived at Tengah yesterday. Come and have lunch."

I said, "I can't come today. My bungalow has just been hit in this morning's raid and we are putting out fires."

I never saw him in Singapore, but we did meet in Java, Indonesia.

Later that day, the woman who I had told to get to the shelter came to thank me for saving her life. I told her that I must practise what I preach, as I nearly lost mine that morning.

Jock Seng said to me, "Master go."

I said, "No Jock Seng, Master stay."

He replied, "No, Master go. Jock Seng stay in Singapore."

He was right! After this experience, I am shaking like a leaf, but I suppose I shall get over it. I am turning in early.

### January 18th 1942

I dropped off into an uneasy sleep last night, and then it happened. There has been a plague of rats lately and I have heard them scampering about on the top of my asbestos ceilings. After yesterday's raid half the ceilings were gone. As the rats ran across they ran into empty space and fell on top of my mosquito net. It sagged down on to me. Was I scared? I just didn't know what to do. All this took place in the dark and I grabbed my torch. I hit out at them and they ran off.

Today, I took my little dog Small to Singapore and had her put down. She has been so terrified lately that it seemed the kindest thing to do. Tony Clarke came with me and took her into the Veterinary Hospital. I have lost a real friend and companion and many who use the bungalow as home feel the same.

Captain 'Hookey' Bell, of *HMS Exeter*, fame is now Captain of *HMS Sultan*. He told us that he had received a telegram from his wife who has been evacuated to Australia. It read, 'Hookey, I am terribly, terribly worried about you. He sent the following reply. 'I am terribly, terribly worried about myself, Hookey.'

### January 22nd 1942

An RN Party of Officers and Ratings, survivors of *HMS Prince of Wales* and *HMS Repulse,* found themselves manning the launches on the west coast of Malaya to oppose the Japs in their small boats. They had their headquarters at the Golf Club at Batu Pahat, a town between Singapore and Malacca. As they had few visitors they asked me to go and spend a few days with them.

At the time I had two Officers, Lieutenant David Fiennes and Sub-Lieutenant Tony Clarke, staying in my bungalow on sick leave. What a place to come to!

I made an early start, having obtained permission to be away from the Base for a day or so, and drove north to a place called Ayer Hittam. Then I turned sharp west and took the road for Batu Pahat. As I went along I was surprised to see cars driving the other way at high speed with mattresses on the roofs. Overhead were the huge Jap bomber fleets on their way to Singapore Island to give the various targets their daily pounding.

The last ten miles I drove through a rubber plantation on a very good

111

road. I had to turn off south by the one mile signpost for the Golf Club. As I drew near I pulled up behind an army truck and got out of my car.

I said to the driver of the truck, "Can you tell me the way to the Golf Club please."

A Cockney voice said, "You won't play golf today chum."

I said, "I don't want to play golf, I am trying to find the Naval Party who are staying there."

He replied, "The Navy have gone with their boats to Sumatra. The Japs have captured Batu Pahat and are on both sides of this road among the rubber trees.

I said, "Whatever do we do?"

He said, "Hop it chum, as fast as you can, just like I am going to do. I am the wireless truck and I know it all. Cheer up and step on it."

I turned my open car round and then did between 80 and 90 miles an hour back to Ayer Hittam. I was very frightened. Now I had a problem. The RN had promised me petrol to return to Singapore. By this time my tank was nearly empty and there was no RN. But I was lucky. Just near by I saw a Royal Army Service Corps sign and so I drove along a sandy road until I came upon the main camp and store. It was an Indian RASC. I met the Officer in Charge, told him of my need and he fixed me up with six gallons.

Then he said, "What's that noise of gunfire?"

I said, "It's the Japs. They are only a few miles away and Batu Pahat has fallen." They quickly went over to an alert and prepared to pack up and move their stores south. I went on my way feeling that I had also done them a good turn.

I had a nonstop run home and my guests were very surprised to see me arrive back. At the Base no one knew that Batu Pahat had fallen to the Japs so I broke the news. Neither did they know that the Chaplain had nearly wandered into the Jap bag! What a relief it is to be back. I still feel very jumpy but a good night's sleep should put me right, Japs, rats and all!

### January 29th 1942

Thank you for all your air mail 'Clipper' letters and the sea mail, which has arrived so regularly ever since I came out here. I can't tell you how sustaining they have been to body, mind and soul over all these months.

The Commander-in-Chief and his Staff left for Colombo soon after the capital ships were sunk.

All women and children in Malaya and Singapore have gone or are going shortly. Some of us are very worried that Polly is still here, but we hear that she should be off to Colombo in a few days.

As many English civilian men working in the Base as can be spared are going and will be employed elsewhere.

We hear that soldiers are still arriving to join in the fray in an effort to stop the Japanese onslaught.

It is not for me, a humble layman, to comment on military affairs but I can't help feeling that, with the Sons of Nippon ruling the skies and their soldiers approaching the Straits of Johore, the military situation must be very serious.

During my 21 months here I have aimed at putting the church life on a firm foundation and to pass on not only an outward looking congregation but also a Christian Church Primary School. In my endeavours I have been well supported by many on the Base, both Service and Civilian personnel.

In the words of the ancient prayer I have tried:- 'To preach the Gospel, to strengthen and confirm the faithful, visit the parishioners, relieve the sick, arouse the careless and convert the wicked.'

During the past seven weeks I have watched the physical disappearance of my flock and congregation. Nevertheless, I am certain that the congregation carry with them their Christian Faith. In the things of the Spirit the results are always intangible.

I think the lesson I am learning these days is that it is not success as we think of it that counts, but faithfulness.

'It is all very well to be happy and bright when life goes along like a song. But the man worthwhile is the man who can smile when everything goes dead wrong!'

And everything seems to be going dead wrong just at the moment.

The Lord's message to the Church of Smyrna (the Book of Revelation) seems right for today. 'Be thou faithful.'

To see these Service folk carrying on the daily round is an inspiration.

There go the air-raid sirens. At least they still work, so do all the electrics and there is still water in the tap. As our shelter has been hit we now use one further away. "We" includes three Officers on sick leave, Jock Seng, his wife and son and me. We now have chairs, electric light and a radio in the shelter and the amazing Jock Seng produces cups of tea and something to eat!

The others are calling me. I must be off. Cheerio for the present.

(So ends the last of the Singapore letters home.)

During the month of December my parents received the following letter from Sub-Lieutenant Tony Clarke, NZ RNVR;

> Dear Rev. and Mrs Pocock,
> I am a perfect stranger to you, but I am taking a leaf out of Lovell's book in writing to you, for does he not write to my wife?
> Let me introduce myself. Name, A. R. (Tony) Clarke of Wellington, New Zealand. Rank, Sub-Lieutenant, NZ RNVR. Together with a friend of many years standing we operate a motor launch, endeavouring to do our humble mite in these waters, to help the case of freedom in this dreadful

turmoil which has beset the world.

In Lovell, we have found a friend of untold merit. In fact we wonder how our unit would fare without his co-operation. Many times has he turned up in response to a telephone call and secured our last minute perishable provisions, which the local vendor had failed to deliver. Upon returning from patrol, a mere ring produces (a) a car; (b) a sadly needed bath; (c) food, not that we do without much, and above all, good fellowship. Believe me, it is well to have a home from home as this is.

I had tiffin with Lovell and Polly and Mike today. She is looking remarkably well and is obviously very, very happy. Polly and Mike have a lovely home at Changi with a wealth of useful gifts that reflect the esteem that they are held in. They both spoke of their regret that the wedding could not have taken place at home, but these are strange times and this is a part of the price we pay.

May good fortune be your lot and your family be reunited in the not too distant future.

Sincerely,
A. R. Clarke.

# CHAPTER VIII

## Chaplain on the run in 1942

*My journey, or retreat, from the Singapore Naval Base took me first to Batavia or Jakarta, Indonesia, and then on to Colombo in Ceylon during February and March 1942. I was then 33 years old.*

"Where are you going?" These words were addressed to me by the Civil Secretary of the Dockyard. He was the Senior Civilian member of the Dockyard, and he and the Naval Captain of the Dockyard both come under the Admiral. It was 9.30 am on January 30th 1942, just as I was entering the main Dockyard Building.

"I am going to the mail office."

"What are you going to do after that?" he asked.

"I am going back to my bungalow at Mata Gate."

"I suppose you know that the Base has to be evacuated by noon tomorrow, the 31st. The Army will be taking over the Base and facing the Japs across the Straits of Johore," the Civil Secretary said.

"This is the first I have heard of it, and I have nowhere to go. In fact I have three New Zealand Officers from the launches staying with me in my bungalow," I replied.

Most of the 12,000 Asians employed in the Base had disappeared by this time, evaporated into the jungle or Singapore after the first heavy raid by the Japanese bombers. This exodus included most of the messengers, mail orderlies, dustmen and so on. Consequently, I was down at the main offices collecting the mail.

The Civil Secretary went on, "All Naval Personnel in the Fleet Shore Accommodation, the Barracks, are going aboard HMS *Durban* and HMS *Dragon*. These ships are alongside in the Base".

The *Durban* and the *Dragon* were two old First War cruisers of about 5,000 tons each which were being used with the other old cruisers on the safe stations such as the east coast of Africa, the Indian Ocean and the south coast of America. They had now come into Singapore and were caught up in the swirling chaos. While we were talking, the Captain of HMS *Dragon* came into the main building. The Civil Secretary told him that most of the Dockyard personnel had gone and Naval personnel in the Barracks were going too. "But the Dockyard Chaplain seems to have been forgotten," he said.

He asked the Captain of *Dragon* whether he could take me.

Curtly and briskly the Captain said, "We sail at 8.30 am tomorrow. Be on

115

board at 7.30". Then he added, "A large number of Naval and Civilian families have been hurried away in a Transport ship. All their gear has been left behind in their bungalows at your end of the Base. There are trunks, camphor-wood chests and suitcases, all roped and labelled, standing in their halls. Could you use your time to get as many as you can down to the Dockyard and I will have them loaded into the *Dragon*?"

That morning we had already spotted a Japanese reconnaissance plane which meant that the big bombers would be arriving at 10.30 am precisely. One advantage of the air raids by the little yellow men was that, because they worked to a strict time-table, we could more or less plan the day. If the recce came over at 8.30 am we knew we should be free until 10.30 when the marauding hordes would appear. They came over in groups of nine and in larger groups up to 81. There were only six targets; the Naval Base, the four aerodromes, the city and docks. The Naval Base was the target for one of the large formations each day and all 81 'let go' together. The arrival of this mass of bombs was nerve-wracking but, once they were down, we knew we should have peace and quiet until the dark hours.

I now hurried to my bungalow with the news that I was closing down. As the majority of the 600 British Dockyard personnel had gone, the residential part of the Base was very quiet and almost deserted. There was no one living within a quarter of a mile of my bungalow, so I was glad to have three Officers staying with me. I have to admit that until they arrived it was a bit lonely. Two of the three had come for peace and quiet and were on sick leave. They were from the launches, which were chiefly manned by the New Zealand RNVR. Each boat carried two white Officers, a Chinese cook and Malay crew.

As a result of the raids so far my bungalow only had a roof. All the walls were gone. It was an improvised open-plan living area. Nothing separated the dining room, the bedroom, the study, the verandah and the bathroom! It certainly simplified movement. All the telephone wires were down but the bungalow remained habitable.

We now had to think what to do. While they were putting their things together I hurried to the Chapel with a suitcase. I stowed all the books in a cupboard and brought away the silver Patten and Chalice, my cassock, surplice, scarf and stoles. Back at the bungalow I packed another suitcase, a small attaché case, a mattress and a mosquito net. In mid-January I had packed most of my gear and a few books into two camphor-wood chests, one inside the other, and crated them. I took them into Singapore and found a small coaster which was sailing for Australia and New Zealand. We could send nothing westwards so one of my New Zealand friends, Tony Clarke, told me to address the crate to his home, near Wellington. The Master of the coaster offered to take this crate for me and one for Tony too. We did this to save everything from being smashed to bits at the Naval Base which was being bombed heavily every day. However, Singapore fell so

116

quickly to the Japanese that the coaster didn't get away, but at least it wasn't sunk in the harbour. (*Early in 1944, two years later, the master of the coaster became so disenchanted with his new masters and their co-prosperity sphere, that he pushed off for Australia. First he called at some Australian ports and then moved on to New Zealand. My chests were looted on the way. Everything had been stolen except my Bible and the chests themselves. In 1946 I received both the chests and the Bible, which has been used ever since back in UK from New Zealand*).

At the bungalow I told the three New Zealand officers to help themselves to anything they wanted. When the morning raid was over and two hours had been spent in the shelter we decided to go to the Naval Club for lunch. It wasn't there. It had been completely destroyed! We returned and ate at the bungalow. At about 2 pm we started our tour of the other homes and spent the next four hours loading trunks, camphor-wood chests and suitcases into my car and running them down to HMS *Dragon*.

At 6 pm my two Royal Marine friends and old ship mates, Major Claude Aylwin and Major Bobby Lang, turned up. Claude was a survivor from the *Prince of Wales* and Bobby Lang from the *Repulse*. Both ships had been sunk on December 10th 1941. A number of my Rating friends also arrived and we had quite a party. My Chinese boy took the extra influx in his stride and prepared a meal for everyone whilst remaining absolutely expressionless. The Marines left about 9 pm in a car they had acquired and took the ratings with them. The four of us left behind turned in early. I slept in my four-poster bed plus mosquito net. They only had camp beds with one mosquito net between them. We had two or three hours in the shelter but managed to rise at about 6.30 am.

At 7 am I was ready to go. First I paid and said goodbye to my Chinese Boy, Jock Seng, who had been so faithful to me for 18 months. I was running away and leaving him behind. I said goodbye to his wife and little child who had become a great friend of mine. He knew one English word and that was Goodbye. From the time when he brought me an early cup of tea, whenever I went out or returned or whenever he met me he said Goodbye. Now I was leaving them all. I gave Jock Seng an extra month's pay as well as additional money and heaps of clothing.

Sadly, leaving my little bungalow which had become home to many of us, we four drove down to the *Dragon*. The quarter deck seemed to be piled high with trunks and camphor-wood chests! I turned over the car to Tony Clarke who drove them back to the bungalow and they stripped it of anything useful. From there they travelled to the base ship in Singapore harbour and unloaded their gear. After that Tony returned to the bungalow, collected Jock Seng, his wife and child, and took them to an address in Singapore. Previously I had purchased 280 lbs of rice for Jock and taken it to an address he knew. I told Tony to use the car until he finally left and then drive it or push it into the drink.

Our days and nights in Singapore and the harbour were frightening. It was a new experience for HMS *Dragon* to be caught up in this sort of situation and the time there was one long nightmare.

Bombs came down in showers day after day, and night after night, but the harbour is a big place. Thankfully neither *Dragon* nor *Durban* was hit. Singapore City was a different matter and the whole area seemed to be ablaze.

The Captain allowed me to go ashore to try to find out whether my sister Polly had left in one of the Transport ships.

Ashore I found the shipping agents open but abandoned. It was very difficult to obtain any positive information but the little bits of news I managed to piece together seemed to suggest that she had left in the *Empress of Japan*. I went on board the base ship to find Tony Clarke. He had slept there but had gone ashore. As I noticed my car was not on the jetty I presumed that he and Bill Mellor were determined to get the coastal patrol boat, the *Hung Joa*, to Batavia if possible.

There were noisy scenes everywhere. Soldiers who had either lost their units or were deserters were roaming up and down streets in a disorderly and drunken fashion. Fires were burning all over the place and heavy gunfire could be heard all the time. I had hoped that I might be able to get in touch with Polly's husband, Mike Halliday, who was, I thought, at the Army Headquarters at Fort Canning. It was just impossible to get there.

I didn't want to be away from the ship too long. The ship's boat came to the jetty every hour to pick up anyone who had been ashore. I must say that it was very reassuring to be with the RN again after all the chaos, confusion and general mêlée ashore. The *Dragon*'s boat crew looked so neat, disciplined and steady in comparison to the rabble who were rushing about the streets with apparently nowhere to go.

It was at this time that the troopship, *Empress of Asia*, arrived in Singapore. The choice of the names of some of these ships seemed to be unfortunate.

First the *Empress of Japan* and the *Duchess of Bedford* were leaving, and now the *Empress of Asia* docked. It seemed unbelievable to many of us that troops should still be arriving and then, after weeks on board, going straight into battle. It was in some ways fortunate that the soldiers didn't know how very serious the military situation was. The other services, the RN and RAF, seemed to be trying to get their men away in the hope that they could launch an offensive from elsewhere. The Navy still in these waters comprised the *Dragon* and *Durban* and a few small craft. The only planes to be seen were Japanese. They were able to roam the Singapore skies at will.

The *Dragon* was the first of the two cruisers to leave the harbour. Although it was with a sense of relief that we found ourselves at sea, it was also with heavy hearts and great sadness. We had left so many of our friends and our kith and kin in such a desperate plight, fighting against the ferocious Japanese. When many miles south, we could still see the pall of smoke rising from the fires in Singapore city. *Dragon*, although a First War cruiser, put on her best speed of about 28 knots. In spite of endless attacks from Japanese aircraft. especially in the narrow Banka Strait, we arrived safely at Tanjong Priok, the harbour nearest to Batavia or Jakarta.

After prayers on the quarter deck one morning, a stick of bombs just missed the stern so the Captain decided not to have them again until we reached Batavia.

At Tanjong Priok, those of us taking passage in *Dragon* left the ship and reported to HMS *Anking*, berthed just ahead. The *Anking* had been a merchant ship plying the China coast but was now the Naval Headquarters and base ship at Batavia. While I was attached to *Anking* some of my delayed Christmas mail caught up with me. It included a Christmas card from the King and Queen which all Service personnel received that year. The card had their photos on one side and Christmas and New Year greetings on the other. Because it was so unexpected I found it most heartening and a real encouragement at a rather depressing time. I still have it!

The *Anking* was very crowded, and acted as a kind of transit ship for Officers and Ratings who had arrived from Singapore or who were survivors from sunken ships. They were then drafted, as soon as possible to any ship sailing for Australia or Ceylon. There was no Chaplain on board and so the Captain and Commander seemed quite pleased to have one. Me! But they really didn't want to accommodate me owing to the shortage of cabins.

Those of us who reached Batavia were the fortunate ones. The Japanese were sinking an enormous number of ships and small craft between there and Singapore, especially around Banka Island. The channel between Banka and Sumatra is not very wide so the Japanese carried out a more or less permanent air patrol over this stretch of water. Their aircraft were stationed at Borneo which they had already captured.

The Banka Strait provided rich pickings. There were something like 150 ships sunk between Singapore and Java. Many of those who managed to scramble ashore from the sunken ships on to the many little islands were either captured or shot. I heard from someone that the *Hung Joa* was sunk and Bill Mellor and Tony Clarke managed to get ashore but Bill Mellor was captured and Tony Clarke was shot trying to escape but this was never verified. Some who landed on uninhabited islands died through thirst, starvation or exposure. The lucky ones were picked up and brought on. When they arrived at Batavia many of them were in such a bad state of shock that they went straight to hospital.

Soon after I arrived in Batavia I attended the monthly get together of the British colony. The outcome of this meeting was that, with the

Captain's consent, I would take on Sunday Services. These included a 7.15 am Communion and an 11.15 Matins for the colony in the English church; a 9 am Communion in *Anking* and a Stand-up Church Service either in *Anking* at the dock-side, or in one of the ships, at 10 am. The British Colony said I could use the empty bungalow next to the church. A further bonus was that I could have the church car for my own use. *Anking* was delighted with the arrangements, because they had a Chaplain but didn't have to accommodate him. Until I had passed my driving test I had the use of a local chauffeur. I passed my test two days later and was glad to be rid of him because when I was not using the car he just sat in it and waited for me. However, as soon as the alerts were sounded he disappeared along with the car keys for hours! The English folk in Batavia hoped that I would open the bungalow as a club for Service men. They seeemed to think that I had come for months whereas I, in my heart, knew that we were all there for a matter of days.

During the latter part of January I had visited some English families living on the outskirts of Singapore City. I was simply appalled at the general apathy. Tea in the garden served by Chinese servants. No hurry and no fuss. While we at the Naval Base were under heavy air attack day after day. A fortnight after I had tea with these people, Singapore had surrendered to the Japanese. Now, it was Java, Indonesia. No hurry and no fuss. Within a month of the surrender of Singapore, Java had gone the same way but this time it was the Dutch. They just wouldn't and couldn't realise how serious the situation was. When they did wake up it was too late and the Japanese were swarming ashore, supported by guns, bombs and a large fifth column. But I am jumping the gun a bit. Let us look back to the second and third week of February.

During these days large numbers of men, women and children were arriving in all sorts of craft at the docks. The fit Service men were taken over to the *Anking* which was preparing men to leave for Australia or Ceylon as soon as possible. The fit civilians were put into ships which were also leaving. The wounded and shocked were taken by Dutch ambulances and cars to hospitals in Jakarta and to schools which had been turned into improvised hospitals.

It was arranged by the Captain and the Paymaster that I should visit the hospitals and schools with a Dutch Officer as my guide. Also it was decided that I should try to get the names, addresses and next of kin of those I visited. The Dutch Officer gave me several more hundred Guilders. I used this to give a small amount of money to each one, which they signed for, to tide them over the coming days. The majority of those I visited were shocked as a result of their experience. A visit and a little money from the RN seemed to buck them up and I offered spiritual help in the way of prayer if they wanted it. The list of patients I gave to the Ship. Most of them recovered very quickly, and were soon on their way to somewhere!

They had no intention of becoming guests of the Nips.

For me it was a long, tiring but well-worthwhile task. The town was eight miles from the docks and the hospitals and schools were scattered all over the place. My Dutch guide and I did a lot of travelling and his help was invaluable. The Japanese also knew their way around alright. The eight miles between the docks and town were littered with burnt out cars and trucks set on fire by the guns of Japanese aircraft. Many of us who had reached Jakarta were frequently at the docks scanning the faces of the new arrivals, day by day, to see which of our many friends and acquaintances had arrived. There was the constant drone of Japanese bombers overhead but they didn't seem to drop many bombs. They just wanted to keep the population nervous by day and then they bombed at night.

Until I was able to move up to the Church bungalow in Batavia I had to suffer with the rest of *Anking*'s ship's company some dreadful nights on board. Each night turned out to be a long nightmare. First of all the bilges were full of mosquitoes which attacked their victims in strength all night and every night. Then noise from the endless and futile ack-ack, which it was hoped would keep the Japanese up. Thirdly there was the constant swish of rockets being sent up by the Fifth Column to guide the bombers in. I wasn't sorry to be offered the luxury of an empty bungalow away from it all. The few nights I was there were Paradise. I then returned to *Anking* for the day, visiting other ships in dock and those arriving.

I remember standing on the dockside at Tanjong Priok when HMS *Durban* arrived. I heard someone on board call out. "There's the Chaplain." It was a member of the *Durban*'s Band whom I had known at Deal in the pre-war days. He had been a Band Boy then but was now a seasoned musician.

Soon after the *Durban* docked the *Kedah* tied up astern of her. It was reported that there was trouble on board. We heard that an odd assortment of troops who had lost their units or Regiments had rushed the ship at Singapore and were now in a mutinous mood. The Dutch stated that no one from *Kedah* would be allowed ashore. I believe the *Dragon*'s Royal Marines took up station on the roof of the go-down opposite to where the *Kedah* was berthed and covered the gangway with their rifles. Led by their Captain the *Durban* detachment of Royal Marines marched on board with rifles and covered their officer and the unruly mob while he addressed them. The long and the short of it was that the *Kedah* left at once for Australia.

One forenoon when in Jakarta I bumped into the Rev. Cyril Tucker. He and I had been at Cambridge together. He had arrived in Singapore early in January 1942 and was RAF Chaplain at Tengah, the RAF Station in the centre of Singapore Island. He had come down from Singapore with a very large contingent from Tengah airfield. They were being housed in a large Dutch barracks near Jakarta. He joined me for a night in my bungalow. After Morning Prayers the next day he left for his barracks and I left for the

121

*Anking.* It was the last time I saw him until after the war when we met accidently outside a telephone kiosk near Bognor. Within a few days of our evening together in my bungalow he was in the Japanese bag and spent his time as a POW in Indonesia and Malaya. After the war, he was Vicar of Holy Trinity, Cambridge, then Bishop of the Argentine. While I was Rector of Ringwould near Deal in Kent, he preached for me. He is now retired in Cambridge.

That morning, instead of going straight to the *Anking* I called on another ship, the *Yoma*, of the Henderson Line. She plied round the ports of the Indian Ocean to Colombo, Bombay, Madras, Rangoon and Singapore. I remember before I climbed the gangway I left my small amount of luggage, an attaché case, mattress and mosquito net, on the jetty. *Anking* was telling all the extra officers to try to get passages fixed up for themselves in other ships in case there was a last minute rush to get away! The *Yoma* officers suggested to me that I should transfer to *Yoma* from *Anking* for sleeping especially as the latter was very crowded and also as I had to return to Batavia each night. More crucially they had no mosquitoes! I thanked them and accepted the invitation. I then discovered that the Captain of *Yoma* had given an order that no one was allowed to leave the ship. The ship had British officers but the crew were Lascars and they were deserting. So here I was without any gear whatsover.

The ship's Quartermaster was sent down to collect my precious oddments. The rest of my wordly possessions were in the *Anking.* I was able to yell across the dock and tell them the situation. I couldn't get off the *Yoma* and that if I could, I would come aboard and collect my two suitcases. If I couldn't, my name was on them. I hoped to meet up again with them at a later date. So that was that.

How long we remained at Tanjong Priok, whether it was hours, days or weeks, I have no idea. One seemed to lose all sense of time. I can't remember whether it was at Tanjong Priok or after we had left and called at the southern tip of Sumatra that we picked up a number of Royal Marines who had escaped from Singapore. They travelled by boat, car and on foot to the very southern tip of Sumatra. They had not seen my friend Claude Aylwin, who had been defending the Kranji W/T Station with his detachment. But they had seen Bobby Lang. He had been wounded in the foot and then captured.

These Marines from his detachment had escaped and the joy of being picked up by the *Yoma* was beyond description. They just couldn't believe it. They came on with us to Colombo. What happened to them after that I don't know. Probably they went on to Bombay before returning to the UK.

I was surprised to find a large number of the RAF already on Board. They had come from the various Air stations in Malaya and Singapore. I suppose the idea was to get as many Service folk away so that they could fight another day. Besides the RAF there were a few Naval types and also a very mixed bag of Eurasians, Chinese, Africans, Malays, Greeks and nationals from other European and Asiatic countries. What they were all doing in Singapore, Malaya, Borneo and Indonesia I couldn't imagine. The ship not only had the responsibility of looking after and controlling this huge mob, but also the task of feeding them. Amongst those I got to know was an Oxford-educated Malay who turned out to be the eldest son of the Sultan of Johore. His father had sent him away in case he, the Sultan was shot by the Japanese. Then, after the war, the son could return and claim the throne. However, the Sultan soon made friends with the Japanese so I don't know what happened to the son, or for that matter to the Sultan's many European and Asiatic wives.

I was devoid of books. The few I had were either at the bungalow in Batavia or in the *Anking*. It was the chief officer who came to my rescue. He lent me a Bible and a hymn book for my own meditation and for preparing for the Sunday church services. He could not have been more helpful. I spent all day and most of the night on the upper deck walking, talking, reading, meditation and sleeping. I had no cabin. The ship had been heading towards Australia but, when south of the Cocos Islands, the Captain received instructions to alter course and proceed north making for Colombo, Ceylon. As we journeyed from the southern hemisphere into the northern hemisphere many of us gathered on the upper deck, leaning against the taffrail and gazing at the Southern Cross, lying low in the sky and surrounded by countless white stars

We thought about and discussed the immensity of the universe, the smallness of our own planet, and the terrible mess the inhabitants of the whole earth had landed themselves in. Many on board had lost wives or husbands and children; drowned, shot or missing. They were angry, bitter and full of hatred.

Men were cursing the Japanese with good reason for the way they were maltreating, beating and killing prisoners. They were cursing the war, the politicians and their own bad luck for getting caught up in this lot. They blasphemed 'God and His lousy world' and, as I was meant to represent His cause, I came in for my share of blame, too.

"You people have had this Christianity business for 2000 years and where has it got us? It is all 'pie in the sky' like that Cross up there. It is time we wrapped the whole thing up," they accused.

There were those on board whose motto was 'eat, drink and be merry, for tomorrow we die' and whose aim was 'wine, women and song'. They were moaning that all three were in short supply on this trip which they realised might end at any moment. However, they buoyed themselves up with the thought that, with luck, there would be all the delights imaginable when they reached Colombo. On this trip they were even saddled with a Parson, which in any case was considered unlucky, and they weren't sure that he could work his ju-ju. When we finally reached

Colombo, they withdrew this complaint! I found them rather fun but I just could not get it across to them that there was another dimension of life. They didn't want to be disturbed or have their life-style altered by paying the price of forsaking wrong doing and sin, which Christian belief and Christian living would demand. Eternal verities did not interest them. Just 'eat drink and be merry for tomorrow we die.'

While we were all gazing at the sea and the sky, someone called out, "Look."

It wasn't a Japanese submarine but the reflection of the Southern Cross on the sea quite near us.

I said, "He isn't very far away after all. The God of eternity whose Cross we can see in the heavens is here with us, in the southern oceans, because his Cross stands for his love."

Even in our dangerous situation because of the Japanese and the sharks, this symbol of our Christian faith, although it was imagery, was a help.

My companions drifted away, most of them lying down on the deck and dropping off to sleep. On this particular night I remained leaning against the taffrail going over in my mind what we had been discussing. This questioning of the Christian faith had been both searching and salutary. How quickly things change in life. Less than three years before I had been sailing in a rather care-free fashion along and across the Norfolk Broads in England in the still halcyon days of peace. Now all was uncertain and unknown. As I stood on the upper deck of the *Yoma*, there was no sound except the wash of the sea against the ship's side and the throb of the engines. Far away in the sky was that wonderful constellation, the sign of our Christian faith, which with the other stars would be moving round the heavens while we slept. Some of the words of Bach's Chorale came to my mind:-

> 'Beneath the cross abiding, forever will I rest;
> In Thy dear love confiding, and with Thy presence blest.'

It was at that moment I recalled a verse of Scripture my father had given me when I said goodbye to him and my mother when I left for Singapore in 1940. I am ashamed to say that I really had not paid much attention to the words, but now they suddenly came to life. The verse was from Isaiah Ch. 43 verse 2.

> 'When thou passest through the waters, I will be with thee;
> and through the fire, thou shalt not be burned.'

I decided that there could be no wavering or turning aside from the Pilgrim Way.

*Years later, looking back on those desperate days, I realised that although we were physically exhausted and mentally confused, Christian Faith was the one sure anchor which sustained many of us during this particular storm of life.*

I stretched out on my mattress on the upper deck of the *Yoma*, with my mosquito net for a pillow, in my shirt and shorts. I had nothing else but my life-belt which I wore all the time in case we were thrown into the sea through torpedo attack. I dropped off to sleep.

*Yoma* was not the only ship trying to escape from the Japanese in this ill-fated convoy. Many others were making their way west towards Ceylon, while still more headed south for northern or western Australia.

During my time as Chaplain of the Naval Base I had tried to call on the merchant ships which came into the Dockyard and so came to know a number of their ship's companies. Amongst them was a Lieutenant RNR who came into the dockyard fairly frequently. After we had reached Colombo and had been there some days I heard this officer's name mentioned when I eventually met him he related a quite remarkable escape.

A few days before Singapore fell to the Japanese he managed to get hold of a large sailing boat. He sailed it with 109 people on board right across the Indian Ocean. It took him three weeks. Some of his passengers died, some went mad and others were ill. They ran out of food and caught the rainwater for drinking in a tarpaulin. What these people must have suffered day after day passes the imagination. This man's efforts in controlling this huge crowd and getting them to Ceylon must rank as one of the finest feats of seamanship, courage and stamina of all time.

Two years later I was to meet this remarkable man again. In 1944 he was an upper deck officer on a Dutch ship, called the *Sibajak*, which the Admiralty had taken over as a trooper. She came into Augusta, Sicily, and took on board a large number of Royal Marines with whom I was serving as Chaplain. We had been engaged in the conquest of Sicily and were being taken back to the UK to prepare for the Second Front. This officer was standing near the gangway watching us as we came on board. He recognised me. When we met he said that he was the only officer who had been caught up in the Far East turmoil. I was the only one amongst our lot who had been out there in 1941/2. This accidental meeting was providential for both of us. We were able to spend many hours together as we journeyed back to the UK going over the events of those catastrophic days, weeks and months.

After our arrival in Scotland, I lost touch with him and never saw him again. Even his name escapes me. I did hear in a roundabout way that he had died young. However, it had been my privilege to have known this remarkable and unassuming man. I don't think his great exploit was ever officially recognised. As I think about him, I am reminded of the Scriptures.

'And some there be which have no memorial who are

perished, as though they had never been. But these were merciful men, whose righteousness hath not been forgotten. Their bodies are buried in peace, but their name liveth for evermore.'

A Cambridge friend of mine, the Rev. Ron Bevington, had gone to Australia in the 1930's to work for the Children Special Service Mission. At the outbreak of war he had joined the Royal Australian Navy and was drafted as Chaplain to HMAS *Perth*. I heard that after the order in HMAS *Perth* to abandon ship, Ron Bevington, with the RC Chaplain, started to swim to a small island ahead of them at the entrance of the Straits. The RC Chaplain made it but Ron Bevington, caught in a strong current, was swept round the island and reported drowned. I find that the faces and names of those days flash across one's mind during the two minutes silence on Remembrance Sunday; that remarkable sailor whose name I forget; Ron Bevington the happy Evangelist; Bobby Lang, the steadfast Royal Marine, Tony Clarke the utterly reliable New Zealander. Their faces are, of course, as one knew them and it gives added meaning to the wonderful words of Lawrence Binyon:-

'They shall grow not old as we that are left grow old;
Age shall not weary them, nor the years condemn;
At the going down of the sun and in the morning, we will remember them.'

Ceylon came into sight at last but by the time we reached Colombo it was sunset and the harbour boom was closed for the night. The ship's speed was about six knots. Just imagine crossing the Indian Ocean at 6 mph! We anchored outside the harbour with other ships and craft and waited patiently for the next day. We were haunted all night by the thought of prowling Japanese submarines and, if the worst came to the worst, ending up in the water with some hungry sharks for company. Why the yellow submarines weren't in attendance we couldn't understand. We were a sitting duck. Perhaps, at this stage, they were outrunning their strength and capabilities.

Morning came at last and, with the other ships, we entered the harbour at once. We didn't go alongside but lay out in the centre. It was Sunday so we had stand-up Church on the upper deck. The words of the Naval Prayer came home to us forcibly.

'Preserve us from the dangers of the sea and the violence of the enemy. And with a thankful remembrance of thy mercies to praise and glorify Thy Holy Name.'

News came through that the *Anking* had been sunk. We also heard that there had been very heavy loss of life. *Later I heard that there was one survivor out of over 400 on board.* Those of us who had been in the *Anking* felt very blessed and fortunate. But for some rather strange circumstances I might easily have been in the ship with my gear! None of us minded the loss of gear, but we were shattered by the terrible loss of life.

About noon, the Captain allowed some of us to go ashore. We lost no time in hailing a native boat near the ship and it landed us at the jetty. While wandering through the town I happened to meet the Captain who told me that if I didn't want to go to Bombay I should have my gear off the ship by 6 pm. I thanked him for getting us all safely to Colombo and returned to the ship with him. I collected my gear, such as it was, and said farewell to the officers who had been such a help to me over the church services. For the second time I left the ship and, having landed, didn't know where to go or what to do. I made a few enquiries and discovered that, being Sunday the Royal Naval offices were closed down.

Across the road was the Grand Oriental hotel so I went in, sat down and ordered some coffee. While I sat there a man and his wife from the Singapore Naval Base saw me, rushed across and hugged me and said how delighted they were to see me as they heard that I had been left behind. But for the Civil Secretary of the Naval Base fixing me up in the *Dragon*, I might well have been! Leaving the hotel, a strange thing happened. I met a man who lived in Colombo whom I hadn't seen since I was about 15. I was surprised that I recognised him. Our parents had been great friends and his brother had spent several school holidays with us when their parents were abroad. We had a chat and then I told him that I had just arrived from Singapore. I added that as the Naval Offices were closed until Monday morning, would it be possible for him to give me a bed for the night. He hesitated. He was very spick and span in army uniform, trousers well pressed, swagger stick and all the rest, while I was a real waif and looked like one.

"There's a war on, you know, and we have got to be ready. I am just off to camp."

However, he rang his wife, told her who I was and that they were putting me up for the night. He drove me to his very nice house where I had a bath, supper and a camp bed. My own rig consisted of my only pair of shorts and a shirt. In the morning he drove me into Colombo and rang his mother who lived some miles away to say that I was there. He told me to leave my address at the hotel so that she could contact me.

Next, I reported to the Naval Office to say that I had arrived. In a letter I wrote to my parents from Colombo and which they showed me after my return home, I said, "Like the rest of the evacuees in the rest of the world, I discovered that nobody wants us." "How many more of you people are coming?" "What's the matter with you all in Singapore?" and so on. I was told to find my own accommodation anywhere I liked, to feed out and report daily. Whether they had been inundated with survivors and by now had had enough, I don't know. Perhaps their resources had been stretched to the limit and they just hadn't room for any more to clutter up the barracks and messes. I was able to draw some money from the Pay Office, which gave me a sense of freedom.

While I was there, I said to the Sub-Lieutenant, "Can you tell me where I can get a suit to go home in?"

"You can have my dark naval uniform for £10, if you like. You will only have to take off one gold stripe. I am here for three years."

I bought it and came home in it plus a dog-collar which I managed to get hold of. *I have worn the trousers of the suit with my dinner jacket ever since.* As I had no clothing I went on a shopping expedition and purchased a suitcase, shirts, vest, socks and a pair of shoes. Later I called on the two RNVR Chaplains. They were pleasant and busy! I told them that, as a survivor, I was not being victualled in the mess and that I had to find my own accommodation, and that I hoped to be returning to the UK shortly in a transport ship. I didn't see them again.

I asked the Captain's secretary, on the first day, about accommodation in Colombo. He told me that owing to the enormous influx of thousands of people, service and civilian, from Malaya, Singapore, Borneo and Java, there was simply nothing available in Colombo. He gave me a list of hotels in the neighbouring towns and villages. The first one I telephoned, Mount Lavinia, offered me a room and so I went seven miles by train at once.

I found that my room overlooked the sea and I discovered a few kindred spirits who had arrived from Singapore. As we felt that we were considered to be not quite traitors, but somewhat suspect, we were glad of each other's company. Each forenoon we travelled to Colombo in the hopelessly crowded trains and we were literally strap hanging. Fortunately for us the RN had told the hotels to send our bills to HMS *Lanka*, Colombo. This simplified matters for us and saved us drawing money from the Paymaster to pay for this splendid accommodation.

I remember thinking to myself at the time, 'The good old British tax-payer! He's not only paying for the war, but paying our hotel bills too!'

The task of dealing with the masses of folk who had arrived unexpectedly must have been immense. The RN suddenly had hundreds of officers and ratings landed on them. They all had to be sorted out. The arrivals included men of all branches. Some were kept for further service, especially if they had served out east under two years. The rest were detailed for the UK by any and every ship available. As considerable reinforcements were reaching both India and Ceylon, there was ample room for those who were homeward bound. We didn't see many Army men around. At least not many looked as if they had come from Singapore and Sumatra.

We could tell those who had by their rather strained looks. Unfortunately most of the Army, caught either in Singapore or Sumatra, were now in the hands of the Japanese. The hundreds of RAF seemed to disappear quickly. They were snapped up to help the RAF in Ceylon. About 600 Admiralty civilians with their wives and children were being sent to Bombay, Mombasa, Durban, Capetown and Simonstown to assist in the dockyards which were all expanding.

Besides all those connected with the Services there were hundreds and hundreds of civilians, men, women and children. The men had been engaged in business, on the rubber plantations and in engineering. Most of those who had come from Malaya, Penang and Borneo had left all their possessions behind. There were endless tragedies of fathers, mothers and children killed, drowned or just missing. What were they to do? Should they try to go to England? Should they wait and hope that survivors might turn up? The longer they waited, the less chance there was of anyone arriving.

During my daily trips into Colombo, from my hotel at Mount Lavinia, I met a large number of Singapore Dockyard famlies and felt that they seemed genuinely pleased to see me. Perhaps the countless hours I had spent visiting the families in the Naval Base hadn't been a waste of time. My organist was missing. His wife and sons had sent for me so that we could talk about the possibilities of his escape but, in the end, we felt that he had been caught in Sumatra. *He died in captivity.*

Some days when I visited the docks, men arrived whom I knew but failed to recognise. They looked so pale, drawn and exhausted. One day after reporting to the barracks I met one of my New Zealand friends. Only two or three of the two dozen had turned up so far. Many of them had visited and stayed at my small bungalow at the Singapore Naval Base, and they told me that they had treated it as home. The two of us spent the day together. After visiting the Docks, to see if there were any more arrivals, we went out to my hotel at Mount Lavinia. As we sat on the verandah, overlooking the sea, we just could not describe the utter bliss of having no Japs above us in the sky and no Japs beneath us in the sea.

Another day I was just wandering through Colombo when I was approached by a total stranger. He told me that he was an Englishman who had retired and was living in Colombo. He asked me if I had just arrived, who I was and where I had come from. The result of the chance meeting was that I was invited to his house and had lunch, tea and supper with him and his wife. We sat for hours in their delightful garden and chatted. I don't know why he spoke to me. Perhaps I was looking rather lost and exhausted at the time but their courtesy, kindness, and generous hospitality helped me to pull myself together and I returned to Mount Lavinia with a firmer tread.

'I was a stranger and ye took me in.'

Like so many who had reached Colombo, we were constantly looking East in the knowledge that so many of our friends, kith and kin were now locked up in the Japanese hell. Besides the thousands of our men there were those from Australia and New Zealand who had so willingly come to Britain's aid and were now caught in the vicious grip of this fanatical, cruel and savage race. It seemed that the only thing they could understand was brute force, and we were not in a position to apply it yet.

We also knew that during March, large numbers of Service and civilian men and women had escaped from Singapore and were on their way across Sumatra. The Army had set up a good organisation with some first class officers and NCO's as guides. It had been arranged that our small ships and other craft would put in at certain points on the West coast of Sumatra to pick up those attempting to get away. However the Japanese moved so fast that, in the end, very few managed to reach the ships. The feelings of the sailors carrying out this difficult task can be imagined when they heard the BBC News from London.

"Our ships are now picking up survivors on the west coast of Sumatra!" reported Aunty.

At some time during the following week I met the mother of the man who had put me up on my first night in Colombo.

She wrote to my parents to tell them she had seen me and that I looked very serene and composed! I am glad someone thought so. Most of us who had arrived had an inferiority complex that we had not done our stuff and, of course, we were very distressed about those we had left behind. I think we all needed a kind word and a little consideration for the vast majority of us were very, very tired.

The days spent at Mount Lavinia, sitting on the verandah of the hotel, gave me time to think through my whole job and vocation. As a priest of the Church of England I was a minister of the gospel and a Chaplain in the Royal Navy. Whether my commissions over the past six years had been successful or a failure was not for me to say. Latterly, the swift collapse of British rule, power and interests in the Far East had to be faced. This included the physical disappearance and disintegration of the church, including my own flock. One cannot blame people for looking upon God as irrelevant, or Christian faith as pie in the sky, or just part of the British establishment. It is a strange thing, but I don't think I ever questioned the basics of Christian faith at the time although, being just a tiny, tiny cog in the wheel, I didn't understand it at all. Perhaps there were so many things to think about at that time. I was surprised to find myself almost buoyant and I put this down to the prayers of my parents and others which were being offered for me on the other side of the world. If I appeared serene and composed to that lady, it must have been due to the spiritual support I was receiving.

There was time to look back on one's upbringing with thankfulness. In the words of Scripture, 'to look to the rock whence ye are hewn.'

I had been blessed with a sound Christian home, praying parents, Christian friends at the University during my years at Cambridge, and involvement in evangelistic missions. These experiences were all underpinned by the solid basis and practice of the Church of England, with its 'Prayer Book to teach and the Bible to prove.'

At Ridley Hall, my Cambridge Theological College, great store had been placed on the Ordinands attending daily Morning and Evening Prayer in the chapel. At times this attendance was considered irksome, a bore and a chore, but we never thought of being absent. This Daily Office, as Morning and Evening Prayer is called, is really the daily square bashing for the budding parson. I realised that it was a vital frame-work to hold on to and to build upon. Besides the daily discipline, it also provided a magnificent Biblical base. Most of the Bible is read once a year, the Psalms once a month, and they are both linked with Thomas Cranmer's Collects which span the centuries. I had been taught to look back with thankfulness; to look to the present with cheerfulness and to look to the future with hopefulness. It was in this frame of mind, that I waited, as did hundreds of other survivors in Colombo, for the next move.

During these days a strange thing happened, recalling an event which had taken place two months earlier. In January I had been talking to dockyard personnel at the Naval Base who were being evacuated and sent home. I asked them if they had any spare room in their luggage. They said that some space was available so they took my golf clubs! Subsequently, I forgot all about them.

While I was in Colombo someone told me, "I have seen some gear of yours in the basement of the Galle Face Hotel."

I hadn't any gear to put there, so I went along to investigate. The couple who had taken my golf clubs had stayed at this hotel while awaiting passage home. When they left they had no room for them so they left them in the basement with my name on. When I finally left for the UK I climbed up the gangway with a suitcase containing the clothes I had purchased, my small attaché case, a mosquito net and my golf clubs. My New Zealand friends said I looked more like a tourist than a survivor!

The day came when we were told the name of our ship and the date of departure. We were to return to England in the Troopship *Staffordshire*, of the Bibby Line, towards the end of March. During March a large Japanese fleet entered the Indian Ocean and in next to no time had sunk two of our cruisers, HMS *Cornwall* and HMS *Dorsetshire*. The fleet advanced on Ceylon. Before it arrived off Colombo the *Staffordshire* had sailed on a course south west for Capetown.

The Japanese sank the aircraft carrier HMS *Hermes* and her aircraft off Trincomalee. There were only four survivors of the ship's RM band. One of them is a friend of mine and lives in my home town of Deal. By the time the Japanese aircraft attacked Colombo our Hurricanes had arrived. The faithful RAF pilots were ready for them and caught them unawares. The Nips suffered heavy losses in aircraft and pilots, possibly more than they could afford. Whatever the reason, after bombarding the Andaman Islands they withdrew to Singapore.

The time came for me to bid farewell to my New Zealand friends, and it was with great sadness that I did so. The majority of those who had come up to Singapore from New Zealand were skilled yachtsmen who sailed in Wellington harbour. Proportionally their losses were very heavy. At least half of their number were dead or missing. Those who reached Colombo were rather bewildered. They didn't know what would happen to them now. They had lost their ships and their gear but they expected to be employed locally by the RN in small craft.

One day when I was aboard one of their boats I heard someone say, "Fancy. He's a Pommie. But he's just like one of us."

I really felt then that they had taken me into their close knit family.

When in Singapore, I recall that on one occasion, I went into my study where one of them was sleeping on a camp bed. He was wearing a sarong and had no sheet or mosquito net. He was sound asleep and was not wakened up by a large rat which was sitting at the end of his camp bed nibbling his big toe! There was never a dull moment. On Sunday evenings they had given full support to Evensong in the Naval Base chapel and made a fine contribution to the services.

By now, sadly, some of them had been shot, some were drowned and some were missing. Those would never be returning to their beloved New Zealand. Now we had to say goodbye to one another. We had been through so much together. When they came to the *Staffordshire* to see me off I think they realised it was most unlikely that we should ever meet again. They did not hang around.

Things happened very quickly. Gear, if you had any, had to be stowed. Cabins were allocated and those of us taking passage had to report.

They said, "Do come and see us one day. You will always be welcome in New Zealand".

They all shook hands with me and were gone. The great charity of those men towards me, an Englishman and their Chaplain, is something which I shall never, never forget.

We had only been on board a few minutes when the first pipe instructed us to collect and put on life-belts and proceed to our boat-stations, according to cabins and messes. While waiting there on the upper deck, to be mustered and checked by the Ship's Officer in charge of our boat, I suddenly realised that it was just over two and a half years since I had left the RN School of Music at Deal in the summer of 1939. Since then I had come safely through the first winter of the war where I was serving in a cruiser on the Northern

Patrol in the Arctic. I had survived the fall of Singapore and Indonesia. I had sailed the North Atlantic Ocean, the South Atlantic Ocean, the Indian Ocean, the China and the Java Seas. And all without a scratch. Now we were about to commence the long haul home again. As I stood there I found myself repeating the verse of a hymn which we had sung in the *Yoma*. It seemed to fit 'my' war although the author, Bishop Heber, had something quite different in mind when he wrote it.

> 'From Greenland's icy mountains, from Ceylon's coral strand;
> From Africa's sunny fountains, roll down their golden sand;
> *I didn't know it at the time but the second line was to be fulfilled in 1943*
> What though the spicy breezes, blow soft o'er Java's isle,
> Though every prospect pleases, and only man is vile.'

I stopped and pondered that this last line is certainly true, especially the last five words, but with some wonderful exceptions. And because of the exceptions, one's faith in human nature is totally redeemed.

The Ship's Officer arrived. After he had mustered, checked us and inspected the way we had put on and tied up our life-belts, we dispersed. We travelled alone and unescorted by any HM Ship. I don't think there were any available. Because of the large Japanese fleet comprising battleships, cruisers, carriers, destroyers and submarines, which was marauding to the east of us, all passengers were requested to keep their eyes skinned when on the upper deck. We didn't need to be told twice.

In civvy street, my journey from Singapore to Colombo would, I suppose, have come under the heading Locum. Now I was trying to work out in mind, how best I could serve the Kingdom of God during my next Locum in my new parish from Colombo to England. As I went to my cabin for the first time I repeated the fine Old Testament word Ebenezer, which means, 'Hitherto hath the Lord helped us'.

# CHAPTER IX

## Locum aboard S.S. Staffordshire

*It was March 1942 and at last we were on our way back to Britain on board the SS Staffordshire. Our travels took us from Colombo, across the Indian Ocean, to Capetown in South Africa. From there we crossed the Atlantic to Ireland and docked in Belfast. The last leg of the journey was by ferry to Stranraer, train to London and Maidstone and a taxi to Teston Rectory and home.*

The first thing I did, when we were dismissed from Boat Stations on leaving Colombo Harbour, was to find my cabin. I had been told it had two bunks. As the voyage home was to last many weeks it was important to know who was to be one's stable companion.

When I arrived at the cabin door a man was already looking in. He turned round to say hello. I said that I had been allocated one bunk in this cabin for this trip.

He said, "Good; I have also been allocated one here, and as this voyage is going to last for weeks, it suits me just fine," and we shook hands.

He was Lieutenant Tom Sutherland RNR and we already knew each other. As the Chaplain of the HM Base in Singapore I had visited his ship, the *Pankor*, several times when she had berthed in the Base. He was the Skipper of the *Pankor*, a Master Mariner, and he had entertained me on board in his cabin.

He had commanded ships of the SS Steamship Company plying between Malaya, Java and Borneo. In those days he and his wife had lived in Penang. While there they had two servants, a Chinaman and his wife. Tom Sutherland told me that when he and his wife dined out, the Chinese servant laid out his wife's clothes and regularly helped her to dress.

One evening as she was being dressed by this Chinese servant she said, "Where is your husband tonight?"

The Chinese replied, "Me husband!" She was quite shocked.

Tom asked me if I had any relations with the same name in Colombo, as he had met a Pocock at the Grand Oriental Hotel.

I said, "No, but I knew there was one."

It happened that one day I went to the reception desk to inquire whether there was any mail for me and I was expecting a local note to be addressed there. I was handed a letter and without looking at the envelope, I opened it. It didn't seem to make sense to me and so I looked at the envelope and saw that it was addressed to Sub-Lieutenant Pocock. I returned the envelope to Reception, writing a few words on the back of the envelope and apologised for opening it. I signed it F. L. Pocock, adding that I hoped that we would meet one day. We never did. Later I discovered that there were only two Pococks in the RN, this Sub-Lietuenant and myself. We were both in Colombo at the same time, using the same hotel, but we missed meeting.

From Colombo, we set course for Capetown, at 12 knots. At this time, there was a large Japanese fleet in the vicinity. As mentioned earlier, they had already sunk the Carrier *Hermes* and the two heavy Cruisers, *Cornwall* and *Dorsetshire*.

The Eastern Fleet of the RN now consisted of old Battleships of the 'R' Class and was based on the Maldive Islands. It was guarded by Royal Marines of the 1st Mobile Naval Base Defence Organisation and now the ships withdrew to Mombassa, East Africa.

Besides the crew of the *Staffordshire*, a number of RN Ratings on their way home joined the 'look-out' watches. They searched ceaselessly for Japanese aircraft, ships or submarines, as we zig-zagged unescorted towards Capetown. In any case, being only capable of travelling at 12 knots, we were very vulnerable. Boat Drill was incessant, just in case! However, there was plenty of time for upper deck competitions including tug-of-war, deck hockey, swimming for which the Officer Commanding Troops had rigged up a small swimming pool, running races round the decks, obstacle races and so on between the RN, the Army, the RAF and the Civilians.

We had a charming Army Lieutenant Colonel as OC Troops. He and his staff could not have been more helpful to me as the Chaplain of this journey. He allocated me a cabin for use as a Chapel for the whole voyage and he had it marked Chapel. It was well placed in the centre of the ship for ease of access by Officers, Ratings and Other Ranks.

In my first interview with him, which took place at his request, he told me that he considered Christian worship, practice and teaching extremely important and that he and his staff would give me every assistance in whatever I attempted to do. We discussed both Sunday and weekday worship.

From previous experience, he suggested 8.30 am for Holy Communion in one of the lounges and I agreed.

For 10.30 am he suggested a popular Service either in one of the lounges or on the upper deck, dependent on the weather.

He said he had plenty of books; a hymn book with popular hymns and a Prayer Book with various Services including a short Matins. He also provided me with a harmonium for the lounge and a piano for the upper deck. The Order of Service, Hymns, Organist, Choir, Church-Wardens and Sidesmen he left to me.

I suggested that I use the Chapel for Holy Communion twice a week and that I have Evening Prayer every night. I might use the Chapel or some corner of the upper deck for Instruction, if it was required. My cabin mate,

Tom Sutherland, told me that he had never shared a cabin with a Chaplain before and that although he was a strict Presbyterian from Shetland, he would do all he could to help me with the Church Services and Church affairs on this voyage home. I appointed him as my Number One Church-Warden!

The Holy Communion Service on both Sundays and weekdays provided many with the opportunity of a quiet half-hour when I was able to administer both the Word and the Sacraments. The Easter Festival took place soon after we left Colombo and large numbers took the Sacrament on that day.

The Sunday Morning Services were rousing occasions. Good Friday, just after we left Colombo, provided a good opportunity to get things going. After Easter Day there was no looking back. Crowds attended and it gave me the chance to challenge all present with the Christian Gospel. Whether the Japs had put the fear of God into them all I don't know, but large numbers came along. After the first Sunday we quickly organised a Choir who relished their work and contribution and went from strength to strength. I think the Sunday Morning Services were something many men looked forward to and valued. They maintained their popularity and enthusiastic spirit right to the end.

Every evening a few of us met for Evening Prayer and Interecessions for the world, our nation and ourselves while teaching or discussions took place as and when asked for.

Besides Service folk from the three Services there were civilians who had been working all over the Far East in Hong Kong, Malaya, Borneo, Singapore, Java and in Sumatra. A few of them had their wives with them, while others had lost both wives and children, either killed or drowned. I think they all considered themselves fortunate to have managed to secure a passage in a Trooper. They had all lost their livelihoods. There were planters, engineers and all kinds of businessmen. They saw no point in remaining in Colombo and this applied to those who had lost families too.

A series of lectures was organised, two or three a week, spread over several weeks. They were open to all personnel and were held either in one of the lounges or on the upper deck.

The aim was to cover the various professionals amongst us who were travelling home to England. Our lecturers included planters, doctors, engineers, traders, businessmen and senior Officers of the Royal Navy, the Army and the Royal Air Force. There were no Royal Marines. Those in the Far East who had not been killed or taken prisoner in the fall of Sinapore were being used to bolster up the weak defences in India, Ceylon and the Maldives.

The lectures were much appreciated as many of us were ignorant of what went on in the Far East. The Service Officers gave us an assessment of the war situation as they saw it. As the Chaplain I found myself included in the Lectures. I was asked to explain the Christian position and how it tied up, or didn't, with a world at war. I tried to keep the Christian Faith personal. I said, "Men are not saved in bundles" but soul by soul and often silently. I found that the majority wanted to stick to generalities and did not wish the discussion to become too personal.

One really had to hand it to the Ship's Company of the *Staffordshire* for the way they ran this ship, and to the whole of the Merchant Service. There was a wonderful spirit throughout. The Upper Deck, the Engineer, the W/T Section, the Paymasters, the Stores, the Chefs, the Stewards and so on, all seemed to go out of their way to help any and all the passengers in any way they could. At the end of this voyage we would be leaving while they would be going all the way back again. Backwards and forwards all the time. We just couldn't help admiring them. At present, of course, we were all going the same way, 'Rolling home to merry England' as the song goes. We knew England wasn't as 'merry' as she should be, but we were all homeward bound. That meant leave on arrival not only for the passengers but for the Ship's Company as well. I might just say that the ship was simply smothered with ack-ack, Bofor guns in case of air attack from the awesome Nazi Condors which flew from Norway, over the Atlantic, before landing in France. They were looking for victims to bomb while out over the Atlantic. *Staffordshire* had already suffered damage from them, hence the Bofors!

As the days and weeks passed there was a general feeling of optimism. Both we and the country had survived so far and the omens were good. There was a feeling that the longer the war lasted, the greater the certainty and the speed of victory. We realised that the ferocious Japs were still advancing, but the Americans were in at last, but at least they were in and with us. The light at the end of the tunnel could now be seen and we all realised that it was a matter of sticking it out until evil men, evil things and evil plans were crushed beyond doubt. Possibly these thoughts which we all discussed came out of some of the lectures we had listened to.

As we rounded the Cape of Good Hope, we passed a huge convoy going to the Middle East or India. Much later, I discovered that my future brother-in-law, David Cummin, was in one of the ships. He was an air gunner in the RAF. On one bombing operation over Burma his aircraft was hit. Both he and his pilot had to bale out. Fortunately there was a strong east wind which carried the parachutes from behind enemy territory to our own and they landed safely behind our own lines.

In next to no time after rounding the Cape of Good Hope, the ship entered Capetown harbour and berthed with Table Mountain in the background. We remained in harbour three or four days.

The Rev. Edgar Rae, who was the port Chaplain, visited me. He was due to have an Assistant Chaplain and here was one, me, on the spot. He begged me to leave the *Staffordshire* and to join him. He even promised me some sea time in one of the many HM Ships which came into Capetown. My answer was emphatic.

I said, "No thank you; I have been away from England since September, 1939 and it is now April, 1942. Whatever happens and whatever is in store for me personally, I am going home."

Just to confirm matters in my own mind I sent a short cable to my parents which said 'Homeward bound. 3rd Epistle of St John, first part of verse 14.' It reads, 'I trust I shall shortly see thee, and we shall speak face to face.' So that was that.

My next visitors were a husband and wife who were quite unknown to me. They came on board, asked if the ship carried a Chaplain, and if so could they see him. When I met them they said that they wanted to take me round the countryside in their car, and then entertain me in their home. They wanted me to bring a friend. I took my cabin-mate, Tom Sutherland.

We had a most delightful afternoon, touring the coast of South Africa first to the east and then to the west. Afterwards we returned to their home for tea and supper. Finally they returned us to the *Staffordshire*. This happened on the second day. I had received the same sort of hospitality in Colombo.

Having lost my Bible and Prayer Book with the rest of my gear, I went ashore in the forenoon to purchase new ones. I was unable to obtain either, but I did manage to get a very fine copy of the New Testament and Psalms which I still have and use. I returned on board for lunch. After tea two of us went ashore to see the film *Dangerous Moonlight* which tells the tragic story of Poland being overrun by the Nazis. The now famous piece of music, the Warsaw Concerto, comes in it.

As I left the cinema I met a Petty Officer from HMS *Ceres*.

He said, "The Ship's in port, Sir; come on board."

I had left *Ceres* in February 1940, and it was now April, 1942. I was surprised that he knew me. I found the ship and went over the for'ard gangway with a rather tipsy Chief Petty Officer.

He said, "Hello, Sir. I haven't seen you round the ship lately."

"No," I replied, "sadly, I left the ship over two years ago, but it is a great joy to be on board once again."

I called on the Wardroom and after about half an hour the Steward came to me.

"A message has gone round the ship that the *Ceres* Chaplain is on board and is on his way to the UK. There are some men outside the Wardroom, waiting to see you."

I went out and there must have been between two and three dozen men, standing there who wanted to say 'Cheerio', or to have a chat, or to ask me to take a letter to the UK for them and post it. By the time I left the ship it had gone 11 o'clock.

As I made my way back to the *Staffordshire* that night I could hardly believe that I had been aboard *Ceres* once more. Being in the Wardroom with some of my Mess Mates and then meeting all those members of the Ship's Company in the Wardroom passage had been an overwhelming experience. My visit to *Ceres* that night had been a real bonus and I was deeply thankful for the unexpected meeting with some of my past flock.

I was on deck in good time the next morning and able to watch *Staffordshire* pull away from her berth and make for the open sea. As we moved towards the harbour entrance I saw *Ceres* and kept my eyes on her until she was lost to my view. *It was in fact, the last time I was ever to see her. After her return to Devonport in 1945, she remained immobile in the Hamoase until she went off to the breaker's yard. It is now 1983, and I still receive a Christmas card from one of her Ship's Company, Commander W. F. May, now retired in Plymouth.*

As we left Capetown Harbour and were mustered at Boat Stations, we were informed over the tannoy that one ship in ten was sunk between Capetown and Freetown. We were also told to be punctual at Boat Stations, always bring a small survival bag with us, always either carry or wear a life-belt, and finally we were to keep a sharp look out for submarine periscopes.

The days and routine were much the same as those from Colombo to Capetown. Leaving Colombo, the weather had become hotter as we approached the equator and gradually became cooler as we approached Capetown.

Leaving Capetown we were told our route but, for a day or so, we appeared to be steaming south-west and it was quite cold. Then we turned north so we presumed that we were sailing well out in the South Atlantic. The one memory I have of those first two days, is the sight of the albatross with its huge wing span. Every now and then one of these wonderful birds acted as a kind of outrider or escort flying alongside the ship. When we turned north they left us. In the Indian Ocean we saw the flying fish skimming along the surface of the sea and porpoises, plunging in and out of the water and somehow, keeping up with the ship. They were most impressive.

Then it was this magnificent bird, the albatross, which held us spellbound. Fishes and birds seemed to restore our sanity and confidence in Eternal things. We spent many hours discussing the everlasting wonder of nature. It made man appear very small and insignificant.

On this section of the voyage and on the next we had a Ship's Officer in charge and in command of every lifeboat. He carried with him a tiny map of the Atlantic Ocean. A pin hole was punched in the map each day to mark the place where we were at noon. If we were torpedoed he at any rate, would have some idea where we were.

We were thankful to be safely behind the harbour boom at Freetown. We, obviously, were not the one ship in ten to be sunk coming up from Capetown.

139

It was rather a matter of 'I'm all right Jack, thank you.' As usual, there was no shore leave in Freetown and what with the heavy, sticky atmosphere and the crowds of ships, it was a matter of being on one's way again as soon as possible.

We departed from Freetown on the same day as a six-knot convoy of about 30 ships. Their escort was just one corvette. We had heard that during the first months of 1942 the German Naval Staff could glimpse victory in the Atlantic. They were sinking ships faster than the allies could build them. Churchill was speaking of shipping shortages as his greatest worry. As *Staffordshire* could steam at 12 knots we went on alone and unescorted. There was no feeling of superiority of extra speed because we knew that these were crisis months in the Battle of the Atlantic. Leaving both the Southern Ocean and Freetown behind we were entering the danger zone. The six-knot convoy was soon left behind and out of sight.

We received a message over the Ship's tannoy, "Take the usual precautions. Wear life-belts. Strict blackout at nights and remember, *we're on our own*."

On the third night out from Freetown the ship's engines failed.

The night was pitch dark and everything went dead quiet. It was an eerie experience. We were informed over the loud-speakers what had happened. The repair of the engines took about two days. During that time the ship just drifted about at the mercy of wind and current. The slow convoy caught us up again and passed us in the distance. They must have wondered whatever we were up to. The tortoise had passed the hare! Once we were under way again the hare gradually overtook the tortoise. We passed fairly near the convoy and gave them a cheer. Whether they heard us we couldn't tell. There was no response!

We were told that we would pass east of the Azores and then steam fairly near the north-west tip of Spain.

On April 23rd, St Georges Day, we noticed tremendous air activity to the east of us. Later, we learned from the BBC News that a British Commando raid had been carried out on St Nazaire. We presumed that the Jerry Air Forces were concentrating their efforts on the raiders and as a result we were spared.

As we passed up the west coast of Ireland we were once more urged to be extra vigilant regarding boat stations, life-belts, lights and so on. Jerry was making an all-out attack on shipping in the north-west approaches. For good measure we were told that a trooper ahead of us had been sunk within a few miles of her destination with heavy loss of life. So it was with a great sense of relief and thankfulness that we found ourselves steaming along Belfast Lough. We had an impromptu Service of Thanksgiving for a safe and happy voyage. My hope was that many who had attended our Services would continue in the Christian Way.

As I mentioned early on, the lectures, competitions and games continued

140

enthusiastically throughout the voyage. Regarding my part of the ship, the momentum and happy spirit of Church Services never flagged. The OC Troops advertised them widely and Tom Sutherland did his best to whip in the masses. I had endeavoured to spread and preach the Word to the crowds who attended. I tried to sustain and build up the faithful, not very successfully, I am afraid. Through our prayers at Evening Prayer, which we had nightly, I laid the needs, the sins and the terrible plight of the whole world before Almighty God. For many or all of us self-preservation was obviously always in our minds!

There was tremendous activity on arrival at Belfast, but I managed to get the OC Troops alone for two or three minutes. I thanked them for the immense help and encouragement both he and his staff had given to me throughout this voyage. He said that he and they were glad to have been of use and in any case, it was all part of the service. He added that the services had been an inspiration to many. I hope so.

For the OC Troops and his staff it was Leave and then back to Belfast and the *Staffordshire* and outward bound again. Humanly speaking, they were unlikely ever to see us again, yet they had gone the extra mile to make the voyage happy, safe and successful. What a wonderful spirit they showed all the time!

We all disembarked and were put aboard a ferry boat to Stranraer, Scotland. It was in Belfast that I had left the *Ceres* in February 1940, making the same journey, Stranraer and then to Teston, Maidstone. Now I was doing it again. The ferry had a barrage balloon high up over its stern, attached by a wire, to ward off attack from the air. At Stranraer we were well looked after in a transit camp. Although crowds of Service folk must have been continually passing through this camp, the staff spared no effort to make us feel at home. The next day saw us aboard a troop train for St Pancras, London. The whole thing seemed like a dream and nearly impossible to take in. Then, for me, it was a train to Maidstone East and a taxi to Teston Rectory. I arrived on a perfect spring evening at six o'clock. It was May 1st 1942.

I had just paid off the taxi, and was standing on the front door step chatting to my parents, when the telephone rang.

I said, "I will answer it."

The call was from Mary's father, Mr Cummin, ringing to enquire whether I had got out of Java.

I said, "Yes; I've just arrived, seconds ago, and I am speaking in person. I have lost everything except the clothes I am wearing, but I have brought my golf clubs just like a tripper."

He said that he would send me some clothing coupons.

I asked, "How are you all and where is David?"

He replied, "He's left England and we think he has gone to India."

Next, I said, "Where's Mary?"

141

She was their youngest daughter and I had known her for years. He told me that she was nursing at the Great Ormond Street Hospital in London. I said that I had to go to London in a day or so to inform the Chaplain of the Fleet at Admiralty that I was alive, back in the UK, fit and well.

"Ring her up" he said, "and take her out to lunch."

I did. I must have given her a good one! We met again and again and again and were married at the end of November just before I went back overseas.

# CHAPTER X

# A Royal Naval Chaplain's Third Battle Front 1942 to 1944

*From May 1942 to June 1944 I was Chaplain of the Second Mobile Naval Base Defence Organisation known as the 2nd Royal Marines Group. I had arrived home from the Far East during the 1st week of May 1942 and a few days later reported to the Chaplain of the Fleet at Admiralty in London that I had returned safely, and was well and fit. He informed me that he was appointing me as the Senior Chaplain to a large Royal Marines Group which had recently been formed and that we would be based initially in the UK for a few months before proceeding overseas.*

The function of the 2nd MNBDO, as it was known for short, I later learned, was to work and defend a port or base which we had captured or re-captured from the Germans, Italians or Japanese, so that the Army could pass through and onwards.

This huge organisation of about 10,000 men had its Headquarters at Alton in Hampshire, with smaller sections based in some of the villages round about. The other parts of the Organisation including the Air Defence Brigade, the Coastal Artillery Regiment, the Landing and Maintenance units, Signals and so on, were scattered all over the country.

The Air Defence Brigade was composed of three Regiments, the 3rd Heavy A/A, the 4th Light A/A and the 12th Searchlights and they were in Cornwall.

The Coastal Artillery Regiment, with Headquarters in Hayling Island, had Batteries on the coast of Sussex, Hampshire and Dorset.

The large L and M Unit covering Supply, Unloading, Transport and Workshops, had some of their men in Hayling and others at Troon in Scotland.

The Signals were, I believe, at Aylesford. They always seemed to be happy and well led. I always had them on my conscience as I didn't visit them as much as I should have done. Their Commanding Officer was Major Hale but he didn't come overseas with us owing to his being over age.

In the organisation there were four Church of England Chaplains. Myself in the Royal Navy and the other three RNVR, one Roman Catholic and one Church of Scotland and one Free Church Chaplain. I relieved an RN Chaplain who was an old friend of mine. He had only just joined the Group, but really wanted to go to sea, so his request was granted. Two of the C of E Chaplains were with the AD Brigade in Cornwall. One was in Hayling

Island with the various units there, and I as the senior Chaplain, was at Group Headquarters at Alton.

My RNVR colleague at Hayling had informed the Chaplain of the Fleet that he had joined the Navy to go to sea and not to live in a nissen hut under the trees with the Royal Marines. His wish was granted. When the time came for him to go we were all very sorry to lose him and he, having fallen for the Royals, left us with a sad heart. It meant that when we finally went overseas we were one Chaplain short.

The Roman Catholic and the Free Church Chaplains joined us some months later. The Headquarters of the 2nd RM Group were at Thedden Grange near Alton, Hants. This could be described as a stately home. It had a chapel, a squash court and extensive grounds.

The senior Officers and the married junior Officers lived out in hirings while the rest of us lived at the Grange. The upstairs rooms were all used as offices. Downstairs was the Officers' Mess and ante-room and more offices. The junior Officers, the Sergeants, the junior NCOs and the Marines were all accommodated in nissen huts. These were also used as the Sick Bay, the Galley, Dining Halls, Workshops and Recreation Rooms. The Chaplain also had a nissen hut, which I used as a Chapel, an Office and a night cabin.

I had a Royal Marine to look after me. He was called my MOA or Marine Officer's Attendant and in peace time he was the Golf Champion of Sussex. Another Royal Marine drove me about and serviced my UV or Utility Vehicle.

During my first weeks at Alton, when my MOA came in to call me in my night cabin he said he often found me lying on the floor and if I wasn't there my bedding was! Those Marines sleeping in huts near to mine told him they heard me having nightmares and shouting and yelling in my sleep. I suppose it was the result of the previous six months in Singapore, Java, Colombo and the weeks and weeks at sea. I was very tired and easily exhausted, not only physically but also mentally, during my first weeks at Group. Added to all this was the effort required in trying to size up this new job. It was something I had not been used to. However my nine months at Deal in 1938/9 stood me in good stead. I had served with the Marines before and because of that I was accepted.

The month of June I spent at Group Headquarters, getting to know both the officers and men. Some of the young Captains I had known at Deal in the pre-war days when they were second Lieutenants. They were happy, full of fun and care-free.

Soon after my arrival I called on the senior Colonel. I hadn't met him before. He had his office on the first floor. I went in and we had a pleasant chat. As I left his office I heard him call me back. I turned round and put my head inside his door. As he spoke to me a young Captain I knew well was coming down the passage towards the Colonel's door. The temptation was too much for him, he applied his boot to my behind and pushed hard. The door flew open and I went headlong into the Colonel's arms. He was facing the door by his desk and although I spent only a second or two in his arms I had time to be impressed by his enormous black moustache! I apologised for this hasty intrusion. His face was blank but he was obviously furious though he realised that my sudden return was not of my doing. Neither of us mentioned this incident again. Occasionally, in the Mess, I found him staring at me as if to fathom who had dared to treat the Chaplain in this way. Once back in the passage I heard hoots of laughter coming from the young Captains' office.

I went in as if nothing had happened and said, "The Colonel wants to see you all at once."

On arrival one of them said, "You sent for us, Sir?"

"No," replied the Colonel, "I didn't send for you."

The young Officer apologised, "Sorry, Sir; we thought you did."

"Get out!" roared the Colonel.

*The Reverend Lovell Pocock in Quassassin Desert in March 1943 while serving with the Second Royal Marines Group.*

I reckon that I won that round. How we all laughed about it in the Mess later, especially as the villain had seen the expression on the Colonel's face when I fell headlong into his arms. He said that he wouldn't have missed that moment for the world. I told him that just becasuse we had been in the Depot Rugger team in 1938/9, I didn't expect him to take liberties with the Chaplain, especially when he had his dog collar on! These young Officers were very good value and helped to brighten up the rather 'heavy' atmosphere of Group.

Perhaps the flippancy of these young Officers should be explained and it may account for the liberties they took with their Chaplain.

In the years 1938/9, they were under training as Second Lieutenants at the Depot Royal Marines, Deal where I was the Junior Chaplain and where I lived in the Mess with them.

Two daughters of the Rector of Ringwould, a village near Deal – I was to be the Rector of Ringwould myself 30 years later – were often invited to parties in the Mess by these young Officers, but the Rector and his wife, Mr and Mrs Maundrell, insisted that their daughters be back at the Rectory by 10.30 pm.

One Friday night they attended a party and it didn't finish until 11.30 pm. I had gone to bed early, but was rudely woken up by several of these Officers at about 11.45. They noisily came into my room shouting, "Get up; get up; welfare case; two peasant women from Ringwould are stranded in the Depot; put on your dog collar and get them back."

As I slowly got up, I informed them that there would be a price to pay for this sort of thing. One of them said, "We will pay you anything you want, but get them back and make it snappy." I told them that I would require their presence . . . all of them . . . in church at the Morning Service the following Sunday, and afterwards they would entertain me in the Mess. They agreed.

I took the Rector's daughters back to Ringwould and faced Mr and Mrs Maundrell on their Rectory doorstep; I was all togged up in my dog-collar. I apologised for bringing their daughters back so late, said that we had had a lovely evening and that next time, I would try to make sure they were back on time.

The young Officers fulfilled their part of the bargain by being in church and I joined them in the Mess afterwards. The Senior Chaplain called across the Mess to me and when I reported to him, he said, "Are you responsible for the presence of these young Officers in church today?" I said, "Yes, Sir." He said, "Well done, you are doing a good job." I said, "Thank you, Sir" and I went back to my hosts; they asked me what the Senior Chaplain had said. I told them, "I am doing a good job on you people, but, if you count yourselves my friends, for heaven's sake be there again next week."

On the voyage from Colombo to Belfast in April 1942 I had shared a cabin with Lieutenant Tom Sutherland, RNR, who was being invalided home. He lived at Privett, seven miles from Alton, and his wife ran a War Nursery. As she wanted an assistant, Mary Cummin, who had just left the Hospital for Sick Children, took the job. About three times a week, I used to cycle over to Privett. The ride wasn't arduous as the road was flat all the way. These outings made a welcome break from Group Headquarters and it meant that Mary and I spent some pleasant evenings together.

All units appeared to be well supplied with transport of all sizes. Utility vehicles were used as the run abouts and all had names. They were called after towns, ports or islands such as Hong Kong, Singapore, Fiji, Colombo, Capetown, Bombay, Trinidad and so on. Mine was appropriately called Jerusalem!

The 3-tonners were named after cricketers; Hobbs, Sandham, Woolley, Sutcliffe and so on. Other types of transport carried other names. The names were printed in fairly large letters on the vehicle. This meant that if a senior Officer saw one speeding, it was easy to identify.

It was nearly three years since I had left the Royal Marines Depot at Deal, and I could easily have forgotten the important lesson of visiting all parts of the 'ship.' In Singapore, I had set about the task of calling on the 600 Dockyard and Naval Married Quarters. I think I did get round most of them.

So at Theddon Grange in June, after spending a few evenings in the Officers Mess and making good use of the squash court, I turned my attention to the Senior and Junior NCO's Messes. I had learned during my Deal days that the NCOs were the backbone of the Corps, as they are of any Regiment, so I gave them a lot of my time. Then there were the Marines themselves. I spent time in their Recreation Rooms, sitting around chatting or playing games. I found that a routine was quickly established.

Each day until about 10.30 am I did my own reading and meditation. From then on until noon I visited the outlying units and sections attached to Group, in the villages. In the afternoons, I watched games or visited offices, workshops, the galleys, the sick bay and so on. Three evenings a week I spent in the various Messes. In the years ahead, when I had left Group and was serving with one or other of the Regiments or Units, I felt that whenever I returned to Group I was treated as a lost sheep returning to the fold.

On Sundays, we used Theddon Grange for 8 am Communion and at 10 am we held the Morning Service for everybody; a Naval Matins. On weekdays I used the Chapel in my nissen hut for anything I put on. Then I would go to one of the villages to take a Service in the camp or join with the local congregation at the Parish Church. The Sunday half-hour Service was, I felt, well worthwhile. Although it was called compulsory there was very little compulsion about and the men appeared to leave the Chapel each week in good heart. I didn't see what more I could do. I was daily trying to carry out my duty to God; praying, and my duty to man; visiting and preaching the Gospel. Above all I tried to be the friend and adviser of all on board.

By July I felt that it was time for me to spread my wings and start visiting some of the other Units. Through the Headquarters of the Coastal Artillery Regiment on Hayling Island I arranged to visit their batteries which were scattered along the South Coast of England.

First I visited Sussex six-inch Battery at Littlestone. I had tea with the CO and his Officers and called on the NCO's Mess. The CO was married to one of the daughters of the Vicar of St George's, Deal. The other daughter was married to our Major General. I understood that these two officers did not speak to each other, except on official business!

A few days later, I called on U Battery, at West Wittering. I arrived about noon in pouring rain. The first person I met was the Company Sergeant Major. I told him that I was the Chaplain from Group and had come to call on the CO, a Captain E. W. J. Bevan. He said that the CO had just returned from seeing his brand new baby, that he hadn't really come down to earth yet and wasn't paying attention to anyone or anything. However, the CSM went with me to the Officers' Mess Tent and reported that someone had come to call on the CO.

I heard one of the Officers say, "Who is it?"

The CSM said, "It's a Chaplain."

There was a dead silence for a few seconds. I was standing outside the tent in the rain while this was going on and could, of course, hear it all.

Then someone said, "Where's he from?"

The CSM said, "Group Headquarters."

The response? Loud groans!

I then went in and apologised for inflicting myself on them, especially as I came from Group. The long and the short of it was that I stayed to lunch, and in spite of this inauspicious start, I always received a warm welcome at U Battery. A day or so later, I visited Dorset Battery at Portland and W Battery at Bridport.

After my visit to these various batteries and units I was deeply impressed by the general spirit of cheerfulness and enthusiasm of both Officers and men and by the care of the COs for the spiritual welfare of their men. The other side of the coin was that the Officiating Ministers I met really enjoyed their contact, often for the first time, with the Royal Marines.

Personally, I didn't really enjoy going round visiting like this. I would much have preferred to have been anchored to one Unit or Regiment. However, this was the job so I had to get on with it. By the end of July I had discovered that anyone from Group Headquarters was considered to be either a bore or a nuisance. This was a pity as there were some very fine Officers at Group Headquarters. I came to know them well and they did their job to the best of their ability. They would have preferred to have been with an active service unit. Most were efficient and reliable. These weeks and visits had provided me with some good contacts, which were to prove invaluable in the months and years ahead.

The Garden Party at Theddon Grange that July took the form of a Musical Concert given by the Portsmouth Royal Marines Band under the direction of Major Vivian Dunn. It was a perfect afternoon with a number of local celebrities present. Chairs were set out on the lawns facing the orchestra. The senior Officers, their wives and guests occupied the front two rows while the rest of us and the other ranks filled up behind.

While one item was being played and Vivian Dunn was conducting with his back to us one of the senior Officers and his wife turned round and chatted to visitors in the second row. Vivian Dunn glanced round, saw what was happening and stopped the orchestra in the middle of a bar. There was dead silence.

The two stopped talking, turned round to find out what happened, and saw Vivian Dunn glaring at them. When all was settled again, the conductor continued.

This was my first meeting with this gifted man, Vivian Dunn. After the war he made the Royal Marines Bands world famous and was knighted for his services. In the fifties I was privileged to be serving with him at Deal and so was able to see him at work. During those years, we became good friends.

In the first week of August, I went west to call on the Air Defence Brigade. This comprised one Heavy A/A and one Light A/A Regiment and a Search Light Regiment.

The Chaplain of the two A/A Regiments was the famous Rev. Geoffrey Beaumont. He was an RNVR Chaplain and a most unusual person. He had a gifted personality and was a talented musician. The first time I met him, he was vamping on a piano in a canteen in Bodmin surrounded by Royal Marines. The next night, he told me, he was booked to play at a pub in Camborne. He had a remarkable way with the Royals and was much loved.

I also met the Chaplain of the 12th Searchlights, the Rev. Dennis Manning. He was a conscientious man who looked after his men well.

I had known the Colonel of the Brigade at Deal in the pre-war days. The two Majors of the A/A Regiments had been Physical Training NCOs at Deal when I was there. They were hard working and forever cheerful. Geoffrey Beaumont spent a considerable time taking me round introducing me to people.

I had the feeling that I was beeing summed up by Geoffrey Beaumont and Dennis Manning. I think they accepted me. They realised that I was unlikely to interfere in their part of the ship in this very self-contained Brigade. I had the disadvantage of coming from Group! The AD Brigade was certainly a long way from the rest of the 2nd RM Group but that suited them. While I was with Geoffrey Beaumont we called at Truro Station, and the Station Master, seeing a Marine standing on the platform, asked him where he was going.

The Marine said, "On leave."

The Station Master asked, "Where to?"

The Marine replied, "England!"

After my three days in Cornwall, I was glad to be back at Group. For me it was now home and I wasn't a visitor any longer.

August 19th is a day which remains in my memory. There were tremendous air battles going on over southern England, the Channel and northern France. It was the day of the Dieppe raid, when the Canadians suffered huge losses. It was the first time since I had returned from the Far East that I had been caught up in this sort of thing. I did not discover until later that the RAF flew 3,000 sorties and the Germans 1,000. The RAF lost about 100 planes and the Germans 50. It was the greatest day battle of the war. Previously when I heard the sound of hundreds of aeroplanes it meant a Japanese attack. We had nothing to put up against them. So it was the sound of hundreds and hundreds of engines that I found so overwhelming. The experiences and exhaustion of the previous months came to the surface again. I felt very, very frightened all day and certainly not battle-hardened.

One August evening some of us went out to watch soldiers come down by parachute from a Whitley. Of the four, two landed perfectly but one landed across electric cables between pylons. He cut off the electricity for some time and he was badly burnt. The fourth's parachute failed to open and he died instantly, landing in a field next to where we were standing.

There were rumours that a German spy had been tracked down and caught in a near-by village. The story was that he transmitted messages to Germany while playing a piano. He played for hours and hours on end and just occasionally passed a message. Nothing was ever verified, but it made a good story in the villages.

September had two aspects for me; one personal, the other Service. On September 18th I asked Mary if she would marry me. Surprisingly she said, "Yes." We would try to get married in the Spring of 1943. Our parents were all very happy about our engagement while Mary's younger brother David, who was in Burma with the RAF, wrote to say that it was the best news he had heard since the war started.

Most of September was spent by the whole of the MNBDO II, all 10,000 of us, under canvas in bell tents at Bordon in Hampshire. I found myself sharing a tent with the Mail Officer, a Lieutenant. I really felt sorry for him. He told me that if the mail was issued on time and his mail services were satisfactory he heard nothing from anyone. As soon as there was a slight delay in a delivery or a shortage of stamps and so on, there was one long moan and he was blasted to blazes, especially by the senior Officers and Unit Commanders, who were more than anxious to keep their men happy and content.

The general opinion of the troops taking part in this month's exercise was that the sooner the word Bordon could be forgotten the better. U Battery of the CA Regiment were responsible for the erection of the 600 bell tents.

Towards the end of the month, the Major General sent for their OC and congratulated him on doing such a splendid job.

The OC said, "Thank you, Sir."

The Major General added, "You did such a good job in putting them up, you can take them all down again."

The OC (Capt Bevan) said, "Yes Sir."

I imagine that the word Bordon, if not written on the hearts of 'U' Battery, was well marked on their hands.

This whole set up was something quite new to me and if I wasn't going to waste the whole month, I had to get on with something quickly. First I had a meeting with the two Chaplains of the AD Brigade. We decided that they should continue to look after their Regiments and men and that I should do my best to cover the rest.

They were well informed by Group HQ of the Church arrangements which applied to all except the AD Brigade. Roman Catholics were looked after locally while the Other Denominations had to put up with me!

On Sundays, I conducted a Holy Communion Service at 8 am in one of the many Tents. Men from any Regiment, Battery or Unit could attend.

At 9.30 and 10.30 am there were Stand-up Prayers for several units and I worked through most of them during the month.

On weekdays, thanks to the co-operation of the COs, I took Prayers with one Battery or Unit and then remained with them for the day while they were on exercise. These days gave me the opportunity of seeing the Royal Marines at work. The way they set about their tasks, although they were only engaged in exercises, was an inspiration to watch. They came from all walks of life and from various occupations in civvy street, yet they quickly caught the spirit of the Corps and did everything with a will. For me there was the old problem! Everybody had a job to do except the Chaplain, so it was a matter of endeavouring to be the man of God, in the words of St Paul 'maintaining the spiritual glow,' and at the same time trying to be the friend and adviser of all on board. It was so easy on the one hand to withdraw into one's self, or, on the other hand, to be just a good Mess-mate and nothing more. The tension was always there.

We were all glad to be returning to our various places by the end of the month. For me, it had been a good experience and a continued education. After Group's return we spent hours going over the whole exercise and discussing it. One of the Officers who seemed to have a bird's eye view of the whole organisation, its function and its ability and possibilites, was the Superintending Clerk. I often found myself going to him for advice although he was an unbeliever!

At the beginning of the month MNBDO were informed of a move to the Midlands during October, to pick up our guns and get ready to go overseas early in 1943.

Group HQ left Theddon Grange in a huge convoy. We went via Oxford to Lutterworth in Leicestershire where we remained for the night. John Wycliffe was Vicar of Lutterworth from 1374 until his death. Some of us from Group put up at the Wycliffe Hotel. The local vicar heard that the Royal Marines had arrived with a Chaplain so he called on us. After supper we went round to the Vicarage for coffee and spent an hour or two with him. He was very proud to be in the line of succession to John Wycliffe, the 'Morning Star of the Reformaton.' It made a very pleasant break for us and I think that he thoroughly enjoyed meeting the Royal Marines.

Next day we pressed on towards our destination at Kirklington Hall where Group was to have its Headquarters. It was a few miles beyond Southwell. As we approached, the convoy stopped for a rest. My car was well down the line of transport, and, while we were resting, someone from one of the leading trucks came running down the line to tell me there was a clergyman approaching the column. Some even thought it was a bishop. I went up the road to investigate and to meet him. It turned out to be Dr Barry, the Bishop of Southwell. He gave us all a warm welcome and hoped that we should be using the Minster. The Marines could not understand why such a small place with a population of only 3,000 should have an enormous Minster. I pointed out to them that all the Cathedral cities were small places when the Cathedrals were built.

As it was probable I would be sent overseas any time after December 1942, Mary and I decided to change our wedding arrangements. We had the Banns called at the end of October and the beginning of November.

We all gathered at Teston Rectory on Wednesday 25th November and were invited to supper at Barham Court with Sir Albert and Lady Stern. The party included Mary's parents – Mr and Mrs Cummin – her sister, Grace, and her husband, the Rev. Keith and Mrs Stevenson, and their daughter Elizabeth, who was to be a Bridesmaid, my parents and my Best Man, Tom Sutherland. Teston Rectory was a large building, so we all fitted in.

We could not muster many of our friends. They were in different parts of the world and Teston was a restricted area for travel.

The two clergymen, Mary's brother-in-law and my father, gave us a first class Service and this was followed by a very happy reception at the Rectory across the road. In spite of rationing, cakes and good food appeared from nowhere as if by magic.

The day was dull but it wasn't raining and a number of photos were taken. We actually managed to get a professional photographer from Maidstone, who played his part well. Some of the pictures are still in very good shape and have lasted well, as have the Bride and her Groom!

We spent the first night of our honeymoon at Salisbury, on our way to

Yelverton near Plymouth. The train finished its journey at Salisbury and, as it was the last that day, we had to stay. After booking our room we went for a walk through the Cathedral Cloisters. The usual blackout was in force but we were able to see our way by the light of the moon.

Continuing our journey we changed trains at Plymouth and went to Yelverton where we stayed at the Rock Hotel. There we managed to borrow two men's bicycles and on them made our way, in spite of the hills, over vast tracts of Dartmoor. We visited bombed Plymouth and attended Yelverton Parish Church on the Sunday. Our week spent tramping and cycling passed all too quickly and, regretfully, we returned to London, where we parted. Mary went back to her parents at Bognor, while I returned to Southwell. Group Headquarters kindly presented us with a silver cigarette case. Once back, I quickly found a hiring for us both and Mary was soon on her way to join me.

We very much enjoyed our evenings together in our one room, in spite of having no heating. We wore overcoats! One evening I was reading aloud to her from a rather amusing book. I stopped while we had a good laugh and, at that moment, the chair I was sitting on collapsed in a heap of dust. The thing was hopelessly riddled with worm. As I sat on the floor we laughed again. On our last evening together our landlady allowed us a fire.

Some afternoons, we were able to attend Evensong together at the Minster, but Sundays were the Red Letter days. In those days there was a Church Parade every Sunday but, for the vast majority of us, the Services were always inspiring and warming. I think we all felt that we were really valued as people and not just pew-fodder.

On Christmas Day every Royal Marine attending the Morning Service of Matins was invited out to lunch by members of the congregation. It was a most generous gesture on the part of the Minster people because there were scores and scores of us. Mary and I were entertained to lunch at the Saracen's Head Hotel by a Southwell family.

It is hardly surprising that the name Southwell Minster had a special place in the hearts of the Royal Marines billeted in and around the town. The people did all they possibly could to make us feel at home during our time there.

For Mary and me it was a wonderful place, seeing that our nation was engaged in a world war and in a life and death struggle, in which to commence our married life. We have found our way back both to Southwell and the Minster several times over the years.

During 1943 the Royal Marines Group were joined by the Roman Catholic Chaplain, the Rev. Father Gilby; and the Free Church Chaplain, the Rev. J Simpson Lee from Scotland.

Other than the life in Southwell, I found my time in the Midlands a rather peculiar existence. I tried to visit the Batteries of the CA Regiments and other Units, who were at Gainsborough, Melton Mowbray, Retford,

Derby and so on. During the last week in January, all the wives left Southwell. However, we looked back on our two months at Southwell with great affection. Mary left for Edinburgh, where she stayed with my sisters for a week or so. One husband was in the Middle East and the other husband was a Japanese prisoner in Thailand.

We left Southwell on the morning of January 31st 1943. All the Officers' luggage was code named Machenry. This was stamped clearly on every kitbag and suitcase piled up on the pavement. As local boys passed on their way to school, one boy was heard to remark, "Mr Machenry is taking a lot of luggage with him!"

We were put on a train at Newark on January 31st and, after travelling all day with endless stops and waits and never a station in sight, we arrived at Cardiff. There we embarked on board the P and O Liner, *Moloja*, with 5,000 other Royal Marines. This tremendous movement of troops was going on day after day, week after week, month after month, for years, practically unknown to the general public. One really has to hand it to the railway companies, the GWR, the LMS, the LNER, and the Southern for their quiet, continuous efficiency.

We were all thankful to climb aboard this huge ship lying alongside one of the jetties. In peace time she carried about a 1,000 passengers. Now she had nearer 5,000 Officers, Other Ranks and Naval Personnel.

The OCs of the various Units and Batteries had a busy time getting their men sorted out into Messes, and their duties organised. Although it was important to have them settled quickly, there was no desperate hurry because the ship remained alongside for two or three days. When we did finally sail, it was by night, and in the morning we found ourselves in the Clyde between Greenock and Glasgow, with the surrounding countryside covered in snow! Again there was no shore leave and we saw other ships both ahead and astern of us. Other Royal Marines were embarked in the *Highland Chieftain* and the *Orduna*.

Boat Drill was held daily for everybody on board. It was considered of the utmost importance that this exercise should be carried out quietly and quickly so that we all knew exactly where to go.

Little did my new bride realise that we were only a few miles apart, but there was nothing I could do about it. The Free Church Chaplain, the Rev. J L Simpson Lee lived at Bearsden, less than a dozen miles away, and quite a number of men came from Glasgow, so we were all in the same boat.

Dr Miller of Group HQ, whom I came to know well, took infinite trouble with a problem I had with one of my feet.

As a result of the long voyage I had had in the *SS Yoma* from Jakarta nearly to Australia, and across the Indian Ocean, I developed a bad sore on one of my feet. We had no change of clothing or socks for weeks. One of the eyelets in my shoe had become jagged. It tore my stocking and then cut my foot between the toes and instep. Nothing seemed to heal this sore. When I joined Group HQ Dr Miller offered to take it in hand and, although his treatment took a year, it finally healed.

We sailed at last in a huge convoy of 60,000. We were told our destination was the Middle and Far East. First we headed north-west towards Greenland in heavy seas. A large number of men were seasick and for sometime, what with the crowded mess decks, the blackouts at night and the portholes closed all the time, life was pretty heavy going. When well out into the Atlantic, the convoy turned south and conditions gradually improved. The escort for this important convoy was the very old aircraft carrier, *HMS Argus*. HM Ships were in very short supply just then. The flat top of this old carrier was rising and falling, pitching and rolling for days, and we often wondered what she could do if she spotted a submarine. No aircraft could possibly have taken off in such stormy seas. We didn't know until after the war that the Germans had broken the Naval Codes and so were able to plot the movements of our convoys, hour by hour. However, where ignorance is bliss, it is folly to be wise.

As we approached the latitude of Gibraltar a few ships left us and were taken under the wing of a destroyer who guided them to the safety of the Rock. There was one U-boat scare for us shortly after this. We heard on the grapevine that a U-boat pack was nearby. That night the convoy circled the Canary Isles and then continued to Freetown, having given the pack the slip. We were glad to be in the anchorage of Freetown, and still for a while. But the place was hot and sultry and we were thankful to be on the move again, wherever it was we were going to.

We were about to turn due east for Capetown when one of the ships in the convoy must have zig-zagged the wrong way. Although we passengers didn't know it at the time this meant that all the ships came near to piling up on one another. Ships' horns and sirens began to sound off. Boat Stations were sounded which meant a controlled stampede!

The convoy slowly stopped and ships' port and starboard lights came on. To our amazement, we saw ships alongside and around us. They gradually sorted themselves out and we got under way again. I suppose some poor wretched Skipper or Officer of the Watch received a full blast from the Commodore of the Convoy. Fortunately no Jerry submarines were around and so no harm was done. When underway again we passengers dispersed to our bunks.

The convoy, having turned to the east, now divided. One half made their way into Capetown while the other half continued past the Cape and made for Durban, about 900 miles to the north. The *Moloja* was in this half and as we approached Durban, we were impressed by the magnificent beaches. We were to remain there for four days.

Life on board took on a recognisable routine. Boat Stations were signalled at least twice daily. The time it took for the ship's Officers to report their boats assembled and ready improved day by day. Bren gun, Small arms and

Rifle Drill seemed to go on continuously, not to mention Square Bashing.

Mess Deck rounds seemed endless but were very necessary. If it wasn't the CO of the Unit or Battery, it was the CO of the Regiment or the No 1 Colonel or even the Major General!

Sport took up a considerable part of the day, commencing with PT, which was never looked upon as Sport. There were Unit competitions, Boxing, Relay Races and Tug-of-War. There were some first class musical concerts. The pianists had a field day which lasted for weeks. Huge crowds listened to them either in one of the large lounges or on the upper deck. These concerts were much appreciated. Many of the Units produced their own Concert Parties. Hours and hours were spent in putting on these rather second-class shows but they were much enjoyed as the characters were well known to the audience.

With all the dead-lights or portholes closed, below decks was very stuffy at night in spite of the ventilation system. So we were allowed on the promenade deck at night. This meant passing through the two blacked-out compartments and, once there, no smoking was allowed. Boat Stations at night was a real test for everyone because we never knew whether it was the real thing or just a practice.

The Regimental, Battery and Unit COs had their own daily meetings with their Officers and NCOs. I think they were all conscious that the eyes of the Senior Officers were upon them all the time so they could not afford to let up. I am sure that they did their best to maintain a high standard of cleanliness, behaviour and morale. The vast majority of Officers and Men, including many of the OCs were only there for the duration so it must have been a new and exciting time for them. All Units had some regular NCOs, who must have been a tremendous strength to their Officers.

Church Events played a very small part in the daily life of the ship but, because this is a Chaplain's Journal, I am setting down in detail what we attempted to do.

There were three of us; the Church of England Chaplain, myself, the Free Church Chaplain, the Rev. J L Simpson Lee and the Roman Catholic Chaplain, the Rev. Father Gilby.

On Sundays Fr Gilby had Mass in one of the large lounges and two weekdays as well. He was also available for his flock at set times during each day.

The Rev. Simpson Lee and I decided to join together as much as possible for public worship and for daily prayers. On Sundays, I had Communion at 8 am in one of the lounges and this Service was well attended with between 30 and 50 coming along.

We arranged to have two main Services at 10 am and 11 am on Sunday forenoon.

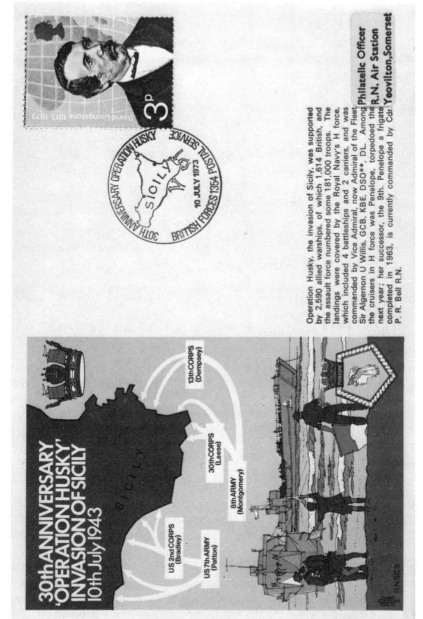

Post Office first day cover depicting the 30th Anniversary of 'Operation Husky' Invasion of
Sicily on July 10th 1943.
(Copyright - The Post Office)

157

Through the Ship's Daily Orders, we appealed for volunteers to play the piano and for men to join in a choir. The response was extremely good. We discovered a very fine pianist who was also a Choir Master, so he took charge of the choir.

We had a choir of between 30 and 40 who not only came to the practice but volunteered to sing at both the main Services on Sundays. OC Troops provided us with hymn books and a fine Order of Service, a kind of short Matins. He had ample supplies of both.

The Pianist-Choir Master taught his choir the first verse of the old Russian Anthem which they sang as an Introit before each Service every Sunday. It became a kind of signature tune. It went like this.

> 'God the Omnipotent! King Who ordainest
> Great winds Thy Clarions, Lightnings Thy Sword; Show
> forth Thy pity, on high where Thou reignest,
> Give to us peace in our time, O Lord.'

After the Blessing and the National Anthem we ended every Service by singing our two Vespers; "For those serving at sea' and for 'Absent friends'. Once again, they are worth quoting:-

> 'O Trinity of Love and Power, our brethren shield in danger's hour;
> From rock and  tempest, fire and foe, protect them wher-soe'er they go.
> Thus evermore shall rise to Thee, glad hymns of praise from land and sea.'

> 'Holy Father, in Thy mercy, hear our anxious prayer;
> Keep our loved ones, now far absent, 'neath Thy care.
> Father, Son and Holy Spirit, God the One in Three,
> Bless them, guide them, save them, keep them, near to Thee.' Amen.

Little could the 19th Century hymn writers, William Whitney and Isobel Stevenson have ever dreamed that their hymns would be sung all round the world, on land and sea, year after year, decade after decade, and in peace and war.

Whereas the Introit proved a very fine and inspiring introduction to worship, the Vespers provided a very moving conclusion to the Services.

We were the 97th Convoy to enter Durban Harbour since the war commenced, with the result that the local inhabitants might well have been sick and tired of convoys. However, we were very kindly and politely received by the populace wherever we went. One afternoon I had left the ship and was strolling through the town with three RM Officers when we met a Mr and Mrs May whom I had known in Singapore. He was one of the Principal Officers at the Naval Base and both were members of my congregation there. They invited us all to supper which, while being a most generous gesture on their part, was a delightful change for us. Mrs May sent a postcard to Mary to say that we had passed through Durban, but that she didn't know whether we were bound for the Middle East or the Far East. Neither did we!

Leaving Durban, the *Moloja*, the *Highland Chieftain* and the *Orduna* were all informed that we were to join the Middle East Allied Forces and that we should be escorted by the cruiser HMS *Hawkins*.

Every day, the *Hawkins* came alongside each of the ships in turn for about half an hour in the forenoon and half an hour in the afternoon. The *Hawkins* RM Band entertained us with music. Their Band Master was Ernie Ough, whom I had known at Deal in the pre-war days. We were near enough to recognise each other and to wave. They always played on the Quarter Deck and were simply delighted to play to 5,000 men of their own Corps. At the end of each performance they stood up and bowed to their audience, who responded with thunderous applause. These twice daily performances for each ship were tremendous morale boosters for the thousands of us cooped up on board, especially as they finished on every occasion with 'Life on the ocean wave' and the 'National Anthem'!

It was a sad day for us all when the *Hawkins* came alongside us for the last time. I remember that they did their very best for us by playing such items as Land of Hope and Glory, Danny Boy, Bluebells of Scotland, I'm Dreaming of a White Christmas and so on. They had escorted us for over 3,000 miles and, as they left us at the Horn of Africa, it seemed that most of the *Hawkins'* Ship's Company were on their upper deck to cheer us on our way. Signals were flashed across to and from *Hawkins* by aldis lamp.

"Good hunting against Jerry and the Ities: Make it snappy. We want to go home." They read. I believe *Hawkins* sailed east while we, with the other two ships, had another 1,500 miles to go to Suez, first through the Gulf of Aden and then through the Red Sea.

We were surprised how much we missed *Hawkins*. We had come to depend on her presence and on her Band. We were also surprised to learn how long the Red Sea was. Once through the Gulf of Aden, Suez wasn't just round the corner, there was another 1,000 miles to go.

I was doing these voyages for the second time. In 1940, at this time of the year, I had come through the Red Sea and the Gulf of Aden, going east. In 1942, I had gone down the east coast of Africa going west, and then back to the UK from Capetown. Before the war was over I was to travel twice through the Mediterranean, first east and then west. But that was still in the future.

We were immediately struck by the large number of ships at Suez, unloading not only men, but every kind of equipment for the desert armies. Arabs in their hordes were used as dockers for this task of unloading which went on unceasingly. My lasting memory of Suez is, however, of something quite different. We all landed carrying packs on our backs, side packs and rifles. As a Chaplain, instead of a rifle I carried my small attaché case, containing Communion Set, wine, wafers, Bible, Prayer Book, altar linen and a number of Service books.

Besides all this everyone of us wore a khaki topee. Just imagine 10,000 men marching ashore in topees! Before we left the ship we were informed that, once ashore, we were to take them off and that we would never be wearing them again. We had to march past three or four marquees in single file and, as we passed, throw our topees in the entrance. After that the Royal Marines wore their fore and aft forage caps while Naval personnel wore their Naval caps.

There were two rumours going the rounds. First that all 10,000 topees were to be burnt, so that they could not be used again and second, that someone in Whitehall owned all the shares in a topee company and was determined to remain in business in a big way and to keep the whole show going as long as possible. With all Service personnel going abroad being issued with a topee, the three Services between them must have provided this individual with a handsome income for life!

Our destination, once we left Suez by train was Ismailia, on the Suez Canal. There we disembarked and went by truck to Quassassin Desert, situated to the west of Ismailia. As there was nothing but desert, there was plenty of room to site large tented camps. These were ready for us when we arrived, set up by the thousands of Italian prisoners and hundreds of Arabs who seemed to abound. These camps had, we discovered, been used by tens of thousands of Allied troops from the UK, Australia, New Zealand, South Africa and various islands of the Commonwealth. The only signs of civilisation were one road which ran north and south and occasionally east and west, and stand pipes situated near both the road and the camps. Every few miles there was a large hoarding which turned out to be a cinema screen. Very ancient films were shown on these hoardings by a Mr Shafty. The audiences sat on the sand in front of these screens. A familiar cry was, "Anyone going up to Shafty's tonight?"

I have no idea how the thousands of Royal Marines were occupied all day and every day. The usual routine of PT, weapon training, kit and tent inspections and games continued endlessly. The RM Galley Staff with 10,000 mouths to feed were at full pressure and did a fine job. One very rarely, if ever, heard any complaints about the food.

On the weapon front I heard that Admiralty, with all their profound and professional wisdom, had sent all the guns of the Coastal Artillery Regiment out in one ship which was sunk. Jerry had put a whole Artillery Regiment out of action for months with one torpedo.

I found it quite difficult to keep any idea of the Church Calendar in front of the men when we were continually moving and when each Unit, large or small, had to be ready for any emergency. Having said that, I have found over the years that the Navy and the Marines always liked to observe the major Christian Festivals. I was able, even when on the move, to maintain the daily habit of Morning and Evening Prayer. Those in authority in MNBDO 2 were no exception to the general goodwill towards the Church so it was up to me to think through and work out the best ways of carrying the Christian Gospel to all the men, especially at the Festivals when they are more susceptible to the Christian Message than at other times.

I was very much on my own. The other two C of E Chaplains were with the AD Brigade a few miles away. I saw very little of them.

The RC Chaplain was polite and friendly but members of his flock weren't even allowed to say the Lord's Prayer with us in those days!

The Free Church Chaplain, the Rev. J Simpson Lee was a Yorkshireman and a Methodist. However, he had lived and worked so long in Scotland that he considered himself a true Scot and an upholder of the 'Kirk'. He was a very fine man, considerably older than most of us, and he had strong principles and views. He and I had worked happily together in the *Moloja* and he was to initiate a fine work in Quassassin Desert.

Ash Wednesday fell while we were passing through the Red Sea, and we marked the day in the *Moloja* with Communion and Evening Prayer.

Lent came during our first weeks in Quassassin. The Free Church Chaplain and I took Prayers with a different Company or Unit each morning. For the Bible reading I sometimes took a suitable passage for Lent and sometimes stories from the Old Testament, connected with the Israelites in Egypt and their deliverance under Moses. Mr Simpson Lee managed to get an evening canteen going in a disused hut and I supported him in this. He provided hot drinks and simple eats, ending every evening with an Epilogue. His over-all contribution was very much appreciated. On Sundays I conducted Holy Communion at 7 am in one camp and at 8 am in another. Then Mr Simpson Lee and I each conducted two main Services, so we managed to cover most of the camps. The Rev. Father had one main Sunday Mass and two during the week.

In 1943, we spent Lent in a desert, just as Our Lord had about 1940 years earlier. I found myself reading and going over the accounts of His Temptation when He was preparing for His wonderful but short Ministry of three years. In 1943 the temptation was for many of us to give up and forget our Christian Faith. The test was to preserve by faith, in the words of Scripture, 'looking unto Jesus, the Author and Finisher of our Faith'.

During these weeks, I was invited by the Landing and Maintenance Company to spend Easter with them at Suez. As the far greater number of men were at Quassassin, we decided that I should spend Good Friday and Easter Day there and go to Suez the following weekend to give them Easter

Communion. The CO of L and M arranged to conduct a Good Friday Service and a Service on Easter Day and I gave him advice on the choice of hymns.

Good Friday was kept as a Sunday, with a Sunday routine. The Rev. J Simpson Lee and I conducted three or four Services in the various camps. The sound of the hymns, 'There is a green hill far away', 'When I survey the wondrous Cross' and 'Jesu, Lover of my soul' was carried across the desert in camp after camp, every one seemed to know what day it was. Being 23rd April Good Friday was also St George's Day.

Sunday is often spoken of, usually in fun, as The Parson's busy day. Certainly Easter Day 1942, in Quassassin Desert, was very busy for me. I celebrated Holy Communion in two camps at 7 am and 8 am, with large numbers of men attending. Then I had two main Services at 10 am and 11 am. These were tremendous occasions with hundreds of men singing the Easter hymns which seemed to take on fresh meaning. Mr Simpson Lee gathered all the Free Churchmen together, while the Rev. Father had no difficulty in mustering his well disciplined flock. Here we were in the middle of a global war and the Christian Message of 'Christ has died, Christ is Risen, Christ will come again' was literally being shouted right across the desert in the middle of a Mohammedan country. It was my feeling that, in spite of having so much against us, the Day was a help and an inspiration to scores of men.

I set out with my driver, Johnny Gunn, in my 15 cwt on the Saturday forenoon of May 1st. We had a journey of about 40 miles to visit the L and M Company at Suez.

On the way across the desert we passed an RAAF Camp and an Airman standing by the side of the road thumbed a lift. We stopped and he climbed into the back of the truck.

The Driver and I were sitting in the front but my gear, consisting of an attaché case containing the Communion Plate, Altar Linen and a number of small sized Prayer Books, and my grip which contained my clerical robes, cassock, surplice, stole, Naval scarf, pyjamas and washing gear were in the back. My Bible and Prayer Book, gifts from my parents to mark my safe return from Singapore, I had with me in the cab as I was reading, meditating and preparing for my visit to L and M.

As we approached Geniffa where the airman wished to be dropped I said to my driver, Johnny Gunn, "Slow down now, and I will go round to the back to make sure that he doesn't run off with anything."

I was too late! by the time I reached the back of the truck he had already gone, taking with him the attaché case and the grip. The airman had mingled with the crowds of Arabs and was lost. We didn't see him. Fortunately Johnny Gunn had his pack with him in the cab beside him and his things were safe. We decided that there was nothing we could do and so we pressed on to L and M.

On arrival, there was considerable sympathy for me and Colonel

Tollemache was furious. They all understood that there was nothing we could have done. If we had reported the loss in Geniffa it would have taken time and by then the things would have been disposed of. The Stores fitted me out with pyjamas, towel, washing and shaving gear and soap.

L and M had their own large Bible and Prayer Book and plenty of small Service Books containing Holy Communion and shortened Matins and Evensong.

The 8 am Holy Communion Service was held in a small marquee. We used a Mess table for an altar, covered by a white cloth. For a Chalice, we used a tumbler and for the Patten, a mess plate. The bread we used had been made in the camp. Although my clerical robes had been stolen, I had arrived wearing a tropical suit and 'dog' collar; so I was covered in that way. Between 50 and 60 men took the Sacrament and as always when ministering to these dear Royals, I found it a very moving experience.

At 10.30 am on Sunday 2nd May we had the main Service, a Naval Matins, for the whole Coy. It was a rousing affair with crowds in a large marquee. The whole congregation seemed to catch fire, especially during the singing of the wonderful Easter hymns. I found it all most inspiring.

A bishop of Salisbury, Bishop Wordsworth once said, "The sermon is the people's Amen". I hope mine was.

I spent the rest of the day around the camp, and although I didn't know L and M very well, I found all Ranks very friendly and chatty. It seemed to me that they were quite glad to have a Chaplain around.

On Monday when I departed the CO and his Second-in-Command thanked me for coming and said they felt that these acts of Christian Worship had meant a lot to the whole Company. There was no need of course, to thank me for coming. It was all part of my duty, which they had made so pleasant for me. I left hoping that I might be able to visit them again but this depended on how long we were to remain in Egypt.

When we reached Geniffa, I left Johnny Gunn with the truck and went off to the market, where I was able to purchase a length of black silk which was to serve as a clerical scarf. My first Royal Naval scarf had been lost in 1942, when the *Anking* was sunk. While at home, later that year, I had purchased another scarf and now that had been stolen.

After returning to the truck, we found our way to the main Army Stores Depot, a simply vast establishment. When I commented to someone on its size, I received a quick and rather superior reply, "You see, Sir, we supply and service the whole of the 8th Army and a lot more besides". I was surprised how easily I was able to sign up for a Communion Set, which was in a compact attaché case. Perhaps they were not used to having Naval Chaplains putting in requests for stores, added to which I was wearing a dog collar which was unusual in these warm climes. So even a dog collar has its uses.

In spite of our huge army of 'Quacks' most men suffered at some time from a Tummy Upset. This particular ailment goes under different names in different parts of the world. In Egypt it is known as Gippy Tummy, in Malta as Malta Dog. In Malaya and the Far East we called it Chinese Cramp or something far worse.

The Heads, which included the latrines, the wash-basins and the baths, were situated about 350 yards away from the camp and to get there seemed like travelling to the next world.

During the day-light hours it was quite common to see men sprinting across this no man's land. It was observed that the 'Upper Classes' made this expedition on bicycles. At night, one could always hear people rushing back and forth, to or from this earthly Paradise. One heard them tripping over a guy rope or a tent peg and then going headlong. Sometimes the individual was on a bicycle so the crash was louder, as the bike went flying too. There were always groans and worse from the wretched man who had tripped or come off a bike and this was accompanied by a cry of, "Halt" from some terrified sentry. The conversation which followed between victim and sentry, while being quite amusing to those who had been awakened by the shouting, was never marked by any lack of sincerity.

Guards were placed round the camps at night to warn off prowling bands of Arabs. It wasn't surprising therefore that the sentries were jittery when they heard noises during the night, even though it was only a Marine tripping over a tent peg. The prowling Arabs would steal anything they could lay their hands on and, as they were never far away, every noise had to be challenged.

An incident took place before we arrived and is worth mentioning. One night, a party of these roving Arabs entered a tent in which 50 or 60 men were sleeping. The Arabs spread abroad some kind of fumes which acted as a drug, ensuring that the sleepers remained soundly asleep and doped. While the soldiers were 'out', the Arabs walked the whole tent away, guys, pegs and all. When these heroic members of the 8th Army awoke, they found themselves gazing at the sky!

During our time at Quassassin another raid was made but on a smaller scale. Two Officers of the Signal Company were sleeping one night in a small tent. During the night one of them woke up and thought he saw the other moving about with a light. It wasn't his colleague, but an Arab who stripped the tent bare. Clothing, kit-bags, cases, camp-washing stand, camp chairs, shoes, everything was taken. When they were woken up in the morning by their Marine all he found were the two Officers in their sleeping bags on their camp beds. Everything was gone including letters, money and washing gear. Fortunately they had no fire arms in the tent. Although the whole affair was considered a joke by everybody, it also served as a warning!

One evening, some of us were passing from one tent to another about 200 yards away when a sentry called out, "Halt." We all stood still. There was

164

still a movement so the sentry called out, "Halt or I fire." The movement continued so he fired but the movement could still be heard. The sentry flashed on his torch. It was a duck which he had missed and which continued its leisured way across the desert. We all laughed, except the sentry.

Mary's sister Elise was in Cairo. Her husband, Dr Douglas Radcliffe, was in charge of the Church Missionary Society Hospital in Old Cairo. One day, I heard that an RM Truck was going to Cairo, and I managed to get a lift.

Once there, I took a taxi to the Hospital in old Cairo. It was a pleasant trip along the banks of the River Nile. I had arranged to meet the RM Truck at 4 pm at Cairo Railway Station for the return journey. My time with them at the Hospital made a pleasant change and the hours passed all too quickly. After I left, Mary's sister Elise wrote to her to say that I had passed through Cairo and was on the way to the desert. It was the last time Mary had any idea where we were until August, when it was announced on the Radio that the Royal Marines were in Sicily.

We all took the mail very much for granted. I was glad that I had shared a tent with the Mail Officer at Bordon the previous September because it gave me the inside knowledge of his job. While we were in the desert he could not be blamed if the mail did not arrive regularly. Sometimes we discussed the problems of the Post Office in London. We all felt their staff did a mammoth job extremely well. There must have been hundreds of ships, regiments, big and small units, of the Navy, the Army and the RAF, but there were very few complaints.

The letters we wrote must have been terribly boring to read because we could give no news whatseover except what had to do with the weather, the food and the same old faces. I suppose the arrival of our mail in the UK meant at any rate that we were still going strong.

A few lines about the Naval personnel with the MNBDO would not be out of place. Chaplains I have already mentioned. Our full complement was four Church of England, one Roman Catholic, and one Free Church. We were one C of E Chaplain short but hoped he would join us before the war was over. The Chaplain of the Fleet had promised to send us someone as soon as he had one available. There seemed to be an enormous number of Doctors, Sick Berth Chief and Petty Officers and junior Sick Berth Ratings. There were also a few Dentists. Added to all these were scores of stretcher bearers! Some peculiar stories went the rounds on the why and wherefore of these vast numbers, but as the stories may not be accurate, I will not repeat them!

On arriving back at Group HQ from my visit to the L and M, there was a message for me, asking me to call on the Colonel of the Coastal Artillery Regiment. By this time I had acquired a red Service bicycle from Stores which I used all day long when going from camp to camp. So I bicycled over to the CA HQ to meet their Colonel. He told me I had now been attached to Group headquarters for about ten months. He asked if I would consider coming to live with the CA Regiment for a while. I told him that I felt very honoured to be invited to join them and that, to my shame, I hadn't given a thought to moving anywhere. I also added that I was surprised that any Regiment or Company wanted to be lumbered with a Chaplain. He went on to say that he had discussed the possibility of my coming with his Battery Commanders who said that, if I came, they would do their best to make me one of the family. When I returned to Group and told them of CA's request they were as surprised as I had been. They seemed piqued that this request had been made to me and not first to them. Whether they considered that I was their property or that I would be prepared to go, I don't know. Anyway it was settled that I should go for a while. All this took place on a Monday afternoon and it was agreed that I should move up the road after Prayer with Group the following Friday forenoon. Now that I was to leave, it was quite a wrench for me. I had settled in with Group and now would have to begin all over again. It was a real Missionary life.

At Morning Prayers the Officers and men were drawn up on three sides of a square while the Camp Commandant, Major W. Newland and I stood on the fourth side. He had done all he possibly could to help me in my work over the past months and had become a constant ally and friend.

After we had concluded Prayers on this Friday morning I was about to walk away when the Camp Commandant asked me to wait. He then addressed the assembled Marines and me saying that Morning Prayers in the Quassassin Desert had come to have a special place in the day's routine. They all appreciated my efforts to make them real and interesting and wanted to give me something to remind me of these desert Prayers and my time with them all.

He then turned to an Italian prisoner who was standing near by. We had crowds of Italian prisoners whom we fed and employed. This Italian was holding a board. On it was a Cross about nine inches high and two Candelsticks, each eight inches high. He took the board from the Italian and handed it to me as their gift. They had been fashioned by the Italian out of pieces of wood from an old packing case with a penknife.

As I stood there, I saw that the Italian was looking at me with a slightly curious smile, as if he knew the significance of what he was doing and was wondering how I would react. At that moment I felt quite overcome. Here was an enemy presenting me, a Minister of the Gospel, with the sign of God's forgiveness, the Cross. We shook hands and I said, "Thank you." I glanced round at the assembled Marines who were watching in dead silence.

Holding the board, with the Cross and candlesticks on it, I turned to the Marines and said, "This Italian prisoner has been preaching a sermon to us all; certainly to me. A year ago, in 1942, I was a survivor in a ship in the Indian Ocean. I lost everything except what I was wearing, and many

166

others were in the same state, including a number of Royal Marines who were survivors from the *Repulse* and the *Prince of Wales*. Then while we were slowly crossing the Indian Ocean God spoke to us all, certainly to me, by showing us His Sign in the sky, that wonderful constellation in the heavens, the Southern Cross. Now He is speaking to me again, to all of us through a nominal enemy, this Italian prisoner, in the gift of his Cross of wood. Thank you for looking after me so well while I have been with you all, and although I am going to live with the CA, I shall often be back. I want to leave you all with a sentence of St Paul which comes to my mind. 'Thanks be to God for His Unspeakable Gift, the Christ and His Cross'. And feeling very sad, I left them.

As I walked away I was joined by my friend, Major Newlands who said, "The Cross I can understand, Love and Reconciliation, but what about the Candlesticks? What are they for?"

I said, "For centuries two candles were placed on the altar so that the Priest could see to read the Prayer Book by their light. With the arrival of first oil lamps and then electric light, the candles have become symbolic, but provide good teaching. Jesus is the Light of the world. One candle represents Him as Son of God, the other as Son of Man".

He said, "Thank you," and left me.

During our time in the Quassassin Desert, we were visited by the Royal Marines 11th Searchlight Regiment, who were based on the Suez Canal. Their purpose there was to spot any aircraft which might attempt to bomb the Canal. They were the most westerly unit of the 1st MNBDO. The rest were in the Maldives in the Indian Ocean while others had been on the Burma Coast until Burma was overrun by the Japanese. They were made particularly welcome by the 12th Searchlight Regiment which was part of our AD Brigade situated about a mile away. The 11th Searchlights specialised in cricket and their teams were organised by their Chaplain, a huge bearded man. His name was Jessop and he was a descendant of the famous Jessop, a magnificent cricketer of former days and a contemporary of W G Grace.

So I left Group HQ and moved to the CA Regiment. They had rigged a small tent for me, set between the Officers and the Other Ranks. Sadly I was to be with them for only a few weeks before the next move came. However, these weeks were invaluable to me in getting to know the Batteries. It is always an education being with people. No two communities are the same and I found the CA Regiment very different from Group HQ. I still went along to the latter for Prayers once a week and remained there for the rest of the forenoon.

On other mornings, I went to Signals and to Supply. In both these Units I had some Deal pre-war friends who made me feel at home. Sport seemed to occupy most afternoons and there was plenty of football, hockey and rounders. The hockey pitch of sand had old oil from the transport poured on it. The pitch was then rolled, which gave it a hard surface.

During my few weeks with CA I was invited to several small Battery parties. They not only invited me to a party but presented me with a serviette ring made out of olive wood with the word Jerusalem on it. They also gave me Acting Temporary Rank and inscribed the word Bishop on it. I have it still.

One night, after I had been in the camp about a week, I had turned in fairly early. It got dark about 6.30 pm. I heard a motorcycle approaching the camp. It was one of the young Officers from Signals bringing a message to the CO. He knew the lay out of the camp but had not visited us since my arrival. He came into the camp with dimmed lights which meant that one saw practically nothing. I heard the noise of the engine getting louder and louder, nearer and nearer, then it happened. It came straight into the end of my tent. He was thrown off one side, while the bike went the other way. Fortuantely, I was on my safari bed at the other end. The tent pole snapped and the end of the tent collapsed. There was a good deal of coming and going and someone called out whether I was still alive. I informed them that I was. I was not amused and I had no intention of moving for anyone or anything. So I was left in peace, in my damaged tent until the next morning. My MOA was quite shocked to find his tent in such a mess. The young Signals officer came along to apologise for his noisy intrusion upon my privacy.

On Sundays I had Holy Communion at 8 am and the main Service at 10 am. I went along to another Unit at 11 am. I was only with them for three Sundays before we moved off again.

I have happy memories of those remarkable Services with the Landing and Maintenance Unit near Suez, and then the final Prayers at Group HQ. Now there were three very moving Services with the Coastal Artillery Regiment. Whether these Services had any effect on the Officers and Men of CA is not for me to say, but they certainly did on me. They were stirring occasions and most encouraging.

In May came the next move. Part of Group Headquarters, Signals, and two Batteries of the CA Regiment formed one party and I was attached to them. The AD Brigade, less the 12th Searchlights, formed the other party and the Rev. Geoffrey Beaumont was attached to them. Strange to say most of us who were going were quite sad to be leaving Quassassin to which, in a peculiar way, we had become quite attached. There was time to rush round and bid farewell to our friends in the other units and the rumour had it that Crete was our destination.

I left with Ernie, my MOA and Johnny Gunn, my driver in my 15 cwt, and we became part of the huge RM convoy. After some hours we found ourselves in another large prepared tent camp some miles west of Alexandria.

Early the next morning a few Officers and Other Ranks joined in a Service of Holy Communion in the open and then after breakfast we departed for the Docks. Ernie and Johnny Gunn went off in my truck taking my gear, a kit bag, a suitcase and my safari bed and sleeping bag.

On that hot May morning the majority marched out of the camp to a railway siding not far away. I remember so well bringing up the rear of these hundreds of men leaving the camp together with the Doctor. We carried packs on our backs containing clothes for a week, a side-pack containing washing gear and mess traps, and I carried my church attaché case. We wore open neck shirts, shorts, stockings, puttees and boots. Some of the lads had put on their puttees too tight and suffered from cramp. So, the Doctor and I waited for them as they dropped out and then encouraged them to join up again, the railway siding seemed fairly near and we were thankful to reach it. Marching in the heat was no fun. There we boarded an open cattle truck and after considerable shunting, we took off for the Docks.

On arrival at the jetty, which was abounding with Military Police, nicknamed Red Caps, we were told to get aboard the ship alongside.

I looked carefully at the ship, and then said to those standing around, "This is the *Yoma*."

The Officer in charge of the Red Caps came over to me and said severely, "How do you know the name of this ship?"

I replied, "I should know. A year ago she brought me safely away from Java to Colombo. And if you want confirmation look at the upper deck."

Many of the ship's staff were leaning on the ship's side gazing at their next consignment of human flesh! And they recognised me. There was no more to say.

As soon as we were aboard, and the gangways removed, we were mustered and told that our destination was Malta. Cabins and Mess Decks were allocated. Boat stations were practised immediately and then again and again. My driver had stayed with our truck and was travelling on another ship but my MOA, Ernie, was aboard the *Yoma* and he had brought my safari bed and sleeping bag, and his own, with him.

The *Yoma* was really a death trap for those down below so we were continually practising rushing up the flights and flights of steps which connected the decks and getting to the boat stations quickly. Back in 1942 I had spent the weeks on deck. Now we were back to the old routine again. Dead lights or portholes were closed all the time and there was a very strict black out every night. Life-jackets had to be worn at all times, day and night. Not only were there German submarines around, but also German and Italian torpedo carrying aircraft, operating from Crete, Greece and Sicily.

The Ship's Staff told me that, in order to mark my second trip in *Yoma*, they wanted to give me a book from their library. I was to choose it. The *Yoma* belonged to the Henderson Line, a Scottish Company. I chose one of their hymn books with tunes. It was a Presbyterian hymn book and contained about 700 hymns.

Once again the Chief Officer and his Staff went out of their way to help me with arrangements for Church. We had one Sunday at sea. We had 8 am Holy Communion at which Service I used my new Army set, and we had a popular Service for everyone on the upper deck at 10.30 am. On weekdays the Chief Officer provided me with a cabin for Evening Prayers.

We entered Grand Harbour, Malta, five days after leaving Alexandria and were all relieved to have arrived safely.

I quote St Paul after his arrival in the year AD 62, 'And so it came to pass, that they all escaped safe to land'.

We were disembarked quickly owing to enemy air raids. The Germans and the Italians had air bases in Sicily and so were only a few minutes flying time away. After two voyages in *Yoma* I felt that I was leaving an old friend and I received a warm farewell from the Staff. She left again the next day for Alexandria with a full complement of troops. Within 24 hours she was hit and sunk by an aerial torpedo off Benghasi with heavy loss of life. A year previously I had left *HMS Anking* and joined the *Yoma* a day or so before the *Anking* was sunk. Now I had left the *Yoma* a day before she was sunk. Being war time we heard and received no details about individuals; just the bare statement 'heavy loss of life'. One piece of the *Yoma* to survive is the hymn book which I still have and treasure.

All our transport, trucks and so on, and most of our gear, came from Alexandria to Malta in another ship. Our gear consisted of one kit bag and one suitcase a man. All this was loaded on to the ship taking the transport by our gallant allies, the Arabs, Palestinians, Fijians and others; the cream of the British Empire we were told. Most of the suitcases and kit bags were broken open, ransacked or stolen. So when we reached our camp in Malta we had nothing except what we carried. In 1946, while serving at the Royal Marines Depot, Deal. I received a torn kit bag, more or less empty, which had arrived from Port Said. It was sodden with sea water but still had a label with my name attached!

Disembarking we piled into trucks and were driven at a terrifying speed by Maltese drivers! We went across the island through Meleiha, to Meleiha Ridge.

The ground was rocky and the tents had already been erected for us to move into with pegs cemented into the rock. Fortunately, our sleeping bags and safari beds had come in the rear of my truck and had arrived safely. Had they come with the rest of our gear, they would have been stolen. Boots were the order of the day and we found the ground very hard on our feet.

By this time I was living with Signals; another kind of flock. The two Coastal Artillery Batteries were about a mile away and the AD Brigade, to whom the Rev. Geoffrey Beaumont was attached, was another mile further on. Our nearest beach was Ghain Tuffeiha which was sandy and provided us with some excellent swimming. We walked or marched daily, both for the swimming or sun bathing. Besides being fit we were always hungry. We lived on rations. The only things freely available were tomatoes, which were plentiful. However, most of us were wary about eating them as Gyppy Tummy, now called Malta Dog, was never far away. Food and manufactured articles were still very short throughout the island. I did hear that the first ship to bring in supplies had nothing but razor blades! The comments aren't fit to print!

Several of us had had all our clothing stolen and the Dockyard was to prove our salvation. I can't speak for others but they went out of their way to kit me up with battle dress, shirts, vests, pants, socks, and shoes. Nothing seemed to be too much trouble for them and as they said, they were determined to send us over to Europe, wherever it may be, well clad.

The Rev. Frank Leonard, whom I had relieved at Alton, was now the RN Chaplain in Malta. It was through his good offices that the Dockyard treated me so handsomely. He came out to see us at Meleiha. His cheerie, happy visit did us all a power of good. Thank you, Frank.

As I left the Dockyard I met Captain Guy Pilcher, Royal Navy, who had been the First Lieutenant of my first ship HMS *Woolwich*. He was now the Captain of HMS *Newfoundland* and he kindly invited me to lunch a few days later. He sent his boat to the Customs House Landing Stage to pick me up and when I came alongside her gangway I really arrived in style.

The cleanliness, the order, the courtesy and the general spirit of friendliness and goodwill impressed me at once. Before lunch Captain Pilcher took me into the Wardroom and introduced me to members of the Mess. I was struck by the white tropical rig. They all seemed cleaner than our rather drab khaki.

After living on rations for weeks, the way the Royal Navy fed really astonished me. We ate like the proverbial Lords. The RN deserves it of course; endless sea time and may they be preserved, as the Naval Prayer says, 'from the dangers of the sea and the violence of the enemy'. This visit to an HM Ship was a real tonic and I returned ashore to Meleiha greatly encouraged by the experience of being on board even for a brief time.

A large number of troops were being assembled all over Malta and at the time no one was supposed to know our destination. It seemed to us that there were two possibilities; Sicily, or the west coast of Greece. One Army Regiment was stationed on the next ridge . . . to the east of us, in and around a village called Wardia.

*Five years later From 1948 to 1950 I was Chaplain of HMS* Liverpool, *the Flagship of the 1st Cruiser Squadron, and we were based on Malta. During these years there was a great housing shortage and Naval families had considerable difficulty in obtaining accommodation. After some months in hotels and flats we were offered a house in the village of Wardia. It was called Casa Manduca and it belonged to a Mr Manduca. It was a country house and it had a garden; a tremendous asset if one had children.*

171

*The disadvantages were that it was 15 miles from Grand Harbour and it was very lonely for Mary when I was away. I think we moved in during October 1948 and the* Liverpool *left for the First Spring Cruise in January 1949. After my departure Mary used to wake up at night hearing a continuous knocking noise and became very frightened. She moved out of the room and on to the landing to sleep. Sue and Andrew were in another room and we often found Sue wide-awake in the middle of the night, screaming. After about six months, for various reasons, we moved into a flat in Attard which was much nearer Grand Harbour and Valetta.*

*When we left the house the owner, Mr Manduca, told us that a Maltese woman had been murdered in it some years earlier by an English soldier. He said that nobody stayed very long there as it was thought to be haunted. We were thankful to be gone!*

While we were on Meleiha Ridge, the weather was perfect, and we were continually walking or marching down to the sandy beach at Ghain Tuffeiha. While there I used to call on the No 6 Army Field Hospital which was near by and I came to know the Captain Quarter Master quite well.

At the beginning of July we were told that we would be on the move within a few days so I decided to scrub my canvas pack, my canvas side pack, with a few other odds and ends. I then placed them on one of the stone walls which were everywhere, about three feet high, and went off with others for a swim at Ghain Tuffeiha. On my return I discovered that they had all been stolen. In my predicament the Captain Quarter Master of the No 6 Hospital came to my rescue. He gave me both a pack and a side pack so when the time came to move off I was fully clad.

Although no one knew exactly when we would be off, or what our destination would be, we were told that it was now a matter of days. I therefore arranged to have prayers for the last time with each Unit before our departure.

It was my custom to read Psalm 46 and follow it with The Naval Collect, from 'Forms of Prayer to be used at sea'. In the Prayer 1662 Book it comes immediately after the Psalms. These Prayers, The Naval Prayer, the Naval Collect and the Thanksgiving after Victory were written by a Bishop Sanderson. He apparently didn't consider the possibility of defeat!

Next came Sir Francis Drake's Prayer on entering Cadiz Harbour in 1585. Then a Prayer for the King, our country, our families and our cause and finally The Lord's Prayer and the Grace.

In the evenings of those July days we occasionally sat around and discussed the war. I suppose there was considerable private and personal apprehension about the immediate and unknown future, but we were all together and we had committed ourselves and our cause to the Lord.

There was absolutely no doubt whatsoever that, however long the war lasted, we must smash the evil Nazis and their puppy dog, Italy, once and for all. In a way, we felt sorry for the Italians led by Mussolini. He was known as Saw-Dust Caesar and was about to receive a terrible hammering.

Somehow the Japanese didn't enter much into our discussions. They were far away and it was realised that once the Americans had got into their stride they would teach the little yellow men a lesson that they would not forget in a hurry. Pearl Harbour still rankled in everybody's mind. Pearl Harbour stood for Treachery!

None of the Royal Marines I was serving with had been in the Far East war so it did not really affect them, except for those who had brothers or friends caught out there. I often had a heavy heart as I thought of the tens of thousands of our kith and kin, including my own brother-in-law and many of my friends, Naval and Royal Marine, who were locked up in this Japanese Hell. Conditions were, in fact, far worse than we realised or could ever imagine.

The words from Psalm 79, verse 12 were often on my lips in those days, 'O let the sorrowful sighing of the prisoners come before Thee. Preserve Thou them that are appointed to die'.

The Russians were considered useful and it became essential to keep them supplied with arms and ammunition so that the Russian Steamroller would keep on rolling west as it was now doing in an encouraging way. However, they were trusted about as much as the Nazis and the Japs. What a terrible, terrible world and as Oliver Goldsmith wrote, 'Where every prospect pleases and only man is vile'.

All that we had discussed had to do with the actual war; the material side of the world's life. I purposely said very little because it might appear that I was merely preaching to them.

They did question the little progress that Christianity had made over the centuries and the little influence it had in the present world conflict. I tried to point out that the Christian faith was an on-going business and that each succeeding generation had to decide for itself whether it would accept or reject it.

They felt it was a good thing to have Christian ideals before us and to have a religion to hang on to. The idea of a personal relationship between God and man through Christ, who lived so long ago, seemed remote and far fetched. I was reminded of the Scripture, 'The God of this world hath blinded the eyes of them that believe not, lest the light of the glorious Gospel of Christ, Who is the image of God, should shine unto them'. At the same time I was conscious that there was a general spirit of goodwill towards the Christian Faith and the Chaplain.

So without forcing my views on any of them, and I think they knew me well enough to know I wouldn't, I had to be ready to help any man who was seeking personal faith.

In the middle of a world war, with the day to day problem of just living, keeping alive and doing one's job, there was rarely time for this sort of quiet discussion and meditation. Politically we were being fed on the Beveridge Report which promised a country fit for heroes after the war.

From my side it was a continual education to be living amongst men who came from so many different backgrounds and jobs and professions. In the Service they had been welded into various Regiments and Units each of which seemed to take on its own personality. To be able to watch them, not only at work, but in their constant care of each other; a spirit which was reflected in all Ranks; and to listen to their constant good humour, was an inspiration and the very salt of life. No wonder their motto was 'Bash on regardless.'

Three events took place during our last days in Malta; events which came from the outside world. They weren't laid on by us.

The first was a visit from ENSA, a professional concert party from England, who were visiting our Forces in North Africa, Malta and the Middle East. They actually came out to Meleiha Ridge and gave us an hilarious evening. Their items included songs, stories, jokes, juggling and recitations. They did us all a power of good and we were most grateful to the party for visiting us as we were not a very large unit.

ENSA were often ridiculed but we were filled with admiration for their efforts, especially as they had to give the same sort of concert over and over again. Thank you, ENSA!

The 2nd event was on a much more serious note. It was the visit of the famous General Montgomery to Malta.

We were herded into trucks, driven into Valetta, and seated in a large hall for a pep-talk from the great man, General Montgomery himself. When he entered the hall we all stood up and in his nasal, crisp voice, he said, "Sit down. No talking and no smoking," and away he went. I heard that there were about 4,000 men present and he let us know that we were on stage two of the Crusade.

"We have driven the Hun (it was always the Hun to him) out of Africa and now we are going to drive him back to Germany, where he belongs."

His theme was, "Onward Christian soldiers," and on to Europe.

The third event was for all of us the most moving of all. This was the arrival in Grand Harbour, Malta of HMS *Arethusa* with HM The King on board. He had reviewed the victorious armies of General Alexander in North Africa and now he had come to Malta to wish us all Godspeed as we prepared to set off to invade and free Europe.

The King toured the island in an open car. He sat in the rear seat and was accompanied by Lord Gort, the Governor of Malta. There were Service men on every road and bend, not as guards but simply to see and cheer the King. We heard that he had Malta Dog poor chap. He certainly looked rather pale but he was determined to let us all see him and he would not have his programme curtailed.

We knew he was on the way by the sound of the cheers which gradually

174

increased in volume and by the singing of the National Anthem which became louder and louder. We had taken up our station on the curve of a steep hill, so his car had to travel slowly round the bend. We stood three and four deep and this whole body of Royal Marines went nearly mad with excitement and cheering. It was a thrilling experience but of course it was all over in a matter of seconds. As we returned to Meleiha Ridge we could hardly believe that the King himself had been so near to us all and had come specially to wish us Godspeed for the coming invasion. We were all greatly uplifted.

At this time a rather amusing story was going the rounds. It concerned the King, General Alexander and General Montgomery. After the King had inspected the Armies in North Africa General Alexander, the Commander-in-Chief, asked the King if he might have a private talk with him.

The King said, "Certainly, what is on your mind?"

General Alexander said that he was worried because he understood that General Montgomery wanted his job.

The King replied, "I shouldn't worry too much. I understand that he is after mine too."

The King didn't stay long in Malta. The *Arethusa* took him back to Gibraltar and then he returned to England by air.

I think it was on July 11th that we left Meleiha Ridge and embarked in a Landing Craft Transport in Grand Harbour. My driver, Johnny Gunn, my MOA, Mne. Earnshaw and I had arrived at the harbour in my 15 cwt truck which, having had its petrol tank topped up and its carburettor sealed, was driven on to the lower deck, while all personnel assembled on the upper deck. Once aboard we were told that our destination was Augusta, Sicily.

The LCT had a Royal Navy crew. Those of us on the upper deck sincerely hoped we would not be hit by a shell, a bomb or torpedo during the crossing because the lower deck was like a huge petrol tank.

Once outside Grand Harbour we found ourselves in company with other LCTs and literally surrounded by a host of HM Ships. It was not only thrilling to see them but also a comforting experience. There were Battleships and I think we made out the *Howe* and the *Anson*. There were Cruisers; *Newfoundland*, *Superb*, *Kenya* and others and a number of Destroyers. As we approached the Sicilian coast, they softened the place up with 14", 8" and 6" shells. It must have been a terrifying experience to have been on the receiving end. Then suddenly, to our consternation, the ships were gone, all of them, moving to another section of the Sicilian coast to soften them up too.

For the last few miles we were all alone and felt both naked and vulnerable. We entered Augusta Harbour between 6 and 7 pm.

The Royal Marine Commandos had preceded us and Jerry had either pulled out or had been pushed out while the Italians, Service and Civilian, had fled under the RN bombardment.

175

Augusta has a wonderful harbour. It had been used by Admiral Nelson over 100 years earlier. It was also a staging post for the Flying Boats of Imperial Airways during the years between the wars.

Much to our relief, it was dark when we pulled to the shore inside Augusta Harbour. Just near the place where we landed there was an enormous aircraft hangar but it was empty. Alongside the harbour there were some large underground oil tanks. We heard that they contained enough oil to keep the whole of our Mediterranean Fleet going for six months. We also heard that the RM Commandos took Augusta so quickly that, when the Italian engineers who were manning the tanks below ground came up at the end of their watch, they found they had a new boss at the top so they were sent below again for another watch!

Our LCT grounded some yards from the shore so the transport had a 3 to 4 foot drop to the seabed. They were well revved up and most of them made the few yards to the shore while the lame-ducks were pushed ashore by willing hands. We were all standing about in the water which was quite warm.

While we were getting the transport and ourselves ashore, there were two or three German bombers flying around above us. As it was dark and theharbour was blacked out they couldn't see us. As no guns were fired at them they were probably unaware that we were there at all. Occasionally a bomb came down but there was no damage and no retaliation. Then it happened! A generator coming off the ramp of the LCT got stuck and nothing would move it. Ropes were thrown round and over it and passed to the huge crowd of men in the water. With a great tug-of-war effort we dislodged the thing and finally dragged it ashore. Whether it was of any use after its soaking and who it belonged to we never found out.

While this was going on an advance party had moved inland and into the olive groves and lemon orchards with white tapes. All the transport, blacked out, followed the white tapes into the groves and orchards. We'd had our evening meal before we came ashore and spent our first night bedded down in our trucks. So here we were in Europe. We had breached what the Prime Minister, Winston Churchill, called 'The soft under-belly of the Axis'.

So the advance party of the 2nd Mobile Naval Base Defence Organisation landed at Augusta. The rest landed during the remainder of July. This great organisation seemed about to commence its true function which was to 'Hold, Protect and Service' this port of Augusta to allow the Regiments and Units of the 8th Army Advanced Headquarters to pass through and on, without let, hindrance or interference from the enemy.

Over the next two or three weeks the main body of the MNBDO arrived, led by Group Headquarters. The others were the Coastal Artillery Regiment, the Landing and Maintenance Company, the Supply Company, the rest of Signals, the 3rd Heavy A/A; the 4th Light A/A, the huge Medical unit and last of all the 12th Searchlight Regiment. The smaller units; Postal Police and so on were attached to Group HQ.

Every Unit or Regiment naturally considered themselves the most important and quite indispensible. For instance Group Headquarters did the planning, handed out the orders and expected an immediate response. Other units looked at this from a different angle and complained that Group were always interfering! The Coastal Artillery Regiment looked upon themselves as definitely indispensible, in spite of the fact that all their guns had been lost at sea on the way out. They captured the Italian guns and had them working so quickly that weapons posed no problem to them. As the First Line of Defence they were able to repel invasion from the sea or the land. They were also in the position to hand it out to approaching aircraft.

The Landing and Maintenance Company and the Supply Company might have taken as their motto 'If it weren't for the likes of us, where would be the likes of you!' They certainly had something and without them the whole show would have stopped!

The 12th Searchlight Regiment were very humble about their contribution. They admitted that they were not really bellicose but gave the gunners an opportunity which brooked no excuse.

So one could go on with other Regiments and Units but I will only mention the Signals with whom I was to live for a short while.

On arrival in Augusta, I went to live with Signals. It was surprising how very different they were from the CA Regiment and Group HQ. Just as families are different from each other, the villages are different, so the various Regiments and Units in this huge organisation were different. Each one seemed to develop its own personality.

Because the various Regiments and Units were utterly dependent on Signals for communication with each other and with Group HQ, Signals could have looked upon themselves as the parents caring for the children. Whether they did see themselves in this light I don't know but that is how it appeared to me.

They spared no effort to see that their charges were cared for properly and efficiently and could communicate with all and sundry. There was a tremendous spirit of service in all ranks.

We had a house to the north of Augusta to use as Headquarters while the whole company, Officers and Men, slept in tents around the house.

Every morning we fell in to be given our ascorbic tablets to counter scurvy or malaria, or both. Twice a week, while they were fallen in, I conducted prayers.

In those days, there were no walkie-talkies so Signals laid miles and miles of lines between the various Regiments and Units, not only in Augusta but all over the surrounding countryside. I came to know the linesmen well and to appreciate their work. I spent hours at the various manned test points which were, I suppose, local exchanges.

The Rev. Geoffrey Beaumont, who had come in with us in the Advanced party, had established himself in an old, empty store at the entrance to the town by the main railway line. He had divided this rectangular building into a Chapel, reading room and rest room. Behind a huge partition, he lived with his MOA and his driver. With the arrival of the main body of the MNBDO at the end of July, they moved out of this building and into an empty hotel in the centre of Augusta. The AD Brigade, to which he was Chaplain, was established in the town with Batteries round and about so he was right amongst his flock.

As a result of his move, regretfully I left Signals after three weeks and moved into the set-up he had vacated. This meant that I could reach the many units which were billeted outside the town.

The Roman Catholic Chaplain, the Rev. Father Gilby and the Free Church Chaplain, the Rev. J L Simpson Lee both lived at Group Headquarters at Villemunde, eight miles in a straight line and on a straight road, east of Augusta.

The Rev. Dennis Manning of the 12th Searchlights, lived with them when they eventually arrived.

Geoffrey Beaumont and I met on Monday mornings to plan our programme for the week and for the coming Sunday. By early August he was looking after his own flock, the AD Brigade less the 12th Searchlights, while I was trying to visit Group HQ, the L and M Unit, the Supply, Signals, the CA Regiment, with their six-inch Batteries, Sussex and Dorset in Catania and Syracuse, and the Four inch Batteries around Augusta and in the harbour.

One forenoon, during the third or fourth week of July I was standing on the jetty of Augusta Harbour watching a number of Landing Craft arrive.

Suddenly I heard someone call out, "There's Lovell Pocock."

It was the Rev. Basil Carver. He and I had been at Emmanuel College, Cambridge together about 1930 and we were both in the Emmanuel Rugger Team. He also Put-the-Weight for Cambridge against Oxford. I called out to him, asking him who he was with.

He said, "I am a Chaplain to the 8th Army Advanced Headquarters and have just got myself a job after the war."

After landing he told me he had come across from North Africa with a Lieutenant Colonel who was patron of the living of Holy Trinity, Sloane Square, London. The living was vacant, and the Patron asked Basil Carver for advice in getting a clergyman to fill it.

Basil Carver said, "Keep it for me and I will take it after we have cleared up this lot."

In 1945 he became the Vicar of Holy Trinity, Sloane Square, and remained there until he retired in the eighties. This is how the Church of

England works!

The same forenoon, one of the Officers of T Battery, the CA Regiment who landed from a Landing Craft with all his Battery, said to me on the jetty "Who came ashore in that Landing Craft ahead of us?"

All the Marines of T Battery were listening as I said, "It was the Naafi Staff."

There was dead silence! Then a great burst of laughter came from the crowds standing on the jetty. Perhaps I shouldn't have spoken, but I had done so in all innocence.

The situation was put right, when a Marine of T Battery shouted out "Permission to go home, Sir." More laughter followed. The Battery, however, were not amused to have landed after the Naafi.

One Sunday morning early in August I was conducting a Service for personnel in the harbour area and I noticed an old gentleman in the congregation. After the Service I spoke to him. It was the Rev. Hyde Gosling. He was a much loved Chaplain of former days who had retired before the war. In 1939 he was recalled for Service and joined his great love, the Royal Marines. Now he was with the Royal Marine Commandos who had just arrived in Augusta with part of the Eighth Army. He was passing 'Through and On' and he remained with his beloved Royals until the end of the war.

A large number of ships and LCTs arrived in Augusta, as well as the Landing and Maintenance Unit, the Supply Unit, the Signals and Large Medical Compound. These all had to be defended by the Heavy and Light A/A Regiments. They all used captured Italian guns, and as they left an abundance of ammunition behind, it was their ammo which was being pumped into the sky.

The Jerry aircraft had a real field day. All the A/A Batteries could do was to keep the monkeys up.

This state of affairs, with heavy raids and the A/A gunners unable to see their targets, continued until the end of July. During the last days of the month the 12th Searchlight Regt. not only arrived from North Africa but positioned their searchlights around both Augusta and the Harbour. Not a searchlight was used until they were all in place.

Then, about August 1st while a heavy raid was in progress and Jerry was using a large number of bombers all flying fairly low, all the searchlights went on at once and caught this great armada in their beams. In spite of the noise from the aircraft engines, and the tremendous racket from the A/A, a tumultuous cheer went up from all around Augusta. Several of the aircraft were hit while the rest dropped their bombs and hurried away. One German pilot reported that, at Augusta, it was like flying into a sea of fire.

By the beginning of August I had worked out my routine for Services and visiting. I was trying to cover all the Units I was responsible for. It was quite impossible for them all to have a weekly Sunday Service, so I visited each Unit once a week and conducted Prayers at some very peculiar times, and gave them a Sunday Service once a fortnight.

I produced a programme to cover the two weeks and had copies run off and sent to every Unit, HQ, and Battery. Then they would know where I was at any given time on any given day, so they could get in touch with me if necessary.

George Formby, the Lancashire comedian and singer was in North Africa and it was arranged that he should come to the Airship Hangar in Augusta and entertain the troops. The show was well advertised and the troops poured in from all over Sicily for the show. At the last minute it was cancelled. But it was too late. The vast audience had either arrived or was on its way and George Formby had had to give up his seat to a Major General.

On Sunday I started with Communion at 8 am in the Rectangular Store which we used as a Chapel, reading room and for accommodation. At 9.45 am I was with the large L and M Unit. This was a popular Service. Next I moved on to Group HQ eight miles away. I used to stand up all the way as, owing to the potholes, one was liable to damage one's spine sitting down.

On one occasion a 15 cwt truck travelling down this road to Group had both its front doors open. They used to slide open. The passenger in the front seat fell out. The rear wheels went over his legs and broke them. After that doors were ordered to be kept shut!

Group HQ had taken over a large house in the village as their Headquarters and across the road was a disused Catholic Chapel. It belonged to the house and the village. The roof leaked. The seats were filthy, the altar derelict and the place housed a few hens!

The Royal Marines attached to Group turned their attention to this Chapel. They repaired the roof, scrubbed the pews, restored the altar and got rid of the poultry.

We used it for our Morning Service, but the local Roman Catholic Priest would not allow us to use the stone altar. Our Priest, the Rev. Father Gilby, was allowed to use it. But not the non-Romans. We used to bring in a wooden table, place it in front of the stone altar, and use it for all our Services. I gave our people Communion after the Morning Service. Naturally the attitude of this Priest didn't do his cause any good but we accepted the situation and didn't make a fuss.

After lunch at Group, I used to move on to U Battery, at Pemiscola Magnisi which was on the south side of Augusta Harbour, arriving about tea time. I had tea with the Officers in a unique stockade they had built, visited the men's messes and had Evensong in the open at about 6 pm. There was no compulsion about these Services. In this case, the CO, Capt. E W J Bevan, was always first to be seated and the majority of the Battery attended. I think the men enjoyed singing well known hymns and the sound of their voices carried across Augusta Harbour. I stayed the night and then after Communion and breakfast, moved on again to Dorset Battery at Syracuse. This sort of routine continued until Thursday.

Friday and Saturday, the truck was off the road for servicing which gave me a day off, a day for being round and about and time for preparation. The second week the same sort of routine took place, but this time we visited Units north of Augusta, ending up in Catania.

While I was visiting the outer units on a Sunday, the Rev. Geoffrey Beaumont was busy with units in Augusta and he usually finished up with a Service in our Chapel. Once a fortnight I got back for Sunday-Half-Hour followed by tea and coffee.

One Sunday night my MOA, Marine Earnshaw and I were clearing up after everybody had gone. I picked up a printed Service and Marine Earnshaw told me it was the one Mr Beaumont had used. It was a Communion Service nicely printed on a card with a few hymns. I read it through carefully, out of interest, and suddenly realised that it was the pure Roman Catholic Mass. Just to make sure I read it through again, two or three times. I really didn't know what to do. Having pondered over it for some hours, I wrote an airmail letter to the Chaplain of the Fleet and stated what was happening. I said that, as the Chaplain of this Group, I could not and would not agree to its use. If he agreed with this Service, and I quoted part of it in my letter, I wished to be removed from the MNBDO II at once. I turned in at 4 am.

Next morning I met Geoffrey Beaumont as usual and we went over the week's routine. I then threw him the letter I had written to the Chaplain of the Fleet and told him to read it. He was very surprised and said he would write to the Chaplain of the Fleet too.

Next I went to Group HQ and told the Colonel-in-Charge what I had done as the Major General was in England. The Colonel agreed with me entirely. Then I visited the Colonel of AD Brigade who was furious with me. He was quite rude and said that he would not have Geoffrey Beaumont removed. The matter of principle which I had raised did not enter his thoughts at all. I informed him that if anyone was to go it would be me and that I was not prepared to give way on what I had written.

Then a strange thing happened. Up to this time, Geoffrey Beaumont had paid very little attention to me in any way. I suppose that I was just part of the Group HQ set up. But from now on, he came to see me regularly and for some days was always hanging round my place and coming in for a chat. I seem to remember that I received a rather non-committal reply from the Chaplain of the Fleet. What he wrote to Geoffrey Beaumont, I don't know and never asked him, but this Service to which I had taken exception was not used again. From now on he always consulted me about his Services. I felt that I hadn't lost him, but rather won him. They say that if you don't stand for something you fall for anything. I stood for the Book of Common Prayer and our Church of England type of Worship. This to me was fighting for Christian Principle and this is what I had tried to do even if it was in the middle of a world war. Hundreds of years before this was the very thing that our forefathers had given their lives for so I had no intention of giving way, no matter how much the Colonel of the AD Brigade pouted and fumed.

Probably what had happened was unknown to the vast majority of both Officers and Men, and, although it had been an unpleasant episode for me, it had done me no harm. In fact, I think I gained from my outburst.

Early in August we heard that our fourth Church of England Chaplain, The Rev. Mike Crooks was on the way to us. He eventually arrived during September. I, with others, felt terribly sorry for him being landed in this huge organisation knowing nobody and starting from scratch.

Although joining us so late in the proceedings, his arrival was a real tonic to us all for several reasons. First, from the Chaplains' point of view, our team increased from three to four. Second, from the various Units' point of view, they would be better served. Most important of all he had arrived fresh, keen and apparently delighted to go anywhere and to do anything. I think that I had got into the rut of war. This was my fifth summer and one can so easily become set, staid and dull. His appearance made us, the Chaplains, look again at our vocation and task.

He spent his first two or three days in Augusta with us. Until he came we hadn't realised how shabby we all looked. He had a very smart uniform almost straight from Gieves.

I well remember taking him round to call on the various Commanding Officers. They were all delighted to meet him. Not only was his a fresh face but he brought a breath of fresh air. Colonel Tollemache of L and M was very interested to meet him and asked me when Mike Crooks would be joining them. I am not sure that it had been decided with whom he was going to live, but this question clinched it. He went to live with L and M.

He arrived with two Chaplains' caps. As mine was in very poor shape, he offered to let me have one of his. My MOA wasn't too happy about this arrangement, as he felt this new cap of mine was too new. He took it in hand for a day or so and made it look as if it belonged to an old hand.

For two or three nights, Mike Crooks bedded down on his safari, sharing my cabin in our place. We were both woken by a noise around the walls. We switched on the lights and saw enormous rats, about three feet long, racing round, while others were gathering nuts from our supply and propelling them across the floor.

Mike Crooks yelled out, "Whatever shall I do?"

I said, "Do nothing. Just turn over and go to sleep."

I was absolutely petrified and my heart was thumping loudly, but I didn't let him know that I was shaking like a leaf. I curled up in my sleeping bag, zipped up all four sides till it was completely closed and having put out the lights, tried to get to sleep. I was certainly glad when the morning came and so was he. We discussed the night intruders and I told him they were quite harmless and not to bother about them!

*In 1972, while I was Rector of Ringwould, Mike Crooks came down from Epsom, where he was the Vicar. He preached at a St Nicholas Day Evensong to a packed congregation at St Nicholas, Ringwould.*

*He started the sermon by saying that he was glad to come to preach for me at Ringwould as I was the bravest man he had ever met! He then told the congregation about the rats. Little did he know that I was so frightened that I could hardly speak.*

After two or three days Mike Crooks moved to the L and M and also took on the Supply Unit and the Signals. His presence was soon much appreciated by all ranks and I hope that he was happy with his charges. Once he had left it meant that we did not see much of him, although we still all lived in the Augusta Chapel. I remember that the Rev. Father Gilby was surprised when we called it The Chapel of St Augustine. I suppose Saint Augustine was a Roman Saint and not a Church of England one and that was the trouble. Geoffrey Beaumont had turned a room in his empty hotel in Augusta into a chapel and he called it St George. We had considered calling ours St Andrew, St David or St Patrick, but we thought that might arouse raised eyebrows so we decided on St Augustine. After all, he officially brought the Gospel to England. Mike Crooks used to visit us on his and our day off, Fridays. I have a photo of him half way up Mount Etna, not to speak of the one where he is with Marine Earnshaw my MOA, my driver, Johnny Gunn, and myself with The Church of St Augustine in the background.

With the arrival of Mike Crooks, who was living in the Augusta area, I was pressed strongly by the Officer Commanding the Medical Unit to move out of my Chapel and into the Medical Compound some miles away. This I agreed to do although we still kept on the Chapel and the reading room. We moved over to the Medical Compound about the end of September. Before we went we experienced an earth tremor. We were not far away from Mt Etna, an active volcano, and I suppose this sort of thing happens from time to time. The tremor took place after breakfast one morning. Our Italian prisoner was doing the washing up for the five of us and had stacked all the crockery on a board, ready for drying. All units have Italian prisoners. All they wanted was to be fed; so they worked very happily with us. It meant that instead of my MOA doing all the chores, he had an Italian to do them for him. Azzapardi I think we called him and he was treated as one of the family. He gave me a present, a Fascist dagger which I used as a penknife. When the tremor commenced all the crockery slid off his board and was smashed to smithereens. Azzarpardi was blamed, of course, for the tremor and for our loss of crockery.

I was surprised that the Medical folk wanted a Chaplain living-in, as the Marines were meant to be young, fit and strong. Sicily was very pretty on the surface but treacherous underneath. There were a large number of men sick with malaria, jaundice and pink eye. Added to these were the stomach troubles, colds and so on. As a result the Doctors were kept fully occupied. Thankfully we had very few battle casualties.

The Medical Unit gave me a fine square tent which I used as a base, for I was out on the trail for five days a week. Life with the Medics was a complete and utter change from any unit I had been living with, and proved both an education and an experience. One learns from every unit and company of men with whom one is privileged to live and work, and the Medical Unit was no exception.

I have one lasting memory of the Church Services in this camp. It was the Holy Communion Service held on Wednesday and Friday mornings. The Service took place in the centre of the camp in the open so all could see what was going on.

It took considerable courage for a man to come and sit on the benches we had rigged and placed in front of the altar. Then he had to kneel to receive the Sacrament in full view of the whole camp. I was surprised, though I shouldn't have been, at the number of men who attended this Service over the weeks.

Because the whole routine was different from an active Service unit or battery, which had to be ready to fire the guns at any moment, I had a Study Group which met in my tent. We were able to study the New Testament and topical questions. I found the meetings both stimulating and helpful. It was, of course, my duty and custom to read Morning and Evening Prayer every day. To these two books I added a few lines from a Latin scholar so my translation of the Latin was very slow and also probably inaccurate. The Bible and Prayer Book helped me, in the words of the Scripture 'to maintain the spiritual glow', while the Latin was a good antidote to the war.

The war receded and moved away from us at Augusta, except for the nightly raids. A party of us decided to climb Mount Etna. We commenced the assault early on Michaelmas Day, September 29th, while it was still dark. We took the truck up to 6,000 feet, where the road ends and then set about climbing the next 6,000 feet on foot.

The lava had poured down the side of the mountain like sand and was very soft. It made the climb both heavy going and slow.

Etna has two craters. When one of them is quiet, the other is active and we were attempting to climb to the crater which was quiet. In spite of our slow progress we were determined to reach the top. At about 10,000 feet, we passed an observatory which was shut. The last 2,000 feet were much easier going and we simply raced to the top and then sat on the bank of the crater, on the inside, which was pleasantly warm. The false bottom of the crater had steam coming out of it and was about half a mile across. From the top, looking east, we could see the coast of Greece including the Corinth Canal.

We spent about half an hour at the top. It was a perfect day for weather, sunny with a cloudless sky, but cold and we felt it as we were wearing shorts and shirts with open necks.

As we commenced the descent – there were six of us – we saw a huge American Bomber Fleet of about 500 aircraft, flying southwards below us at 5,000 feet. They were returning to North Africa after bombing the Rumanian oilfields. At 6,000 feet we found our truck safe and sound, although our driver, Johnny Gunn, was fast asleep. We stopped to eat some sandwiches and drink the tea we had brought and we arrived back at camp about 5 pm. I don't think anyone had missed us; I personally was very disappointed, while my colleague, Mike Crooks, thought it was wonderful as everybody thought that we were 'out on the job.'

I said that the war moved away from Sicily during September, but the month was an anxious one for all of us in that island. We knew there was to be an allied assault on the Bay of Salerno, south of Naples, and it began on September 9th.

Men of many Regiments, including the Royal Marines, took part in the landing and they were subjected to a murderous attack from the German guns situated in the hills inland and to continuous bombing from German aircraft which were only a few minutes flying time away. Allied losses were very severe in dead and wounded and there was doubt as to whether the bridgehead would hold. But it did and, with the Eighth Army advancing from the south, the Germans withdrew.

During October we had very heavy rain. The roads, which in any case were in poor shape, now became much worse. Many were no better than a quagmire and others were already a mass of potholes. Travelling was both slow and dangerous.

The Rev. J L Simpson Lee, our Free Church Chaplain, was anxious to establish a canteen. He found some empty sheds on the Villemunde Road, about half way between Augusta and Group HQ. Somehow he furnished them, moved in and, by the begining of October, opened his canteen for the men. It was well placed just off the main road. Unfortunately it was in a dip and, owing to the rains, it was completely surrounded by water. It became known as Noah's Ark and the flooding remained, off and on, during the whole of our time in Augusta. In those sheds he also had a chapel, a reading room and his own quarters. Once it became known, it was used by many Marines not only for its canteen but also as a place of quiet and rest. In spite of continual problems owing to the rains Mr Simpson Lee remained there and his efforts were much appreciated by all Ranks.

One day in September, my driver and I were travelling south to visit Dorset Battery at Syracuse, when we were waved into the side by Red Caps, the Army Police. While we were stationary General Montgomery passed us, travelling slowly north in his open white car.

At that time the Pioneer Corps were widening the road so that it would take our tanks. Monty had stopped to talk to the men and handed round smokes to them. One member of the Pioneer Corps we spoke to showed us the cigarette Monty had given him. He had no intention of smoking it but said he would keep it and have it framed one day. There is no doubt that this great man, Monty, inspired confidence, hope and loyalty wherever he went.

A Rest House was established for the MNBDO on the slopes of Mount Etna, overlooking the town and harbour of Augusta. It was in the charge and care of a Royal Marines Officer Captain Armour who had a small administrative and galley staff to help run the place. I think it could take four Officers and about 20 men at a time and they went there for three day periods.

I was up there for three days myself in November and was fortunate to have as my cabin companion a simply charming Captain, Royal Marines of the 7th Battalion. I never found out why someone from the 7th Battalion was in Augusta. This particular Officer went out of his way, throughout the three days, to make our stay pleasant. Those days were some of the finest I had in Sicily. Somehow we borrowed a jeep and were able to drive right round Mount Etna, including going through the Bronte country. He was a splendid companion; Captain, later Colonel, J T O Waters.

*We met again in the fifties when he was serving at the Royal Marine Barracks at Eastney and I was at HMS Siskin, Gosport. Some day I hope we shall meet again.*

The months of October, November and December slipped quickly away and except for the regular air raids on the town, harbour, ships and jetties, there was little war activity.

I think the Chaplains found it difficult publicly to keep the Church Calendar before the men, but we seemed to come into our own at the Festivals.

Harvest Festival and Thanksgiving gave us the opportunity of some fine Services all round Augusta. The Harvest hymns were sung with great gusto with oranges, lemons, figs, grapes and nuts much in everybody's mind. There seemed to be a wave of thankfulness towards nature while the world was in its arid climate of war and hate.

Remembrance Sunday was another occasion which brought us up with a start. Possibly, as never before, the sacrifice of 1914/18 came home to us all. The Lessons seemed to have a greater significance this year and were listened to quietly and thoughtfully.

> 'Let us now praise famous men and our fathers that begat us.
> Their bodies are buried in peace and their name liveth for
> evermore.'

There was a general demand that we sing 'O valiant hearts' and from somewhere we managed to get copies. This wonderful hymn by Sir John S Arkwright was sung at most unit Services. For many of us, Remembrance

Sunday, 1943 in Augusta, was an occasion we should long remember.

In December I found myself in another 'Chaplain's crisis' but this time it was not of my making.

The Rev. J L Simpson Lee, the Free Church Chaplain, decided to have a Christmas Morning Service in the cinema in Augusta. He had it well advertised with posters and a signal from Group HQ to all Regiments and Units. He had forgotten to consult anyone or even mention what he intended to do.

The first thing to happen was that I was approached by the Rev. Geoffrey Beaumont. His Regiments and 12th Searchlights wanted to know if the Service was for all Free Churchmen or for anybody. What were the four Church of England Chaplains doing? What about the majority of men who would not be able to leave their particular place of duty? And so on.

I had to tell him that I knew nothing about it until I saw the signal. I went to Group HQ eight miles away and discussed it with the Colonel. The other Regiments and Units had got in touch with me and asked me to clarify the Christmas Services.

Nearly every Battery and Unit wanted their own Carol Service and Communion. We sent out a general signal stating that the four Church of England Chaplains would be visiting all Units for a Christmas Day Service and Communion. The Service in Augusta was for all Free Churchmen who could be spared and for anyone else who wanted to attend.

Having made all our local arrangements with the Rev. Mike Crooks looking after L and M, the Supply Coy, and part of Signals, he went down with fever and was taken to the RN local Hospital near Augusta. As a result the three of us, Geoffrey Beaumont, Dennis Manning and I, divided his Services between us and so far as I know every HQ Battery and Unit had a Christmas Day Service.

On the Christmas Evening, another Officer from AD Brigade joined Mike Crooks in the local Hospital. He arrived with violent stomach pains. The RN Doctor was convinced he had appendicitis and decided to operate at once. In fact his appendix was in perfect condition. It was placed in a bottle and on Christmas morning was handed round the ward for inspection. The Officer's stomach pains were due to his having drunk an extra bottle of Marsala! Later, during the forenoon of Christmas Day, the Parson and his Officer were placed in an ambulance and bumped all the way to Syracuse via the Villemunde Road, which must have been quite an experience for them both, especially for one who had his stomach cut open the night before and had been 'tatted up without much care or expertise,' as someone was heard to remark!

In an HM Ship there was a discussion about which Officer has the least to do, the Major of Royal Marines or the Chaplain. It was agreed that the Major of Royal Marines has the least to do because, whereas the Chaplain works on Sundays and other Holy Days, the Major of Marines has a

Company Sergeant Major and a whole detachment of Marines to help him do nothing!

On Christmas Day, 1943 in Augusta, the Chaplains worked hard and, speaking for myself, we were richly rewarded by the spirit of the Services. The Christmas Message, 'God was in Christ', went across well but the other half of the sentence, 'Reconciling the world unto Himself', was still a long way off. The evil things we fought were still powerful. I had the feeling that there was great faith in our cause, and Faith in God Himself, to see us through.

The Americans were in Sicily using the Catania airfields for their aircraft. We came across them from time to time. Our Supply Officer used to exchange crates of corned beef, the staple standard British diet, for crates of spam, the American diet. This made a pleasant change for us all. The Americans seemed to be well supplied with Flying Fortresses and Liberator aircraft. We heard that many of their air crews and personnel indulged in the luxury of flying to America for the week-end! First stop Portugal, second stop the Azores and third stop the States; and then back to war on Monday!

Having lived with the Mail Officer at Bordon before we left the UK, I was always welcome at his small unit and occasionally used to spend a few hours with him. We discussed his part of the ship which had been running fairly smoothly since our arrival in Sicily.

The Great British Public had been informed by the BBC in August that the Royal Marines were in Sicily, a month late, and as a result our mail home should have been more interesting and intelligent because we could say where we were. We even managed to send parcels of fruit and nuts to our families. Most of the fruit, oranges and lemons, was bad by the time it arrived, but at least it showed we cared!

I remember sending home a glowing account of our climb of Mount Etna. This was not received with the enthusiasm I had expected.

'I thought we were paying for you all to fight a war and to get it finished and not for you all to go sight-seeing round the Mediterranean, being fed and getting paid for it,' was the answer I got!

One Battery I visited had just received some papers from England, and one of the lads was reading aloud a paragraph about the Royal Marines in Sicily. It was his local paper. It stated that all the Royal Marines were hand-picked. This produced hoots of laughter, especially when one member of the Battery said that about half were ex-jail birds and he was one of them!

About the turn of the year, 1943-1944, we heard that we would be returning home, disbanding and then reforming for the Second Front. The night air raids still continued but, with the fierce barrage put up by the A/A Regiments, ably supported by the Searchlights, not many German aircraft got through. One night a stick of bombs hit an ammunition ship in the harbour and caused considerable damage.

During these days and weeks, men who had been serving outside Augusta were gradually being assembled in Augusta, ready to embark. One night, during a heavy raid, a number of bombs hit a barracks where the men were being housed prior to joining the transport home.

A large number were killed and others wounded. We had a mass funeral, in which all the Chaplains took part with representatives from every Regiment and Unit. A wave of sadness swept through the whole of MNBDO that this should happen during our very last days in Sicily.

We had been fortunate to have had very few battle casualties although there had been a large number of men sick. Now we had been smitten in a most unexpected way at the very last minute.

At the end of January 1944 we embarked in a Dutch ship manned by British Officers and Crew. She had been taken over by the Admiralty and was being used as a Trooper. She was the SS Sibajak,

Once more we were back to the sea routine of endless boat stations, all dead lights closed all the time, black-outs at night, and cramped conditions. But we were going in the right direction.

Training of all kinds, which had been a top priority on the outward voyage, was now done with little enthusiasm. We were now, after living more or less together for so long, closer to each other than on the way out. There was a mutual respect, trust and confidence.

Battery and Unit competitions were still the order of the day. The Atlantic Ocean was kind to us and the submarine menace was on the wane. Mike Crooks and I did our best to keep the Church Flag flying with Sunday Services and with meditation and prayers on weekdays in a small room allocated to us.

I doubt if any of us realised that this journey home was, in reality, the end of the Commission and that it was the last time so many of us would be together. The one longing was to get home. Every day brought us nearer and we couldn't see much further than that.

I have mentioned elsewhere that I was fortunate to meet one of the Ship's Officers I had known in Singapore in 1941/2. After the surrender of the Island to the Japanese, he escaped and brought 109 people across the Indian Ocean in an open boat. We spent many hours of the voyage together going over the tragic events of those days.

This was my ninth transport or trooper since 1939. I had also served in four HM Ships and taken passage to Sicily in an LCT. At least one of the transports or troopers and two of the HM Ships had been sunk. Thus far I had survived so the omens were good. In the words of the great Apostle, 'I thanked God and took courage.'

After arriving at Greenock with the two other ships bringing the MNBDO home, the whole organisation dispersed to billets of various kinds. They went into towns and villages in and around Glasgow including Hamilton, Motherwell, Paisley, Kilmarnock and others. The billets included condemned Barracks, camps on race courses and even prisons.

Leave was granted to practically everyone immediately and, on our return, this huge organisation gradually began to disband and form up again for the Second Front.

I found myself living with Group HQ once again and seemed to have my time taken up keeping in touch with all ranks now scattered far and wide. I would have liked to have returned to Signals, with whom I had been happy for three weeks in Sicily, but the Staff now wanted a Chaplain at Group HQ. Week-end leave was not given regularly, but we continued to have Sunday Worship for those left behind. All the married men did their best to have their wives up in Scotland, but for many who had children, schooling and houses, this was extremely difficult.

Mary and I lived first in Hamilton, then in Kilmalcolm, which nobody liked and I don't think they liked us, and finally on a farm south of Greenock.

I saw little of the other Chaplains who were living with their families in other towns and places. Afterwards I wished that we had seen more of each other during those weeks.

On Easter Day, a large number of us attended the Morning Service in the Episcopal church, and this Service left a deep impression on us all. The Easter flowers and decorations, the singing of the Easter hymns, not to speak of the dignity of the Service, helped to produce an immediate impact on us all and it was a wonderful ending to our time in the MNBDO which disbanded altogether soon afterwards.

I think the grandeur of the Services, the magnificent building, a robed choir, and the gracious welcome we received from the Churchwardens and Sidesmen, all came home to us after our own rather stark and meagre efforts of the past years.

Soon after this I received a letter from the Chaplain of the Fleet that I was to take a few days leave and then join the Royal Naval Barracks Chatham to await my next appointment.

The ending of the MNBDO II was a terribly sad affair although we didn't realise it at the time. All those months hundreds of us had been locked together through all kinds of situations. Now the vast majority of us have more or less disappeared into thin air and only a few of us, a very few of us, would ever meet again. For myself, it was most unlikely that I would ever be working with my brother chaplains again. The realisation of this came home to me too late. I was deeply grateful to each one of them for the particular contribution to the cause of the Christian Gospel and the high standards they had maintained in this great Royal Marines organisation. In the voyage out we had sung the first verse of 'God the all-terrible' as an Introit to the Sunday Services, The last verse, I think, sums up the hopes, desires, friendship and prayers of the Chaplains.

190

'So shall Thy children in thankful devotion,
Praise Him Who saved us from peril and sword;
singing in chorus, from ocean to ocean,
Peace to the nations and praise to the Lord.'

A year or so after the break up of the MNBDO II, I received a letter from one of the Officers. This is what he wrote.

'D'you know, I always thought and felt that the disintegration of the MNBDO 2 was a tragic affair. Not that it may have been necessary; but it all happened so casually. People just drifted piecemeal as if the spirit and comradeship of three years' building had never been. It was in vain that we looked for a comparable spirit, or even the time and opportunity to develop it, in the various formations to which we were posted. Certainly, in my consequent travels, I often longed for just a few of my old "S" Company lads.'

So I went on leave. Mary and I had no home of our own yet, so we spent part of the time with her parents and part with mine. We made the most of our days together and I was reminded of words written by Ronald A. Hopwood in his poem, 'The Laws of the Navy'

'When the ship that is tired returneth,
With the signs of the sea showing plain,
Men place her in dock for a season,
And her speed she reneweth again.
So shalt thou, lest perchance, thou grow weary,
In the uttermost part of the sea,
Pray for leave for the good of the Services,
As much and as oft may be.'

During this short leave I licensed, and put on the road, my little open Morris Eight. I was allocated a number of petrol coupons for Foreign Service Leave. It was quite fun to be driving about the countryside in May in an open car on the more or less empty roads. As we went through Kent and Sussex, people stared as if to say, 'What right have they to be driving a car on the road in war time?' As the car did about 50 miles to the gallon, we went fairly long distances. We did enjoy it, especially while eating ice-cream cornets, whether people stared or not.

On arrival at Chatham, the Chaplain informed me that, as my stay was likely to be short, I would have no official duties. He wanted me to man the Chaplain's Office for a few hours every day and to help him with the Sunday Services.

I was glad to be able, once again, to assess the role of the Chaplain;

perennial question for Naval Chaplains! Looking back, one had to try and sum up what we had done and what one had not done. Looking forward, to try and prepare for whatever the future held.

It had been my custom to read and think through the Ordination Service in the Prayer Book once a year and these days at Chatham gave me the opportunity to do just that. I quote the Exhortation which is very challenging.

> 'Ye are called to be Watchmen and Stewards of the Lord; to teach and provide for the Lord's family; and to seek for Christ's sheep that they may be saved through Christ for ever.'

That gave me enough food for thought!

I realise that it is much more difficult for a Chaplain to carry out his duties when he is on the move than when he is static in a shore establishment, a Barracks or a Ship. I came to the conclusion that the most important thing for the Chaplain is, in the words of Scripture 'to maintain the spiritual glow' by reading and meditating on Morning and Evening Prayer daily, as set out in the Prayer Book. This all Clergymen are ordered to do.

Several things happened while I was in the Barracks. As they are connected with happy memories of men from the MNBDO 2, I will mention them.

One day, I was manning the Chaplain's Office, which was situated in a very busy corner of the Barracks. People passed to and fro all the time rather like one of the London main line railway stations. I saw a man staring at me through the window. He had just driven his utility vehicle from Cockfosters, in north London, bringing his Chaplain to visit someone in the Barracks. As we were talking, the Chaplain came out and asked the driver if he knew me.

He said, "Yes, Sir. He has been my Chaplain for the past two and a half years." This Chaplain was with a section of the disbanded MNBDO and they were forming up for the Second Front, Beach Party, I think.

The long and short of it was that I went back with them both and spent two days with the Officers and Men of this Beach party. The Chaplain was the Rev. John Long who, after the war, became Domestic Chaplain to Archbishop Fisher.

I introduced him to all the Officers in their Mess and then to all the Other Ranks.

I hope that my visit to my Royal Marine friends was of use to their new Chaplain, and helped to get him off to a good start. This visit to these fine men had left me much refreshed and had been an unexpected bonus to my time at Chatham.

The Barracks' Chaplain gave me a couple of days off each week, when I was able to spend the time with Mary at her home near Bognor.

One day, I had my Father over to lunch in the Wardroom. It just happened that the Barracks was being visited by the Senior Roman Catholic Chaplain of the RN, Rev. Father Dewey, that day. The Father had not only been Priest in my Father's parish in Devonport, 24 years earlier, so they knew each other well, but he was the Fleet RC Chaplain in the Mediterranean in 1936/7. He was accommodated in *HMS Woolwich* where I was the Chaplain. So this was a happy occasion.

When I arrived back from Cockfosters my appointment awaited me. I was to return to the Royal Marines Barracks at Deal. It was just five years since I had left. I had come through those years without a day's sickness and without a scratch. I received this appointment with a very grateful and thankful heart. It was like going home.

My appointment just said 'on St Peter's Day'. Perhaps the Chaplain of the Fleet imagined that I would have to scurry off to find a Church Calendar and look up 'St Peter's Day'. I knew it was June 29th!

The first thing I did was to ring up the Drafting Officer, an old RM friend of mine, at the Royal Marines Office at Admiralty in London to ask him what had happened to Marine Earnshaw, my MOA over the past two and a half years. He told me that he was listed for a Beach Party on the 2nd Front. Everybody seemed to be joining Beach Parties! I told the Drafting Officer that I was returning to Deal and that I would be pleased if he could arrange for Marine Earnshaw to be drafted back there as my MOA. In fact he arrived at the Royal Marines Depot, Deal, before me.

The morning after his arrival he reported to the Second-in-Command, who asked him why had been drafted to Deal.

Earnshaw said, "I am the next Chaplain's MOA."

The Second-in-Command said, "Since when have Royal Naval Chaplains had Marine Officers Attendants?"

Earnshaw replied, "This one has had me for over two years".

The matter was settled!

Next, I went off to Deal and managed to rent a house in Upper Walmer. Having had no home, we had no furniture or linen, nothing. Mary's parents at Bognor and mine at Teston offered us furniture and other household necessities, but how were we to get it all to Deal in war time?

Next door to us in Walmer there lived an old gentleman with his two daughters. Soon after our arrival, he died and a Royal Marines Officer and his wife moved in at once.

Years later, I met this Officer again and he said, "I shall never forget our arrival at this house. The old fellow died in the morning. We moved in during the afternoon. The bed was still warm!"

Capt. Edward Bevan of the MNBDO, who was getting together a Unit for the Second Front, came to spend a day or so with me at Chatham Barracks. He travelled between RM Barracks, Eastney, Portsmouth, RM Barracks,

Chatham, and the RM Depot, Deal, fixing up his men and his supplies and stores. He had his own Service transport.

He offered to act as our Furniture Remover on his journeys between Eastney and Deal. Bognor and Teston were also on his route. I think it needed three trips to complete the whole operation which he did with the help of his MOA. He brought furniture one way and took men and stores the other.

During these weeks at Chatham the south of England was under attack from Flying Bombs. These unmanned missiles were blasted off from the Calais area. At Chatham we could hear the roar of their engines as they winged their way towards London. They were so designed that their petrol ran out by the time they reached the capital. Occasionally we saw our fighters chasing them, giving them a burst, and then sheering off to avoid the explosion.

The Barracks were responsible for the Service personnel, and ground staff manning the Barrage Ballooons. These balloons were strung out in a long line from east to west in an effort to catch the Flying Bombs. It was hoped that they would get caught in the wires of the Balloons, and then blow up before they reached the built up areas of London.

I went out to take a Service for these people. There was a regular roar from the engines of the Flying Bombs as they passed overhead. If they went on, all was well from the point of view of those below. If the roar remained over head, it meant that a Bomb was caught in the wires and, when its petrol was used up, down it would come and explode. It was a nerve-wracking business and I was thankful to be safely back at Chatham. The Barrage Balloon crews certainly deserved full marks for their courage and steadfastness.

So I returned to Deal. I relieved a much loved Chaplain, the Rev. Lancelot MacManaway, and had a lot to live up to. His assistant, then mine, was the Rev. Michael Brown. He left for Holland shortly after I arrived. There, he was badly wounded and returned to the UK. He was serving with the Royal Marines at the time. He was followed by the Rev. N L Cribb, who did a good job with the NCOs' Courses, until he was demobbed. After him, for a short time, came the Rev. L Janes until he, too, was demobbed.

Deal was a veritable hive of activity, mostly taken up with the training of hundreds and hundreds of Recruits. There were PT Courses, Small Arms Courses, NCOs' Courses, Young Officers and so on. In spite of all this, after being in the Front Line for almost five years, I felt that I had been relegated and exiled to a backwater!

When I had been at the Depot for about six months, an Officer of the MNBDO turned up.

He said to me, "What's it like here?"

I replied, "I have been here six months, very busy, but I don't seem to know anyone."

He said, "That is because you are no longer living close to men as we were in the MNBDO. How do you face it?"

I said, "As you know, I used to read my Bible and Prayer Book every day, but also I used to read a few lines of Latin verse. I came across some that so appealed to me I have typed them out and pasted them in the back of my Prayer Book."

Then I quoted to him these lines.

> 'Even though others may form the first line, and your lot may have placed you among the veterans of the third, do your duty with your voice, encouragement, example and spirit. So help me God.'

He said, "Thank you. Give me a copy and I will do the same. I am in a backwater too. Cheerio."

* * *

*Looking back over the mists of time, all sorts of names and faces come crowding into my mind and memory. There were the outstanding figures of Colonels V. D. Thomas, Tollemache, "Tolly" to the MNB, Gunner Paine, Barclay Grant with his huge voice and great laugh and Geoff Sherman, always so reliable. In the pre-war days of 1938-39, he and I had quarters next door to each other. They said that he was on the Depot Staff in those days because he was a fine bat in the Depot side! There was John Salter too, the helpful Staff Officer and Squash player. Wilfred Newlands, the Group HQ Camp Commandant, was always so helpful to the Chaplain and Major Don Burrows took as his motto (to misquote Charles Dickens) 'Burrows is willing'; he, of course, was part of the well supplied 'Supply Unit'.*

*Col Chang Holford said to me, "I shall never be promoted, but I love the Corps."*

*Alan Alcock used to sing to us about the Armenians and the Greeks, or was it the Argentinians? Edward Bevan with his flute was the bane of U Battery. Teddy Dunn was Officer Commanding by far the noisiest Battery. Jock Downey was the silent Scot. Tom Macafee booted me into a Colonel's arms and Halliday was his confederate! Titch Langford, in Sicily, not only had his own Service car but an aeroplane placed at his disposal by the Yanks! The Signals Group included Ian Harrison, the great Corps sportsman. He was a Second Rugger Team. There were Pantlin, Farquharson and many others. I remember Ginger Muir and Tommy Lenham from AD Brigade, both of whom we had taught to play rugger at Deal in the pre-war days. Before we went overseas, Tommy Lenham went to call on one of the junior Officers in his billet. When he knocked on the front door, he made a* hole in the panel. The landlady was not amused with Major Lenham. There were members of the Police, the 'Posty' Lieutenant Roberts, always hoping that the wives had written! That tower of strength, Captain Robson, was our outstanding Superintendent Clerk and a first class shot. And so one could go on.

I felt really sorry for the Italians and the Germans facing such a formidable array of Leaders. They seemed to be indestructible.

It wasn't surprising that the other Ranks of the MNBDO 2, led by such magnificent men, had such an unbreakable spirit, which still persists 40 years on.

After the Falklands victory in 1982, a senior Officer and a Senior NCO made their comments, as follows, after their 40 mile Yomp.

The Senior Officer said,

"The bearing, the spirit and the caring comradeship of our young men was an inspiration to the older generation."

The Senior NCO said,

"They did the right thing without prompting, and they remembered their training."

\* \* \*

After he left the Service, The Rev. Geoffrey Beaumont went back to St John's, Waterloo Bridge. As I was at Deal, I used to let him know when the next Squad of RM Recruits were arriving at Waterloo Junction and joining the train for Exeter and Lympstone. He would push a tea trolley on to the platform for the benefit of the Recruits. I sent him, as a gift, a Book of Common Prayer and a New Testament with the Royal Marines Crest of the Globe and Laurel on them. I received the following letter from him.

'Your present of the New Testament and the Prayer Book with the Corps Crest is most touching and I am delighted to have them both and the Old Crest as a constant reminder of those few happy years of Service with you. They will be a joy. I often see Deal boys at the YMCA at the Station and get news of you from time to time. There are one or two nice little places for lunch up here at Waterloo Station if you phone or write. Do come.' It would seem that the Chaplain's crisis over the Roman Mass had done no harm. And I did have lunch with him as invited.

In the fifties Geoffrey Beaumont, who was always trying to make Church Services understandable for the man-in-the-street, produced his Folk Mass. It was the Communion Service set to a modern rhythm, with some of his own hymn tunes, using familiar words. He produced it as a record and it had a good market. I have a copy.

I like to think that my theological confrontation with him in Augusta put him on the right Church of England lines. The Folk Mass was quite orthodox in its teaching of the Sacraments, so the uproar was probably all

196

for the best, and I didn't lose his friendship.

After leaving St John's, Waterloo Bridge, he went first to St George's, Camberwell and then to the College of Mirfield in Nottingham, where he became an Anglican monk and changed his name to Father Gerrard.

From Mirfield he went to South Wales for a short time before moving to South Africa where he died, aged 62.

Looking back, I feel fortunate and blessed to have known this very gifted Christian man. His personality and musical gifts made him much loved by the Royal Marines and I am sure that there are many men who had little or no time for the Church or the Christian faith, who would contribute to both because of Geoffrey Beaumont.

I am ashamed to say that I lost touch with The Rev. Dennis Manning during the post-war years. I know that he had several Livings in the north west Midlands. In 1981 his family suffered an appalling tragedy. One evening, Dennis Manning had driven his daughter to a party in a village a few miles away from their home. On the way back, he gave a lift to a young man who murdered Dennis in his car and there seemed to be no motive. I had known him as the Chaplain of the 12th Searchlight Regiment. He looked after them well. They didn't want to lose him and were very glad of his sincerity and thoroughness.

Although Mike Crooks joined us very late in proceedings, he did his utmost to be one of the team and I hope that, in looking back, he felt that his time with the MNBDO 2 was a worthwhile experience. After leaving the Service he worked in East London, then moved on to Cobham, Epsom and Haslemere, places which, to many of us lesser breeds, looked very much like the famous stockbroker belt. My own feeling is that these sort of places are much more difficult to handle from the Christian and Church point of view. 'How hardly shall they that have riches . . .!' During his distinguished Service in those towns, he was made a Canon. I remember, when visiting him at Epsom, he showed me his church which was the size of a Cathedral. On coming out I saw a church notice board on which were the names of five or six clergymen.

I said, "Who do all these clergy belong to?"

He said, "They are my Curates and it is a full time job training and looking after them. I won't say more!"

His final Living was in the Isle of Wight, and after retiring, he has remained on the Island. We understand that he spends most of his time sailing round the coasts of Britain in his large and well equipped yacht. He even carries a radio-telephone.

We haven't seen each other for years but we keep in touch by phone and through letters. He is another Chaplain in the MNBDO 2 whom I was fortunate to know. During his short time with us all he made many friends and struck a powerful blow for the Gospel.

When he joined us, none of us knew that he carried a Canon in his *knapsack! The rest of us have just slummed along, in Bishops' terminology, as The Inferior Clergy.*

*Well done The Reverend Canon F W (Mike) Crooks, MA, and thank you. 'Dominus vobiscum semper.'*

\* \* \*

*The Cross and Candlesticks presented to me by the HQ Company of MNBDO 2 in the Egyptian Desert made out of some old pieces of wood by an Italian prisoner, have been used over the years.*

*During my time as Rector of Ringwould from 1967 to 1977 I used them at the Primary School Assembly every Wednesday morning. Two of the children used to prepare an altar on which they placed the Cross and Candlesticks. They have also proved invaluable for private Communions. I still have them.*

\* \* \*

*The Holy Communion set we used at the Naval Base Chapel in Singapore, I took with me when we left in February 1942. This set was lost at sea, with all my gear, when HMS Anking was sunk in March 1942.*

*On my return to England in May of that year, I obtained another set from the Admiralty. This I took with me when I went overseas with the MNBDO 2. It was stolen while we were in the Egyptian desert in 1943.*

*The Army loaned me a further set and I managed to keep this one and returned home with it in 1944.*

*Later, in 1945, I saw a notice in one of the National Daily papers which stated that anyone who had an Army Communion set on loan could purchase it for £10. This I did.*

*Over the years I have used it during my various Commissions and since 1963, when I retired from the Royal Navy, for private communions in the village where I have been the Incumbent.*

*In September 1981 I was invited by the Rev. Peter Gregson, Royal Navy, the Chaplain of the Royal Marines Barracks at Stonehouse in Plymouth, to stay with him. While I was there, I presented him with this particular Communion set.*

*In February 1982 he left with the Royal Marine Commandos for the Falkland Islands. His wife told me that the last time she saw him before he embarked was marching out of Stonehouse Barracks carrying the attaché case with the Communion set.*

*He landed at Carlos Bay in the East Falklands and, while there, administered the Sacrament to his Royal Marines.*

*We considered it quite remarkable that he was using the same set which I had used and he was administering to the next generation, the sons of the fathers with whom I had served.*

*A quotation from 'The Pilgrim's Food' comes to my mind.*

> *'We have Bread and His Word, and God's Cup of red Wine,*
> *To share on our journey with all of mankind.'*

* * *

*Having been overseas since before the war, at sea and on land, I had never heard of the MNBDO until I joined this organisation in May 1942.*

*While in Colombo in March and April 1942 we did hear that the Royal Marines had been in action against the advancing Japanese army, off the coast of Burma. Also, they were protecting the Fleet anchorage in the Maldive Islands. What we didn't know was that they were the 1st MNBDO.*

*What the 2nd MNBDO accomplished in the years 1942 to 1944 has been recorded elsewhere. Whatever tasks they were set to carry out, they did to the very best of their ability.*

*One of the greatest things to come out of this organisation was the friendship and comradeship between the men, not to mention the confidence and trust. The patient caring of men for each other and the continual good humour was unceasing.*

*It was, and still is, almost incredible to me that in the middle of the materialistic and cynical 20th Century, and with the whole world engaged in a savage and ruthless war, the Christian Faith, our Christian Faith, should not only be accepted by the Royal Navy and the Royal Marines, but that it should play such a vital part in the lives of so many of their personnel. The Christian living, the Christian devotion, the patient and cheerful endurance of so many who practised their Faith was to me a continual encouragement and wonder.*

*The Chaplain's task seemed to me to be five-fold. First, to give Christian Leadership to the whole organisation and to give guidance to the various and many Commanding Officers. Next, to provide opportunities for Christian Worship, the Word and the Sacraments, and to advertise the Christian Festivals with popular Services. Then, to seek out opportunities of presenting the Christian Gospel and Message, to the masses who, although continually on the move, are also so approachable. Fourth, to endeavour, through constant visiting, to be the friend and adviser of all on board.*

*The final task, it seemed to me, was for the Chaplain to maintain the Spiritual glow himself, by the daily reading, study and meditation of Morning and Evening Prayer, as set out in the Book of Common Prayer.*

*'It is a strange thing that sometimes, when I'm quite alone, sitting in my room with my eyes closed, or walking through the lanes, the people I've*

199

seen and known are brought before me, I hear their voices and see them look and move almost plainer than I ever did when they were really there in the flesh. I feel that I could touch them and my heart is drawn towards them. I feel their lot as if it were my own. I take comfort in the Lord, resting in His Love on their behalf as well as my own.' Quoted from Adam Bede

\* \* \*

### The Royal Marines Prayer

O Eternal Lord God, Who through many generations has united and inspired the members of our Corps, grant Thy blessing, we beseech Thee, on Royal Marines, serving all round the globe.

Bestow Thy crown of righteousness upon all our efforts and endeavours, and may our laurels be those of gallantry and honour, loyalty and courage.

We ask these things in the name of Him whose courage never failed, our Redeemer, Jesus Christ our Lord. Amen.

the Rev. F L Pocock

\* \* \*

### The Royal Marines Band Service Prayer

Almighty and Everlasting Lord, in Whose sight are treasured up the memories of many generations of men who have served Thee in the Band Service of the Royal Marines; we thank Thee for the rich heritage of music placed in our hands, and for the joy and inspiration which it brings to men.

Enable us, Thy sons, truly and godly to serve Thee, that by Thy help and through our music, we may continue to inspire, help and lead men. We ask these things in the Name of Him Who is our Saviour and our Leader, Jesus Christ Our Lord. Amen.

the Rev. F L Pocock

\* \* \*

### The Naval Collect

Prevent us, O Lord, in all our doings, with Thy most gracious favour, and further us with Thy continual help; that in all our works begun, continued and ended in Thee, we may glorify Thy Holy Name, and finally by Thy mercy obtain everlasting life; through Jesus Christ Our Lord. Amen.

### The Chaplain's Prayer

*O Eternal and Everlasting God, Whose never failing Providence watcheth over all from the beginning to the end; keep under Thy care and protection all those who have been committed to my charge.*

*Grant that the ties of friendship and trust formed between us may never be forgotten; and that whatsoever good I may have been permitted to communicate to them from Thy Holy Word and everlasting Gospel may, by Thy power, bring forth in them the fruit of Christian living and in the end Thy gift of Everlasting Life; through the Love and Cross of Thy Son; Jesus Christ our Lord. Amen.*

* * *

*The following are a few comments by the Rev. Canon F W Crooks, MA, taken from a letter he wrote to me.*

*'On the day of the Earth Tremor which accompanied the Augusta Earthquake in the autumn of 1943, my MOA had gone to the galley to fetch me a bag lunch. He found somebody under a pile of bully beef tins, which had been stacked against the wall. I was glad when he returned and told me about it, because I had felt the bungalow, where I was at the time, moving to and fro. I made a most undignified exit down the steps only to find an unearthly stillness in the orange grove. The question then struck me, "Had it been my imagination." I looked round to see if anyone had witnessed my wild dash. I then returned full of misgivings about my sanity. Luckily at that moment my MOA arrived with the good news about the unexpected burial of the cook!*

*On my way to join you in September 1943, at Augusta, I spent a few days at a Transit Camp at Araria in the Western Desert. We went there by train in which there was a young Army Lieutenant who let fly all kinds of abuse about General Montgomery. The reason for this was never known to me but what he said was perhaps deserving of a Court Martial because it was a scandalous way to speak of a superior Officer. I was glad to notice how you spoke, in your journals, so admiringly of this great man for he was great in spite of certain characteristics which could be offensive. During the Ardennes counter attack, he stormed into General Bradley's US Headquarters and one of the US Officers described his arrival as being like "Jesus Christ about to cleanse the temple".*

*It was an extraordinary feeling, after our return home, almost of desolation in having no real purpose. (So I wasn't the only one to have this experience.) I was living in Cambuslang where the local Vicar was most helpful and hospitable in allowing me the use of his church for the troops.*

*We also had Services in various huts in camp but it was forever a joy to minister in a Church Building free from the smell of stale beer and cigarettes. This ignites memories of conducting some Services in the huge Airship Hangar at Augusta for the Landing and Maintenance congregation. There was also a lingering smell of beer or was it Marsala?*

*Anyway, I wouldn't have missed serving in the MNBDO for worlds. Not only was my time with this organisation an education and an inspiration. The comradeship and the friendliness beggars description and is life long!*

\* \* \*

*'Thank you Mike. You have stated briefly and well what so many of us thought.' (Author)*

\* \* \*

*My camphor-wood chests, containing my Bible, arrived by sea from Wellington, New Zealand. They had been sent by Mrs Rita Clarke, widow of Lieutenant Tony Clarke, New Zealand RNVR, in 1946.*

*She came to England in 1947 to visit relatives and, while here, she came to see us at Deal. I was able to give her his sextant which he had given to me for safe keeping when the war commenced. I had stored the sextant in my golf club bag which had, by sheer good fortune, turned up in Colombo as I have described. When I found the bag in Colombo, I brought it home with me plus the sextant. So, after her visit to us at Deal, it went back with Mrs Clarke to New Zealand. Their daughter came with her to England and I was glad to have the opportunity of meeting both of them.*

*In 1953, while travelling in a corridor train in the Portsmouth area, a gentleman looked into the compartment where I was sitting and said, "I believe you are Mr Pocock, the Naval Chaplain who was at the Singapore Naval Base when it was taken over by the Japanese early in 1942".*

*I said, "Yes, that is right".*

*He went on, "I heard that you were responsible for getting my trunks and camphor-wood chests and suitcases away from my bungalow to HMS Dragon".*

*"Yes," I said, "I was one of the people involved in that particular operation. Later, I did see them in Dragon at Batavia, but had no idea what happened to it all after that."*

*"On behalf of my family and myself, please accept our sincere thanks for your efforts. Eventually, they all reached us safely in England," he said.*

*He moved on and I was left to reflect on the events of years ago. I was glad to have been of help to these people, dozens and dozens of them, and to have been one of the team who got their personal possessions away. I then recalled the terrifying loss of life. I remember at the time that it was not*

202

*until I saw the piles of luggage some people managed to take with them, that I began to miss my own. How easily one's mind and desires become centred on things. Actually, this man's appearance was a warning to me not to become obsessed with possessions. Some words of Scripture came to my mind as I sat in that railway carriage:-*

*'A man's life consisteth not in the abundance of "Things" which he possesseth but rather, seek ye first the Kingdom of God and His Righteousness.'*

*I reached Portsmouth Harbour Station and alighted. I crossed the harbour by ferry to Gosport and made my way back to the Royal Naval Air Station, HMS Siskin, where I was serving. The Word of the Lord had come to me in an unexpected way, as it usually does.*

*Recently, I met a man whom I had not seen for about 50 years.*

*He said to me, "What, you still around? I heard that you were lost at sea in the Far East in the forties".*

*I replied, "Yes, I'm still around".*

*"Well," he said, "would you believe it." Then before I had time to say any more, he said, "Well I must be off; see you some time".*

*I have just heard . . . June 1985 . . . the reason why YOMA was suddenly ordered NORTH to Colombo, instead of making for Perth, Western Australia.*

*A Rating, who was in a small ship heading for Australia, was in the vicinity of Anking when she was sunk en route for Australia. There was a large Japanese Squadron on the loose between Java and Australia. Anking was sunk, but had time to warn Admiralty . . . hence, Yoma was instructed to turn round for Colombo.*

*The Rating in this small ship picked up a survivor from Anking . . . one of his messmates; they had both been survivors from HMS Prince of Wales!*

*I received the following letter in July 1946:-*

*Pocock Esq From Jock Seng*
*c/o The Chaplain of the Fleet 140 Middle Road*
*Admiralty Singapore*
*London 15 June 1946*

*Sir,*

*I have much pleasure in sending this esteemed and grateful note to you as a token of my honour and great respect in you which you incurred and highly striked in me in my continuous years of service under you in the Church, HM Naval Base, Singapore.*

*Again I do remember in my poor memory how you showed me your pure and simple sincerity in confidence towards me, which I can not forget for ever, at the time of your departure from here.*

*Further, to my great joy, I have to mention here, full heartedly, my joy in meeting you again in Singapore, and hope that in the not too distant future, your presence will be decorated in the same place. Now, I am unemployed, staying in Singapore, No 140 Middle Road, in a fairly well being position, and eagerly hope you are doing well with your family.*

*Let long live you, Sir, by the grace of the Almighty and I often pray to Him for the same. Eagerly awaiting for a kind reply and thanking you in anticipation.*

*I beg to remain, Sir, Yours most obediently*

*Jock Seng*

*Jock Seng was my faithful Chinese boy. I wrote to tell him that the Admiralty wouldn't let me come back to Singapore, even to allow him to join me again.*

# CHAPTER XI

## Peacetime Chaplain in HMS Liverpool 1948 to 1950

*Following my appointment as a Chaplain with the Royal Marines in their Second Mobile Naval Base Defence Organisation in and around the Mediterranean I went to their Depot at Deal in Kent. Here I remained throughout the last stages of the war and the first years of peace. I watched hundreds of Recruits being trained to serve at home and overseas, afloat and ashore, at war and in keeping the peace.*

*We had all prayed for peace in our time and now our prayers had been answered. There was rejoicing everywhere.*

*Then, at the beginning of 1948 I was appointed Chaplain of HMS Liverpool, Flagship of the First Cruiser Squadron, Mediterranean Fleet, based on Malta.*

I was instructed to join HMS *Liverpool*, my new ship, at Chatham in March 1948. As the Commission was to last about two and a half years, families could come out to Malta. We were warned that there were no married quarters and that accommodation was both scarce and expensive. At Chatham, on the first night when all the Officers sat down to dinner in the Wardroom, I put up my first black! The President banged his gavel on the table for Grace. I was caught off guard and by mistake I said, "For what we have received, thank God". We hadn't received anything! It cost me a round of port and I didn't use that Grace again!

During the second week of March, *Liverpool* sailed from Chatham for Portsmouth for the Commissioning ceremonies. Our journey took us past Sheerness, commonly called 'Sheernasty' by the Matelots, past the Forelands, through the Straits of Dover and westwards to Portsmouth.

I asked the Navigating Officer, Lieutenant Commander Antony Fanning, whether he would be taking the ship inside or outside the Goodwins. I said that if we went inside, I felt sure that the Royal Marines at Deal would like to see the ship pass. He said that he would take *Liverpool* inside the Goodwins, through the Downs and close to the Deal-Walmer shore. I rang the Adjutant of the RM Depot at Deal, Captain N. L R. Griffiths, gave him the news, the date and time. He arranged for most of the Recruits, under training at Deal, to be on the Walmer front, by the capstans, to watch this great ship sail past. Many of their families were there too.

I should say that Captain Griffiths was a tower of strength to us at the Depot Church and a great encouragement to me personally.

Before we leave Deal, one incident connected with Captain (now Major) N. L. R. Griffiths must be mentioned. The Adjutant employed a recruit from one of the many squads under training to be his Orderly for the day. This Recruit had to march about five yards behind the Adjutant wherever he went in the Depot. One day, the duty Recruit was informed by his Squad mates that if the Adjutant mounted his horse the Orderly was to mount too, behind him on the horse. It happened. The Adjutant mounted his horse and the Recruit tried to mount as well. The horse turned his head round towards the Recruit, curled his lip and kicked out with his rear right hoof. The Recruit suffered a bruised and skinned shin. The horse trotted off with the Adjutant and the incident produced a laugh from all the recruits.

At Portsmouth Captain Kenneth Mackintosh read the Commission to the Ship's Company and their families, many of whom were present. Then followed the Commissioning Service which I as the Chaplain led. We had two or three Farewell Parties. These were friendly, quiet and in some cases rather sad occasions, especially for those families who were saying goodbye to husbands or sons for two and a half years. After a brief call at Gibraltar we reached Malta early in April.

After living ashore for a few years it takes time to shake down and settle into the life of a Wardroom, and of a ship.

Within a few days I can remember thinking to myself; 'O my word! Fancy being locked up for two and a half years in this steel box with some of these people!'

For in a Wardroom one lives pretty close to one's Mess Mates. You soon know how many bites they take to each mouthful!

Then a strange thing happens and you begin to think, 'There is something awfully nice about this man.'

By the end of a Commission, a unique and wonderful bond has been formed and forged and so we have the expression, 'Shipmates forever.'

The Squadron was made up of four Cruisers; two heavy, *Liverpool* and *Newcastle* each of 9,000 tons; and two light, *Phoebe* and *Euryalus* each of 5,000 tons; all four with a Captain in command and a Rear Admiral commanding the Squadron. While *Liverpool* was in the UK in early 1948 for re-commissioning, the Flag was transferred to *Newcastle*. The Rear Admiral at the time was Rear Admiral Symonds-Taylor, and he remained in *Newcastle* until October 1948 when he returned to the UK.

With the arrival of *Liverpool* back on the Mediterranean Station, Admiral Sir Arthur John Power, Commander-in-Chief, Mediterranean Station, decided to come and live in her with his staff. He used to pay his official calls round the Mediterranean. First it was to Algiers where the Admiral called on the French Commander-in-Chief. While we were there Mary's uncle, the Rev Harold Cummin, North African Secretary for the British and Foreign Bible Society, came on board to see me. Next it was to call on the Italian Commander-in-Chief in Naples. While there we were visited by the Italian Roman Catholic Cardinal and I was asked to take care of him. As he spoke no English and no one in the ship, including myself, spoke Italian, we had an interesting afternoon.

It was piped round the ship, "The Chaplain is conducting the Roman Catholic Cardinal round the upper deck. He can't speak English so help the Chaplain with smiles and nods." Our first stop was the ship's laundry. The Cardinal stepped inside and was met by a Rating carrying an armful of dhobie. The sight of this scarlet clad figure was too much for the Rating, who dropped the washing and ran. I decided, after this episode, not to enter any more closed spaces. The ship's company went out of their way to help me and even produced cups of tea for us both.

*Liverpool's* first stop, after leaving Malta for the Eastern Mediterranean, was Pireas, the port of Athens where Admiral Power called on the Regent of Greece, Archbishop Damastinos. The Archbishop was a huge man, six feet nine inches tall, he allowed the sailors to take a photo of himself, with his hand on the Admiral's shoulder, at the same time looking down on him from his great height. It was quite an occasion. Next time *Liverpool* came to Athens, Greece had a King and Queen! From Athens we sailed east, north of Crete, and then along the south coast of Cyprus. By coming close in shore, we were able to see the camps which housed thousands of Jews waiting to enter Palestine. From there we went on to Port Said, the Suez Canal, the Bitter Lakes and Geniffa where the Admiral, and some of us lesser mortals called on the British Army. Egypt was still more or less ours.

On the return voyage, we went into the Adriatic with the first stop at Navarino Bay where the Fleet Regatta took place. *Liverpool's* new Ship's Company were competing for the first time. The long and the short of it all was that *Liverpool* won most of the pulling races and returned to Malta with the Cock of the Med (The Regatta Trophy). When we entered Grand Harbour all the trophies were on a table, placed on the fo'c's'le, with a large silver Cock in the centre. The winning of the Fleet Regatta had a tremendous effect on the morale of the Ship's Company, especially as we had only been in commission for six months. From there we sailed on to Venice where we remained only a few days. Then we set out for Malta. It was while we were on this return journey that I had my first personal test as the Chaplain and it came about in the most unexpected way.

There are certain Ship's evolutions which have to be carried out in all HM Ships serving on the Mediterranean Station once a month. (Med. Fleet Standing Orders.) They had not been carried out in *Liverpool* during August 1948. Someone forgot!

We sailed from Venice during the morning of Sunday August 31st and those in authority decided to have the evolutions during Sunday forenoon. As a result the Church Service, which was in the ship's cinema, was completely spoilt. We could hear the evolution orders coming over the ship's loud speaker system, loud and clear. I was very angry indeed and blew my top. I scrapped my prepared sermon and gave a lecture on 'Sunday'. The congregation was larger than usual that morning because those who attended Church were excused evolutions! I said that first of all it was a pity those in authority in *Liverpool* hadn't carried out the instructions in King's Regulations and Admiralty Instructions which laid down that ships' companies were not to be employed on Sundays. Second, and far more important than KRAI, was the Christian and Church teaching on 'Sunday'. I said that most of the British nation had ditched both God and Sunday. However, we in the Royal Navy still honoured God every Sunday forenoon. Finally I added that the behaviour on board *Liverpool*, the Flag Ship of the First Cruiser Squadron, had set a thoroughly bad example not only to the Squadron but also to the whole Mediterranean Fleet.

*HMS Liverpool, Flag Ship of the Mediterranean Fleet, entering Grand Harbour, Valetta, Malta on April 25th 1948.*

Admiral Power, who was present with his staff and *Liverpool*'s Captain, sat glaring at me during my tirade which he had to listen to. Immediately the Service was concluded he left without speaking to anyone. The infuriating thing was that I was quite right and had given his 'part of the ship', the executive, a good old bashing. I understand that the Ratings loved every minute of it. They would, of course!

Perhaps I can jump the gun and complete the Sunday Evolutions episode. My friends in the Wardroom kept asking me whether I had been 'sent for' about my sermon. I did wonder myself whether there would be any repercussions from my explosions. One was that there were no more Sunday evolutions during that Commission! Another I heard from the wives after our return to Malta. Apparently my stocks had gone up by leaps and bounds and what I had said was the talk of the ship. The Admiral, I heard, was furious, not with me but with the Captain and Commander for arranging these Evolutions on a Sunday and for giving me the opportunity of delivering this broadside. Strange isn't it? The result was quite the opposite to what I had expected. They say that 'If you don't stand for something, you will fall for anything' and, quite unexpectedly, this Chaplain had stood up for Sunday!

Travelling south, we visited the Greek Islands on the west coast of Greece which were once British. One island we visited for a few days was Cephalonia. The capital is Argostoli, and we, the RM Officer and I, visited the cemetery. In the nineteenth century there were colonies of British living in these islands. We found the gravestones of the postman, the schoolmaster, the vicar, the shopkeeper and many others. During the war a stick of bombs had fallen across the cemetery and most of the headstones had been flattened. So with the co-operation of the Commander, we took a party of sailors and Marines ashore and spent a whole day repairing the graves and the headstones. A few of us from the Wardroom climbed the highest mountain on the island, Mount Nero, over 5,000 feet high.

On the Sunday, Admiral Power invited all the British residents to Church on board. Amongst those who came was an English lady married to a Greek. They invited me back to tea and showed me a Greek Ikon of Our Lord tied to a whipping post. A year or so later there was an enormous earthquake at Argostoli, with considerable damage. In the mid-fifties I had a letter from this lady and she asked me to visit her in Woking as she had something for me. Her husband had died as a result of the earthquake and she had come back to live in England. It was their wish that, if she was able to trace me, I should have this Ikon and she gave it to me when I visited her in Woking. A special feature of Argostoli was the water-mill which was driven by the sea, which ran and disappeared into the earth! Of latter years this had been silting up.

The month of October, 1948 produced a change for *Liverpool*. Rear Admiral Earl Mountbatten of Burma relieved Rear Admiral Symonds-Taylor as Admiral of the 1st Cruiser Squadron in *HMS Liverpool*. Admiral Power moved back to *HMS Surprise*, the Commander-in-Chief's yacht.

The first thing the Admiral did was to address the ship's company on the quarter deck. He said that from now on *Liverpool* would work hard and lead the first Cruiser Squadron. He said that the days when *Liverpool* looked upon themselves as the C-in-C's private yacht, and superior to the lesser mortals in the other ships, were over. They would no longer be sailing about the Mediterranean quietly on their own. He said that from the moment we left Grand Harbour we should be working with every other ship on the Med. Station! This is what the Ship's Company thought they had been doing, but The Noble Earl wanted a greater effort. He also pointed out that every ship was using fuel paid for by the splendid, generous and great British public so no time or fuel would be wasted. Finally he said that we had to be ready for any eventuality. It was the time of the Berlin airlift and so, as usual, relations with Russia were strained. He demanded immediate obedience, utmost loyalty and every man's best effort.

Earl Mountbatten arrived in Malta in October to command the First Cruiser Squadron. Later in the month, his wife Countess Mountbatten, and his younger daughter the Lady Pamela, arrived too. The appearance of the Mountbatten family so soon after their service in India, where he had been Viceroy and India's first Governor General, was a great thing for the Maltese, for the Mediterranean Fleet and particularly for *HMS Liverpool*. Over the next year and a half all the top people of the countries *Liverpool* visited wanted to meet Earl Mountbatten. These countries included France, Italy, Greece, Lebanon, Syria, Egypt, Algeria and so on. For this reason *Liverpool* seemed to go to the more important parts while the other ships of the squadron had to make do with rather second-rate ports or even deserted Greek islands!

*A map of the journey of HMS Liverpool on her Second Summer Cruise as Flag Ship of the Mediterranean Fleet in September 1949. Left; HMS Liverpool. Right; The late Lord Louis Mountbatten, the Vice Admiral Earl Mountbatten of Burma.*

In Malta endless people, service and civilian, used to call on the Mountbattens by signing the Visitors' Book. The Mountbatten family used to return these calls by inviting them to cocktail parties in *Liverpool*. Officers and wives of *Liverpool*'s Wardroom used to act as hosts for all these hordes who came to the gatherings on the quarter-deck. Our RM Band played at all the parties. We met all sorts of people who, in the ordinary course of events, would never have come our way. So for the Wardroom it was really a fascinating experience, which went on throughout the commission. One evening, while talking to Lady Mountbatten, I happened to say, "Do you know all these people?"

She replied, "No, I have never seen them in my life before. I expect they have signed the book."

During these months the ship was in and out of harbour exercising not only with the other ships of the squadron but with the rest of the ships of the Mediterranean Fleet and with the RAF too. Admiral Mountbatten had told the Ship's Company that we had to be ready for any eventuality and he saw to it that we were.

In *Liverpool*, we usually had about 50 Officers and Ratings at the Morning Service on the quarter deck or in the cinema. When we were in Malta, families came in good numbers. The 50 was composed of about 25 Officers and 25 Ratings. The Captain and Heads of Departments used to discuss Church with me. They used to say that whereas *Liverpool* had between 20 and 30 Ratings at Church every Sunday, the other cruisers had between three and ten. However this was really no consolation to me, and I considered the position absolutely terrifying.

During December 1948, Captain Mackintosh for reasons of his own, sent every Officer a little note to let him know how he thought they were getting on. One of the Engineer Lieutenants, Lieutenant (E) Geoff Cornish, came to me with his note. It merely said, "St Luke 12; 48".

He said, "What does this say?"

I said, "Come up to my cabin and we will look it up."

I read it to him, "For unto whomsoever much is given, of him much shall be required; and to whom men commit much, of him will they ask the more."

Geoff Cornish said, "What has he sent this to me for?"

I said, "The Captain thinks, or knows, that you are not giving of your best and he expects a lot more from you."

Geoff Cornish said, "And would you believe it! I spend most of the day below decks. He rarely sees me and if he does, he hardly ever speaks."

Of course, the exercise was a very clever move on the part of the Captain. He was going to get the very best out of every Officer. On mine he put, 'A good preacher and in close touch with the ship's company.' I wasn't a good preacher. I knew that. But I decided that I really must try to improve. Also, I wasn't in close touch with the ship's company. How can one be in close touch with between eight and nine hundred men. But I decided that there were parts of the ship I ought to visit more, if I was brave enough. So his little note had done its work on me!

One Sunday, while we were in Malta, we had Church in the ship's cinema; we used the cinema during the winter months; and I had a Baptism afterwards. I had the ship's bell, inverted, for the Baptism and it was standing at the front of the nave in a wooden structure made in the ship for the occasion. My sermon that morning was on Baptism. After the Baptism, the Captain sent for me. I wanted to discuss a rather complicated welfare case. He sat at one side of the desk in his day cabin and I sat on the other side. I should think we were about 40 minutes thrashing out this case. About every five minutes the Captain's Secretary, Lieutenant L. Townsend, drew back the curtain of the doorway to see if we had finished.

We finished eventually and as I got up to leave the Captain said to me, "A very good sermon this morning. Let us have more of this dogmatic stuff."

I said, "Thank you, Sir."

I left his cabin, walked across the flat, poked my head into Leslie Townsend's office and said, "He's free now; you can go in."

He said, "What has the Captain been talking to you about all this time?"

I replied, "If you really want to know, he has been telling me what a wonderful sermon I preached this morning and he wants more on the same lines."

He said, "Wonderful sermon! I have never heard such unadulterated rubbish in all my life."

I said, "Lieutenant Townsend, the Captain wants to see you at once!"

In the spring of 1949 Captain Mackintosh was relieved by Captain Shaw-Hamilton. Whereas Captain Mackintosh had left me more or less alone; I think he saw I was trying to do my job, so he did not interfere; Captain Hamilton took a keen interest in my routine and would ask me how and when I went about my work. Occasionally he sent for me to discuss some individual or some ship's problem. Perhaps I can jump the gun a bit and describe what happened to me in Toulon when I went for a walk with him. I think it was the autumn of 1949.

He was a great walker and one Saturday after lunch, while we were berthed at Toulon, he came into the Wardroom and it happened that I was the only one there, reading a paper.

He said, "Would you like to come for a walk with me and climb the hills behind Toulon?"

I said. "Thank you, Sir. Certainly, let's go."

There was no option; I had to go. We set off at 2 pm and returned to the ship about 6 pm. We were met on the gangway by the Officer of the Day. I had a bath, then supper and it being Saturday, I retired to my cabin to prepare for Sunday.

About 8.30 pm there was a knock on my door and the Officer of the Day burst in and said, "What have you done to the Captain? He is in a foul mood and is complaining about his feet."

I told him that I had been compelled to go for this beastly walk; that it was far too long and that my feet were sore too.

He said, "Well next time you go, keep it short. I have never known him in such a filthy temper."

So that was all the thanks I got for doing the Wardroom's work. Next morning the Captain read the Lesson at church. He never mentioned the walk and he never asked me to go with him again, except when we were at sea. He often used to send for me and I had to walk with him up and down the quarter deck. On those occasions he would dismiss me when he had had enough. I suppose the Chaplain was a safe person to chat to and I presume he thought me trustworthy. He was a fine man to have as Captain; very straightforward and fair with the Ship's Company and I could not have wished for a better Captain. In his confidential report on me, I understand that he said I was fearless. Little did he know with what trepidation his Chaplain used to face visiting the Mess Decks. And it was a job which never became easier.

Soon after Captain Mackintosh left us, it was the turn of Commander Nigel Pumphrey to go. I was extremely sorry to be losing his faithful support and I naturally wondered how I would fare under his successor. I needn't have worried. Commander Robin Topp was another fine Christian man who was sympathetic both towards the Chaplain and the Church. If we ever had a poor congregation on a Sunday, he would always try to cheer me up. He was very short and completely bald. Throughout the ship he was affectionately known as 'Curly Topp.'

Another Officer, who was a faithful friend and ally, was the Navigating Officer, Lieutenant Commander Antony Fanning, commonly called 'The Pilot.' He had charge of all the midshipmen and was called their Nurse! He would frequently discuss them with me. On one occasion, one of them was very rude to me. I forget the details.

I asked 'The Pilot' if I might send for this young man and tear a strip off him for being rude.

He said, "I can think of nothing better for the young man. Please do."

So he sent this midshipman to my cabin where I rebuked him for his lack of manners. I enquiried how he had been brought up, where he had been brought up and who had brought him up. I dismissed him and forgot about it. But the young bounder won in the end. On the following Sunday night, when we had guests on board, imagine my surprise when this same midshipman introduced his mother and father to me. He did it with a wicked twinkle. His father was a Naval Captain!

When I told 'The Pilot' about this, he said, "That will teach you to tear strips off my dear Snotties."

During the Commission, I baptised Antony and Mary Fanning's baby, Peter, on board and years later I attended his sister Jane's wedding at Old Windsor.

Here perhaps I can add a few lines about some of our dear wives. The Fannings had a flat overlooking Grand Harbour. Every time the ship sailed away on a cruise my wife Mary, Joan de Courcey-Ireland, the RM Officer's wife and Mary Fanning used to retire to the Fannings' flat to have a united weep over the departure of their husbands. It is nice to know that we were missed. When Antony Fanning left the ship, he was followed by Lieutenant Commander John Blake, another fine Christian man who gave me constant support. He and his wife Betty came from Deal and we were to meet again in the sixties when we returned to the area and he became Mayor of Deal. He was one of the School Managers of Ringwould Church Primary School while I was Rector and Chairman of the Managers. It was such fun to have him on the Committee.

In *Liverpool* there seemed to be crowds of Engineers! Officers, Warrant Officers, Chief and Petty Officer Stokers, Engine Room Artificers and Stokers. They were well led by the Commander, (Engineer) Joe Little and the Senior Lieutenant Commander, Jeremy Sedgewick. These two and others used to give me every possible encouragement as Chaplain. I had a happy relationship with the many Lieutenants. As a branch, the Engineers made a fine contribution to the life of the ship. At least, I thought so. They had plenty of hands to man their boats in the Fleet Regattas and they received strong vocal support from their great buddies, the Royal Marines.

*Her Royal Highness the Princess Elizabeth, now Queen Elizabeth II, aboard HMS Liverpool escorted by Vice Admiral Earl Mountbatten of Burma in April 1950.*

It would be easy for the Chaplain, when visiting round the ship, to forget about those who spend many hours below decks. However, the Divisional Engineer Officers kept me up to scratch by inviting me down to the boiler rooms regularly.

Regarding church, the Engineer Officers used to come as a body, sit together and act as an unofficial choir. They led the singing and used to tell me that they expected a good sermon, about God and about ten minutes!

One Sunday, in the Wardroom after church, I heard an Officer from another branch say, "Why does the Priest allow these plumbers, (he meant the Engineers) to decide at what speed we shall sing the hymns? After all they are only plumbers." This Officer had his trousers removed by the plumbers present and they did not appear to be too gentle in their approach to him.

Strange to say Commander Nigel Pumphrey, was the only member of the Wardroom I had met before.

When I joined the Royal Navy at Devonport in January 1936, he was a Lieutenant serving at the Boys' Training Establishment at St Budeaux, Devonport. One Sunday I was sent up to St Budeaux to take the Service for the Boys as their Chaplain was preaching at the RN Barracks.

Just as I left the Barracks Chaplain said to me, "You will be well looked after up there by Lieutenant Pumphrey, he's another black Protestant."

When we met at the beginning of *Liverpool*'s Commission, I reminded him of this incident.

He said, "I haven't changed one little bit and I hope you haven't either!"

To my mind, Nigel Pumphrey had a very good relationship with his Chiefs and Petty Officers and led by example and his cheerful spirit. The Ship's company thought him a fine hard working Officer, one who was always fair in his dealings with defaulters. I think he told me after we had visited Villefranche that he had 74 defaulters!

His little daughter, Phillipa, came to stay with us for a night at Wardia, St Paul's Bay. He told us that it was her very first night away from home. The Pumphreys had a delightful flat, called Villa Sultana at Tax Biex. When the time came for them to leave, they gave a farewell party for both Officers and Ratings, something rather unusual in those days. They called it a Farewell Fling and there was optional fancy dress.

I dressed up as a Royal Marines Corporal with my hair made grey with a little ship's flour. I can remember entering their flat on the first floor, I passed through a large hall and then, as I ascended the wide marble staircase the *Liverpool* Master-at-Arms and his two Regulating Petty Officers were coming down. I heard the Master say, pointing at me, "Is that one of ours?"

One Petty Officer said, "Yes," while the other said, "I'm not sure," but they didn't stop.

As I entered the front room which was full of Officers and Ratings, one of the Officers, a Lieutenant Bence Trower called out to me, "Corporal, come over and take this order from these Officers and Ratings!" My disguise was never discovered and my friends on the Royal Marines Mess Deck thought the whole thing a great lark, especially as I had danced with the wife of the Gunnery Officer. She remarked that she had never danced with a flunkey before! I replied that I hoped not, but that there was always a first time.

After he left *Liverpool*, Nigel Pumphrey was promoted Captain and appointed to Vienna. Early in 1950 *Liverpool* visited Venice and Trieste, and while we were there, he paid us a visit. Of course, we were delighted to see him. I do hope that we meet again one day.

The Bishop to the Forces, Dr Cuthbert Bardsley, visited the three Services in the Autumn of 1948. All Naval personnel who wished to meet him and hear him speak mustered in a large hall in the Dockyard. The audience included Officers, Ratings, Royal Marines and Chaplains. After the Bishop's address, the meeting was thrown open for questions. The whole of the time was taken up by a CPO Writer, of the C-in-C's Staff, who made a violent and vicious attack on the Naval Chaplains.

This man was an old shipmate of mine, when we had both been serving in *HMS Woolwich* in 1936/37 on the Mediterranean Station. We had often had some thoughtful discussions regarding our Christian Faith. I made a point of seeing him afterwards and told him that I was simply appalled and shocked by this public attack on Chaplains. He said he had no idea that I had been present. I told him that the damage was done and I felt I had been kicked in the teeth by an old ship-mate. I ended up by telling him that I left the meeting deeply saddened and disappointed and now I would have to go back to *Liverpool* and try to repair the damage.

There is one incident connected with Lieutenant Peter Bence Trower which remains in my mind. It was late one night, and this Officer, generally known as 'B-T' was Officer of the Day. He was waiting for the late Liberty Boat to return and I was walking up and down the quarter deck with him.

After the Liberty Boat had arrived, the men fell in for inspection at the top of the gangway, and the Petty Officer reported to B-T.

"Liberty men ready for inspection, Sir," he said.

B-T went down the line, and as he passed one sailor, he noticed that his 'silk' was out of place. He went to adjust it and, as he did so, the sailor shook hands with him and said, "Good evening, Sir," and wouldn't let go his grip.

B-T merely said to the Petty Officer, "Dismiss Liberty men and get them below!" Well done B-T.

Besides being our First Lieutenant, Commander Ian Garnett was also the Gunnery Officer. To me he appeared to carry out his duties happily and with little fuss. He was a good churchman and gave me his full support and encouragement. During the Commission he was promoted Commander and left us. He and his wife had followed the Pumphreys into their very nice flat at Tax Biex and we were fortunate to have it after their departure for the United Kingdom.

On one occasion, when the ship was under sailing orders, all Officers' Leave finished at 8 am. the Officers' Motor Boat left Customs House at 7.45 am. There was a fairly heavy sea running that morning, even in Grand Harbour.

When the boat came alongside the ship's gangway, hands on the quarter deck lowered lines for any suitcases to be hoisted up before we disembarked. One suitcase belonged to an Officer of the Admiral's staff. When it was about halfway up it suddenly burst open. Amid cheers both from the boat and large numbers of the Ship's Company who were lining the upper deck the complete contents, which included a dinner jacket, trousers, shirts, socks and all the rest of the clobber, fell into the water and went floating away, down Grand Harbour, assisted by the strong sea.

After that, those of us who had suitcases in the boat watched anxiously lest ours should suffer the same fate. Fortunately, all was well and it had been left to a member of the Admiral's staff to give the Summer Cruise a spectacular send off.

The Archbishop of Canterbury, Dr Fisher, visited the Mediterranean Fleet during the Autumn of 1949 as the guest of the Commander-in-Chief, Admiral Sir John Power. The naval Chaplains had the privilege of a whole forenoon with him. We were greatly encouraged by his stirring address and the confidence he radiated. He was well supported by his Chaplain, the Rev John Long. He and I had met previously during the war when he joined an RM Unit including many men with whom I had just served.

I officiated at several ship's weddings during the Commission, but will only describe one or two. First Lieutenant Joe Mills married Sheila. He sent home for her and I officiated at their wedding which was followed by a reception on board. They went to Taormina, Sicily for their honeymoon.

Soon after their return, the ship was due to go on a long cruise, and his Mess Mates were saying, "Poor old Joe; can't you get the Parson to have a quiet chat with the Captain and arrange for you to be left behind in Malta during the cruise?"

Joe came to me and said, "Any suggestions?"

I said, "Yes; come to my cabin and let's see whether the Good Book can give you any help and guidance."

I opened the Bible at the Book of Deuteronomy Chapter 24 and told Joe to read verse five aloud to me. He read: "When a man hath taken a new wife, he shall not go out to war, neither shall he be charged with any other business; but he shall be free at home one year, and shall cheer up his wife which he hath taken."

I said, "That is the best I can do. If your wife is really worth it, then face the Captain with this Scripture."

It just happened that, the next day, the Captain came into the Wardroom at midday, and one of the Officers said to him, "While you are here Sir, Lieutenant Mills would like a word with you."

Joe Mills, who now carried his Bible with him like a real Bible Thumper, had it open at Deuteronomy Chapter 24 and he asked the Captain if he would please read verse five.

When he had read it, Joe said to him, "Under the circumstances, Sir, might I apply for shore leave while the ship is away?"

By this time, the whole Mess was watching and listening.

The Captain replied, "As I expect you know Mills I have the greatest respect for Holy Writ but, as the ship will not function at her best without your presence, your request cannot be granted."

He was silent for a moment and then he added, "It rather looks as if the Parson has thought this one up, and I have to admit it is a good effort. As you cannot be spared I will give you a drink, if that is any consolation, and I will give the Parson one too for his valiant efforts."

Major Bill de Courcey Ireland of the Royal Marines used me more than any other Officer in the ship. This may have been due to my long association with the dear Royals over the years. He and I often went ashore together.

Surgeon Lieutenant Commander Anthony was our Medical Officer. The doctor and I had a close liaison. With about 900 men living together in unnatural conditions, there was bound to be some mental problems. He took the name of many a man who went to Sick Bay to see him. Then he would ask me to make a point of having a word with the man when on my rounds, and report back with my comments. I think that he and I were able to assist many men in this way.

Midshipman Simon Crawley, who joined us during the second half of the Commission, was a fine Christian lad and a good influence in the Gunroom. Eventually, he left the Royal Navy as a Lieutenant and was accepted for the Church of England Ministry. He went to Emmanuel College and Ridley Hall, Cambridge.

We were to meet again when I was Rector of Ringwould, near Deal. While we were there, he was first Vicar of Holy Trinity, Margate and next Vicar of Holy Trinity, Folkestone. During one of our Flower Festivals he provided music for the visitors by playing his guitar. Now he is Rector of Patterdale, in the Lake District. He has invited me to do several locums for him and we stay in his Rectory.

I found the Warrant Officers a splendid lot and utterly reliable and also, most of them, God-fearing men. I had many friends amongst them and valued their wisdom and advice.

As the RM Band played at church every Sunday their Bandmaster was an important person to me, the Chaplain. In HMS *Liverpool* I was greatly blessed in having Captain Bill Fitzerald as the Bandmaster. No one could have been more helpful, co-operative or encouraging. We had considerable fun in arranging and choosing the hymns. He finally retired to Deal and I was privileged to give the address at his funeral in 1979 at St George's, Deal. Several members of that Band have been in the Deal area over the past few years. Band Sergeant Douglas Haig became a Captain and brought an ensemble to play at some of our Ringwould Church Services. Band Sergeant Tom Merritt retired to Deal when a Lieutenant. Bandboy Mason, who was the youngest man in the ship, rose to become Principal Director of Music, Royal Marines at Deal. He became a great friend of Earl Mountbatten.

In the New Year we went off to the Combined Fleet Exercises in the Atlantic. On the way we called at Naples, a place I always found exciting, with Mt Vesuvius, Pompei and Puteoli nearby. At Gibraltar we met the Home Fleet before joining them in the annual Fleet exercises.

For these exercises HMS *Phoebe*, one of our Squadron, was to be lent to the Home Fleet. Before the transfer took place Admiral Mountbatten, who was leading the Mediterranean Fleet, sent for me. He told me what was happening, and asked me whether there was an appropriate verse of Scripture we could send to the Home Fleet regarding *Phoebe*. I gave him St Paul's Epistle to the Romans, Chapter 16, first part of verse one and verse two. It reads, "I commend unto you, *Phoebe*, our sister. Receive her in the Lord, and assist her in whatsoever business she hath need of you; for she hath been a succourer of many, and of myself also."

When *Phoebe* joined the Home Fleet, Admiral Mountbatten was clever enough to 'plant' his own signal bo's'n on board as a spy. During the exercises, this Rating was able to signal to the Mediterranean Fleet all the Home Fleet's movements. The umpires had no difficulty in announcing that the Home Fleet had been soundly beaten by the Mediterranean Fleet. Later I heard that Admiral Mountbatten's planting of his signal bo's'n in *Phoebe* had not gone down too well with the Home Fleet.

But, as he said, "It might have been war."

After the exercises, both Fleets spent a day or so at Gibraltar giving the opportunity for friends of both Fleets to meet. The Royal Marine Officers all met together for a dinner, and they were kind enough to invite me to dine with them as their guest. This was probably due to the fact that I had served with them all for so many years. Then, after a brief call at Tangiers, we returned as a Fleet to Malta.

\* \* \*

As a Royal Naval Chaplain I tried to make it a rule to read three things at the beginning of each Commission. The first part of 'The Ordering of Priests' from the Book of Common Prayer, including the Bishop's Exhortation and the Veni Creator Spiritus. Next I read Chapter 12 of King's Regulations and Admiralty Instructons which is headed 'Discipline.' Paragraph one deals with Sunday work, paragraph two relates to the Chaplain. Finally I liked to read 'The Diary of a Country Priest' by Georges Berganos, pages 27 and 28.

Chapter 12 of the Regulations, in its first paragraph, deals with Sunday work. 'The Ship's Company is not to be employed on Sundays unless absolutely necessary', it says. By August 1948 I had already faced Authority with this paragraph and I think I had won. The second paragraph deals with the Chaplain whose 'Duty to God' requires that he is not given any executive duty which shall hinder his carrying out the duties of his Sacred Office.

The reading and meditation of Morning and Evening Prayer, besides being a duty, is also a wonderful framework on which the Chaplain can begin to build his own spiritual life. I have discovered, over the years, that nothing can take the place of 'The Daily Office' as Morning and Evening Prayer are called. It helps one, in the words of St Peter, to be 'Steadfast in the faith.'

As far as his Duty to man is concerned, 'The Chaplain is not to be given any executive duty which shall interfere with his being considered the friend and adviser of all on board.' It is a whole Commission's work to try to become 'the friend and adviser of all on board,' for he is 'a man with a Message', the Christian Message, and so he has to try to spread it, by life and lip, while having the privilege and confidence of so many men.

There are dangers! The Chaplain can easily become the spy of the Wardroom. One word spoken unadvisedly or out of place will travel round the ship in a matter of minutes, with telling exaggerations. Also he can easily fall into the habit of only visiting those of the Ship or the Messes that he likes. I had to be very stern with myself.

Living in a Wardroom is exciting and demanding. The Chaplain has to fit in with, to get on with, to work with and to get to know a variety of persons and personalities. It is a heart-warming and never-to-be-forgotten experience. As one of my Mess Mates said to me years later, "The memories of past Commissions simply glow when re-kindled."

Each of the Cruisers had a Chaplain, but we saw very little of each other. When visiting around the Mediterranean we usually dispersed to different ports while, once back in Malta, we used to spend as much time as possible with our families. In fact, only two of us were married. Two of them seemed quite happy to keep to themselves. The other one and I used to meet to discuss our work and problems and to have our prayers together. He used to become very depressed about his work and the lack of support he received from the Wardroom. I on the other hand was richly blessed by having a number of Christian Officers, who gave me every possible support and encouragement.

The Heads of Departments, and other Officers, discussed with me, ad infinitum, the perennial problem of the non-church going sailor. In the end, of course, it was my problem but they gave me all the help they could.

Various factors contributed to the sad and unsatisfactory position of the non church-goer. Sailors 'like a church to stay away from.' All of a ship's routine is compulsory for everyone. About the only thing that is voluntary is church! Therefore, church is not on.

A man has to have strong Christian convictions to face his Mess and let his Mess Mates know that he is going to church on a Sunday. While he is changing, he will probably be jeered and laughed at. Few men could face this. As the Scripture rightly says, "The fear of man is a snare."

Surprisingly, the vast majority of men join the Royal Navy without Christian Faith. I would like to quote a much loved Chaplain of former days, the Rev. Howard Gosling. I first met him at Alexandria in 1936 when I was serving in my first ship, *HMS Woolwich*, and he was serving with the Royal Marines ashore. He travelled home to England in an army transport and it occurred at the start of an open air debate on the Upper Deck. The subject was . . . 'Whether a man loses his Christian faith on joining the Service, or joins the Service without Christian faith.'

He said, "Every particle of space was crowded. Men listened from the decks over their heads. For two hours the debate raged. Men of every rank spoke and even boys joined in. Finally when a vote was taken, it was decided by an overwhelming majority that men joined the Service *without* Christian Faith".

Perhaps a few comments on Admiral Mountbatten's attitude to the Church would not be out of place at this stage. I had several long talks with him about church-going and the Church. Possibly, because he had spent years in Destroyers, he had not had much to do with Chaplains. Now he was living pretty close to one, and we saw quite a lot of each other. As a result, our relationship was always open and friendly.

He felt that the abolition of compulsory church was a bad thing for the Navy and for a ship. He said that a whole Ship's Company at worship did something for them all and for the individuals. He was a great Church of England man and thought that the Established Church was a tremendous asset to the whole nation.

He used to say to me, "The Roman Catholics say, 'You will go to church.' The Church of England says, 'You should go,' and so it is up to you, my dear Parson!"

Years later, when he was Chief of the Defence Staff and visited Naval Establishments, he always had 'Old Ships' fallen in so that he could meet them. We met several times and he used to call me out for a chat, making enquiries about the family and church life on the Station or in the Establishment.

He usually ended by saying, "Have you another clerical story for me?"

By April 1949, for me, almost half the Commission had passed and what had I achieved? What was the 'church' position?

On Sundays, between 10 and 15 of us used to meet for Holy Communion at 8 am in our tiny Chapel, which was also the Ship's school. On the whole those who came did not want to join in any kind of Fellowship.

The main Sunday Morning Service, held either on the quarter deck or in the Cinema, was kept going and was in good heart, with good support from the Wardroom, between 25 and 30, and the Ratings, between 20 and 30, and the splendid Royal Marines band.

I had gathered together about 20 men, two or three Officers and the rest Ratings, into a loose Fellowship. Some of us used to meet together to read the Bible and pray, in the Chapel, several days a week. However they were all rather fearful and needed constant help and encouragement.

So, here I was, in this great ship carrying 900 men; men who for the most part arrived in the Service with no Christian faith; serving under a famous Admiral and travelling all round the Mediterranean. I realised that my task was to build up the church and preach the Gospel to the Ship's Company.

I was determined to stick to my daily praying and meditation; to stick to my regular and systematic visiting of the various parts of the ship; and to try to shepherd my rather fearful flock who could easily err and stray when ashore in the various ports we visited.

A sentence from a book on the Battle of Midway, the battle which changed the course of the war in the Pacific in 1942, written by an American was, and has been, a great help to me over the years.

He wrote, "A battle is only a battle when there is a crisis. Until then it is only an engagement." I was in crisis and therefore engaged in battle. To quote John Bunyan, it was "The struggle for mansoul;" for the souls of HMS *Liverpool*.

How was I to break through on to the Mess Decks where there appeared to be so little Christian Faith? What more could I do? All was not gloom! The Wardroom, the Gunroom and the Warrant Officers were helpful. The Ship's Company were friendly. I was welcome in many of the Messes, but that was as far as I seemed to get. The message of the Cross was irrelevant to most men.

The prayer which Admiral Sir Francis Drake had composed and used at Cadiz in 1585 was continually before me.

> 'Grant us to know that it is not the beginning, but the continuing
> of the same until it be thoroughly finished that yieldeth the
> true glory.'

So after a year, I seemed to be getting nowhere. I was in crisis in my work and I suppose I faced defeat, although I wasn't down-hearted. I wanted something to happen in the spiritual realm and it had to happen quickly. Time was not on my side. Arthur Hugh Clough wrote:

'Say not, The struggle naught availeth,
The labour and the wounds are vain;
The enemy faints not nor faileth,
And as things have been they remain.
For while the tired waves vainly breaking,
seem here no painful inch to gain,
Far back, through creeks and inlets making,
comes silent, flooding in, the main.'

On our first summer cruise to the Eastern Mediterranean in May 1949, our first stop was Athens, where the King and Queen, the Admiral's relations, came on board as his guests. The Royal Marines Band stole the hearts of the Athenians by their Beating Retreat in the main square of the city. Some of us, on a run ashore, climbed Mars Hill.

### St Lawrence, Patron Saint of Cooks

Leaving the Pireas we sailed north along the east coast of Greece. While on my rounds I happened to enter the galley. The CPO Cook asked me, in front of his staff, why St Lawrence was the Patron Saint of cooks.

I said, "All come to church next Sunday and I will tell you."

The following Sunday we were anchored off one of the many Greek Islands. It was a pleasant morning. Church was held on the Quarter Deck and, for some reason, we had a large congregation including the Galley staff.

Admiral Mountbatten was sitting in the front row of the Officers, and I was about two yards away. I was facing the congregation and, in my sermon, I commented on the presence of the Galley staff who had asked me to talk about St Lawrence, their Patron Saint.

I told them the story of St Lawrence and how he ended up by being placed on a grid iron by the Roman authorities and roasted. After some time, Lawrence said, "Turn me over, I'm done this side." At this moment, the whole congregation, to my complete surprise, roared with laughter. All except Admiral Mountbatten who glared at me as if he wanted to cut my throat. The laughter died down and then, quite suddenly, the Admiral threw back his head and laughed aloud. And the congregation laughed again!

Admiral Mountbatten didn't forget this incident. The following August, when we were back in Malta, his Flag Lieutenant came to my cabin one morning with a newspaper cutting and note attached.

'I hope you didn't miss this!' signed Mountbatten of Burma. It was an account of the roasting of St Lawrence in the *Times of Malta*, dated August 10th. They write about a Saint every day. I had been correct.

223

Next we called at Salonika where the East Surrey Regiment was stationed. We had an exchange of visits and I put my name down to be one of the members of the Wardroom to visit their Mess. On arrival they made me particularly welcome as my brother-in-law was an East Surrey Officer. I had conducted the wedding service of Mike Halliday to my sister Polly in Tanglin Church, Singapore, just before the Japanese war. Polly got away, leaving Singapore in the *Duchess of Bedford*. But Mike Halliday went into the Jap bag, serving on the infamous Burma railway for three-and-a-half years. He survived, no thanks to the Japs, and now lives near Moretonhampstead, Devon.

Leaving Salonika, we sailed east and then north-east through the Aegean Sea into the Dardanelles and the Sea of Marmora. Turning south, we went past Mitylene, Smyrna, the Island of Cos and on to Rhodes, where we anchored and remained for a few days. Countess Mountbatten and Lady Pamela had flown in from Malta and they joined the Admiral for church on Sunday, the next day. Also present for this Service was the Consul's party and most of the English community.

This Service, which was to be quite remarkable, was held in perfect weather on the quarter deck. The arrival of the British community meant that there would be a good turn out of Ratings, who were always glad to see new faces. The Royal Marines Band were playing their voluntaries long before the Service commenced and, with their fine rendering of some well known hymns, we were off to a good start. The Lesson read by the Captain described St Paul's voyage along this very coast. There was a great stillness during the Captain's reading of this Lesson, during the prayers and during my sermon. The whole congregation seemed to be strangely moved and uplifted.

Immediately we had finished, the Admiral sent for me. He and his party wanted to discuss the Service. They all seemed to be at a loss to say much. On returning to the Wardroom, I found that they, too, were discussing the Service, and it appeared that the Ratings had been affected in the same way. Here we were in the very steps of St Paul and the same Spirit was at work in our hearts. We left Rhodes the next morning and as we sailed towards Cyprus I listened to what men were saying about the Service. I wondered how I would be able to follow up what seemed to be the first break in the clouds. But before we leave Rhodes I want to describe the Admiral's Dinner Party on the Sunday night to which I was invited.

The Dinner Party and its aftermath should be described in detail. Besides the Admiral, Countess Mountbatten, the Lady Pamela Mountbatten, the Consul and his wife, a few local dignitaries, the Flag Lieutenant, the Captain, the Commander and the Gunnery Officer, there was also the Greek Archimandrite and myself. The dinner was finished, the pipers had completed their piece and we were to proceed to the quarter deck for coffee, where the Wardroom Officers were waiting for us.

The Archimandrite joined the Captain and me. The Captain showed him his bathroom. The Archimandrite just nodded and said, "Si, si," went in and closed the door. He spoke no English and we spoke no Greek. We walked up and down the flat and waited for him to come out.

After about five minutes, the Flag Lieutenant arrived and said to the Captain, "Sir, the Admiral says you are to bring the Archimandrite at once."

The Captain said, "Sorry, we can't. He's in the bathroom."

We continued to walk up and down the flat. Then the Captain tried the bathroom door from the flat, and from his night cabin, but they were both locked!

After another five minutes, the Flag Lieutenant arrived again and said, "The Admiral is getting impatient. You are to bring the Archimandrite at once."

The Captain replied, "Sorry, we can't. I've tried both the doors and they are locked."

A few minutes later, the Flag Lieutenant arrived for the third time and said, "The Admiral is frantic and is going up to the quarter deck without him".

The Captain said, "There is nothing we can do except wait."

So once more the Flag Lieutenant hurried away. As we stood waiting, the door of the bathroom suddenly opened, and the Archimandrite appeared.

He was all smiles and all he could say was, "Si, si."

The Captain had a quick look round his bathroom, and reckoned that the fellow had had a bath. News soon spreads in a ship, and the idea of the Greek Archimandrite having a bath in the Captain's bathroom produced the biggest laugh of the Commission!

It was the custom of HM Ships, when visiting a port, to have a Cocktail Party on the quarter deck. It takes place on the evening of arrival or the second night, for the local residents. All who had any claim to be British tried to get an invitation. It always appeared to us that there were an enormous number of British nationals living in every port we visited! However, it does give the locals an opportunity to meet members of the Ship's Company and to invite them to homes and to dances, outings, cocktail parties, tennis parties, football matches, and other social activities ashore.

At the Ship's Cocktail Party, if we were alongside, the Royal Marines Band would Beat Retreat towards the end of the party and conclude with Sunset and the National Anthem. If we were anchored out, either in the harbour or at sea, the RM Orchestra provided the music and concluded the evening the same way. Although I have heard Sunset played in practically every port around the Mediterranean, on the jetties or on board, it never seemed to lose its moving appeal and provided a wonderful ending to these everlasting parties. After the National Anthem the guests slowly made their way ashore, many of them obviously deeply impressed by the whole evening. To us the parties varied like the people. Some were quite fun. Others were the most terrible bore.

We anchored off Limassol, on the south coast of Cyprus, one Tuesday forenoon and the Wardroom Party was due to take place on the Tuesday evening. During the afternoon the Quarter Master, who was on the gangway, came to my cabin.

"There is an American clergyman on the quarter deck and he wants to see you," he said.

I went up to see him and he said, "I am an American Presbyterian clergyman working in Limassol. We have a school, a hall and a church for the Cypriots. Can we be of any use to you while you are here?"

He had been to the other cruiser which was also anchored off Limassol and put the same question to their Chaplain who had declined his help with thanks but said, "Try Mr Pocock in *Liverpool*," which he did.

I thanked him and asked him if he was in a position to provide an evening meal for about two dozen men and follow the meal with a Gospel Meeting. He agreed and we arranged that I should take the men ashore to the jetty the following evening at 7 pm. He would meet us and take us up to the Mission.

At the Cocktail Party that Tuesday night on the quarter deck, I was approached by two Englishmen.

They said, "We are Christian doctors working in Cyprus. Besides our ordinary work we run a Soldiers' Home in Famagusta."

One was Dr Shelley, a GP, and the other was Dr Campion, a dentist.

They went on, "Famagusta is 25 miles away, but we can arrange transport. Can we do anything for you while you are in Limassol?"

I told them what the Americans were doing and so we arranged that I should take about 25 men over to Famagusta on the Saturday afternoon and again on the Sunday afternoon. They agreed that we would have time to just sit around and look at papers and magazines. This is something sailors really enjoy. Then they would provide us all with a meal and follow it with a Gospel Meeting.

Twenty-five of us went ashore at 7 pm on Wednesday and the American clergyman met us at the jetty to lead the way to their Mission. The Quarter Master was one of my Christian team so, as he went round the ship piping the orders, he was able to pipe my invitation to the members of the Fellowship. About 80 of us, which included the Cypriot congregation, young, middle-aged and old, sat down to supper in one of their halls. There must have been a lot of work involved in preparing this meal for us and all the rest. Then came the meeting. It consisted of hymn singing, a solo or two, a Bible reading, prayer and then the address by the Minister. He presented the claims of Christ to us all and exhorted us to serve and follow Him. I am sure the evening proved a blessing to these men and, as we returned to the ship, they appeared anxious for more. I had the Minister to lunch on the Friday which gave me the opportunity to thank him for the generosity of his congregation. I was able to take him round the ship so he could meet some of the men again.

On the Saturday afternoon, about 20 of the 25 came again. The others were on duty. I filled up their places and 30 of us went ashore. The news had spread round the Messes and many were keen to come. Whether it was the mixed company or the good meal or the Gospel Meeting I cannot say. Two three-tonners were waiting for us at the jetty, plus drivers. They were Army lorries but why army I have no idea and I never did find out. An hour's run took us the 25 miles to the Soldiers' Home. We spent the first hour in their reading room, looking through magazines and papers. Next the two Doctors and their staff provided us with a first class meal which, much to the sailors' delight, included bacon and eggs! Then came the meeting and this time my flock were eager and ready for it. Things were run on much the same lines as the American evening with plenty of hymn singing, a prayer, a reading from the Bible, and finally, the earnest Christian Gospel appeal by Dr Shelley. All this had its effect on us and we left determined to return the following day if possible. This communal approach was beginning to have its effect and most of the 30 were at church on the Quarter Deck the next morning.

Sunday aftrernoon found us all ashore and once again we were met by the Army three-tonners and their drivers. We enjoyed the 25 mile run across the island. Our hours at the Soldiers' Home passed all too quickly. The sailors were glad of the further opportunity to sit and read quietly for an hour before the high tea or supper which our hosts provided for us. We all enjoyed this generous hospitality and the meeting which followed was a heart-warming experience. The way the two Officers, the Ratings and Marines said goodbye to the Doctors and their helpers brought home to me how many of their hearts had been touched by the Everlasting Gospel. As I left I asked the Doctors whether I might be allowed to contribute towards the cost of the thirty suppers two nights running. They wouldn't hear of it and said it was their privilege and joy to be allowed to be of service to the Christian Fellowship in HMS *Liverpool*. Further, they said that the Church in this great ship would be remembered in their prayers reguarly. Added to this were the prayers of the Americans in Limassol, and we should probably never see any of them again.

My Church Fellowship meant that I had no time at all for any of the many social activities and parties laid on for the Officers and Ratings while we were in Limassol. This was of no consequence to me. Far more important was the fact that this considerable number of men should decide to serve the Lord and be built up in the Christian Faith. On reflection I realised I was only touching the fringe of the Ship's Company.

We sailed early on the Monday morning. When the 'locals' woke up and looked for us, we had gone. For many of my Fellowship it was with mixed feelings. Joy for the refreshing, enlightening and positive time we had experienced with these fine English, American and Cypriot people, and sadness that we should not be seeing them again. For some, Christian Faith had begun. For others, it had been strengthened. To me it appeared to be just like Apostolic times, but the other way round! Here we were in the very steps of St Paul but, instead of Paul preaching to the people ashore, the Christians ashore were preaching the Gospel to us in HMS *Liverpool* and my dear flock was responding. The same Spirit was at work in our hearts as He had been working in the hearts of the people in this same area in the first century. I was reminded the of words of St Paul to the people of Ephesus, not far from where we were. He wrote:

> 'I know not what things shall befall me, except that the Holy Ghost witnesseth in every city' (in our case Rhodes, Limassol, Famagusta and soon Beirut) 'and when he had thus spoken, he kneeled down and prayed with them all and they accompanied him down to the ship.'

The next stop was Beirut where we remained from the Wednesday until the followng Monday morning. On the first evening there was the usual party including the whole of the Lebanese cabinet who came on board as guests of the Admiral. It gets dark early in the Middle East and during this particular evening, the Royal Marines Band Beat Retreat on the jetty under the ship's flood-lights. The Band gave a first class performance and an American Colonel, the American Army Attaché who was standing next to me, said, "This is one occasion when I wish I was British!"

I was called on by the British Chaplain, Rev. Tommy Atkins. On the Sunday, he came on board and preached for me while I took his Service and preached ashore. I was wise enough to tell him that my congregation loved long sermons, anything between 30 and 40 minutes.

When I returned on board, the Wardroom said, "Thank heaven you are back after what we have been through this morning."

I was also visited on board by the Head of the British Syrian Mission. This is an Inter-denominational Mission working in Lebanon and Syria through a number of Christian schools. He said that they were anxious to help us in any way they could and, if we had a Church Fellowship on board, they would be pleased to entertain us. In fact Beirut was to be another landmark in the build up of the Church in the ship. The members of the Mission were generous in every way; the time they gave us; the meal they provided for 30 of us; and the meeting they inspired us with. These missionaries, men and women, seemed surprised and delighted to meet a cross section of Officers, Ratings and Royal Marines from one of HM Ships. The other side of the coin was that the sailors much appreciated meeting the men and women from the various missions around the Mediterranean.

228

After Beirut the next stop was Alexandria and, as you can imagine, I was curious and anxious to know what lay in store for us there. What about my flock? Would there be anything for them? The Ship's Company always seemed glad of a few days at sea to recover from the hospitality of the previous port. However, with Admiral Mountbatten driving the squadron, there was little time to recover and we invariably exercised all the way. By not overstaying our welcome anywhere the locals were sorry to see us go, hoping that we would return. That, of course, we never did. Even if the ship returned, it would be with a new Ship's Company.

In next to no time we were tied up alongside the jetty in Alexandria harbour. At the Cocktail Party on the first or second night, a gentleman approached me and asked me whether we had a Church Fellowship on board. So this was it! When I informed him that we had, he said that he and a number of his friends would like to entertain us for an evening, that they lived at the eastern end of Alexandria, and that they would provide transport both ways. The day, time and numbers were fixed.

During *Liverpool*'s stay in Alexandria, it was arranged that Admiral Mountbatten should call on King Farouk in Cairo. Somehow the Admiral heard that Mary's sister was at the hospital in the old town. He sent for me and asked if I would like to go up to Cairo with him and his staff. I thanked him for his kind thought and jumped at the invitation. So off we went. Lord Louis to call on the King while I went to call on my sister-in-law, Elise Radcliffe. All of us went in an aeroplane laid on by the British Army, as we still had our bases in Egypt.

On the way up, the Admiral and I again discussed church-going in the Navy.

Once again he said to me, "The Church of Rome says, You will go to church. We in the Church of England say You should go."

"If," he said, "You can make the message living, urgent and vital, you will have a living growing church."

I agreed and realised the fact only too well. Whether at this time he saw any change coming over our Sunday Services, I don't know. He never said so.

We landed at Heliopolis, 10 miles from Cairo and all the Top Brass in the Middle East was present to meet the Admiral. He descended from the aircraft and met the reception committee. Next came his Staff Officer, Lieutenant Commander David Dunbar-Nasmith, then myself, the Chaplain and finally, his Flag Lieutenant, Lieutenant Commander Peter Howes. The Admiral introduced each of us in turn. Meet my Chaplain, Mr Pocock. Meet my Chaplain, Mr Pocock, all down the line to an Admiral, a Lieutenant General, an Air Vice Marshal, RN Captains, Colonels and Group Captains. I was approached by a Group Captain who offered to drive me wherever I wanted to go. I thanked him for this very generous officer and said that I wished to go to the CMS Hospital in Old Cairo. He had never heard of it but I told him I knew the way, and off we went. Once we reached

Cairo, he was lost so I directed him down the banks of the Nile to Old Cairo. I remembered the way from my visit in 1943. I think he was fascinated with the experience of driving through the native quarter while I was deeply grateful to him for so kindly bringing me all this distance. I had a pleasant day with Douglas and Elise (Douglas was a Doctor at the CMS Hospital) and I returned to Alexandria the next day by train.

Having returned safely from Cairo I mustered the Church Fellowship and we were met on the jetty by a fleet of cars. It seemed that most of the Ship's Company were watching as we piled into these limousines, so we went on our way to cheers and cat-calls. We travelled to the eastern end of Alexandria along the Corniche; a very pleasant trip. Our hosts and hostesses were kindness itself. We were entertained in a lovely house and had a relaxing time chatting and reading. They had provided a buffet supper for us all so we were able to move about freely. After the supper came a very informal meeting. We sat in comfortable chairs all round the room. There was some singing, a reading from the Bible and then three or four of our hosts spoke briefly of their Christian experiences. There was a final prayer and it was time to return to the *Liverpool*.

We all returned to the Ship that night deeply grateful for the kindness, the hospitality and the Christian encouragement we had received from all these people, not only in Alexandria, but also in Beirut, Famagusta and Limassol. There was no more they could have done for us. For me the cruise had been overwhelming and had taken a course that I could never have dreamt of. The members of the Fellowship seemed to be absolutely astonished that I knew people in every place we went to. I didn't really, but the way we were entertained made it appear that way.

As we sailed west for Malta next day I realised that it was up to me, with God's help, to hold on to, keep together, teach and encourage in the Christian way, my enthusiastic and increasing flock. It has been said that the actual Mission is the easy part of the church's effort, while the follow up is the difficult part.

> 'It is not the beginning, but the continuing of the same until it be thoroughly finished that yieldeth the true glory,' said Sir Francis Drake.

One of the matters I had to think through carefully during the days at sea was how the continuing was to be tackled.

I think it was while we were at Alexandria that the Gunroom, as the Midshipmen's Mess is called, invited the Admiral, his Staff, the Captain, a few members of the Wardroom including myself, to their Mess after church. Some of them were leaving the Ship. It just happened that while I was telling some of the Midshipmen a rather amusing story, Admiral Mountbatten was listening.

230

Afterwards, he called me to one side and said, "While we are at sea during the next few days on the way back to Malta, use the time to build a sermon round that story for the great day."

I had no idea what he meant by the great day but I decided that I would give it a go. So besides having to think through how I could best deal with the growing Church Fellowship, I also had to try to put together a sermon round this particular story.

We arrived back in Malta on a Friday and on the Saturday forenoon, the Flag Lieutenant came to my quarters.

He said, "The Admiral wants you in his cabin."

I went along and discovered that the Captain and the Commander were also there.

The Admiral said, "What are the hymns for tomorrow's Service?"

I thought, 'This is a strange inquiry . . . he had never asked before.'

I told him that I had chosen the hymns in consultation with the Bandmaster, Captain Bill Fitzgerald and gave him the list.

He said, "Not bad. And have you got that sermon ready for the great day?"

I replied, "I am afraid that I didn't know what the great day is, but I have had a go at building a sermon around that story."

All the others were listening.

He said, "Good. The great day is in fact tomorrow, Sunday. Princess Elizabeth has just arrived to stay with us in Malta and she will be coming to church in *Liverpool* tomorrow morning."

This was very exciting news for us all; the families and the Ship's Company. The families came on board in good time and hundreds of Ratings crowded on to the quarter deck for the Service. The Admiral, Captain Shaw-Hamilton, and Commander Robin Topp were waiting at the head of the gangway to greet the Princess when she alighted from the *Liverpool* motor boat, accompanied by her Lady-in-Waiting, by Countess Mountbatten and by Lady Pamela Mountbatten. I was standing somewhere nearby ready to take the Service.

While we were waiting for the boat to come alongside Commander Topp came over to me and said most movingly, "My dear Parson, I hope that you can make the most of this great opportunity to preach the Gospel not only to the Princess but also to these hundreds of sailors."

I didn't answer for a few seconds and then replied, "I shall do my best."

He said, "I'm sure you will. Good luck," and he left, giving me a delightful smile.

It is not for me to comment on the Service. The singing of well known hymns by hundreds of sailors is a great experience in itself. The whole of Grand Harbour was ringing with the Lord's Praises that morning. To have the Princess in our midst added to the joy and enthusiasm. After the Prayer for the King, the Prayer for the Royal Family which included the words,

'The Princess Elizabeth' had special significance for all present.

I gave the sermon that I had prepared. My text was "He that endureth to the end shall be saved." And I wrapped it up around several little stories.

Later in the week, the Admiral met me and said, "Tell me another story sometime and I will tell you whether you can build a sermon around it!"

The Princess came to church in *Liverpool* several times, including Christmas Day when we had the Ship's Carol Service. She also attended two or three of our Wardroom receptions. Mary and I often had the privilege of a chat with her after church on Sundays. There is one incident, connected with one of her visits, which remains vividly in my mind. Some of us, including Mary and me, were talking to her when the Flag Lieutenant approached the Admiral.

He said, "Admiral, Sir, the King is on the phone from Buckingham Palace and would like to speak to the Princess."

The Admiral took her down to his cabin aft, where she spoke to the King. This was rather early days for long distance telephone calls and we were all fascinated that the King was speaking from Buckingham Palace to his daughter in *HMS Liverpool*, anchored in Grand Harbour, Malta.

Mary, and our two children, Sue and Andrew, had come out to Malta in the early summer of 1948. After several months in hotels we managed to rent a nice country house called Casa Manduca belonging to a Mr Manduca! It was at Wardia, a village high up behind St Paul's Bay. On its credit side, the house was in the country, it was large and airy. On the debit side was its loneliness when I was on board, its distance from Valetta and Grand Harbour, 10 miles away, and its lack of facilities. The water came up from an artesian well, with a pump dependent on the wind! There were paraffin lamps for lighting and cooking. The hot water for the bath was heated by a paraffin geyser and used to light with a tremendous bang. The nearest telephone was hundreds of yards away and was a field telephone from the Dockyard in Grand Harbour to the Wardia Armament Depot. It was in the care and charge of a miserable, lazy Maltese dockyard matey. My only means of communication with Mary when we returned to Grand Harbour was to ring this fellow and try to persuade him to go the 300 yards to our house to ask her to bring the car down to Grand Harbour. I never knew whether he would deliver the message even if, in a surly voice, he said, "Yes."

When we were away on cruises, the wives used to love to come out and visit Mary for a day in the country. However, we really wanted to be nearer civilisation.

At the end of May 1949, we left Wardia and moved into a dreadful flat in Attard, only four miles from Grand Harbour. Mary was expecting her baby in August and so we wanted to be near the King George the Fifth Hospital in Valetta. The first summer cruise was imminent so we had settled in Attard just before the squadron sailed. We were back again at the end of July and then moved again, this time to a delightful flat called *Villa Sultana* at

Ta'x Biex, between Valetta and Sliema and overlooking Marsamascetto Harbour. It had previously been occupied by Lieutenant Commander Ian Garnett and before him by Commander Nigel Pumphrey, both of the *Liverpool*. At this time we had a young nannie named Muriel living with us so she was able to look after Sue and Andrew when Mary went into hospital.

Charlotte was born on Sunday August 14th 1949. I had been to the Barraca Church for Evensong at 6 pm and then went down to the hospital near by. Mary had her new baby in her arms when I went in and I was able to stay with her for a while. Mary was very well looked after. It was a Christian Hospital and Charlotte seemed so very, very tiny.

*Liverpool* was in harbour for three weeks after that. Mary and Charlotte came home after a week so we had about a fortnight together before I sailed for the second Summer Cruise.

The Sunday after Charlotte was born, we had Peter Fanning's Baptism on board after the Morning Service. As the hospital overlooked Grand Harbour, Mary was able to watch the people coming on board and the Christening on the quarter deck. A few doors away from our flat was Whitehall Mansions where all the WRNS and Naval Nursing Sisters lived. One of the Sisters, Annie Webster, had been at The Hospital for Sick Children with Mary so she was also a frequent and welcome visitor.

While the ship was on the Spring Cruise to the western Mediterranean we spent several days at Nice. There was an Anglo-American Hospital here and Lieutenant Leslie Townsend and Surg. Lt Toothy Montgomery visited and got to know most of the nursing staff quite well!

When we left, Toothy announced, to the utter astonishment of the whole Wardroom, that he had asked Miss Daphne Briggs, one of the staff, to marry him and she had accepted. He had kept his secret so well that not even Leslie Townsend suspected anything!

Daphne came to Malta and the wedding took place in St Paul's Cathedral, Valetta, well before our second Summer Cruise in the Mediterranean. Lieutenant Harvey, who had been best man to Joe Mills, was chosen by Toothy to be best man at his wedding too. I had the honour of officiating. The Reception was held on board and was a very happy occasion, after which the happy couple left for their honeymoon in Sicily. After their return from Sicily, Robert and Daphne soon settled into the life of Malta. He had been a regular member of our Sunday Services, and now they both joined the Officers' and Ratings' wives and crowds of children who came on board for church.

The second Summer Cruise was to take us to the western Mediterranean. The first stop was Palermo, where I christened the American Consul's baby. While we were in Palermo harbour various other cruisers of the Commonwealth Navies were passing through the Mediterranean. Admiral Mountbatten managed to have them all come into Palermo. He had the

*Liverpool* Band on the jetty to greet each one.

There were cruisers from Australia, Ceylon, Pakistan and several from our own squadron. It was a most remarkable sight. All these ships were flying their own national flags at the Jack Stay and the White Ensign at the stern.

I happened to be standing next to a German and, as we were watching all these ships berthing, he said to me, "Whose Navy is this? Who do they all belong to?"

I replied, "They are the White Ensign Navy and they all belong to our Commonwealth."

I thought it was quite a good answer and he seemed satisfied.

From Palermo, we sailed along the coast of Sicily and on to Naples. I didn't, on the whole, do much organising of outings for the Ship's Company. Someone else usually did this but on this cruise, I was fully occupied arranging trips for the ship. For example, while we were in Naples, I organised Ship's Company trips to Vesuvius, Puteoli, Sorrento and Rome.

One of the duties of the Chaplain and the Royal Marines Officer at each port is to visit and report on the British cemeteries. At Naples, Major de Courcey Ireland and I visited Sorrento together. The size of the cemetery and the number of headstones was terrifying. There were literally hundreds and hundreds of men of the Army and Royal Marines buried there as a result of the Salerno landings. The place was beautifully kept by an Italian working for The Imperial War Graves Commission. We both came away very moved, yet grateful that the cemetery was so well looked after.

Leaving Naples, we crossed to the Isle of Capri and anchored. We understood that Gracie Fields lived there so the Captain sent me ashore to invite her to come and sing to the sailors. She was in London doing a show but I arranged to meet her husband, Monte Banks, in the Square at the top of the island at 6 pm. The young soldier, Lieutenant Johnny Harwood insisted on escorting me. Johnny was unfortunately killed later in Korea. We went up to the Square in a huge lift with three or four sailors and two or three English tourists.

These people said to our sailors, "Aren't you young men lucky sailing round and round the Mediterranean for two and a half years, visiting lovely places like this. All found and you get paid for it."

I must say that we all found Capri very pleasant driving round the island and bathing in the Blue Grotto. Two nights later, the ship was pounding along in very heavy seas towards San Remo. As I passed along the upper deck, very late, those same sailors were duty boat's crew, standing there, soaked to the skin.

They called out, "Sir, those English tourists should see us now. We are tired out and soaked to the skin while they are tucked up in their lovely beds!"

At San Remo I took Evensong at the English church. The Major of Marines came along to support me. We made up most of the congregation. Also while we were there I went for a trip on the over-head railway, cable car, up to the mountains. It broke the following week!

So far, I had not been able to arrange anything for the members of the *Liverpool* Church Fellowship and this Cruise was to set certain problems for me. Nowhere did I find a church group to whom I could have introduced them, so I had to make sure that they were all at church on Sundays. On the whole they were bearing up well. Some were beginning to join in the Communion Services. In Nice I dined with others from the ship, with the Mayors of Cannes, Villefranche and Toulon, where the Captain took me for a walk! At St Tropez we all enjoyed the beaches. I think I managed to arrange outings at all these places. They meant considerable work and time, but on the whole the Ship's Company were satisfied customers.

A few of us were invited by an English lady to lunch in one of the big hotels in Monte Carlo. A terribly boring hour and a half was saved by one amusing remark our hostess made.

She said, "You poor English sailors away from your loved ones for so long. The least we can do is to offer you a little hospitality."

The wives, who were stuck in Malta with the children and never a day off had other ideas about these 'poor English sailors' who were being wined and dined all round the Mediterranean ports! I understand that the English Church always had a good morning congregation. It was rumoured that they ran a sweepstake on the numbers on the hymn board each Sunday!

There were usually a number of men in the Sick Bay. I could never understand why there were so many. The Navy is a young Service and the majority should have been well and fit all the time. My friend the Doctor asked me to arrange an outing for his walking patients and this I agreed to do. He told me he wanted me to go with them and I reluctantly agreed to this as well. Before we left he addressed the whole coachload of them and told them what I was doing for them. He said he wanted a report of good behaviour on their return and that no one was to touch alcohol. They promised. On this particular day I took them on one of the favourite tourist trips to the Gorge de Loups. I had a very difficult time. They managed to get hold of all sorts of alcohol, with many of them arriving back at the ship in a very poor shape. It was the last outing the Doctor and I arranged for his dear patients.

As we returned to Malta during the second half of September and looked like remaining there for October we decided, after consulting the Commander, to have Charlotte christened. The Service was to be on the quarter deck after the morning Church Service on Sunday October 30th, which was also Mary's Birthday. Lady Pamela Mountbatten consented to be one Godmother; Colonel Paine, Royal Marines, who lived practically next door to us in Malta and with whom I had served in Sicily in 1943, consented to be Godfather and Beatrice Little stood proxy for Elizabeth

Stevenson, Mary's niece. On this Sunday the weather was perfect. The whole of the Wardroom and Gunroom and a large number of Ratings were present as well as a number of our shore-side friends, including several Royal Marines families. It was a very happy occasion for all of us and I hope for the rest of the congregation too.

The vast majority of the Ship's Company did not have their families in Malta for this Commission for various reasons, such as housing, schooling or family. So two and a half years is a long time to be away. We were now well over half way through the Commission. 'Downhill' the sailors call it so most people were thinking of home. October saw the ship in harbour except for a few days carrying out gunnery practice. In November, we sailed for Algiers and Oran for a week. While we were there I managed to organise an outing to the French Foreign Legion at Sidi-Bel-Abes. While there we bumped into the Admiral who appeared surprised but delighted that some of the Ship's Company had been able to visit this interesting place. He had also invited Army personnel from Malta to join us for this trip and he arranged for them to watch *Liverpool*'s gunnery. Something went wrong and *Liverpool* bombarded a native village by mistake Fortunately, there were no casualties but the Noble Earl was not amused. It was reported that some of the tiny shells landed in the sea amongst Arabs who were bathing. The Ship's Company were highly amused.

Now that we had a pleasant flat, not too far away from the ship, Mary and I felt that we should use it for the *Liverpool* Fellowship. It is the custom in the Navy for the Officers to have guests on board for supper on Sunday evenings. We decided that one week we would go on board; we didn't want to cut ourselves off entirely from our Mess Mates and their wives; and the other week we would have the Fellowship at our flat. Over the months, we were able to entertain to supper Colonel and Mrs Paine, Colonel and Mrs Houghton; he was in the *Woolwich* with me, Major Freddie and Mrs Pam Clifford and Major Sandy and Mrs Nora Macpherson, all friends from Deal days; Captain and Mrs Charles Verdon whom we knew from Deal and Singapore, and many friends whom we had known over the years.

We were fortunate in our ground floor flat mates. They were kindness itself. They might easily have objected to a large number of sailors and Marines passing through their flat and having to listen to them singing hymns, but they didn't.

The lads usually arrived about 7.30 pm, when the children were in bed, and they stayed until about 10.15 pm. We had a large supply of old magazines and papers which they were delighted to read and look through. Supper followed. This was Mary's contribution and it proved to be a large one with between 20 and 30 to cater for. Occasionally I got the Wardroom Messman to help us out. Hymn singing followed, with readings from J. B. Phillips' Letters to Young Churches. This in the '40s was something quite new for us. Over the coming months we were to read through and discuss several of these Epistles.

Two friends of ours, Harold and Mary Burridge serving with the RAF, used to come along regularly and Mary Burridge was our soloist. The Burridges made an enormous contribution to the regular meetings of the Fellowship. When Mary and I were on board, the Fellowship was transferred to their house. These meetings, in one house or the other, continued for the rest of the Commission. Those who came from the *Liverpool* began to bring their friends and these included men from other ships. In this way our flat, or the Burridges' house, became the centre for a large number of Christian men. It is impossible to remember them all. Many were not only a help to me but to other younger Christian men. I have put down a few names for my own benefit, because one forgets so quickly. There was Lieutenant David Harding, 'Chippy' Hunt, Don Parsons, Leading Seaman Reg Ogles, who was one of the ship's Quarter-Masters and my messenger for getting my own news around the ship, Stoker 'Lucky' Luck, Able Seaman Pinkney, Junior Musician Jimmy Mason, who was to become the Principal Director of the RM School of Music and many, many others.

After the turn of the year, as men were being drafted home, we lost some of our members but we seemed to gain others including men from other ships.

One result of the regular Sunday evening gatherings was the change which came over our Sunday morning Services on board, on the quarter deck and in the cinema, both in quality and numbers. It needed considerable courage for a Rating to change his rig and come to church. Now, that fear had largely gone and the regulars were bringing their friends. The Commanders of the ships of the squadron, who had regular meetings to discuss their own affairs, were not slow to notice what was going on in *Liverpool*. Commander Robin Topp told me how fortunate and blessed we were to have such a good congregation. During these weeks I was well supported by my faithful few and we were determined to maintain the spiritual glow. It was a real test of endurance. When in dock the ship seems hollow! Power and water are supplied from the dockyard. All washing facilities were ashore and there was no heating. All those who could get ashore  did so. During the day the ship was swarming with Maltese dockyard maties, while there was the continual noise from hammers, drills and so on.

By the end of the year, several members of the Wardroom had been relieved. They included the Fannings, the Sedgewicks and the Cruddas family, all good friends of ours. The Sedgewicks retired near Monkton Combe and we saw them when we visited our younger son, Stephen, at Monkton Combe School. We are in touch with Rennie and Betty Cruddas and in, 1962, their son was a member of the crew of a yacht of which I was skipper on the Norfolk Broads.

Christmas had passed off happily and busily and January saw *Liverpool* off to sea again. Her departure from Grand Harbour, Malta, for Greece and the Adriatic was dramatic. A *gregalli,* a Mediterranean storm blowing from east to west throughout the length of the sea, had been raging for a day or so. Nothing had been able to enter or leave Grand Harbour. *Liverpool's* Ship's Company hoped and hoped that our sailing would be postponed until the gale subsided. But no! The King and Queen of the Hellenes were to come on board *Liverpool* at the Pireas, Athens for the last time on this Commission and The Noble Earl, Admiral Mountbatten, said that nothing . . . not even a *gregalli* must prevent us sailing on time. The news soon spread to all the other ships in Grand Harbour that *Liverpool* was about to sail, and so they all literally cleared lower deck to see the fun. (For the first and last time *Liverpool* was cheered madly as she sailed out of Grand Harbour.) I am told no sooner was she through the breakwater, than she was lost to sight. I must admit that it was a most uncomfortable trip and the whole Ship's Company were thankful to be at anchor in the Pireas.

After a visit from the Royal guests and a day or so in Athens, where the Royal Marines Band Beat Retreat in the main square, we proceeded up the Adriatic and anchored in the Grand Canal opposite St Mark's Square. It was pleasant to be there in January. There were few trippers and the place didn't smell as it does in the summer. Besides visiting St Mark's Cathedral and Square, the Doge's Palace, the English Church, which was closed, and travelling around in Venetian Gondolas under The Bridge of Sighs, some of us visited the Island of Murano and its glass factory to make a few purchases.

At the end of January, the whole of the First Cruiser Squadron, *Liverpool, Newcastle, Phoebe* and *Euryalus,* put to sea with Admiral Mountbatten for the last time. Probably because it was a perfect day for weather he invited Princess Elizabeth, Countess Mountbatten, his daughter the Lady Pamela, and the Princess's Lady-in-Waiting to embark in *Liverpool.* We did some exercises, and then the other ships of the squadron 'marched' past with the Princess taking the salute on the bridge. Standing with her were the Admiral, the three other ladies, Captain Shaw-Hamilton, Commander Topp, Commander John Blake, the Navigating Officer, the Officer of the Watch, the Chief Signal Bo's'n, the Flag Lieutenant, and two or three junior Ratings. I too managed to find room to squeeze in with this distinguished company!

The plan was to sail round to the south west of the island to land on one of Malta's few sandy beaches, called Ghajn Tuffieha. *Liverpool's* Royal Marines Detachment was to land first in one of her Liberty boats. The RM Officer invited me to join their boat to land with them. Naturally, I was only too pleased to be joining the fun.

As we approached the beach, the young Royal Marines Officer Lieutenant Johnny Harwood called out, "There's my horse. I wondered what Prince Philip wanted her for."

The Duke of Edinburgh, who was First Lieutenant of the Destroyer HMS *Chequers* had borrowed about 20 horses and had them taken to Ghajn Tuffieha beach. As we came up in *Liverpool*'s boat, a concourse of 20 horses came galloping along, the riders dressed as Red Indians, with the object of opposing the landing. Prince Philip led the attack. Behind him two Red Indians who were mounted carried a huge banner between them. On it was printed in large letters, 'The Duke of Edinburgh's Light Of Horse!' Having charged past us yelling and screaming, they charged back again. We heard that the Royal Uncle, the Admiral still aboard *Liverpool*, was not amused!

Two small dinghies were provided for the Royal party to come ashore. The sea was quite rough and to me it seemed highly dangerous. I can't think what the Monarch would have said if he had known that his Daughter and Heir was coming ashore in Malta like a Cockleshell Hero.

Soon after this Lord Mountbatten, his family and the Princess returned to England. It had been an inspiring Commission serving with this famous sailor and statesman. While he was in *Liverpool* his Indian mail was about 60 letters a day. We had an Indian Lieutenant on board who used to tell me that no one in India could understand why he had returned to sea to command a Cruiser Squadron. The answer was, of course, that he loved the Sea and the Royal Navy. It had also been quite wonderful for us in *Liverpool*, in the Squadron and in the Mediterranean Fleet, to have the Princess amongst us. She had often come to church on board. Both before and since it has been my duty, privilege and joy to pray for her twice a day when saying Morning and Evening Prayer.

Admiral Mountbatten lowered his Flag in *Liverpool* at the end of January 1950 and his relief was Rear Admiral Mark Pizey, who had been my first Commander in HMS *Woolwich* in 1936.

As *Liverpool* went into dry dock at the beginning of February, Admiral Pizey hoisted his Flag in *Phoebe. Newcastle* had gone home to re-commission, which left only *Phoebe* and *Euryalus* at the ready. *Phoebe* had been without a Chaplain for some months so the Chaplains of *Liverpool* and *Euryalus* had been helping out. I think it was because I knew Admiral Pizey that I was invited to take the first Church Service. There was a good muster of families and I felt that there was a very good spirit in the Service held on the quarter deck. They used an altar which had been made in the ship and also a Prayer Desk from which I took the Service. Admiral and Mrs Pizey lived near us in Ta'x Biex so we saw them from time to time.

Life in dry dock is no fun for anybody, but it is surprising how the whole Ship's Company rallied round and made the best of it.

I still have a vivid memory of our Good Friday Service on the quarter deck in dry dock. A wonderful spirit prevailed. The Sub-Lieutenant of the gunroom sang a solo, 'Were you there when they crucified my Lord?' It was very brave of him to sing to the whole congregation of Officers, Ratings and Families, with many people in the dockyard stopping to listen as they walked past. He had learned it from a 78 gramophone record.

After the Service our Commander, Robin Topp, asked me, "Where was the Holy Spirit at the Time of the Crucifixion?"

He was a very thoughtful Christian man. Thinking over our Church Services while in dry dock and during the last part of the Commission, a fine spirit seemed to permeate them. I am certain that their meaningfulness, liveliness and joy was almost entirely due to the presence and prayers of the members of the Fellowship. They never wavered or faltered, especially during the run down of the Ship's Company and the rigours of dry dock.

During the spring there were further changes in the Ship's Company. Most of the key Ratings had arrived, followed by the new Wardroom and the mass of the Ratings. They were all getting to know their part of the ship. It must have been a very difficult time for the Captain, especially as the Commander, Robin Topp the Captain's right-hand man, was relieved in May. The month saw the ship in and out of harbour with the gunnery, torpedo and signal officers all exercising their men.

In July it was my turn to learn that my relief had been appointed and was about to arrive. His name was the Rev. Alwyn Wragg. Strange to say, the last time we had met was in this very ship, in November, 1941 in Singapore.

I wondered how he would cope with returning to the same ship.

He told me, "The Ship's Company is completely different from 1941, and it is quite nice to be taking over my old cabin once more."

Our passages were booked in the *Empress of Australia* for the second half of July. Our Vauxhall was going home on the upper deck of HMS *Ocean*, an aircraft carrier. Back in England I met two of our *Liverpool* Ratings who had taken passage home in *Ocean*. They told me that they visited the upper deck every day to see that our car was well secured. I thought it was very thoughtful of them. Mary and the children were ready and pleased to be leaving Malta.

Much as we had become attached to the place and to the Maltese, two and a half years is long enough in spite of the pleasant weather, the glorious sunset over Grand Harbour and the comradeship. There was the summer heat and the Sirocco winds from Africa to contend with, not to mention the Gregallis in the winter. January and February are really cold with rain and strong winds. There are no fires and no heating in the houses. Most of the windows are warped by the sun in the summer with the result that rain pours in through them in the winter.

The end of a Commission is a sad time both for the Ship's Company and the families. Although they are all glad to be returning to England there is sadness that the communal life of the Commission is gone for ever. In the future, we might serve with one, two or even three of them once more, but the majority we would never meet again.

Most people are tired at the end of a Commission. I once asked an Officer we had inherited from the previous Commission, who went home fairly early, whether he was ready to go.

He replied, "Yes. I am exhausted physically, mentally and spiritually, and I look forward to my Foreign Service Leave."

I think we all felt this way, though we would not on any account have missed the past two and a half years with its joys and sorrows, its hopes and fears, the rough and the smooth. The discipline, the loyalty, the friendship and, above all, the great, great charity, have to be experienced to be believed. It is hardly surprising that naval folk look upon every Commission as something precious and never to be forgotten.

Such words as 'He is an old ship of mine', 'We served together, in the China Seas, in the Mediterranean, on the Northern Patrol, in the Arctic, at Yeovilton, in Ceres'. . . and so on, carry a depth of meaning which the landsman finds it hard to understand. So we should leave this Commission with the hackneyed phrase 'Shipmates for ever'! The last ship is always the best ship. In this case that means . . . *LIVERPOOL*!

By the beginning of July I was the oldest inhabitant in the Wardroom of the old Commission. With the arrival of the new Chaplain, the Rev. Alwyn Wragg, I was glad to be leaving. It was a great comfort to me, as I left the ship, to know that the work of the Church and the Kingdom in the new Commission of HMS *Liverpool* was to be in the hands of this capable, faithful, wise and well-tried Chaplain.

*Years later, I was standing at our front garden gate talking to an old friend of mine, a retired Royal Marine, when a retired senior NCO passed on a bicycle. He called out, "Mr Pocock, Sir, don't take any lip from that Royal Marine; I was his Regimental Sergeant Major years ago."*

*My Wardroom Attendant in* Liverpool *was a certain Bill Merritt; he used to bring me a cup of tea every morning at 7.30. Now, he only lives round the corner, but no longer brings me any tea!*

Early in the morning of July 20th we watched the *Empress of Australia* steam into Grand Harbour. The view from our flat at Ta'x Biex looked straight out to sea so we were able to watch all the shipping which entered and left the Harbour. Some friends kindly drove us down to the Custom House and from there we were taken out to the *Empress* by ferry.

At 11.30 am, the *Empress* slowly left her anchorage and proceeded out of Grand Harbour. Life in *Liverpool* would continue with the Daily Routine, with one and all on board quite oblivious to the departure of the *Empress* who was taking with her, amongst others, the very last members of the old Commission.

Astern of *Liverpool*, lay *Phoebe* and *Euryalus*, while in other parts of Grand Harbour were the light carriers, *Triumph* and *Glory*, destroyers, submarines and Depot ships; 'A safeguard unto our most gracious Sovereign Lady, Queen Elizabeth, and her Dominions, and a security for such as pass on the seas upon their lawful occasions,' to quote The Book of Common Prayer.

The Commission was over and my work as Chaplain in this ship was finished. It was a strange feeling. In the words of the Prayer Book. I had been called 'to be a Messenger, Watchman and Steward of the Lord, to teach, admonish, to feed and to provide for the Lord's family; to seek for Christ's sheep that are dispersed abroad, that they may be saved through Christ for ever.' I could only hope and pray that the Seed, the Word, sown in weakness would bring forth fruit unto Eternal Life.

After Gibraltar, we sailed into the Atlantic, known as the Western Ocean to sea-faring men, and then across 'The Bay' through St George's Channel and on to the port of Liverpool. I had hoped we would berth at Southampton. The last time I had returned home and come up the Channel was in 1937 when the *Woolwich* came home to Spithead for the Coronation Review of King George VI. That voyage home took place in the middle of *Woolwich*'s first Commission and was a pleasant surprise and a great morale booster for the Ship's Company, except for those who had their wives in Malta. I can remember being very moved by some words from the poem 'The Ending' by John Masefield as we came up the Channel.

'The Lizard, the landfall beloved of the homecoming men,
The first light of home they behold, after long months away,
An outpost of England, sea-fronted, uplifting her lamp.'

But this time it was Liverpool, from which port Mary had sailed with the children two years before. In next to no time we were all ashore and aboard the Services train which took us to London. We were met by Mary's mother and brother and off we went to commence our Foreign Service leave and to await the next appointment.

*The Liverpool's Family Song*
Oh! What a wonderful morning; Oh! What a wonderful day,
*Liverpool* comes into harbour, Having been two months away.
Children and wives of the 'natives', watch from house-top and roof,
Everyone seems so excited, No one remaining aloof.

Children have grown and developed, Wives have remained just the same,
Families once more united, Loneliness banished again.

Oh! What a wonderful morning; Oh! What a wonderful day,
Oh! how I wish you'd remain here, Never to sail away.
                    (one of *Liverpool*'s Ship's Company)

242

\* \* \*

*The Naval Collect . . . Used daily*
Prevent us, O Lord, in all our doings, with Thy most gracious
favour, and further us with Thy continual help; that in all our
works begun, continued, and ended in Thee, we may glorify Thy
Holy Name, and finally by Thy mercy obtain everlasting life;
through Jesus Christ Our Lord. Amen.

\* \* \*

*A Prayer for old Shipmates of past Commissions . . . 15*
*Commissions, each remembered (twice a month)*
O Eternal God and Everlasting Father, Whose never failing
providence watcheth over all from the beginning to the end;
keep under Thy protection, all those who at any time have
been committed to my care; and, grant, I beseech Thee, that the
ties which have been formed between us may neither through
sin be broken, nor through multiplicity of cares be forgotten; and
that whatsoever good I may have been permitted to
communicate to them from Thy Holy Word, may by Thy power
bring forth the fruit of Christian living and in the end
Everlasting Life; through Our Lord and Saviour, Jesus Christ.
Amen.

\* \* \*

*A Prayer for Perseverance in the Christian Way*
O Lord God, when Thou givest to Thy servants to endeavour any
great matter,
grant us also to know that it is not the beginning, but the
continuing of the same until it be thoroughly finished that
yieldeth the true glory; through Him, who for the finishing of
Thy work laid down His Life, even Our Redeemer, Jesus Christ
Our Lord. Amen.

\* \* \*

*Hymns or Prayers used every Sunday in the Royal Navy, in the*
*Fleet Air Arm, and in The Royal Marines*
O Trinity of Love and Power, Our brethren shield in danger's
hour;

From rock and tempest, fire and foe, Protect them where so'er
they go;
And ever let there rise to Thee, Glad hymns of praise from land
and sea.

* * *

*The Fleet Air Arm*
Strong Son of God, save those who fly, Swift winged across the
uncharted sky;
Each anxious hour, each lonely flight, Serenely challenged
day or night.
O'er land and ocean safely bear, All those in peril in the air.

* * *

*A Prayer for all Seasons*
O Saviour of the world, Who by Thy Cross and precious Blood
has redeemed us;
Save us, and help us, we humbly beseech Thee, O Lord.

*Lieutenant (S) Leslie Townsend rose to be Rear Admiral (S). I think I am
correct in saying that from 1981 to 1983 he was an Equerry to Her Majesty
the Queen. I heard that when she said Goodbye to him at the end of his
time with her, she thanked him for his services and said that she wished
to give him her own Christmas present. It was December when he left her
Service. She created him Knight Commander of the Victorian Order. Those
of us who have served with him thought it was quite wonderful.*

# CHAPTER XII

# HMS Siskin, Royal Naval Air Station at Gosport 1952 to 1955

*In July 1952, I received an urgent message from the Chaplain of the Fleet that he wanted me to join HMS SISKIN, RNAS at Gosport. On arrival at Siskin, I met the retiring Chaplain briefly before he departed.*
*I can remember him saying to me, "Everything goes along very smoothly at Siskin; no problems; no difficulties and no worries."*
*Mary who heard this pronouncement said, to me later, "If everything goes along so smoothly, something must be wrong. The church must either be asleep or dead."*

HMS *SISKIN*

In the 1850s a number of Forts were built around Portsmouth to defend the area against possible attacks by Napoleon III of France. These Forts were known as Palmerston's Follies. There are three to the west of Gosport running towards Stokes Bay along the Military Road.

The Forts are called Rowner, Grange and Gomer. Opposite Fort Rowner was the Garrison Church, a huge timber building with a very steep roof. Next to that, going south, The Red House which was the Commander's Residence then, after a gap, six Officers' Married Quarters and the Ratings' Living Site covering a couple of acres. Opposite all these on the other side of the road and between the Forts, were the Administration Offices, Workshops, Hangars, Fire Section, the Control Tower and so on.

In 1919, the Army moved out and the area was taken over by the RAF. The fields behind the Forts became the airfield.

In 1945, there was another change. RAF Gosport became a Royal Naval Air Station, HMS *Siskin*. There were about 800 Naval Personnel and also about 250 RAF Personnel who shuttled back and forth to Culdrose, Cornwall on anti-submarine work.

Fort Rowner was used for Naval Stores and Lecture Rooms. Fort Grange was used to accommodate 250 RAF personnel and Fort Gomer was empty.

We moved into 4, Officers' Married Quarters on the Military Road in September 1952. Sue, Andrew and later Charlotte went to Alverstoke Church of England Primary School, while Stephen was only seven months old. The other Quarters were occupied by the Commander of the Station, a Group Captain, RAF, the Doctor, another Commander who was an Engineer and the Commander of Flying.

On the Station there was a Station Squadron, a Helicopter Squadron, an

Avenger Squadron, who were very noisy, a Training Squadron and various other odd aircraft.

At the 8 am Communion service on my first Sunday the Captain, one other Officer and a number of civilians were present.

At Morning Service there were . . . Captain and Mrs Hawkins, two or three Officers and their wives, no service families other than ours, no Ratings and about 150 civilians. Next to the Church, which seated about 350, was the Chaplain's hut. On Sundays the under eight-year-old children of civilians commenced in church and sat in the south aisle. They faced a side altar of carved wood, which had been the altar in the chapel of the old carrier, HMS *Furious*. About half-way through the Service these under eights trooped out of one door into the Chaplain's hut, while the over eights, who had been in the hut, came into church for the rest of the Service. They were under the command of Mr Fred Gaze, who was also the local Scout Master. The choir was composed of about 10 boys and 10 men and women, all civilians.

There was Evensong at 6.30 pm with about 15 present. Not a single Rating entered the church all day and this was the Station church!

The Verger was a Mr Donald Dunbar. He had been gassed in Flanders in 1916, invalided out of the Army and, paid for by the Army, became Verger of Siskin Church. In 1919 he remained as Verger paid for by the RAF ranking as a Messenger. From 1945 the Admiralty paid him as a Head Messenger.

My second Sunday was the Harvest Festival. During the previous week I was in the vestry office while the choir was practising, when one of the choirmen came in.

He said, "We have a Harvest Supper at Siskin in the hut, and as you and your wife are new, we invite you both as our guests," and he gave me the tickets.

I thanked him and said, "How many sailors are coming?"

He replied, "Tickets are half-a-crown each. They can buy them if they want them."

I said, "I will have half-a-dozen for Ratings now."

This wasn't appreciated and the Ratings weren't welcome when they did come. I wasn't off to a good start, especially when I told civilian Church Leaders that my first duty was to the Officers and Ratings of HMS *Siskin*.

Near the end of September I was informed that, from October until March, there would be no Evensong on the first Sunday of the month and I was to have a Children's Service instead. I wasn't prepared to accept their orders so I had to act quickly. I discussed the matter with the Captain who was deeply concerned that very few Officers and no Ratings attended the Station Church. With his support I announced that there would be a Family Service at 3.30 pm on the first Sunday in the month; that I would be making all the arrangements and also that I would inform the organist and choir which hymns and psalms I wanted.

I also visited the Leader of the Salvation Army in Gosport, told him of my difficulties and he offered his full support in anything I arranged. His Band would provide the music on this first Sunday and my organist agreed to co-operate.

The Salvation Army Band and their supporters, with a number of naval families, left their Citadel at 3 pm with banners flying and they also carried a huge sign stretched across their ranks which read 'Join us for the Siskin Family Service today at 3.30 pm.' Crowds followed them and there were about 400 people by the time we were seated in the church. With popular hymns we had a first class Service and the choir, in spite of being practically taken over by the Salvation Army, thoroughly enjoyed it. The civilians who ran the church were both astounded at the response and furious that I had got away with it. At the end I advertised the November Service which maintained the momentum. We were, of course, without the Salvation Army, but we had a large number of Service Families present.

After the first Family Service in October, Donald Dunbar and I walked into trouble. When we came to collect the hymn and prayer books we found about 200 of them torn. I went to the Supply Officer of *Siskin*, and told him what had happened.

He said, "No problem, Padre. We will return them to the Dockyard and exchange them."

We did, but unfortunately the same thing happened in November. Once more I went along to the Supply Officer and told him the bad news.

He said, quite rightly, "We really can't keep changing the books every month."

We sent this lot back and I promised it would not happen again.

One of the naval families attending the Family Service in November was a Lieutenant Hinckley, his wife and children. He worked in a huge drawing office just across the road from the church, with him were between 30 and 40 Chief and Petty Officers engaged in designing aircraft alterations to engines, wings and so on. After the destruction of the November books I asked him if he could help me by allowing his team to print, in large type on large sheets of stiff paper or cardboard, the Creed, the Lord's Prayer, some Collects, and Choruses.

He put the idea to them and they were delighted. It made a pleasant change from what they spent their time doing. Soon the whole office was engaged in this work for me with unexpected and extraordinary results. There was practically a religious revival. I was invited to the office for Chaplain's Hours and we had earnest discussions on the Creed, the Lord's Prayer and some of the Collects. Several men brought their children to the Family Services to see Daddy's beautiful work.

By the end of 1952, I was getting into my stride with a regular weekly programme. I conducted Morning Prayers with various units and parts of the

Station, including the Young Officers Training Class, the Fire Section and the Engineers where Lieutenant Commander Mike Hayward was always so helpful. He had a remarkable influence over his men and it was always for good. I took prayers with the personnel of the Control Tower, the RAF, the Galley, the Squadrons and others. During the forenoon I usually visited the unit where I had conducted prayers. There were also visits to be made to the hangars, the workshops, the offices, the Married Quarters and the caravan site. One of the RAF helicopter pilots was a friend of mine and he frequently gave me a flip round the airfield before depositing me at the particular unit that I wished to visit!

The first Sunday in December was Bible Sunday. I divided the scores of children into age groups up to seven years, eight to 10 year olds, 11 to 14s and over 14 years. They were to make something and attach a suitable quotation. Fathers could help and the response was astonishing. There were over 400 people present with crowds of fathers! We had rigged tables all round the Church to take the objects and texts of the various age groups. The Captain and Mrs Hawkins, the Commander and Mrs Ridley were the judges and we had prize-giving at the end of the Service. The prizes were Bibles, New Testaments and Prayer Books.

A group of the civilian women met the Captain afterwards to complain about what I was doing and not doing.

He said, "Look at this Service! Have you ever seen anything like it before? Have you ever seen so many Naval families?"

The answer was "No;" but they were furious and didn't like the way 'their' church was being taken over by the Chaplain and the Station.

The First Sunday in January 1953 came within the 12 days of Christmas so we had a Family Carol Service. This was in addition to the Station Carol Service, the Midnight Communion Service with over 200 communicants and the Christmas Day Services.

In February the Church was dark enough for us to have a Film Service, again with large crowds, while we finished off the season with a Mothering Sunday Family Service in March.

Captain George Hawkins, who had been such a strength and encouragement with the problems during my first months, left us. His place was taken by Captain H. C. Browne, who was the sole selector for the Royal Navy Rugger Team. He held a Heads of Department meeting every Monday morning. At his first meeting he reproved me, his Chaplain, for the noise the children made in church during their change over. By this time we were getting huge crowds for the Morning Service.

At his third meeting, he said, "I wish to apologise to the Chaplain for my remarks at my first meeting. I now appreciate the position and congratulate him on these heart-warming Services."

Perhaps I can jump the gun a little and say that by the summer of 1953, all the families of our Married Quarters were coming to church regularly on

Sunday mornings. Also we now had a study group meeting weekly at our own Married Quarter. This meant that Mary, besides having the four children to deal with, also had a fairly large group of people occupying one of the rooms for about an hour and a half, with tea or coffee at the end of the evening. A confirmation class was also under way, meeting either at the church or in our Quarter.

As with many churches, there was a Women's Sewing Bee. The one at *Siskin* also ran the church until my arrival, and the Chaplain's hut. The only person who could not get in on any night of the week was the Chaplain although it was heated and lit by the Admiralty and cleaned by my verger, Donald Dunbar.

There was a general whist drive in the hut every Monday evening. The Brownies used it on Tuesdays, the Cubs on Wednesdays, the Guides on Thursdays, the Scouts on Fridays and someone else on Saturdays. The proceeds of the Monday whist drives went to each of these organisations in turn. As I was determined to have the use of the hut one night a week, I decided it would be mine on Mondays. The various organisations could give up one night a month for a whist drive.

What I didn't realise was that the Monday night whist drive was for the whole of Gosport. These same people went somewhere else for a whist drive every other night of the week. When they suddenly found that their free hall was taken away from them on Mondays, there was the most awful row. The Mayor of Gosport approached the Captain of *Siskin* about it. The Captain told him that his Chaplain only wanted it one night a week.

"It is the Chaplain's hut," he said, "and he has my complete confidence to do as he sees fit." I didn't quite know what to do. I also felt that I was losing the confidence of the Captain. Mrs Browne his wife, who always attended the sewing Bee, asked if she might come to see me.

"Mr Pocock," she said, "You have been very patient and tolerant with the sewing Bee. If I were you, I should close it for a few months and open it again in the autumn."

I did, and we reached an uneasy truce for the sake of the church.

The North Sea floods, which particularly affected the east coast of England and parts of Holland, brought international fame to 705 Helicopter Squadron, which was based at Siskin. When the full extent of the flooding and tragedy in Holland became known, 705 Squadron, under the command of Lieutenant Commander Spedding, took off under Admiralty instructions for Holland and remained there for weeks carrying out their rescue work. Many Dutch folk were rescued from upstairs rooms or the roofs of houses. The choppers based over there were able to assist with moving people, stores and equipment when all else had failed. It was a great day at *Siskin* when the Squadron returned en masse to receive a rapturous welcome from the *Siskin* Ship's Company.

The Queen's Coronation was a very happy occasion with the whole

Station on leave for the day. The Wardroom celebrated with one of their delightful parties and an enormous firework display. Added to the general celebrations was the conquest of Mt Everest by Sir Edmund Hillary and Sherpa Tensing.

After the Coronation, came the Naval Review at Spithead. There is a railway, used for goods traffic, which runs from Fareham to Gosport Ferry, passing through Gosport itself.

The Queen came down this line by train to Brockhurst Halt, which is alongside the Siskin Church. The Halt had a fresh coat of paint and it was a great day for the Station Master. The Queen alighted at the Halt and drove very slowly down Military Road passing all our Married Quarters and the crowds of Naval families who had gathered to cheer her on her way. She drove as far as Stokes Bay where the Royal Barge took her off to the Royal Yacht *Britannia*.

Queen Victoria had this railway built because she had had a disagreement with Portsmouth Town Council and refused to go there. So this Branch Line took her from Fareham to Stokes Bay where she crossed to the Isle of Wight by ferry. It must have been rather fun to let a town council know just what you thought of them.

Most naval establishments put on a fine show on Guy Fawkes' Night when they use up all the previous year's flares as an extra to the fireworks.

We always thought that Siskin excelled in this spectacular show with crowds from all over Gosport to watch the display. The evening closed with all the messes celebrating with hot soup and drinks, which helped everyone on their way warm and satisfied.

The Admiralty Officers Selection Board was held from time to time in the *Siskin* Wardroom. It consisted of a Rear Admiral as chairman, a Captain, a Commander (S) a Lieutenant Commander (E), a Major Royal Marines and a civilian school master.

The following conversation is reputed to have taken place at one of these Selection Boards. The Candidate had been interviewed.

The Admiral said, "Has any Officer any further question to ask?"

The Lieutenant Commander (E) said, "Yes Sir. I would like to ask the candidate to give us his views on the various classes in society."

The Candidate said, "There is the upper class; the upper middle; the middle; the lower middle; the artisan and the working class."

The Officer said to him, "What am I, upper middle?"

The Candidate replied, "No, Sir, you are lower middle."

The Officer said, "How do you work that out?"

The Candidate replied, "You see, Sir, the upper middle are the Jaguar Belt. You only have a Vauxhall, so you are only lower middle."

The floor of the church had bare boards and, after the winter of 1952/3, I felt that some kind of covering was needed. In spite of the two old fashioned stoves, which Donald Dunbar lit every Friday afternoon and attended to on Saturday morning and again at about 10 pm every Saturday evening, the church was always cold during the winter months. Draughts came up through gaps between the floorboards. Donald Dunbar and I agreed that lino would do the trick.

The *Siskin's* Supply Officer arranged for someone from the Dockyard to come and measure the amount needed. They said about 3,000 square feet. This I was told was simply out of the question.

Sometime in the early summer, I went oveh to a church store in the Portsmouth Dockyard to pick up a lectern, some Hymn boards and other odds and ends. To get into this store, I passed through another store FULL OF LINO!

I said to the head storeman, "Who does all this lino belong to?"

He replied "Any establishment that wants it."

I said, "Thank you; thank you very much."

I went straight back to the Supply Office and said, "Will you please order 3,000 square feet of lino from the Portsmouth Dockyard at once." I added, "Ask them to deliver it to the Siskin Church immediately."

He said, "Certainly, Padre."

It arrived in a Dockyard truck about two days later, rolls and rolls of it. Dunbar and I got it all into the vestry somehow and locked the door whenever we weren't there. Next we ordered two lino layers from the Dockyard. These two men had only one job in life and that was to lay lino! They arrived on a Monday about two weeks later and it took them several days to get it all down.

We bought Donald Dunbar an electric polisher and he became very proud of his highly polished floor which was completed by July so we were ready for the coming winter. Some time in October, there was a high level meeting between the Chief Dockyard Stores Officer and the Supply Officers of the various Naval establishments.

When *Siskin* came up for discussion the Chief Officer said, "We are very sorry, but we shall not be able to supply any lino to your Chaplain."

The Supply Officer replied, "Cheer up, chum; our Chaplain has got your lino and had it laid, 3,000 square feet of it. It now has 400 chairs on it and on Sundays 400 pair of knees kneel on it. You will never get it back." How we and the whole station laughed when we heard the story.

It always distressed me that, with about 400 people in church every Sunday, whether sitting or standing, they were looking at four long lights, or panes of glass, in the east end of the church when eyegate is such a powerful weapon for teaching.

Stained glass windows are to teach the Faith, and I wanted the Crucifixion in some form for everyone to see and think about every Sunday.

One day I was talking to members of the Station Canteen Committee made up of representatives of the various messes of the Lower Deck. The Station Church came under discussion and I said I would really like to put some stained glass windows in the east end of the church.

When one of them said, "What for?" I said, "To teach the Christian Faith. That is what the church has been doing for hundreds of years, especially for people who cannot read." I added, "Any church worth calling itself a church has stained glass windows."

I don't suppose many of them came, but because it was their church, they thought it was a wonderful idea and they offered to pay, out of their canteen funds, for any windows I decided to put in, whatever the cost.

We got a designer down from London and I requested him to let us have an historic Crucifixion scene, 'There is a green hill far away,' which would cover the two centre lights. Later, I thought we could tackle the two outside lights. We placed the design on view somewhere in the Station and it was agreed that we should go ahead. The cost was to be £300 and they said they would raise that sum.

At the Dedication Service the Captain of the Station, Captain H. C. Browne, requested the Chaplain of the Fleet, Archdeacon Noel Chamberlain, to dedicate the windows. The large congregation included Rear-Admiral Torless from Flying Training. Many civilian members of the congregation came to me after the Service to congratulate me on beautifying the church, first with the lino and now with these windows.

There were six families in the Officers' quarters in Military Road, where we lived. Our immediate neighbours were Dr Foster the Station Doctor and Commander (E) Webber, Commander at Fleetlands. There were also Lieutenant Commander Nigel Ball and Lieutenant Commander Lough. All had families with children of the same age as ours so there was considerable activity going on between the quarters.

The Station Commander lived in the 'Red House' next to the church, while the Captain had a house near the *Siskin* Wardroom, overlooking Stokes Bay. Lieutenant Commander Lough and Lieutenant Commander Ball were in charge of the Young Officers Flying Course. One incident connected with those young men remains in my mind. A cadet was killed in a road accident. The funeral took the form of a Memorial Service which was attended by the lad's family, the whole course and representatives from the various sections of the Station. Afterwards I received a letter from the boy's brother. He said that he had come to the Service with a feeling of black despair, but that there had been such a spirit of determination and hope about the whole Service that in spite of himself, he left with a feeling of hope and almost cheerfulness.

*Lieutenant Commander Nigel Ball later died at Doulting in Somerset whilst we were at* HMS *Heron, Yeovilton. Pat, his wife kindly invited me to conduct the funeral. Then after cremation, I took the Committal Service from a helicopter, south of Portland Bill, while his ashes were committed to the deep by Commander Randle Kettle our neighbour and the Commander (Air) at Yeovilton.*

Throughout the year the church Services maintained their momentum and, by the summer, all the families in our Married Quarters were coming regularly on Sunday mornings. Through the support of these Officers and many others I was having Chaplain's Hours across the Station and had a Confirmation class under way.

For me, 1953 had been a turbulent year, and I just wondered whether Captain Browne wanted a change of Chaplain.

On Christmas Day, after the Morning Service, he said to me, "I would like to see you in the Mess at about 12.30 when I have finished visiting all the Messes."

I thought to myself, "Good heavens, he wants me to go, but I hope he doesn't tell me on Christmas Day."

Mary was at home with the children who all had measles so I went up to the Mess alone.

When Captain Browne arrived, he drew me to one side, and said, "I have received a Christmas present from their Lordships at Admiralty this morning."

I thought it was a rather odd remark to make, but I replied, "I am glad their Lordships have time to think of their Captains at Christmas."

He said, "They have offered me the job of Captain of HMS *Ocean*, a carrier in Far Eastern and Korean waters. Will you come as my Chaplain?"

I was so taken aback at his invitation, as I had half expected my marching orders, that I didn't reply for a few seconds.

Then he said quickly, "Don't answer now; go home and discuss it with Mary, and let me know at the Wardroom Cocktail Party on New Year's Eve."

I thanked him for the honour he had done me, and told him that my silence was due to the fact that his offer was so unexpected, as I thought he was going to sack me. We discussed his invitation at home; I had never asked for a job and had never refused one. Being a man under authority, we decided that I should accept and go.

At the New Year's Eve Party, the Captain told me that he had seen the Chaplain of the Fleet, who told him regretfully, "No." The Chaplain of the Fleet said that I had had a difficult time at Gosport with the civilians and that he wanted the whole thing seen through before I left. So that was that. We had become very fond of the Brownes, who had appreciated my problems in trying to get the Station church to be a real Station church. They had both given us every possible support.

Captain Browne was followed by Captain Ian Sarel. I think he was well briefed on church affairs and my battles. The church was still packed every Sunday, much to the annoyance of the Vicar of Forton, Gosport.

It didn't take long for Captain and Mrs Sarel to settle in and they were soon beloved of the whole Station. He at once gave me his full support, while Mrs Sarel went along every Wednesday to the sewing bee.

"Oh dear, it's always Wednesday," she remarked!

At the beginning of March 1954 a strange thing happened. We were visited by Dr Shelley who had run a Soldiers' Home in Famagusta, Cyprus in 1949, when I was serving in HMS *Liverpool.*

Now Dr Shelley was on his way to the Isle of Wight. He had lunch with us and then I took him down to the Gosport Ferry.

Just as he was about to leave, he said to me, "Are you going to Harringay?"

I said, "What's on at Harringay?"

He said, "Dr Graham, the American Evangelist is coming to speak there; you must take your men."

I said, "I know nothing about Dr Graham, but have seen his photo on the back of some magazines."

He said, "You must go. Goodbye."

A few days later we went on our Easter leave to Mary's Brother-in-law's Rectory at Fyfield in Essex.

The day we reached Fyfield a farmer called at the Rectory and said to Keith and Grace, Mary's sister, "I have a spare ticket for Harringay for tomorrow night. Any of you want it?"

I said, "Yes please, I would like to go."

I went and after the experience of being in an Evangelistic meeting of 14,000, of hearing the singing and listening to Billy Graham I decided that this was just what I had been waiting for. First it would give the *Siskin* congregaton a lift, if I could get them there; I felt that as a congregation we were rather stuck and second this sort of approach would have a real impact on the whole Station.

After the leave, we took cars to Harringay as a try out. In mine, I took Donald Dunbar and two others. A Warrant Officer took the Commander Bill Ridley and two others. The Meeting began at 7.30 pm.

We left at about 2.30 pm, and arrived safely at 7 pm. The Meeting finished at about 9 pm. We began the return journey three quarters of an hour later and, after stopping for a bite of food somewhere, arrived back at about 1 am. The next night, there was a Cocktail Party at the Captain's Residence, and the talking point was Billy Graham.

I well remember the Captain saying to Commander Bill Ridley, "Well, Bill what do you make of it all?"

He replied, "The whole thing is still with me. I can't forget it and I feel as if I have been whipped."

News soon spread round the Station that some of us had been to Harringay and I had the feeling that many would like to go. I told the Captain this and he said, that with his and the heads of departments co-operation, I could go ahead and organise parties for anyone who wished to go. This meant that those attending would have the afternoon off. With the Commander's consent a note about the Harringay trips was put in Daily

Orders. The Canteen Committee owned a bus, affectionately known as 'The Brown Bomber.' It was available for hire by anyone on the Station or any organisation or club at very reasonable charges.

The charge for a Harringay trip was £10 return so we charged 10/- a head. We organised one, or two or three trips a week and the lists of names came to me.

We usually left Siskin at about 2.30 pm for the Meeting at 7.30 pm. Owing to the enormous number of cars leaving after the Meeting it was about 10 pm before we were clear of Harringay. On the return journey we stopped at a café for some food which meant that we were not back until the early hours of the morning. For me it was a tiring and exacting trip. Not only had the numbers to be organised, but also the drivers. There were long hours, late nights, my usual work around the Station and of course Sundays. It is quite impossible in a few words to describe the events of those days and weeks or to pass on their spirit. I can only say that the impact of the Mission both on the Church and the Station was enormous. The whole spirit of our Sunday Services changed very rapidly. There seemed to be quality, depth and joy in the worship which we had not had before. The people told me that I was preaching with more confidence, conviction and fire.

There was a new interest in the Station Church and men who had never been before came regularly. While all this was going on our problems seemed to get left behind. With the Christian life of the church moving on to another plane we were getting numbers of people coming along for study groups, singing groups and prayer groups. The Scripture, 'Love the brotherhood,' took on another meaning. Service and civilian folk were now mixed together. Lots of people were in and out of our Married Quarters. Mary used to say that if serving cups of coffee and tea contributed to a place in the glory she would be, without any doubt, in the front row of the stalls.

Three or four weeks after I had taken Donald Dunbar to Harringay, I met Mrs Dunbar.

She said to me, "What have you done to Don?"

I said, "I haven't done anything to him; why?"

She said, "He is so different since you took him to Harringay. He is so happy. Thank you for taking him."

Donald Dunbar was a remarkable man in so many ways. He had served and suffered under Chaplains of the Army, the Royal Air Force and now the Royal Navy. Never mind the Chaplains, he loved Siskin Church. The Church had no Patron Saint and in Gosport, this wooden tabernacle which in turn had served the Army, the Royal Air Force and now the Royal Navy, was known as Dunbar's Church.

Besides keeping it swept and tidy, he looked after our two old coke stoves. This was heavy work, constantly carting coke and cleaning out. He was responsible for the cleanliness of the Chaplain's hut too, and in the winter months he always had a blazing fire burning in the Vestry. On his way down Military Road to the Administration Offices where he picked up the Chaplain's mail, he often called in at our Married Quarter. He doted on our son Stephen and called him 'My Boy.'

It was my custom to read Morning and Evening Prayer daily either at my Prayer Desk or in the winter in the Vestry. After a while he stopped work while I was reading the Office and joined me. Later on he regularly read the Lessons and finally he occasinally read the Service and I read the Lessons. There is no doubt that Harringay was a rich experience for him and after his return he did all in his power to encourage the *Siskin* matelots to go. When I left *Siskin* in April 1955, I went without relief as *Siskin* was to close down as an Air Station. The Lee-on-Solent Chaplain, The Rev. Frankie Leonard, a friend of mine, was going to care for *Siskin* during the rundown but I felt that the church building and the people were in good hands with Donald Dunbar there. He had developed into a fine Christian leader and could help and advise and pray with any young Rating who came along to the church. And they often did. We had become good friends over these years and I couldn't have wished for a more faithful Verger and adviser.

For one of our visits to Harringay a Chief Petty Officer volunteered to be our driver. Our party of 24 all had tickets, but when we arrived inside the building, there were no seats left. We were then ushered down flights of steps towards a basement.

I said to the steward who was leading us down, "Where are we going?"

He said, "You are going to an overflow meeting where you will hear everything."

I said, "No, that's not for us."

I called out to all our sailors: "Stop."

They all stood still.

I said to the steward, "We haven't come 88 miles just to hear. We have come to see the show. Please take us to the arena."

Another steward took pity on us and said, "Follow me."

Up we went again. He divided us up into twos and threes and sat us down on the steps of the various entrances where we all had a fine view of the whole stadium. I sat on the steps next to two Chief Petty Officers, one of whom was our driver. It was the usual moving meeting; wonderful singing by 14,000 people; the solos by Beverly Shea and then the simple stirring message by Billy Graham. Finally came his appeal for decision to serve the Lord. Men and women were moving steadily from all over the stadium to the front just below the platform where Billy Graham was standing. Suddenly one of our Chiefs stood up, picked up his burberry, gave me a steady look and was gone.

After Billy Graham had closed the meeting all those who had gone forward were taken below for counselling. The *Siskin* contingent mustered at the *Siskin* bus and we waited for our driver. At last he came, apologising for being so late. We arrived back at Siskin about 1.30 am. It was Friday morning.

On Sunday he was at the 8 am Communion. He told me he had been confirmed at the Boys Training Establishment, HMS *Ganges*, but had not been to church since he was seventeen and a half.

Later I said to him, "Why did you get up out of your seat and go forward?"

He said, *"It was my night, I had to go."*

From that day he became a tower of strength to our congregation. He lived on the Ratings caravan site which was further down from our Married Quarters.

Early in July he came to me and said, "Why don't you have an open air Evensong on our caravan site one Sunday instead of in the Church? If you agree I would like to read the Lesson and I will have the whole caravan site present."

We did.

On that Sunday afternoon Donald Dunbar and I carried about 150 chairs, a lectern, hundreds of books and a harmonium down to the caravan site in Naval Transport.

At 5.30 pm a Naval bus took the Choir, in their robes, down to the site and we commenced Evensong at 6 pm. True to his word, this man read the Lesson and had the whole site present. It was a perfect summer's evening and we were joined by the Sunday crowds returning on foot from Stokes Bay. We had familiar hymns such as 'Jesu, Lover of my soul;' 'The King of Love my Shepherd is;' 'Eternal Father, strong to save' and 'Abide with me.' The choir also sang one or two pieces on their own.

It was a remarkable and unexpected Naval Occasion with an estimated congregation of between three and four hundred.

On one trip to Harringay, we arrived for the Meeting at 7.30 pm and, when we reached the door, I discovered that I had 24 tickets dated the previous day. The uniformed Commissionaire at the door refused to let us in. Our driver that night was 'Paddy,' the Concert Hangar Manager. He was a hard-drinking Irishman who had no time for any kind of church and he had done me a real favour by driving us up that night. As I argued with this Commissionaire Paddy watched. The Commissionaire told me that the queue waiting to come in was a quarter of a mile long, four deep, and that those at the very back had come from Newcastle! I told him that I didn't care who they were or where they came from.

I said, "I have brought 24 sailors from the other side of Hampshire and we haven't come just for the ride."

There was a clergyman standing nearby listening. Unknown to me, he was one of the Committee which had invited Billy Graham to London.

He said to the Commissionaire, "Let Jack in."

That was enough and before the poor old Commissionaire had time to answer we were all inside. What happened to our lads at the meeting that night I can't remember. But something quite unexpected did happen. The next morning when I went along to thank Paddy for driving us, he said to me, "After seeing you battling for our sailors last night, I decided that you were genuine. From now on, if I can help you in any way, you only have to ask."

Dear Paddy. He became a real friend and couldn't have done more to help me and my work in any way he could. I learnt a lesson. One is watched all the time.

One week, we went up to the Saturday afternoon meeting. Our party included some of the RAF lads. At the end of the meeting, an RAF Corporal went forward. We waited for him in the car park. He eventually joined us and asked to be dropped off on the way back as he was going home to Bournemouth until Monday forenoon.

During the following week, I received a letter from the Minister of a Congregational Church in Bournemouth. He said in his letter that before the 11 o'clock Service an RAF Corporal from HMS *Siskin*, whose parents attended this church, came with them and asked for permission to address the congregation about his visit to Harringay. The Minister gave him leave and briefly he spoke of what had happened to him at Harringay. He told them of his response to Billy Graham's appeal, how he had gone forward and of his firm determination to serve the Lord. The Minister added that he spoke with such power and conviction that he literally set the congregation on fire, and that the whole spirit of the service was affected. On returning to *Siskin* he joined one of our groups.

In the Spring of 1953 I received a very late Christmas Card from an American Presbyterian Minister and his wife from Jerusalem. They had been very good to me and a party of sailors I took ashore at Limassol in Cyprus, where I also met Dr Shelley. These Americans had now moved to one of their Mission Stations in Jerusalem. A month or so later, I answered this card by writing a very factual letter stating what had been happening at Harringay in London with 14,000 a night for 12 weeks attending. I wrote of the effects at Gosport and of Dr Shelley's visit, whom they knew. A little later, I received a letter back to say that they had read out my letter to their church in Jerusalem. It had made a deep impression and had started a Christian revival. Things like this, the RAF Corporal's visit to his home church, Donald Dunbar's influence on his neighbours at Elson in Gosport, a CPO's witness to a whole caravan site and the change in a whole congregation were just a few of the fruits of these extraordinary days.

Dr Graham's final meeting took place at Wembley Stadium on Saturday, 22nd June. We took a full coach, the Brown Bomber from Siskin. This bus with HMS *Siskin* painted on the sides and on the bows had become a familiar sight at Harringay, causing considerable interest and inquiry; "What ship is HMS *Siskin*?" I personally had never seen a *Siskin*. It is a

258

small bird, with green and yellow plumage, with a black crown and chin. It is resident in the wooded parts of Scotland, Ireland and Wales and occasionally in Southern England so I hope to see one. (We have them in our garden at Walmer, 1984.)

One of the men anxious to go was a Petty Officer of the Station Photograhic Unit. We fitted him in. It is difficult to describe the impact of the singing of this vast crowd, the final address of Billy Graham and the closing Blessing by Dr Fisher, the Archbishop of Canterbury. It all made a lasting impression. He seemed to be under the spell of the Spirit and spoke what he felt and how he felt. When the end came, it seemed that no one was going to move and when we finally did it was with a feeling of deep joy and of great sadness; of joy for being allowed to be a small part of this wonderful movement of the Spirit; of sadness because we should not be meeting in this way again.

I suppose it was the experience of thousands that over the weeks we had been to a modern Pentecost. Who in that huge crowd will ever forget 120,000 people singing such moving hymns and songs as 'How great Thou art,' 'This is my story, this is my song;' and the wonderful setting of Malotte's 'Lord's Prayer.'

As we made our way out I heard someone call out, "There's Lovell Pocock with his *Siskin* boys. We heard you were coming."

It was the Rev. Will Sandey with a party of sailors from HMS *Vernon*. He always had a good following. We only met for a matter of seconds, but he had time to tell me that the Rev. Launcelot MacManaway was present with a party from HMS *Collingwood* at Fareham. I thought to myself, "Well done the Naval Chaplains. They are doing their stuff today."

Next I bumped into a Naval Officer, Commander Ronald Oliver. We had known each other for years. We had sailed the Norfolk Broads together in the '30s and served together in the Mediterranean in the '40s.

He saw me first, and said, "Lovell, where have you come from?"

I said, "We are all from *Siskin* at Gosport," and added, "What are you doing?"

He said, "I have been a steward every night for 14 weeks at Harringay."

He was serving at Admiralty at the time.

He just had time to quote Psalm 84:11 "I had rather be a door-keeper in the house of God than to dwell in the tents of ungodliness."

Then he was gone.

On the way back to Gosport, I was sitting next to the Photographic Petty Officer.

He said to me, "I wish I'd had the courage to go forward today and now it's all over."

I said to him, "You don't have to go forward to serve the Lord and to give your heart to God. You can do it anywhere, anytime."

He was in church the next Sunday morning and continued to come until he left for RNAS Eglington, Northern Ireland. I didn't pass him on to the Chaplain, but in November, I received a letter to say that this Petty Officer had asked to be prepared for Confirmation. This was 1954.

*Later in 1961, Bernard Briggs, who was with me at Yeovilton, flew to HMS Goldcrest, Brawdy, S. Wales to relieve the Chaplain there who was away for two or three weeks. While he was there, this same man approached him and asked him if he knew where Mr Pocock was. Bernard told him that we were serving together at Yeovilton.*

*The Petty Officer said to him, "Please tell him that I am still continuing in the Christian Way which I began when I attended Dr Graham's final meeting at Wembley in 1954."*

I should like to record here part of Dr Fisher's assessment of the Harringay Mission conducted by Dr Graham. He wrote in the Canterbury Diocesan Notes as follows:-

> 'That the Blessing of the Holy Spirit has been upon this campaign cannot be doubted. The mission itself has beyond doubt brought new strength and hope in Christ to multitudes, and won many to Him, and for this God be praised. I have spoken to many who went to Harringay. Always they have spoken of the simple sincerity of it all; the direct presentation of God's word to man in Christ; the restrained but deeply moving impression given by it. Always there was the same testimony to an experience which could injure none and which spoke to all in a movement of the Spirit, some portion of the wonderful works of God.'

In the aftermath of Harringay and Wembley, we were able to maintain considerable interst, both in the Station and outside, in Christian and church matters. We booked the Concert Hangar, thanks to Paddy, for three Billy Graham evenings. In September and in October we put on two Harringay evenings, which were recorded Meetings from the Harringay Mission.

In November we showed the Billy Graham film *Oiltown USA.*

Each of these evenings made a forcible impact on the Service and civilian personnel and there were about 600 people present on each occasion.

After the rather exacting and exciting summer months, we as a family were more than glad of our summer leave spent in Norfolk. We went first to West Runton and then to the village of Horsey, where we joined some friends in caravans and tents. While there we made good use of both the lovely beach and the Broads.

In the autumn, the Chaplain of the Fleet, The Venerable Noel Chamberlain, visited *Siskin* again. He told us that we should be returning to the RM Depot, Deal in April 1955. It was a great joy to be going back to

Deal and a tremendous help to know in advance. In November Mary and I visited Deal to find somewhere to live. We also arranged for Andrew to enter Tormore School, as a boarder, where Mr F. G. Turner was headmaster, and for Sue and Charlotte to enter Leelands as day girls.

The *Siskin* Wardroom was the scene of very many extremely happy parties and occasions. There were the annual Official Cocktail Parties, Christmas Parties, Children's Parties, the Coronation Party, the Guy Fawkes Night Party, Summer Parties and New Year Parties.

One thing that always surprised those of us who attended was how cheap they were per head. In fact, as time went on we seemed to pay less and less. I remember a Mess Cocktail Party in the autumn of 1954 and that was free, and our invited guests came free too. It seemed too good to be true.

Then it happened.

*Siskin* lunches were always good value and Officers of other Naval Establishments often came to *Siskin* for lunch, paying of course. There were numerous training courses going on all the time including helicopter, air traffic, fire fighting, young officers and so on. All those joining were checked in by the Supply Officer who received an Admiralty cash allowance for messing for every Officer while he was on his course. The audits of all accounts took place annually. If I have got my dates and facts correct, one of the schoolmasters who was auditing the Supply Officer's accounts asked to see receipts which no one had bothered about before. What he discovered was that the Admiralty cash allowance which was credited to the account of every Officer joining a course had not been cancelled when the Officer left the Station. This situation had been going on for two or three years, with the result that the Wardroom's balance grew larger and larger. So we, as members of the *Siskin* Wardroom, were able to have, first cheap parties and then free ones. For months and months this unique and wonderful state of affairs had existed and no one bothered to try to find out the reason. It would probably have continued except for this schoolmaster.

This astonishing and magnificent error reached the ears of the local Admiral and Admiralty. Overnight and, much to the disappointment of the *Siskin* Wardroom, all parties were stopped until further notice.

The sum added to the Wardroom account ran into thousands of pounds. The Wardroom general and the Wardroom wine funds were confiscated in an effort to recover this vast sum. The whole thing was considered to be a tremendous joke by the Navy in the Gosport area. There was a Court Martial with *Siskin* Supply Officers of by-gone days being brought from all over the world. I am uncertain of the final outcome. The *Siskin* Mess account and Wine account went broke but the Wardroom still had their New Year Party. Finally, *Siskin* lunches still remained popular and continued to be patronised by Officers and neighbouring establishments.

During the early part of 1955 we received a visit from the next Chaplain of the Fleet, The Venerable Darrell Bunt. *Siskin* had been in the news and we think he wanted to have a close look at us all. He spent the Saturday night in Portsmouth and came to preach at our Morning Service. After visiting one or two Messes, we were to have him to lunch. He was reputed to have a weak stomach.

Mary had made a soufflé for lunch and had left it ready while we went to church, all except Stephen, who was just three and who we judged would be better off left at home. We judged incorrectly. Somehow he got hold of the washing up mop and smothered it with soap powder. He then stirred up the soufflé with the mop.

It was too late for Mary to do anything. I forget what happened to Stephen. We just carried on. The soufflé was served in the normal way and we all ate it. None of the family was any the worse for this unique dish and we hoped that the Chaplain of the Fleet's weak stomach gave him no trouble. Perhaps, when Chaplains of the Fleet are on their rounds, they should think twice before accepting their Chaplain's hospitality. In this case Mary received a charming letter from him thanking her for the delicious meal. It made her feel worse than ever.


The Rev. Will Sandey, whom I met at Wembley, was serving at HMS *Vernon*, the Torpedo School in Portsmouth. He was a first class Chaplain and had a good following on the Lower Deck. While he was in Vernon, he and I sometimes joined together to put on something of an Evangelical nature for our sailors. I hope it was all worthwhile. I enjoyed working with him.

The Rev. Launcelot MacManaway, was Chaplain of HMS *Collingwood*, a large electrical establishment at Fareham. He was another fine Chaplain. He and I , with intervals of years in between, covered the Royal Marines Depot at Deal for nearly a quarter of a century. I was there '38/39 '44/48 and '55/57. He was there '42/44, and from '61/63. In 1961 he invited me back to preach at the Depot Centenary Service which was a magnificent occasion with Parades and Bands, not to mention the parties! Lance was a happy soul who worked hard and whose advice and friendship I much appreciated over the years.

With my departure from *Siskin* in April 1955, and with no relief, The Rev. Frankie Leonard, of HMS *Daedalus*, Lee-on-Solent became responsible for *Siskin*. I personally could not have wished for a more sympathetic Chaplain to care for my dwindling flock. Although he had a full time job at Lee, he put himself out to look after *Siskin*. He was a tremendous support to Donald Dunbar the Verger. I felt that we were all fortunate to have him there. He was at the right place and at the right time. Thank you, Frank.

The Rev. Peter Chapman joined the Service a few months before me, in September 1935, and was a very High churchman.

On one occasion, the Chapmans had been to one of our *Siskin* parties.

Afterwards, they came back to supper with us. Churchmanship was under discussion.

I remember Mary, who knew nothing about Peter Chapman's High Church ritual, saying to him, "Peter, surely you are not one of those people who ring the bells?"

He replied, "My dear, you are not yet educated, but I fear that as you are married to a Black Protestant, there is no hope for you."

Peter left the Service shortly before I did and I had a very warming letter from him on his departure.

Although The Rev. Jack Holland was serving only two-and-a-half miles away from *Siskin* at HMS *Daedalus*, Lee-on-Solent, we didn't see very much of each other except for an occasional lunch together. In fact, one saw very little of one's clerical brethren. I suppose we were all well occupied in our own parishes.

Jack's first ship was HMS *Shropshire* which he joined in 1935. She was a Chatham ship. My first ship was HMS *Woolwich*, which I joined in 1936, also a Chatham ship. Chatham ships had few rugger players compared with West Country ships which could muster two or three teams. Perhaps because of this paucity of rugger players, he captained the *Shropshire* team and I captained the *Woolwich* team. We used to meet on the so-called Rugger fields at the Marsa Malta. As the pitches were mostly shingle and stones with a few blades of grass, our knees and elbows used to get bruised and cut to ribbons.

While we were together in the Gosport area, Jack came to preach for me at *Siskin*. It was the Second Sunday in Advent, Bible Sunday. His text, the prelude to a powerful sermon, has remained with me over the years. It was from 2 Tim. 4:13. 'When thou comest, bring the books, but especially the Parchments.' He left the Service rather early to become the Chaplain of the Naval School at Holbrooke. I hope we meet again.

Commander (E) Roy Webber, one of our immediate neighbours, had a very difficult time while we were at *Siskin*. His wife Pru was in a Nursing Home at Midhurst. This meant considerable travelling for Roy. Thankfully, Pru recovered and when we were serving in that area in 1958, she was back to health.

Captain Ian Sarel, who was the first Naval captain to fly Jets, was an excellent Captain. Both he and his wife were a great help to me as Chaplain both on the Station and at the Church. Also he was always approachable.

I remember on one occasion when I knocked on his office door, he said, "Come in."

On entering I said, "I hope that I am not disturbing you, Sir."

He replied, "No, I am only reading a novel. I did in fact slip it into this open drawer when you knocked. I thought it was my Personal Assistant. (She was an Officer WRNS in this case). She is very strict with me, and I daren't let her catch me reading a book, so I keep this drawer open."

His assistant married an Officer serving at *Siskin* at the Station church. Afterwards, during the reception, Ian Sarel made a very amusing speech in which he mentioned the rough time the Bride had given him when she was his PA, and he wished better luck to the Bridegroom.

As already mentioned Commander Mike Hayward, Senior Engineer at *Siskin*, had a wonderful influence over his men, and nothing seemed to be too much trouble for them. If the day finished at 3.30 pm, and Mike was still flying, there was never a shortage of men to bring his aircraft in. As a result I had some good Chaplain's Hours in his department. He and Betty lived on Hayling Island, a long way away, but they used to make the effort and the journey to come to church on special occasions.

Many of the Petty Officers, if not most, went to HMS *Royal Arthur* at Corsham for the Petty Officers Course. The Chaplain there was the Rev. Bernard Briggs. As I went round the Station, the Petty Officers invariably remarked on their time at Corsham and how they enjoyed the discussions and lectures given by the Chaplain. For several, it was a first look at the Christian Faith and the Church with the results that they were more favourably disposed towards the Church at *Siskin*.

The following notes were passed to me by Bernard Briggs:-

> 'It was when the 1st Sea Lord (at the time the late Earl Mountbatten of Burma) was visiting *Royal Arthur*. He said that with the Chaplain of the Fleet's approval, he was going to ask me to give some talks to the Courses on the Christian Faith; and that they would be included in the 'Seamanship' lectures. He warned me that they would only succeed by popular vote. At the end of each course, the members voted on what was worth keeping and what should be dropped. He wanted to see whether I could get it voted on by common consent.
>
> My heart sank at such an impossible challenge, until I remembered this was just how Moses felt when he had to face Pharaoh. I also remembered that the Lord told him to seek help from others. Accordingly, I went to see my brother Officers and they promised wholehearted support. The brilliant Instructor Officer, the "Headmaster" of the Course, said that he could not see what I was worrying about as I had the best of all Messages to proclaim . . . how the whole world could be saved . . . he added that his Officers would get together and help and think out with my guidance a programme for my lectures.
>
> The Course which was about to leave took the Sunday Service; and so through God's grace, the support of my

brother Officers and the fervent prayers of my supporters and myself, Christian Worship was not only established, but I was able to preach the Gospel to every Course. Christian Lectures and Worship were voted back every time.'

Well done, Bernard; few of us could have measured up to this challenge.

Lieutenant Commander Jack Welpby and his wife had two boys aged eight and six. The younger one developed cancer of the liver and eventually died. It was a terrible tragedy for them, and indeed for the whole Station. Jack came to see me the day after the little lad passed away and it was the day after Ascension Day.

He said to me, "We realised that we were going to lose him. There was nothing anyone could do. As he had to go, what a wonderful day for him to go, on Ascension Day; wonderful for him and for us."

They were both in Church a few days later, and I remember saying to myself, "What remarkable faith and hope."

Such are my memories of a few, a very few of my shipmates; men I was privileged to serve with. So many of them went the extra mile and nothing seemed to be too much trouble in whatever they turned their hand to. It is a sad day, therefore when the end of a Commission arrives.

When the time came for us to leave *Siskin*, it meant that we should be leaving the civilian congregation for good, while there was a chance that we should be meeting and serving with some of the *Siskin* Ship's Company again. We had a lovely last Sunday at the Church. After Morning Service the congregation gathered in the now famous Chaplain's hut to wish us Godspeed as we set out for our next Commission at Deal.

The date of our departure was to be April 5th.

The day before, the 4th, we placed all our personal belongings, trunks, boxes, bits of furniture, bicycles, garden chairs and four hens in the garage ready for Pickfords' vans to collect in the morning.

We attached the caravan to the car, ready to move off directly Pickford's had loaded all our gear. The caravan had all our camping equipment, including an army bell tent which we had purchased from the Dolphin Canteen Naafi Manager for £5!

At 8 am on the 5th, the Dockyard Maties arrived to check the inventory and to take over the Quarter. This operaton took about half an hour. Then they departed and we were locked out and left sitting on the doorstep and in the garden to await the arrival of Pickford's van. To leave us, the whole family, just sitting on the doorstep, seemed to us both impersonal and inhuman. After all, the Quarter had been our home for two and a half years. However we all saw the funny side of it and so did our Naval neighbours. The Dockyard Maties didn't, especially as we weren't too polite to them I am ashamed to say. Fortunately the day was fine and as we sat and waited our Naval friends literally showered us with hot drinks and refreshments.

Finally Pickfords arrived and we watched them load all our gear into their van. They moved off. We followed and then as we came opposite the Church, Donald Dunbar was waiting to say his farewell.

As he was talking to the children, I thought to myself, 'Another Commission completed. For us and for these congregations it is now all past history.'

After the Blessing at the Morning Service we always sang our Naval Vesper for those serving at sea, 'Eternal Father.'

After Evensong, we sang an Evening Vesper which I had taught them and which they came to love.

> 'Light that groweth not pale with day's decrease,
> Love that never can fail till life shall cease;
> Joy no trial can mar; Hope that shineth afar,
> Faith serene as a star, and Christ's own peace.'

A postscript to the *Siskin* Commission.

*The spiritual movements in both Liverpool and Siskin were greatly helped by Dr. Shelley of Cyprus. In HMS Liverpool and at the Fleet Air Arm Station, HMS Siskin, I was holding the Gospel candle, but it was Dr. Shelley who lit it. It was the Scripture repeating itself. It reminded me of Philip in the Acts of the Apostles Chapter 8, suddenly turning up and preaching the Gospel to the Ethiopian as he crossed the desert. The man believes and is baptised and Philip is gone. Dr. Shelley appeared to help us in preaching the Gospel in HMS Liverpool, in the Mediterranean. Five years later, he turned up again to help us at Siskin, in Hampshire, and then, like Philip, he was gone again.*

# CHAPTER XIII

# Depot Royal Marines and School of Music at Deal 1955 to 1957

*In the autumn of 1954 we had learned that we would be returning to the Royal Marines at Deal in May 1955. We had much enjoyed our previous Commissions at Deal from 1944 until 1948, and the Chaplain of the Fleet's news seemed too good to be true. In the pre-war days I had been the Assistant Chaplain of the Depot and Chaplain of the Depot and Chaplain of the Royal Naval School of Music, as it was then called. So this would be my third Commission at the Depot.*

*I remember the Archdeacon had visited us at Chatham early in 1952 when I was Chaplain of the Dockyard. There we lived in one of the 'Stately Homes' in the Dockyard Terrace. 'Harmony Row' it was called! I had a very large and long study. I kept all my boots and shoes in a line along one of the walls, including a pair of black boots, highly polished, which I had used overseas when serving with the Royals and at the Depot during the years 1944 to 1948.*

*The Chaplain of the Fleet said to me, "Why do you keep those highly polished boots in that line?"*

*I replied,"For the day when we return to Deal!"*

*Now we were going.*

There were no Married Quarters in those days and no houses for letting in Deal, so we had to buy. Thanks to the help of the Abbey National Building Society, which to us seemed like a fairy godmother, we bought a house called Taplow at 1, Cornwall Road, Walmer. From the first floor bedroom windows we looked on to South Green in the South Barracks. There was plenty of room and it was to prove a very useful happy home and house.

We all arrived in Deal from Gosport early in April, 1955, and I was able to remain with the family while we settled into Taplow, our new home. Amongst our gear we had brought four laying hens. Two were lost en route, so the two remaining hens had to work overtime. After the Easter leave I had to return to HMS *Siskin* at Gosport until May and by the time I returned to Deal, all the children had started school.

The Depot consisted of South, North and East Barracks. South Barracks contained the Officers', Sergeants' and Corporals' Messes; the main Office Block, the Gymnasium, the Drill Pitch, and the Church.

North Barracks contained the Guard Room, the Supply Offices and Stores; the Globe Cinema; the Transport Section, the Naafi Recreation

Rooms and bar; the Men's Dining Hall and Galley; Five Officers' Married Quarters, the Detention Quarters, the Stables; a small Cemetery; the main Accommodation Blocks, the larger Parade Ground and Drill Shed.

East Barracks contained the Clothing Store; the Instrument Store and Repair workshop; many rooms for Musical Instruction and Practice; the School of Music Administration Offices; a large Practice Room and the disused Cemetery with goal posts for football practice and the large Parade Ground on which we rigged some tennis nets for the boys.

Outside the Depot, just across the road from North Barracks, were the Sick Bay and the Dental Surgery and the Depot School for the Recruits and Junior Musicians.

The function of the Depot, as I the Chaplain saw it, was to train Royal Marines Recruits from scratch for 26 weeks and then send them on to Lympstone for the second part of their training; to train Junior Musicians from scratch, 400 of them from the age of 14 years, and turn them into musicians in three to four years to serve in RM Bands in the UK, at Naval Establishments, in HM Ships and at Naval Stations overseas. There were also PT Courses, Small Arms Courses, Band Masters Courses and Bands to train from Commonwealth Navies.

The Commanding Officer was the late Colonel Bertie Lumsden whom I considered a fine leader, inspiring confidence and zeal. His wife Betty fulfilled her role extremely well. She had a happy disposition and got on well with all ranks and their wives. Colonel Lumsden gave me his full support.

The Second in Command was the late Colonel Dickie Griffiths who backed up his Commanding Officer well. He and I were old friends from the pre-war days and it was the third time we had served together at the Depot. I found him most helpful, happy and amusing!

Among the many extra duties which fell to the Second in Command was that of the Depot Piggery. The pigs were fed on Depot waste.

I still remember him saying, "Well, I'm just off to the Depot Piggery at Coldblow to get the pigs lined up and sized up for the Major General's inspection."

The Staff Officer was Major Ken Morriss who was quiet, efficient and helpful. He and I had two or three battles but they were always settled amicably and we were very fond of the Morriss family. Years later I had the privilege of conducting Sue Morriss's wedding at Haslemere.

The School of Music Staff Officer shared the same office as Ken Morriss. He was Captain John Lee. He was another Staff Officer with a quiet and deliberate manner. I remember on one occasion I entered the office while he was talking to someone at the Royal Marines Office in London on the telephone. A Royal Marines Band had returned from Malaya and apparently one of their number had become a Moslem. The telephone conversation seemed to revolve around how many wives a Moslem might have, how many this particular Bandsman had brought home with him and how many Married Quarters he might expect to be allocated!

Young men who were accepted for the Royal Marines arrived at Deal in batches. I never did discover where they came from . Perhaps they were told to catch a particular train from Charing Cross, so they might all arrive at Deal together. The new Squads seemed to form up every two or three weeks. Their first few days were spent being fitted for uniforms and being marched about the Depot by their Instructor. It always astonished me how quickly, how very quickly, they developed or caught the esprit de corps of the Marines. They came to Deal for the first part of their intensive training of 26 weeks and then moved on to Lympstone for the second part. Training came under the direction of the Adjutant, Captain W. B. Mansell (later Colonel), whose assistant was Captain Ronnie King.

Captain Bill Mansell set a fine Christian example, not only to his Staff and Recruits but to the whole Depot. Captain Ronnie King supported him well in his quiet way and was also a member of the Depot Church Choir.

It seemed to me that the whole of the Adjutant's Staff from the Adjutant himself, his assistant, the Regimental Sergeant Major, the First Drill Sergeants, the Instructors and the Rear Rank Instructors, to the clerks and the orderlies, worked at full pressure from morning till night. By the time the Squads moved on to Lympstone they all, particularly the Instructors, hoped that they would see the fruits of their labours.

As a result of the Daily Prayers on Parade and of the Religious Instruction in the Church to which all the Instructors brought their charges, I developed a close relationship with the whole of the Training Staff and they could not have done more to help me in my part of the "ship." The Cadets of the RMVCC and their training also came under the Adjutant and his Staff. This was evening work and it came at the end of a hard day on the Parade. It always seemed to me to be a real chore for them all, but they went through with it all with zest and enthusiasm. Major Martin Pound, now Colonel Pound, and his Staff from the Gym looked after all the PT training and the games. They also ran PT Courses for Royal Marines from all over the country. The Gym was always a hive of industry with PT Instructors working with either Recruits, Junior Musicians or those on the courses. The various pitches for soccer, rugby and hockey seemed to be in permanent use by someone. The late Captain Robson, another very old friend of mine, was in charge of the Stores and the Galley. Robbie to his friends, and I had served together overseas and I looked upon him as a very fine Officer. He was absolutely straight, good humoured and to me a wise friend. He was an unbeliever but we understood each other well and strange as it may sound it was a Godsend to have him at Deal.

Lieutenant Colonel Vivian Dunn was the Principal Director of Music for the whole of the Royal Marines. He had an office next to the Colonel on South Barracks, but was away a lot. He conducted the Depot Orchestra in Church on special occasions and conducted and introduced the Winter Concerts in the Concert Hall. He was a fine leader, a magnificent musician and an inspiring conductor.

The Officer Commanding the Junior Wing of 400 Junior Musicians was Major Louden Macleod. He and I had served together at the Depot in pre-war days and also in Malta.

He had four House Masters, Lieutenants, responsible for the four houses. There were about a hundred boys in each house. One was Lieutenant John Walter, a fearless Christian man who had an influence on the whole School. The Company Sergeant Major was Mr Jennings, another good Christian man who, although a keen Baptist, did all he could to help me at the Depot Church both by his influence and his presence.

The late Captain Ernie Ough was the Director of Training for the School of Music. He and I had served together at Deal in the pre-war days, in the years 1944 to 1948 and in the Mediterranean in the late '40s so we had a happy and trustful relationship.

Lieutenant Paul Whitehead, the Transport Officer, was another Christian leader while one of his section, Sergeant Rowing, was to become a regular lesson reader at Kingsdown Church in years to come.

When the Junior Musicians passed out and became Musicians, they joined 'M' Company. Their Company Commander was Captain Bill Fitzgerald. He and I served together in HMS *Liverpool* in the 1948/50 Commission. He had always been most helpful to me in arranging the Sunday Church Services so it was a Godsend to me to have this fine man as Company Commander of 'M' Company. His Second in Command was Lieutenant Tom Merritt, who had also been with us in the *Liverpool*. In fact I was his Chaplain when he joined the School of Music as a boy in 1938.

Lieutenant Commander Willie Golding RN was in charge of the Depot School situated in the Sick Bay area. He was a regular member of our Sunday congregation and joined our Depot Church fellowship when we got it going.

His RM writer was Lance-Corporal John Slegg who did a considerable amount of typing for me. Later, he was ordained, and became an Army Chaplain.

I realised that I was greatly blessed in having so many splendid Christian men around me. I was determined to do all I could to build up the church life of the Depot; to assist and encourage these men and to present the Christian Gospel not only to the Recruits and the Junior Musicians but also to the whole Depot.

During my first Summer term from May to August, 1955; (we work in Terms in Service Training Establishments, Spring, Summer and Autumn) I was trying to assess the type of men I was working with, what they were aiming at and what my own  particular role was in this exciting Royal Marines Establishment.

By the end of the term I was simply staggered by the magnificent quality not only of the Senior and Junior Officers that the Commanding Officer Colonel Bertie Lumsden had  gathered around him, but also by the quality of the Senior and Junior NCOs who made up the team. The CO drew a tremendous response from the Depot Staff and this spirit had its effect on the whole Depot including the Chaplain. So what was my task in the Depot?

Besides ordering the worship and visiting members of the establishment the Chaplain has to maintain his own spiritual life in spite of what is a very busy and exacting daily round and common task. He needs regular times of quiet, meditation and preparation, day in and day out. It was summed up in the command of the great Apostle, 'Maintain the spiritual glow.'

The Chaplain of the Fleet informed me that when I joined the Depot Royal Marines I would be relieving two Chaplains. Before I joined he had discussed church Services with the Commanding Officer and they had agreed on a few changes in the Services.

He suggested that the Sunday Services which he understood would  be acceptable to the CO, should be 8 am Holy Communion, 10.30 am Morning Service, 6 or 6.30 pm Evensong. On my arrival at the Depot at the beginning of May, the CO wanted me to commence the new routine at once, but as one of the Chaplains remained until the end of the month, we started in  June.

Church is compulsory for Recruits for six weeks and for Junior Musicians until they pass out aged 17 and a half.

Church was killed by the Parade which preceded the Service. However the Parade Staff, the RSM, the CSM, and the NCOs did all they could to cut the time of the Parade down to a few minutes. Often they were defeated by the Recruits and the Junior Musicians themselves, who arrived for the Parade late or untidy or both.

The CO informed me that Training Establishments were allowed to have one Church Parade a month or 12 a year. We worked out our programme with one a fortnight in the Summer Term for the benefit of visitors, holiday-makers and parents. In the Autumn or Michaelmas Term there was one for Harvest, one for Remembrance Sunday and one for the Boys' End-of-Term Carol Service.

It hardly needs to be said that the spiritual place of the Church in the life of the Depot depends very largely on the quality, the liveliness, the attractiveness and the meaningfulness of the main Church Service on Sundays. Therefore it was vital that care, time and thought be given by everyone concerned to each and every Service.

I found that dealing with the Recruits was far easier than dealing with the Junior Musicians. The Recruits were at the Depot for a matter of weeks under strict discipline and behaved well both at Instruction and in Church. The Boys, on the other hand, were at the Depot for between three and four years. They knew it all! They knew all the dodges whether it was cutting church, gym, the parade, games and anything else they didn't like. Also in church they could be as difficult as they dared to be, whether it was Instruction or Church Service. Sometimes I used to think that the Parade Staff, with whom I had a very happy relationship and many of whom were my friends, tended to forget that they had the easy job in being only with Recruits. Those of us who had the Junior Wing to deal with as well were brought to the end of our tether and further before the end of a week.

At 8 am Holy Communion we had a few Officers, wives and civilians.

One House of the Junior Wing attended. Those who wished to take Communion sat on one side and those who didn't were on the other. This gave the Chaplain some idea of the numbers when he was preparing the Communion. That House did not attend church again that Sunday.

It was easy to be taken in by the boys. One Sunday they arrived in good time, at about 7.50 am. They sat quietly, with heads bowed. I thought this was very encouraging. The boys were quiet and reverent. Perhaps they were reading through the Gospel for the day. On walking down the church between the pews, I discovered they were indeed quiet. It wasn't the Gospel for the day they were reading, but the *Sunday Mirror*, the *People*, the *News of the World* and the *Sunday Pictorial*. What is more, every boy seemed to have his own paper!

The 10.30 am Morning Service was a short Matins with plenty of well known hymns, or Psalms, one Lesson, a set of prayers and a sermon. The Service ended with the Royal Marines Prayer, the last verse of 'Eternal Father' and the Blessing. It lasted about 40 minutes. At 2.30 pm there was Sunday School for children of Royal Marines and a few others and at 6.30 pm we had Evensong.

The Headquarters Company consisted mainly of trained marines and they 'ran' the Depot. This company included the clerks, writers, police, cooks, the Guard Room personnel, the grooms, and the orderlies and so on. I found they were a most reliable group of men, hard working and conscientious. They could easily be overlooked, forgotten or neglected by the Chaplain but they received my attention.

There was a continual Ministry to the never ending Squads of Recruits training in the Depot before moving on to Lympstone.

Regular Religious Instruction took place in the church. Every squad came along once a week for nine weeks. I gave them simple Christian teaching based on the Bible, the Prayer Book and the Catechism. On the whole the Recruits listened well except when they fell asleep through utter weariness from their Parade work. It was my custom to visit a new Squad on their first night in the Depot. For some of them, for most of them, it was the first time that they had spoken to a clergyman. I used to visit the Barrack Rooms at least three times a week. During these visits I sought out the Christian believers, volunteers for the Choir and Confirmation candidates.

I didn't have the whole 400 every week but various classes or houses came to me in the church every two or three weeks. Visiting them in their rooms, in the Recreation Room and watching their games helped to win their confidence. I like to think that the Chaplain became the friend and adviser of many of them. We managed to gather a number of them into a Christian Fellowship. They also provided several choristers for the Depot Choir and I had a regular Confirmation class going on, sometimes there were two or three classes at once with different groups of boys.

But it wasn't only the boys one had to deal with. There was the Admin. Staff, both in the main offices and in the houses. There were the numerous music Instructors, Service and Civilian, not to mention the Bandmasters' classes and the various Bands forming up for ships and establishments both at home and overseas.

I tried to set aside one evening a week to visit the many families living in Married Quarters, in hirings and in their own homes. This visiting included both Officers and other Ranks. From the visits came Baptisms, Sunday School, Choir and Confirmation.

I made a point of visiting the Works Department and their people during working hours. Depot folk usually only visited the Works Department when they wanted something done. I made a point of visiting them when I didn't want anything! They were most friendly.

A large number of civilians attended the Depot church more in the Morning than in the Evening. To me, it seemed that they played a vital part in the Service by their regular presence, when the Depot personnel were continually changing, except the boys. Many of them told me that they prayed regularly for these important Sunday Services. I often had the feeling that this contribution, this spiritual contribution, underpinned, strengthened and hallowed our Worship. As the Commission went on, the Depot Christian Fellowship upheld our Sunday Services when we had on occasions five, six and seven hundred Service and civilian people present.

The late Mr Ernest Stride had been the Depot Church Organist in the pre-war days when I was the Junior Chaplain, so I knew him well. In those days he used to work in the Labour Exchange in Deal.

During the war he was with the School of Music and when I returned to the Depot in 1944, he was serving with a Royal Navy Band at Lowestoft. Thanks to the efforts of all concerned, we managed to have him drafted back to the Depot as a member of the Depot Band and as the Church organist. Only those who knew him can visualise the expression of horror on his face as he marched up and down North Barracks Parade ground, in a musician's uniform, clanging symbols.

He said, "It is worth it. Just to be back at the Depot Church organ".

So in 1955 it was delightful for me, on returning to the Depot as the Chaplain, to find Ernest Stride still organist of the Depot Church and also a Professor in the School of Music. He inspired every Service with his playing. He was respected both as organist and as teacher. For me to have this dedicated Christian man helping in our weekly Worship was an extra bonus.

The late Mr George Dowdell the Verger had joined the Royal Marines in 1899 as a Recruit. The Rev. A. Miller, our Free Church Officiating Minister had joined at the same time. George and I had served at the Depot together in the '40s so we were both back in our original jobs!

He was always at church early, looked after the heating and the cleanliness of the church. Having been a Royal Marine, he was rarely taken for a ride by the Band Boys, the Recruits or anyone else. He was utterly reliable and set a fine Christian example. In 1956, he was taken ill and died in Deal Hospital.

Again, we were fortunate, Mr Bert Featherstone, another retired Royal Marine who worked at the swimming bath, volunteered to take on the job as Verger. He proved like George Dowdell to be another real pillar of the church. Nothing was too much trouble for him and he was another man who did not allow the Band Boys to push him around. It was my custom, on arrival at the church every morning, to read Morning Prayer in the Lady Chapel. At first Bert Featherstone used to stop work while I was there; later he used to join me and occasionally read a Lesson. The late Rev. A. Miller, the Free Church Officiating Minister, was a Baptist. He was an old friend of mine. We used to play chess together in the '40s. As he was also a friend of George Dowdell, we were a good team. He was a magnificent Christian man and knew his job. He retired in 1957 and was relieved by the Rev. M. Tribe of Walmer Baptist Church. He was another conscientious Chaplain.

The Free Church Ministers came in about once a week to visit their flock.

The late Rev. Arthur Baker was my assistant and Officiating Minister. The Chaplain of the Fleet had told me when I joined the Depot that I would not be having an Assistant Chaplain, but that I could have a Church of England Officiating Minister to help me with the week-day Instruction, if I could find one. I was fortunate to find the Rev. Arthur Baker, Rector of Sutton. He was an elderly man of wide experience and threw himself heart and soul into the job. He came in three forenoons a week, so we were able to have Morning Prayer together before the battle commenced. I took all the Recruits' Instruction and we divided the Junior Musicians' Instruction between us. We endeavoured to join a different unit in the Depot for stand-easy and coffee each day. In this way, we managed to get round the whole place. Like me he found the boys quite a handful with 20 or 30 of them and very few really interested in what we were trying to put across. All too often he would come to the Vestry during one of his classes and ask me to come and deal with a boy who was proving a problem. They were usually the older boys who had been receiving the Chaplain's Instruction for two or three years.

The usual complaint was, "I am not really interested. I am wasting my time. I joined the School of Music to learn music and I want to get back to it."

Many of them, the vast majority, were quite happy to be quiet for half an hour and away from the normal rush of life. This sort of thing did us no harm. In fact it was salutary and we did all we could to make the Instruction varied and interesting with 'Fact and Faith' and other films. Also we enlisted the help of local laymen to give a talk on some Christian subject or topic.

Arthur Baker was a great help and support to me. We kept in touch with each other long after I had left the Depot and he and Mrs Baker came to my Institution and Induction as Rector of Ringwould by Dr Michael Ramsay, the Archbishop of Canterbury in 1967.

From the beginning of June, I was on my own. Arthur Baker didn't join me until September. It meant that I was literally at full stretch, trying to cover or fulfil the various aspects of my duty to man. I felt that I had been dropped into a whirlpool and just had to tread water as the whole thing went flying round.

There was not only the daily Instruction, but there were these great Services to prepare for on the Parade Sunday with ever increasing numbers attending. Besides the Officers, their wives and children, there was the regular civilian congregation plus several Squads of Recruits, scores of Junior Musicians and hundreds of visitors and parents. My aim at these Services was to have inspired singing, assisted by the organ, the choir and the Royal Marines Orchestra and a simple challenging presentation of the Christian Gospel.

I was conscious that the Depot Staff, Officers, NCOs and Bandmasters were all watching the new Chaplain. I suppose the Recruits and the boys took the Chaplain for granted. I had to try to give my best. Besides the usual routine of Prayers on the Parade on Mondays, Wednesdays and Fridays and the Instruction, there were the cells and the sick bay to visit regularly, Baptisms to arrange, weddings and their preparation, the very enjoyable social evenings and parties. We met someone who had been to one of the Queen's 'Meet the people' lunches. Those present had asked her how she arranged her daily timetable with so many State duties. She told them that she divided her day into three parts, the morning, the afternoon and the evening. Her plan was to give two parts to affairs of State and one to herself and her family. For example, if she had an Investiture or some interviews during the morning and a reception or dinner in the evening, then she kept the afternoon free. In this way, she said, she didn't become over-tired or stale.

I tried to work to this routine and, although it wasn't always successful, it was a good model to work to. I found the forenoons taken up with Instruction and with visiting the various parts of the Barracks. The evenings, or most of them, were taken up with visiting both inside and outside the Barracks, when possible. I didn't go in during the afternoon except to watch games. This gave me a certain amount of time with the family.

After a few weeks with his Squad the Instructor, who was Father and Mother, indeed almost God to his charges, could see a remarkable change in them. Long hours on the parade ground with the Adjutant and the Regimental Sergeant Major keeping a close watch on them had their effect. Instead of being a number of rather raw, scruffy individuals in an assortment of ill-fitting uniforms, they were transformed into a keen, proud and up-standing Squad, smartly turned out, marching about the Depot with their heads held high. The miracle had happened and I frequently envied the Instructor.

With the Chaplain it was different. He saw them for 45 minutes a week and in the mass for about 40 minutes on Sunday. My aim and purpose was to try to present the Christian Gospel and challenge in a simple, powerful and understandable way. Many of those arriving at Deal had no spiritual teaching whatsoever, and so much of the Instruction to Recruits was very elementary. I was aware that the Gospel seed falls upon all kind of soil, human hearts, and I had to see that it grew. How they responded was their concern not mine, although I hoped and prayed that many of them would decide to serve the Lord. I hoped that when they left Deal they would not be just Royal Marines, but Christian Royal Marines.

My predecessor had arranged a Service of Holy Communion for the Junior Musicians every Wednesday at 7.30 am. As he wished that they should take Communion fasting, he arranged with the Galley that those who attended should have a late breakfast at 8.15 am in the Dining Hall. During this late breakfast they were able to sit and watch the rest of the Juniors being inspected by the Colonel! The CO asked me if I would look into this Wednesday Communion as he was not happy about it. The same day Mr Dowdell, our Verger, told me that there were some funny goings on at the Wednesday Communion when there was a huge congregation. He told me that not only did everyone who was Church of England come along, so that they could have a late breakfast, and miss the Parade, but the Baptists, the Salvationists and all the rest of the Christian religions also enjoyed sitting quietly on their behinds in church before partaking of this late breakfast!

A day or so later, Captain Robson of Supply asked me if I would look into the Wednesday Service as his Galley were 200 breakfasts short every Wednesday. It turned out that the young monkeys had a double breakfast every Wednesday. They all had one on the way to church before their fasting Communion then, after sitting quietly for half an hour, they had another on the way back, with the added joy of watching the CO's Parade functioning without them. One has to hand it to them for their efforts.

Throughout this term I had been finding out who would join some kind of Church Fellowship which would be open to all ranks. I felt that we needed a forum where the Christian men could share their problems of Faith and where we could discuss the whole question of presenting Christianity to the Depot. There was considerable potential but it needed mobilising to see what part each individual could play.

At the beginning of August the whole Depot went on leave and the Pococks, as was their custom, winged their way to the Norfolk Broads to their tents and boats.

We had now settled into the routine of one House of the Junior Wing coming at 8 am each Sunday for Communion and then they were free for the day. At this Service there were also a few Officers and civilians. The members of the Church Fellowship made a point of coming to either the 8 am Service or to Matins and it was a great source of strength to me to have them there. Amongst the Recruits it was rare to find anyone who had been confirmed so this Service did not really touch them.

Except for the Parade Sundays, Harvest Festival, Remembrance Sunday and the End-of-Term Carol Service, the Sunday Morning Services were poorly attended by both Officers and NCOs. Having said that, the majority of married Officers, their wives and children set a good example. Many of these, I felt, came for the benefit of their own children who really seemed to enjoy themselves.

The Parade Services were always inspiring occasions, chiefly thanks to the wonderful contribution made by the organ and orchestra. Lieutenant Colonel Dunn always saw to it that the orchestra was in good form and their music and playing was of a high standard.

Harvest Festival was held in September and was a happy affair. The church had been decorated by the wives. The produce was sent along to Deal Hospital.

On Remembrance Sunday 1955, the Mayor and Corporation of Deal attended with various Service organisations including the Royal Marines Association, The Royal Naval Association, the British Legion, the Coast Guards, the Women's Service, Youth Organisations and others. There was also a full turn out of Officers, NCOs, wives and civilians.

From the Chaplain's point of view, the preparation for this Service was not all plain sailing. I had to insist with the Staff Officer that all regular members of the normal Sunday morning congregation had seats allocated to them. I had to point out to him that I considered it was sheer hypocrisy to give seats to all and sundry, whether it was the Mayor and his party or anyone else, and not to care for the regulars. After considerable pressure on my part the Staff Officer agreed that I was right, although he told me that Remembrance Day was a national occasion.

For our preacher I had invited a very old friend of mine, the Reverend Martin Harvey, DSC, MA, of St Lawrence College, Ramsgate. In pre-war days we had sailed the Norfolk Broads together and, during the war, he had been an RNVR Chaplain. He filled the bill well and was on the wavelength of the congregation.

It was difficult for anyone attending the Service not to be moved when such hymns as 'O God our help in ages past' 'How bright these glorious spirits shine' and 'O valiant hearts' were played and sung.

The End-of-Term weekend was a great occasion for the Junior musicians. Hundreds of parents arrived and found accommodation locally.

First they all attended the Christmas Concert in the Globe Cinema in the Depot. They followed this by attending the Carol Service on the Sunday morning. The whole of Junior Wing were in the parade while the boys also provided the orchestra. With plenty of singing and well known carols the term ended on a high note from the church point of view.

The biggest chore of the term was writing the 400 End-of-Term reports for the Juniors. This exercise at the end of July had caught me unexpectedly. However by this time I was getting to know the boys so I had my own ideas about most of them. Whatever I wrote on the report, I also wrote on the back of a card index. It really meant shutting myself away for about two days in the Vestry or at home while I worked through them all. After the first term I made up my mind what I intended to write on the report before I looked to see what I had written the previous time. I was encouraged to discover that my next assessment of the boy tied up with the previous one. The Chaplain always received the reports first and so he had no chance to see what anyone else had written. Having done my stint I passed them on to Captain Jeff Beadle, Second in Command of the Junior Wing.

After about a year, I suggested to him that he should have them first and then he could pass them on to me.

He said, "Good heavens, No. I read what you have put down and then I put the same thing down in different words!"

I officiated at the Daily Prayers for the Recruits and Juniors on North Parade on Mondays, Wednesdays and Fridays. They consisted of a hymn led by the Depot or Boys Band; a reading from the Bible read by myself, the Adjutant, an NCO, a Recruit or a Junior; and the prayers.

Prayers for the Headquarters Company took place in the South Drill Shed on Thursdays. It was my custom to take the whole of the Service, reading from the Bible and prayers. If by any chance I was away I left everything ready for the CO, Colonel Lumsden. It happened that on one occasion when I had arranged for him to take them he too was called away suddenly and so it fell to Lieutenant Colonel Dickie Griffiths to officiate. Unfortunately Colonel Lumsden had not passed on to him the prayers and reading which I had left ready. It was the first time the Clerical Mantle had fallen on him. All he had at hand was a Prayer Book. Apparently his taking of the prayers was a unique and never-to-be-forgotten occasion. He opened the Prayer Book at Morning Prayer and read all the Sentences of Scripture. He continued with the Exhortation, the General Confession, gave all the Old Soldiers the Absolution and continued with the Lord's Prayer and Responses. He then read the Venite and called it a day. The Royal Marines of Headquarters Company took it in their stride. There were no complaints, but the following week I was back and so they had to put up with Iron Rations!

Church flowers were arranged by the ladies under the guidance of Mrs Lumsden the CO's wife, and Mrs Dowdell, the leader of the Depot Mothers' Union. The latter met once a month for Corporate Communion in the Lady Chapel.

I invited all those in the Depot who were interested in some kind of Church Fellowship to come to our house one evening early in September. I was hopeful that those who came would be a cross section of the Depot and the Junior Wing.

In this I think that we were fairly successful. There were representatives of the Parade staff, Officers and Non-Commissioned Officers, members of the Transport Section, Naval Officers from the School, two or three Depot NCOs and Marines.

From the Junior Wing we had Officers, Senior Non-Commissioned Officers, Instructors, L/Corporals and Musicians. Added to all these a few civilians also came along.

If I could unite all these people, they would be a powerful force for the Church, the Kingdom of God and the advance of the Christian Faith in the Depot.

Those whom I had approached and were willing to come were quite new to this sort of thing and to this approach, but I was convinced after my experience at HMS *Siskin*, RNAS, Gosport, that the possibilities were enormous, and must be seized at once.

I had invited Mr Bernard Pratt, a master at Tormore School to open our first meeting by talking to us on Christian Leadership.

We then got down to discussing what we should do, when and how! We tried to think through our aim and purpose. The discussion was very frank and open and I think everybody made some contribution. In the end we decided that all members would suport the Depot Church Services, and the

Chaplain, by attending at least one of the Sunday Services. Next it was considered vital that we meet to discuss our Christian Faith and its relation to our everyday life in the Depot. I was asked to initiate discussions on the Bible. They also asked for guidance on how to pray and what to pray for. It was agreed that these meetings for the Fellowship should take place once a month and we provisionally fixed the dates and place of meeting for October, November and December.

Several felt strongly that we should meet for prayer during the week and that we should start at once. We decided that we would say Evening Prayer on Mondays, Wednesdays and Saturdays each week. I was to lead this on each occasion. I suggested that after the Third Collect we should pray for one or two parts of the Depot each evening. When I suggested that one of them might take these prayers, they asked me to continue for the rest of the term and after that someone else might take my place. We were to meet in the Lady Chapel of the Depot church at 6 pm and members were asked to do their best to attend at least once each week.

There was a strong feeling that we should make one supreme and combined effort each term to present the Gospel to the whole Depot in a dramatic way. They asked me to put forward suggestions.

Naturally, this first term was in the nature of an experiment. We were very much beginners and learners.

During the next term one of our Officer members came to me and said, "I have always tried to live as a Christian, but I have always been rather ashamed of my Faith. Now, I am afraid no longer. I wonder why?"

I said, "Because the Spirit is with us."

A few days later a Senior NCO said to me, "I have been a believer ever since I joined the Service, but rather a secret one. Now it's different. I am no longer afraid and I want people to know. What's happened?"

I said, "The Spirit is with us and He gives boldness."

The Fellowship became a great strength to me on the non-church parade Sundays. They could always be relied on to be there.

At Evening Prayer I was surprised at the way the Fellowship came along. They seemed to value this short time of prayer, reading the Bible and meditation. Our prayers covered Depot personnel, the Recruits, Junior Wing, the Training Staff, the Families, Works department, the Sunday Services and all involved as well as one another. On Saturday evenings our civilian friends always attended and by the end of term these Evening Prayers were firmly established.

To me it seemed almost out of this world that our Fellowship should include Capt. W. B. Mansell, the Adjutant of this great Establishment. He was a man who had such far-reaching influence on the young men joining the Royal Marines, the Marines of the future, the Training Staff and indeed the whole Depot. I had already decided that I must assist, support and try to strengthen him for his great work. Then there was Company Sergeant Major Jennings of Junior Wing, again, a man exercising vast influence over hundreds of boys. He needed my prayers too. There was a House Master, the Head School Master, Officers in charge of Units, Instructors on the Parade and in the School of Music.

The possibilities of this fine team of Christian men were enormous and I was determined to do my utmost to inspire their Christian service and witness.

The brickwork of the Chancel was red in colour but it seemed that the mortar had been mixed with salt water and the salt had stained the bricks. We asked the Works Department if they could repaint the bricks and they were doubtful. However the fact that we had His Grace, the Archbishop of Canterbury coming to preach in January, 1956, turned the scales and they carried out the work during December.

At the October meeting of the Fellowship, I told them that I had the 'Fact and Faith' film *God of the Atom* for a night in December and also that I had booked the Globe Cinema for it. On the night there was a fair number of both Recruits and Junior Musicians, about a hundred altogether. The impact was good and those present would, in my opinion, come to the next one and probably bring some of their friends with them. The Depot personnel were, however, conspicuous by their absence. This meant that we were making no impact on the Depot whatsoever. We would have to think again and persevere. The Vicar of Sholden, the Rev. C. G. Stapley was always most interested in what the Church Fellowship was trying to do in the Depot and always enjoyed coming along to our meetings.

The Christmas leave period was a very happy time for the many families in the Deal area, with parties of all sorts for all ranks and for all ages.

To me, the two outstanding Services at the Depot Church were the Midnight Communion and Carols with about 200 Communicants, and the Family Carol Service on Christmas morning with the families of Service personnel and civilians present in great strength.

On the altar we had an illuminated Nativity Tableau which had been made by Mary, my wife. We kept it there for the 12 days of Christmas.

The New Year of 1956 was to prove a momentous one in the life of the Depot Royal Marines at Deal with several outstanding events. For those of us involved with the Christian Faith there was never a dull moment.

The Depot Church had been opened for Worship and dedicated to St Michael and All Angels by the then Archbishop of Canterbury on Sunday January 26th 1906. We invited Dr Fisher, Archbishop of Canterbury to preach at the 50th Anniversary on 26th January 1956. The Commanding Officer, Colonel Lumsden saw to it that all Officers with their wives and children, the Depot Staff, every Recruit and every Junior Musician was informed of this great occasion. The result was that the Archbishop was presented with an enormous congregation. Colonel Vivian Dunn conducted the orchestra. Ernest Stride excelled himself at the organ and so, with plenty of well known hymns, the whole Service was an inspiration to all who were there. As Chaplain I conducted the Service and, when introducing the Archbishop, was able to tell the congregation that it was one of his predecessors who had opened our church 50 years ago to the date and day. I was also able to inform them that our Cross bearer, Mr Arthur Kidd, had been at the opening service in 1906 as a member of the choir.

The Archbishop opened his sermon by saying how deeply moved he was to be present on this unique occasion, and how encouraging it was to him, as Archbishop of Canterbury to be involved in such a remarkable service. He went on to say that on this same day, after lunch, he was going to Dover to dedicate a chapel in the prison.

Half to himself and half to the congregation he said, "I wonder what the difference is between this place and a prison?"

The 400 Junior Musicians, who of course think the Depot is a prison, cheered wildly! The Archbishop, although he had been a Headmaster of a public school, was obviously taken aback.

Slowly he removed his spectactles, leaned over the pulpit, glared at the boys and said, "I wonder how many of you will end up in prison?"

And so they all cheered again.

When the noise died down he put his head back and roared with laughter. And everybody laughed! He gave us the simple and straightforward message 'Fear God and keep His Commandments.'

After the Service he met Mr Ernest Stride, the Choir and Mr Arthur Kidd, and Colonel Dunn introduced members of the orchestra. The Archbishop visited the Corporals' Mess, the Sergeants' Mess, the Officers' Mess and then had lunch with the Colonel who was kind enough to invite Mary and me to join them. At this luncheon we had pancakes for the sweet. The Archbishop asked if it was Shrove Tuesday. We all laughed. It was 26th January and a Sunday! This from the Archbishop of Canterbury!

It was obvious that his visit made an immediate impact on the whole Depot, and I could only hope and pray that it would be lasting. He met many of the Officers and NCOs and their wives and they were deeply impressed by his human approach. We gave him a book he asked for by which he would remember his visit.

As we commenced this new term and year, I was conscious of the fact that the whole life of the church would depend on the support I received from the Depot Church Fellowship. I had no need to be anxious as to whether the members would rally round.

From the very beginning of term several of them turned up for Evening Prayer in the Lady Chapel and they never wavered. As time went on I asked one or other of them to lead us in the prayers after the Third Collect. These were for the various parts of the Depot. I had prepared the prayers for them to use. Besides this spiritual power house I knew that my friends at HMS *Siskin*, Gosport were praying that the blessing we had received would be passed on to Deal.

At the first Fellowship meeting in January, we fixed the dates for our meetings in February and March. They wished for teaching on Prayer and Worship.

We also discussed the formation of a Junior Wing Church Fellowship, under the leadership of Lance-Corporal David Squibb. Thanks to the support of housemaster Lieutenant John Walter, CSM Jennings and Band Master Peter Sumner among others, this effort got off the ground and continued over the next two years.

The Evangelistic effort aimed at the whole Depot was to be the powerful Billy Graham film *Souls in Conflict* in the Globe Cinema, RM Depot on Friday March 1st 1956. The evening was introduced and closed by the Rev. Maurice Wood, DSO who was Vicar of Islington and who had served with the Royal Marines during the war.*He is now Bishop of Norwich.*

After talking it through with the CO, he invited members of the Officers' and Sergeants' Messes and their wives to give the Chaplain their support on this occasion. I think many of them wanted to see Billy Graham, besides having a look at what the Chaplain was up to!

The Fellowship made this particular evening a priority in their prayers. The Rev. Maurice Wood informed me that, on the night of the showing, there would be 10 different groups of men and women at prayer in his parish with the sole object of supporting him and his presentation of the Gospel.

The Rev. Clifford Davies, the Chaplain of the RM Camp at Lympstone, who used the same film a few weeks later told me that over 60 groups of men and women in the west country would be praying for the RM Depot, Deal on the 1st March.

The Adjutant did his best to get support from the Parade Staff and the Recruits.

Lieutenant Walter, CSM Jennings, B/M Sumner and Lance-Corporal Squibb all did their best in 'J' Wing. I did my best with the various congregations. In the end, we issued tickets to civilians wishing to attend with all sorts of people coming in, writing in or phoning in for tickets.

There was a full house of 400 people in the auditorium and the sound and the picture were excellent.

Before we commenced, I introduced the Rev. Maurice Wood, and turned the evening over to him. He spoke to the audience briefly and told them that he would speak to them again before they left at the end.

The story of the Vicarage family, the characters which were portrayed, and the Harringay meeting with Billy Graham's sermon were all enjoyed by the audience. Rev. Maurice Wood had no difficulty in keeping their attention for a few minutes at the end.

First he asked the Chaplain to come and stand below him on the floor of the house in front of the first row of seats. This was quite an ordeal for me!

He said that we had all enjoyed this particularly unusual film. He invited anyone who wished to know more about the Christian faith to come and stand with the Chaplain. About 30 came out.

"There will be another Billy Graham film in the autumn," he said, and added, "Except for those standing in the front with the Chaplain, you can all go home. Good-bye and good luck."

After the cinema had emptied, he led all those who had come forward over to the Depot Church.

First he addressed us all then, after a prayer, he spoke to everyone there for a minute or so, which gave me time to note down who they all were.

Those present were quite a cross-section of the Depot. There was one Sergeant who later obtained commissioned rank in the Corps. There were two musicians who never looked back in their Christian Pilgrimage. Later, after leaving the Royal Marines Band Service, they were ordained into the Ministry of the Church of England. Also amongst the 30 were Royal Marines and Recruits. The Recruits were leaving for the second part of their training at Lympstone within a few days and so I was able to pass them on to the Rev. Clifford Davies their new Chaplain. There were also a few civilians, two or three who were quite unknown to me but who had managed to get a ticket for the showing of *Souls in Conflict* in our cinema.

Next day I happened to meet the CO and he asked me whether I was satisfied with the evening. I thanked him for his support and he added that the Christian Gospel had gone across to many in the Depot in a new and unusual way. He hoped that many would respond to its challenge. I thought this was a tremendous thing for the CO of this establishment to say. I replied that not only the film, but Maurice Wood, had stirrred many and time would tell what the result would be. In the immediate future much would depend on me, the Chaplain!

When we met together, I thanked the Fellowship for the support and encouragement they had given me. They said there had been widespread discussion of the film and they felt that, for the first time, the Christian Gospel had rocked the Depot. I would certainly like to think so.

I had arrived for the summer term of 1955. Then came the Michaelmas Term with the beginnings of a Depot Church Fellowship. Now I had come to the end of the third, the Lent or Spring Term. What was the position?

I realised that the Church Fellowship, though not very strong numerically, was united in Faith, Hope and Charity. In Scripture language it was indeed 'The Beloved Community' and 'The Household of Faith.' By their regular attendance at one or more of the Sunday Services, their regular support of our weeknight Evening Prayer in the Depot Church Lady Chapel, and by their enthusiastic backing of our evangelistic efforts, they had been a great encouragement to me personally.

There was considerable discussion amongst Officers and NCOs as to the value of some of these great evangelistic films and meetings, but they had no suggestions as to what I could do instead.

I had to complain to the CO occasionally about the lack of leadership and Christian example by the Officers and NCOs in the matter of Divine Worship. I had to remind him that we were a Training Establishment and that meant more than square bashing. He was always sympathetic and did his utmost to help and encourage me.

About a week after our film I received a letter from a Methodist Minister in Deal, who wrote that one of the fringe members of his congregation attended the film, *Souls in Conflict,* and was converted. In future would I please let him know when this happened to members of his congregation. There was no message of thanks for giving one of his congregation a good shake up! What would have happened if we had turned him into a full-blooded non-believer I wonder?

In May, the Bishop of Dover, the late Dr A. W. Rose came to the Depot for Confirmation. The candidates were chiefly from the Squads and Junior Wing. There were a few choirboys, one or two from the Sunday School and two adults. He was a very good friend of the Depot. I had seen him conduct such a service there in 1939 and several times in the years 1944 to 1948. It must be a very exacting Service for a Bishop. This time Dr Rose told us that he had been taking Confirmations for 21 years. He said that he tried to make each one seem like the only one he would ever take. By doing that, he didn't become an automaton or a machine. He always seemed to be at home with us and he told me how much he appreciated not only the visits, but the way he was looked after. I was able to pass on the Recruits who had been confirmed to Clifford Davies at Lympstone.

The purpose of the Queen Mother's visit to the Depot in June 1956 was to open a new large block of living accommodation in North Barracks.

Some months before the event, the CO invited comments from the various departments of the Depot regarding the visit. I suggested that this new Block should be treated as a ship and should have a Commissioning Service. For some time, he resisted the idea. Whether he sought advice from higher authority or the Chaplain of the Fleet, I never discovered, but one day he sent for me and told me to prepare an appropriate Service for the occasion. Ernest Stride and I had already discussed a Service and had one ready!

Her Majesty's visit took place on a perfect June day. The whole Barracks were assembled on North Parade, facing the new block. A dais had been erected nearby on which the Queen Mother, her party, the Colonel and a few other celebrities were to stand. Between the dais and the body of Royal Marines stood Colonel, then Major, Martin Pound, with his Guard.

The Depot choir, were under the direction of myself with Ernest Stride and the Baptist Minister, the Rev. A. Miller. We were all drawn up alongside the dais. The ceremony commenced with the Service. The choir sang Psalm 23, unaccompanied. Mr Miller, looking very smart in dog-collar and black gown, read the Scripture. I took the prayers and then, led by the Depot Band, the whole Parade sang the last verse of 'Eternal Father strong to save.' After the Blessing we all sang the first verse of the National Anthem and the choir walked off.

The Queen Mother inspected first the Guard and then the Parade. Then the CO led her to the door of the new block and she declared it open. After inspecting the building, she was taken to South Barracks.

On South Green a number of Officers and their wives were presented to her, including Mary and myself. She visited the various Messes before lunching in the Officers' Mess with us all. In the afternoon, she had some function to attend near the Walmer Lifeboat and finally left for London in a RN helicopter.

Mr George Cansdale, the Zoo Man, was well known to the general public, especially the children, owing to his TV programmes with animals. Added to this particular gift with God's creatures he was also a Christian Evangelist.

I managed to persuade him to come and see us. For his visit, he chose the 'Fact and Faith' film, *The Prior Claim*. I remember that 'King Cricket' was ruling on South Green and the Drill Pitch at the time, with lovely weather; I had my doubts whether Depot personnel would want to go into the Globe Cinema. I had booked the Globe for the dog watches and was pleasantly surprised at the response. There was no doubt that George Cansdale was a box-office attraction. There were not only Recruits and Juniors present, but also a number of parents with children. All were anxious to see the 'Zoo Man.' He introduced the film and afterwards spoke very simply and plainly to his audience about our Christian Faith.

During these weeks Mr George Dowdell was taken ill and died after two or three weeks in Deal Hospital. His passing was a tremendous loss, not only to me personally, but also to the church and the whole Depot. He had been a good friend and adviser to me; absolutely reliable and he never minded going the extra mile. On one Sunday morning, when we both arrived at church at 7.30 am for the 8 o'clock Service, we discovered that there were no altar flowers. We went round the church garden, helped ourselves, filled up the vases with a lavish supply and said nothing. We were both much amused to hear members of the congregation say how well the flowers had been arranged. *Recently in 1981 I received a letter from a friend of mine who knew George Dowdell. I would like to quote from his letter. He says,*

286

*"Remember me very kindly to Mrs Dowdell. Her husband was one of the Saints; a typical Anglican, quiet and unostentatious, but deep in faith". What better testimony can one require than that?*

The Adjutant and his Staff, with the Band outside the church, myself and the organist and the choir with the orchestra inside the church, all did our very best to see that each Parade Service was of a high standard and of good quality. Literally hundreds of visitors attended these Services. I often received letters of thanks from those who came along. Let me quote from one letter.

> 'Dear Mr Pocock, We are indebted to Mr Waters the NAAFI Manager for suggesting that we attend the Parade Service yesterday, which we did. My wife and I greatly appreciated worshipping with the large number who attended that Service and I should like to say that the way you presented the Gospel Message in the Service and the sermon deeply impressed us. Realising the tremendous possibilities of the work which you and the Christian men around you have been called to amongst the nation's young men, you may be assured that we shall remember to pray for you all.'

As a result of our discussions on Prayer the previous term, the Fellowship asked me to introduce a Card which would give them a prayer for each day and so unite us in our thoughts and prayers. This I did and gave one or more copies to each member. We had them printed just in time, because some of our original members soon received Draft chits and left us. As we heard that several were leaving or about to leave, we decided to give each of them a little book of daily Bible Readings for Morning and Evening called *The Daily Light*. These little books were to prove a help to many.

During this term Band Master Peter Sumner taught the whole of the School of Music The Lord's Prayer to Malotte's wonderful setting. They all came to the church for three practices. The Officer Commanding Junior Wing, was rather cynical about it and hoped that the Juniors weren't wasting their time. However, at the Service itself the 400 Juniors, under the direction of Peter Sumner, rose to the occasion and gave the vast congregation a splendid rendering of this setting. It seemed to me, from my Prayer Desk in the Chancel, that the whole congregation was deeply moved by their inspired singing. Mrs Betty Lumsden, the Commanding Officer's wife told us all afterwards that it was the most moving experience she had had in the Depot Church. It certainly made a deep impression on the congregation and was a good note on which to end the term. We decided that they should sing it at the End-of-Term Service.

The Depot did not, of course, stand still. Squads were moving on to

Lympstone at regular intervals and new Recruits were joining all the time. In the Gym, courses were continually coming and going. The Kingsdown rifle range seemed to be well booked up with courses, and the School of Music had their regular Bandmasters classes. The Concerts every fortnight were in full swing.

Juniors were continually being rated up to Musicians while new boys, who had passed their audition conducted by Captain Ernie Ough, joined the School. So the Depot routine continued as usual with each department keeping up their momentum.

Whether the following incident was connected with Captain Mansell, the Adjutant I can't be sure. It certainly happened to one Adjutant while I was serving at Deal. The Major General from Eastney used to inspect Deal once a year. His inspection of Recruits included half a dozen kits which were laid out in the Drill Shed. The Adjutant was naturally anxious that the Recruits who had the best kit lay-outs should have theirs inspected on the day. He addressed all the Recruits and told them that it didn't matter who the General chose, the ones he, the Adjutant, had chosen beforehand would lay out their kits. The inspection of the Squads took place during the forenoon. The General chose the six Recruits who were to lay out kits and said he would inspect them in the Drill Shed after lunch.

While the General was at lunch, the six the Adjutant had chosen laid out their kits in the Drill Shed and waited. The General came along and inspected them with the Adjutant watching.

As he walked away, he said to the Adjutant, "The lay-out of the kits by these Recruits is first-class."

The Adjutant said, "Thank you, Sir."

The General then added, "But it is a strange thing. The Recruits I chose all had red hair!"

And he walked away.

At the November Fellowship, Major General Haffenden came to speak. On this occasion the Adjutant and Mrs Mansell kindly invited us to use their married quarter for the meeting. Because of the identity of our guest speaker, we had a number of Officers and NCOs present who didn't usually come. Names elude me but I think several senior and junior NCOs came for the first time.

Evening Prayer continued three times a week and the members appeared to appreciate these times for quiet and meditation.

Our film for this term was another Billy Graham one called *Oiltown USA*. The Rev. Clifford Davies, the Chaplain at Lympstone, came to introduce and close it for us. He had an easy way with the Recruits and was able to meet those who would be joining him in a week or so. Two Musicians responded to his talk and as a result joined our Fellowship.

At the end of one period of Instruction, the class went to the gym. It so happened that I kept one Junior for a minute or so. I then sent him on to the gym. About 10 minutes later a Corporal came to church to inquire whether I still had this boy.

"No," I said. "He left several minutes ago."

The Corporal departed.

A few days later I saw this boy and said to him, "Did you go straight to the gym when you left the church the other day? They were enquiring after you."

He said, "No Sir; I don't like gym so I went and lay on my bed for half an hour!"

The Junior Musicians looked down on the Recruits who appeared to spend all their life Square-bashing. If there was an opportunity to take the micky out of them, they did so. I think I am right in saying that Recruits were not allowed out of Barracks for the first four weeks. When they went to Deal, they had to go in uniform and march in good Royal Marines fashion. It was not unusual to see them marching three or four abreast. The Juniors are aware of this.

On one occasion, a Junior in uniform marched behind one of these lines of Recruits who, by this time, obeyed orders immediately. When the Junior called out from behind, "Recruits halt," they all halted! He informed them that he had been sent to take them back to Barracks. He turned them about, marched them back down Canada Road, and having turned them into North Barracks, he beat it!

At one of the Corps Reunions at Deal, I chatted to a Royal Marine, now in a civilian job, whom I had served with many years before in Egypt. He was very talkative, and I said, "How is life treating you?"

He said, "Fine, better and better; I am in the same profession as you are."

I said, "Is that so; what do you actually do?" (I wondered whether he was a Vicar or a Hospital or Prison Chaplain.)

He said, "I am an undertaker!"

I said earlier that the Instructor is like God to the Recruits. He is probably one person of the Trinity, but there are two others. The Number One God is the Old Soldier in the Barrack room.

I visited a Barrack Room one evening, and the Old Soldier called out, "I wish I was a Naval Chaplain. Nothing to do all day and take your time in doing it."

The Recruits stopped cleaning their uniforms and all looked at me.

"All of you come here a minute," I said to them.

They gathered round me.

I said to the Old Soldier, "You come here too," which he did.

I then directed my remarks to him and said, "There is nothing, nothing in the world to stop you being a Naval Chaplain, but you have got to have one thing which I have, and you have not."

He said, "What's that?"

I pointed to my head and said, "You have got to have it up there."

I then left the Barrack Room, and I heard a great laugh. I had no further trouble with the third person of this Trinity. This particular Old Soldier became a friend of mine. He realised that I had given as good as I got so he did all he could to help me.

Later, I heard that my standing amongst all the Recruits had gone up because I had seen off this particular member of the Trinity, the Old Soldier in this barrack room.

During this Commission there were several of what the Prayer Book calls 'Occasional Services' which remain vividly in my mind.

I baptised Mark, the son of Captain William and Mrs Jane Mansell, and Linda, the daughter of Lieutenant James and Mrs Alice Mason. At the Mason's reception, which was held on the first floor room of their hiring in Victoria Road, there were about 20 to 25 people in the room. It is probable that the room was not meant to take the weight of this number but, when we were about to commence the tea party, the floor began to give way. There was dead silence for a few seconds and then we all moved out into the hall with the baby and the cake! We went downstairs to another room in the basement to continue the festivities!

I also baptised Paul, the son of Captain Jeff and Mrs Connie Beadle. Captain Beadle had come over to the church to enquire about Godparents. I told him that the baby boy should have one Godmother and two Godfathers who should be 'trusty men and true.'

He said, "We are inviting you to be one of the 'trusty men and true', so I was one of Paul's Godfathers and have been able to keep in touch with him, or at any rate his Father over the years. *In 1983 I officiated at the wedding of Flight Lieutenant Paul Beadle.*

I was privileged to officiate at the wedding of John and Ann Walter in the Depot Church on Saturday August 27th 1956. It was an extremely happy afternoon.

Major Macleod was relieved as OC Junior Wing by Major A. D. MacPherson . . . 'Sandy' to his friends. It was the third time Sandy and I had served together at Deal; first, in 1938/9; next in 1944 and now in 1957. It was splendid to have Sandy and Norah, his wife, back again at Deal and it did not take them long to enter into the life of the Depot; added to this they both gave me full support at the church. *Years later their son who was at Sherborne School bicycled over, more than once, to see us at RNAS Yeovilton where we were serving.*

Major Wainwright, affectionately known as 'Skinny' Wainwright, was retired and had lived in Walmer for many years. He was a regular and welcome member of the Mess. He used to travel vast distances by moped. On one occasion he went to visit some friends in Birmingham and while there, sad to say, he died. The funeral service took place in Birmingham and cremation followed. His ashes were returned to us at Deal and, at his wish, were to be scattered in the Downs. The Memorial Service took place in the Depot Church. The Rev. W. H. Maundrell, who had been Chaplain of the Depot from 1928 to 1933 and Rector of Ringwould from 1935 to 1940, gave the address. The Commanding Officer read the Lesson and I conducted the Service.

A few days later, Major Willie Aston and I went out in one of the Deal boats to scatter the ashes. It was a fine day but blustery, and the sea had a fair lop. When we were some way out, the Coxswain brought the boat into the wind and, as I said the words of Committal, Willie Aston emptied the ashes from the casket into the sea. At this very moment a huge wave hit the boat slewing her round and the ashes, instead of falling into the sea, blew all over Willie.

All three of us were thrown over the thwarts and I heard Willie Aston say, "Blast old Skinny. He's won in the end!"

A room just inside the Cavalry Gate, opposite the main offices, was allocated to the Chaplain and was used by the Depot Brownies, the Guides and the Mothers' Union. The walls were bare except for two or three large posters which I had hung on them. One of the posters read, 'What kind of a Churchman are you? A pillar on the inside or a buttress on the outside?' Willie Aston was the Barrack Master and part of his job was to visit the various rooms and stores in the Depot. I met him one day when he had been into the Chaplain's Room.

He said, "I have just carried out my inspection of the Chaplain's Room. I am a buttress on the outside!"

At the beginning of 1957, the Right Reverend S. W. Betts was consecrated Bishop of Maidstone in Canterbury Cathedral. The Bishop of Maidstone's Diocese, or responsibility was Bishop to the Armed Forces of all three Services. He was an old friend of mine. He rang me up from Canterbury and said he was free on Sunday February 2nd and would I like him to preach at the Depot. So he came and preached his first sermon as Bishop in the Depot Church of the Royal Marines.

Our friend, the Rt Rev. A. W. Rose, the Bishop of Dover, retired in the Spring and his place was taken by Bishop Meredith who had previously been the Vicar of Bognor. He came to the Depot for Confirmation in May. It was his first Confirmation as Bishop. So we had two firsts!

During the summer Bishop Betts, and The Rev. Professor Charles Moule, Professor of Divinity at Cambridge University, a mutual friend, paid me a call at the Depot. They came to the church and listened while I gave Religious Instruction to about 30 Recruits. On this particular day I was talking about parts of the church, namely the Lectern and the Prayer Desk. These lads were sitting in the rear three or four pews of the church, in the nave, and I was standing in the pew in front of them with my back to the altar. The Bishop and the Professor sat on seats behind the Recruits. I sent a lad up to the Chancel about 20 yards away and told him to kneel down at the Prayer Desk. The other I sent to the Lectern and told him to read the Bible. I suppose I was about 15 minutes talking to them, telling them that at the Lectern, where the Bible is, God speaks to us; while at the Prayer Desk, where the Prayer Book is, we speak to Him. A few questions followed taking, I suppose, another 20 minutes. Then I told them that we were fortunate in having our Bishop with us and that I was going to ask him to speak to us. I went to sit with Professor Moule and saw to my horror that the two Recruits I had sent to the far end of the church were still there. One was kneeling at the Prayer Desk, the other was standing at the Lectern. I had completely forgotten them. I recalled them and there were no repercussions either from their Instructor, the Adjutant or from their MP!

Later they both joined the Church Fellowship at Evening Prayer in the Lady Chapel.

Afterwards the Bishop said to me, "You have all taught me something tonight. You have turned your Evening Worship into an Evangelistic Meeting by the way you all prayed for various parts of the Barracks."

I came to Deal for the first time on October 1st 1938 as the Junior Chaplain and Chaplain to the RN School of Music. The Rev. W. R. F. Ryan was the Chaplain and he was very good to me. I had an extremely happy nine months before going off to sea as Chaplain of the 11th Cruiser Squadron aboard HMS *Ceres*, whose war station was the Northern Patrol in the Arctic.

I returned to the Depot as Chaplain in 1944 and remained there until 1948.

Early in 1947 we placed two small Stained Glass Windows in the west wall of the church to depict the Nativity and the Presentation of Our Lord in the Temple. In September of that year we invited Mr Ryan to return to the Depot and to dedicate these two windows during the Sunday Morning Service. He appreciated being asked and enjoyed meeting a number of old friends.

In 1957, when I was back for the third time, we put in two more windows just inside the north door and in the corner of the nave. These depicted Our Lord as a boy in the carpenter's shop and His Baptism in the River Jordan by John the Baptist. I told the Commanding Officer what had happened in 1947 and we decided to invite Mr Ryan back again to dedicate these two windows. I also informed the Chaplain of the Fleet what was happening. I received an immediate reprimand. He informed me that it was the prerogative of the Chaplain of the Fleet to dedicate windows in Service Chapels. I replied that I would cancel my invitation to Mr Ryan and he, the Chaplain of the Fleet, could do the job instead.

He replied, "Mr Ryan can do it this time, but in future . . ."

So in September, Mr Ryan came for the Harvest Festival and dedicated the two windows at the same time. I told everybody that I had been with Mr Ryan at the Depot in the '30s, and that we had invited him back in the '40s. Now he was back again but by 1967, I would be 'on the beach' myself! I think he found it a very moving experience to be back at the Depot.

Talking to the CO one day about George Dowdell, he said, "What a pity we can't do something practical to remember him. Have you any ideas?"

I said, "Yes. What about a small stained glass window?"

We had worked out a plan to depict the Life of Our Lord on the north side of the church in windows and the Acts of the Apostles on the south side. The plan was in fact never carried out.

I said, "If we could raise the money, we could have the very last window in his memory. It would be St Paul on Mars Hill."

So we raised the money and had the window put in. The CO decided that he would unveil it and that I should dedicate it.

The dedication took place at a Morning Service with all the Recruits and Juniors Present and many others too. The CO spoke very movingly from the Chancel Steps about George Dowdell; from the time he joined as a Recruit in 1899 until his death as the Verger of the Depot Church in 1956.

I remember him saying, "We are here today, to honour this Christian gentleman. Our purpose in the Depot is not to turn out just Royal Marines and just Musicians but Christian Royal Marines and Christian Musicians."

Mrs Dowdell, and her friends who were present, joined the Commanding Officer and myself as we went to the rear of the church. The whole congregation stood while we unveiled and dedicated the window.

In November 1957 I heard from the Venerable Darrell Bunt, Chaplain of the Fleet, that I would be returning to the Fleet Air Arm; to HMS *Daedalus* at Lee-on-Solent, Hampshire. I was to change places with the Chaplain at Lee, the Rev. Frank Leonard, an old friend of mine.

I felt both thankful and happy that Frank Leonard would be taking over as Chaplain at Deal. In 1942 I had followed him in the Second Royal Marines Group, an organisation of about 10,000 men. In 1955 he had taken over HMS *Siskin*, RNAS Gosport, from me as Chaplain.

So, once again, we would be on the move, home, schools, caravan, tents, and all the rest of the clobber!

This move meant that we should never return to the Royal Marines Depot at Deal again as I had only two more Commissions to do before retirement.

I had been fortunate and blessed to have served at Deal three times. First, in the pre-war days from 1938 to 1939. Secondly I was there from 1944 to 1948 when I returned with the 2nd MNBDO from overseas.

We had been delighted to be continuing with the Corps and they were to prove busy and exciting years at the Depot. One of the celebrities in one of the 'Y' Squads was David Steel, now Leader of the Liberal Party. He was in 'Y' 8. This reminds me of a recruit I knew in 'Y' 7.

At our Church Services in the years 1956 and 1957, all sorts of things had appeared in the Offertory bags from the Band Boys. Such things as matchsticks or nails or messages. One read, 'Hard luck, Parson; better luck next week'. On another occasion there was a note, 'I owe you 6d'. This one appeared in the National Press and received a practically world-wide fan-mail. Gifts of money arrived because God had been robbed. One letter I received was from a 'Y' 7 Recruit, now working in Rhodesia. It read 'Am appalled to read of the behaviour of RM Recruits or Band Boys. If the boy was out here I would whip him. It would never have happened in my day!'

Thirdly we were back again for these years, 1955 to 1957, when I was Chaplain of the Depot and also of the RM School of Music.

If one adds the years with the MNDBO and the years with the RM at Chatham, it meant that 12 years of my Service life had been spent with these fine men. We, as a family, had become very fond of them and amongst them had made many life-long friends.

Now that my Commission was ending; and the word 'Commission' is significant as it means 'Mission together'; I decided to ask myself what I had set out to do in the Spring of 1955. How had it all worked out? Had I maintained a straight course or had I strayed? Had the sails been set properly to catch the Wind of the Spirit or were they all over the place, flapping here and flapping there?

The Church Fellowship, the Church Crew, had worked like beavers, and their faith, happy spirit and determination, while never flagging or wavering, had sustained me continually. Often we were overtaken by the many events which crowded upon the life of the Depot. We endeavoured to buy up the moments and make the most of the endless opportunities to forward the work of the Gospel, the Kingdom and the Church, day after day.

Looking back, a Commission is always full of precious memories; of people and events. The same set-up will never happen again. There were the tremendous Church Services, Parade and non-Parade Sundays, the Corps Remembrance Sundays: the Annual Remembrance Sundays: the 400 Junior Musicians singing Malotte's setting of the Lord's Prayer: the huge crowds turning up to the Evangelistic films in the Globe Cinema: the inspiring Church Fellowship with its sense of purpose and its earnest discussions about our Christian Faith and how to present it to the Depot: the never failing chore of the term's 400 Reports: the exhausting periods of Religious Instruction with the Juniors: the continual enthusiasm and courtesy of the Parade ground Instructors: the long discussions on the Parade while watching the Bands practising, with Ernie Ough and many others: the impact of Archbishop Fisher's visit on the Depot: the goodwill and support of so many Officers and Other Ranks who were not really Churchmen: the Queen Mother's visit with its sense of pride, joy and happiness: the glorious evenings sitting in the Pavilion on the Drill Pitch watching and listening to the Bands.

Then there was the Tattoo on South Green which took place in a thunderstorm, and the retired Royal Marines Officer who, sitting on a hard seat in the open, yelled out, "Thanks very much everybody for a first class performance, both the tattoo and the thunderstorm. We have only come 80 miles and so we should dry by the time we get home again!"

It is not for the Chaplain to decide how he has done or not done. The CO's assessment of his Chaplain is sent off in his Confidential Report to Admiralty and to the Chaplain of the Fleet. This may affect his future appointments. The Chaplain's work and character is also summed up by his Mess Mates and the Depot Staff but this can only be superficial.

In the end the Chaplain, to whom has been committed the Eternal Gospel and the oracles of God, and who is the 'official agent' of the Gospel in the Service, will be responsible to God and to God alone.

St Paul tells us that every man's work will be tried by fire at the Judgement seat of Christ.

As one translator puts it, "There is going to come a time of testing at Christ's Judgement Seat, to see what kind of material each builder has used. Everyone's work will be put through fire, so that all can see whether or not it is of lasting value, and what was really accomplished."

This is the severity and terrifying price of being a Christian Minister and Believer.

Five or six Royal Marines and Musicians whom I knew at Deal in the years 1955 to 1957 are now serving in the Ministry of the Church of England. Several Chaplains, the Rev. Frank Leonard, the Rev. Lancelot MacManaway and I, were their Chaplains so I suppose we all had a hand in their decision. They included Lance-Corporal John Slegg; Musician John Watson; Musician Barry Sucksmith; Musician P. A. Self and one or two others whose names I regret to say I have forgotten. So far as we know, they have all been a credit to the Royal Marines, the Church of England and to ourselves.

During our first few days at Fareham, while we were unpacking and before I joined HMS *Daedalus* at Lee-on-Solent, I had time to think through my approach to my new appointment.

I went back in my mind to Devonport where, as a youth, I used to cycle with other boys to Mount Wise to watch the Fleet either entering or leaving harbour. We used to sit at the foot of Captain Robert Scott's Memorial; 'Scott of the Antarctic'; and I used to read and re-read Lord Tennyson's words, carved on the Memorial.

'To Strive, To Seek, To Find, But Not To Yield.'

I never could understand what he meant. Now I understand quite clearly. As the Lord himself said, "No man having put his hand to the plough, and looking back, is fit for the Kingdom of God."

# CHAPTER XIV

## HMS Heron, the end of an era, 1960 to 1963

*After leaving the Depot RM in January 1958, we were 2½ years at HMS Daedalus, Lee-on-Solent. In June, 1960, I was appointed to HMS Heron, the Royal Naval Air Station at Yeovilton in Somerset. I had just two days with my predecessor before I took over.*
*There were about 2000 Officers and Men on the Station as well as wives and children.*

On my first Sunday there were only two people present at the 8 am Holy Communion Service. At the Free Church Service at 9 am there were six. This was taken by a visiting Officiating Free Church Minister, and the Roman Catholics went into Yeovil by service transport. At our main Morning Service at 10.30 am there were only nine of us in all. These included the Captain and Mrs Simpson, Commander Wedderburn, the Organist, myself and four others! No Ratings were present at all. My own family had not yet arrived from *Daedalus*.

During my first week, I had a visitor. I don't know who he was or where he came from. We stood talking on the Parade Ground of the Ratings Living Site.

He suddenly said to me, "What are all these buildings?"

I replied, "That huge building is the Gym. That long one is the NAAFI Heron Club and that building is the YMCA".

Then he said, "What is that little building?"

I replied again, "That is the Chapel."

He stood staring at me and then said quietly, "God must be a very small Person on this Station."

I said, "Yes, I am afraid He is."

He stood still staring at me and then suddenly said, "Well, I must go and Good Luck."

He left me standing there and at that moment I determined and vowed that, before I left Yeovilton, God would be writ large all over Yeovilton and right across the Station.

The Battle was on and the Struggle, the Struggle for the soul of Yeovilton had commenced.

After walking around the Station for a few days, I came to the conclusion that the place was a spiritual wilderness and I wondered just where I should start to organise the Church and the Christian Fellowship here at HMS *Heron*.

During the leave period my family came from Fareham and we moved into No 1, the Wardroom Site. We stored our own furniture in two rooms of Yeovilton Vicarage, an enormous building!

I wrote to the Chaplain of the Fleet and requested the help of another Chaplain. He said that Bernard Briggs, a very old friend of mine, had a year to do before he retired from the Service and would be delighted to come and join the battle. This was a great joy to me. Bernard had followed me in my first ship, HMS *Woolwich*. It was his first ship, too.

Bernard arrived and we surveyed the Station. We decidedto meet in the Chapel three times a day for prayer, from Tuesday to Saturday, every week.

At 9 am we had Morning Prayer together and at 12 noon, we joined in the Litany, or something else and then, in the first Dog watch, we met for Evening Prayer.

We divided the Station up into 10 sections of Squadrons, Units, and so on. We prayed for one each day, covering the station in a fortnight. We then visited the Squadron, Unit or Quarters we had prayed for.

Bernard was still living in the Mess and went home to Box, near Bath, every Sunday after Morning Service and returned on Monday night.

We both did the visiting every forenoon around the airfield and then in the afternoons we visited the Married Quarters and the hundreds of naval families on the Caravan Site. Every Married Quarter and Caravan was systematically visited. After Evening Prayer, we turned our attention to the Ratings' Living Site, Chiefs', Petty Officers' and Ratings' Messes and huts.

I was responsible for arranging and preparing the Sunday service, while Bernard arranged the Chaplain's Hours with the Squadrons and Units, chiefly with film shows.

By the end of the Michaelmas Term, the Sunday morning congregation had increased to about 30 souls.

In November, the Captain wanted to stop weekend leave and have an enormous Remembrance Day Service in one of the hangars. I told him that the whole idea was impossible and would be a disaster, especially for the church. He agreed.

In fact, we could not accommodate the numbers who came along to the Chapel and the same thing happened at the Carol Service at Christmas. It was obvious we wanted a larger building for worship.

During this term, others began to join us at the weekday Evening Prayer in the first Dog watch, while we had Holy Communion at 12.30 pm one day a week; and also the Fellowship was growing in numbers. In spite of all sorts of problems, the Captain, the Commander, the Commanding Officers of the Squadrons, and the Heads of Departments were giving us every possible encouragement and support. We always began by visiting the COs, to let them know we were around and then proceeded to visit the crew rooms, the hangars, the stores, the airfields, the Sick Bay daily, the offices, the civilian transport drivers and workers, the canteens, the school, the gym, the Naafi clubs and everywhere else we could think of. When end of term came, we were more than glad of the Christmas leave.

The Christmas 1960 Leave Period was a happy time for the Wardroom Site, commonly called Skid Row. There were the Shells, the Wedderburns, the Kettles, our great friends the Mackonochies and Captain W. Simpson and his family. The children were home from both day and boarding schools and spent most of the time in each others' houses. Besides a few parties for the adults, we had family parties which included Father Christmas arriving by helicopter for the children. On Boxing Day, which was very cold and bleak, a number of us took the children and went to Glastonbury to climb the Tor. Then we went on to Wookey Hole to explore the underground caves which were quite warm. We were the Attendant's only customers that day!

Bernard Briggs and I stuck to the same relentless routine of praying together three times a day and remembering in our prayers the various parts of the Station. Chaplain's Hours, which usually commenced with a film, were now being asked for and also included the Caravan Site, where we used the Social Club in a Nissen hut about once a fortnight. We now, thanks to the Captain, had our own projector, and so could move about freely at any time. We often put on a film in the Sick Bay during the first Dog watch. Previously, we had to borrow a projector from the School or from one of the Squadrons.

During Sunday services, we now had a choir of Officers, WRNS and Ratings and the numbers during this spring term at the Sunday service were ranging from 45 to 70. The number attending Communion was also going up. Confirmation candidates were coming forward and being prepared. The Sunday School was taking shape and took place in the YMCA, during the latter part of the Church Service.

Before the end of term, I told the Captain that we wanted a larger Chapel.

He said, "Put in for it."

We did.

At the beginning of May, I showed a Billy Graham film, *Souls in Conflict*, to a Squadron, who lived on the far side of the Station. We felt we had rather neglected them. This Squadron was paying off as their particular type of aeroplane was going out of service. The whole Squadron turned up for this film.

It made a tremendous impact and the result was that they asked for a Paying Off Service. They wished to present their Squadron crest to the Chapel. They chose the hymns, read the Lessons, arranged the flowers, read the Naval Prayer, provided two Churchwardens for the Service and acted as hosts at the Coffee Party in the Heron Club afterwards.

They also invited another Squadron.

It was a wonderful service and at the Coffee Party afterwards, the Commanding Officer of the invited Squadron asked me if they could have a similar kind of service as they, too, were paying off. This service took place at the end of May and was another splendid naval occasion. In June, we had a 21st Thanksgiving Service (the Station was 21 years old) taken by the Engineers. They always do things in a big way, and on this occasion it might have been Harvest Festival.

The Admiral and his Staff attended and at his party afterwards he said to me, "You are on to something. Keep it up."

I said, "What about the Admiral and his Staff doing a Sunday?"

He agreed.

Every year, headquarters of the Fleet Air Arm allocate a sum of money for improvements on the five Air Stations.

Every department, of course, puts in for something and this year the Church was added to their list. The Committee at headquarters at Lee-on-Solent comes under the Maintenance Captain. At the time, he was an old shipmate of mine, Captain Pat Bowden. He rang up to tell me that he and his Committee were coming to Yeovilton in a few days time but they didn't want to give any money for the Chapel extension. I had seen the Works Department and they wanted £1,000 for the suggested extension. Pat Bowden was a Sub-Lieutenant in his first ship when I was a young Chaplain in mine.

He said to me, "Play your cards cleverly and boldly, and I will do what I can."

He brought his Committee to the Chapel and introduced me. There were a Commander, a Lieutenant, a Chief Petty Officer, two Petty Officers and two or three Seamen.

The Commander explained that they were really there to provide operational requirements and that the Church was very low on the Amenity List. He said that the Squadrons, the Sports Officer, the School, the Medical Department and the Band all wanted improvements, but they were prepared to listen to my case.

I said, "I am simply appalled that you and your Committee have relegated our Christian Faith to an amenity. I take it that you all consider that the Lord God Almighty is an amenity."

I turned to Captain Bowden and thanked him for bringing his Committee to the Chapel and then I left and played the old naval trick of disappearing for the day. I returned when they were all safely tucked up in their aeroplane and on the way back to Lee.

Two or three days later Captain Pat Bowden rang me up and said, "My dear Parson, you have your Chapel. Well done!"

I thanked him for his help and told him that I should be putting in for a further extension next year. We got it too, although it wasn't completed in my time. HMS *Heron* is now considered to have one of the finest naval

Chapels anywhere.

Besides the Air Display by the Squadrons at the 1961 Station Air Day, there were several hangars given over to Static Displays showing the work of the various departments. In one of the hangars we rigged up a very attractive Chapel with a considerable amount of church furniture; Prayer Desk, Lectern, Communion Rail, Pews, hymn board and a large bookstall. This contained a variety of Bibles, Prayer books, portions of Scripture and paperbacks for sale. There was also some free literature and leaflets giving information about the Royal Navy Lay Readers' Society.

The general interest surprised us. We sold an enormous number of books, every one we had, including all the Bibles. Many visitors used the Chapel both as a resting place and for saying their prayers.

Afterwards we received a number of letters saying how encouraging it was to find the church present in the midst of this exciting Air Station. We felt that all the effort of organisation and the preparation and the humping of all the gear was worthwhile. At the start of the Summer term we produced a Church Calendar for all members of the Station giving general church information and coming events. It meant that the fact of having a Chapel, Chaplains, Church Services, Film Shows and other news went into all Departments and into every Married Quarter and Caravan and brought us to everyone's attention!

The Chapel extension was soon completed. An area had been added to the rear of the building giving us an extra 25 to 35 seats.

The Station routine gave us a short weekend from Saturday noon until Sunday night one week and a long weekend from Friday 4 pm until Sunday night the next.

The various units – Air Divisions, Supply Unit, Medical Branch, and other Departments were responsible for the services on the short weekends, while the three lots of Married Quarters, the Caravan Site and the Admiral's Staff looked after the long weekends. This meant that every Sunday was covered by one section of the Station. This programme was now worked out one term ahead so the Church Calendar for the coming term was made out and delivered in good time. If, by any chance, we missed out a Squadron or unit, they wanted to know why!

In order to bind together the faithful, and also help them, we produced a *Heron* Church Fellowship Prayer card. Numbers of Officers, Ratings and Wrens took these cards which provided a prayer for each day of the week. This meant that we were all united in thought day by day.

Thanks to the co-operation of the Master-At-Arms, we had a large Notice Board erected near the main gate of the Living Site. It proclaimed; Next Sunday, The Morning Service will be led by . . . and here we changed the name each week: The WRNS, The Air Division, The Juniors, 766 Squadron, 893 Squadron, 700 Squadron, The Supply Unit, The Medical Staff, The Admiral's Staff, The Caravan Site, The Married Quarters,

Wardroom Site, Married Quarters – Ilchester.

All was not plain sailing, of course, and we seemed to be in continual trouble. In the words of Archbishop Fisher "the work was both exhilarating and exhausting."

*The Commissioning Service of 899 Squadron at HMS Heron, RNAS, Yeovilton in 1961. Right; Commander Jack Carter and, left, the Reverend Lovell Pocock, during his last commission before his retirement from the Service in 1963.*

The congregation on Sundays now consisted of a growing number of regulars plus the particular Unit leading the Service. Throughout the term, both Bernard Briggs and I continued the daily visiting of the Air Station every morning. Chaplain's Hours and the visiting of the Married Quarters and Caravan Site went on relentlessly. It was my routine to visit the Caravan Site every Tuesday afternoon, commencing at 2 pm.

I would arrive at exactly the same time as the Butcher and say to him, "It is easy for you, as everybody wants what you have to sell, but I find that there are only a few who want my wares!"

At the end of September 1961, Bernard Briggs retired. This was a great loss to me personally and also to the Station and Service. He had been a splendid colleague, friend and adviser. On one occasion, I had been sent for by Captain Simpson who was strongly opposed to a suggestion I had made to him. I informed the Captain that I could not give way.

He dismissed me from his office. It was 12 noon and time for our midday prayers which Bernard took. Afterwards, he could see that I was still very worried about the matter.

He said, "For heaven's sake come over to the Mess. We've said our prayers. We must leave something for the Lord to do."

Just before he left Yeovilton, Bernard said to me. "There is one thing I can never understand."

I said, "What's that Bernard?"

He replied, "I have been watching you for about 25 years, and I can never understand why their Lordships at Admiralty took you on and turned me down!"

I said, "Your engine is running, you're wasting petrol. Good-bye."

*Bernard Briggs had applied to join the Royal Navy in 1934 and was turned down.*

*I applied in 1935, was accepted and joined in January 1936.*

*In 1937 Bernard tried again and was accepted, joining in 1938. He took passage to Malta in August 1938 to relieve me as Chaplain of HMS Woolwich. We had two days together before I departed for the UK.*

That very afternoon, the Captain sent for me and as I went along I said to myself, "What now?"

On arrival at his office he said pleasantly "Regarding our talk this morning, I am sorry. I was wrong and you were right, so carry on."

For the rest of the term I was on my own, and I did my very best to keep the whole show going.

In the east end of the Chapel there were two stained glass windows, one above the other in one light, with a sheet of frosted glass between. One window was in memory of a Squadron and the other in memory of the WRNS who had lost their lives in the war.

I went to the Captain to discuss them. I told him that as windows they weren't bad but they had no business to be at the east end of the Chapel for us all to look at all the time.

He said, "Why not?"

I replied, "Stained glass windows were placed in the east end and in all the walls to teach the Christian Faith by picture before people could read. These particular windows of the Squadron and the WRNS teach us nothing."

He said, "What do you suggest?"

I said, "We must have Faith in the East wall and these two windows can be placed elsewhere. We must have, in some form, the Cross."

He agreed with me enthusiastically and said, "Let's get on with it."

A representative from a stained glass window firm, with headquarters in the east end of London, visited us and listened to our suggestions. These were that he should design three lights. He was to bring in a Pilot, Crewman and a Carrier in one; a member of the WRNS, a mechanic and an aircraft in another and in the centre, a Crucifixion scene, not necessarily historic but possibly futuristic.

Just as the man was leaving the Captain's office, the Captain said to him, "Do a Resurrection scene too," and he left.

When the designs arrived the Captain sent for me and we agreed that the two outside ones were good and that we would ask for comment from many of those interested. These people agreed that they were fine and that they should be accepted as they stood. Regarding the Crucifixion scene and the Resurrection Captain Simpson said to me, "I have decided to have the Resurrection scene."

I replied, "You said that you accept the advice of your Chaplain. I am not dogmatic about this particular design of the Crucifixion, but the Crucifixion must come into the window."

The Captain said, "I am the Captain of this Station and as we aviators believe the Lord is alive, I have decided on this one."

I said, "Other people besides aviators believe that the Lord is still alive. Your decision is taken against my advice," and I left his office.

My explanation for wanting the Crucifixion in the centre window was quite simple, really. The Cross, the Roman way of killing men, shows us God's love. 'For God so loved the world that He gave His only begotten Son.' 'While we were yet sinners Christ died for us.' 'He loved me and gave Himself for me.'

I said, "The Cross reveals God's love. The Resurrection reveals God's power. Power, without love is hopeless. Look at history. Look at Russia. Look at Nazi Germany."

I said to the Captain, "When you come to Communion; when you kneel at the Lord's Table; when you receive the Sacrament; you are thanking Him for His love, not His power. You hear the words, 'Take and eat this in remembrance that Christ died for thee'."

The Captain said, "Thank you, Lovell. You were right to hold out and I am glad you did."

I said, "I could do nothing else."

We shook hands and I left him.

Both designs were returned with instructions to produce one from these two. The result was the Risen Lord over His Cross. I was quite happy about this one but before the order had been placed, Captain Simpson left the Station and was relieved by Captain Rodney Carver. He sent for me and said that I could do as I liked. I said I should like to stick to the latest design and when this one was put on show it was agreed that we should go ahead with it.

The cost of the windows was raised by private subscription from individuals and firms. A list of the names has been placed on a brass tablet in the Chancel of the Chapel.

Prince Bernhard of the Netherlands was to fly in to Yeovilton, change aircraft and then fly on somewhere else. Captain Simpson decided that while he was in Yeovilton, he would give him coffee in the Control Tower. He sent for the Supply Officer, Stores, Commander Graham Chambers and told him what was happening.

He said, "In your stores you have a spare set of fluted bone china".

Commander Graham Chambers said, "No Sir, I haven't. The Chaplain has it."

The Captain said, "The Chaplain has no right to have it."

Commander Chambers replied, "Yes, he has, Sir. Naval Captains and Chaplains with over 22 years seniority are allowed fluted china, a silver teapot and silver candlesticks. He has the bone china but not the silver teapot or the silver candlesticks."

The Captain said, "Have the book with all this in it sent to me."

Graham Chambers answered, "Very good, Sir."

He left the Captain's Office and sent him the book. The Supply Officer, Stores, heard no more about the affair and I, of course, knew nothing about it until it was all over. Then I heard about it from Graham Chambers.

The Prince of the Netherlands arrived, was met by the Captain and taken to the Control Tower, where he was offered a cup of coffee. There was no fluted china so the Prince had to drink his coffee out of a thick Service cup! If the Captain was so keen on the Prince drinking from fluted china why didn't he send for his own set?

The Captain never mentioned this incident to me. It was considered by the Mess to be a huge joke, especially as the Prince had to drink out of a thick cup!

In mid-November 1961, the Chaplain of the Fleet informed Captain Simpson that he would be sending the Rev. Jim Sharpe to Yeovilton as Assistant Chaplain and that he would be coming from RNAS Anthorn in Westmorland. If possible he wanted him to have a Married Quarter, as he had been unaccompanied at Anthorn. His family were at Weymouth.

Accommodation was duly allocated, and his family settled in well in their Married Quarter at Ilchester. They made a good contribution to the church, while Mrs Sharpe was much appreciated in the Quarters. He remained with me until June 1963, when the Chaplain of the Fleet drafted him to the Naval Base in the Persian Gulf.

So many people were involved in the church life at Yeovilton. Some are remembered well. There was Captain Willie Simpson with whom I had many battles, but who was always prepared to listen and was very helpful. Captain Rodney Carver, was such a strength to me; I Christened his infant daughter, Victoria, in Podimore Parish Church. Podimore was part of the Station, as was also the parish of Yeovilton. Victoria became the hundredth Christian in Podimore. The population was 99 until her arrival!

One incident in the Station Chapel illustrates Captain Carver's happy and thoughtful approach to life. He used to sit in the front row in Chapel, and the choir stalls were at right angles facing inwards. One Sunday, it just happened that our younger son, Stephen, aged nine, was the only boy in the front row of the choir, and he was sitting at the far end near the altar. When the collection was taken, it was obvious to Captain Carver that Stephen, who had searched his pockets in vain, had no collection. The Captain took a coin from his own pocket, flicked it along the choir pew and it came to rest right in front of Stephen. He gave a lovely smile to the Captain who replied with a merry twinkle.

Commander Michael Blake had a great love of horses and ran the Saddle Club and his voice could be heard sounding 'Whey, Woa' all over the Station. I can still hear Commander Ian Wedderburn's voice coming over the Station Tannoy, when all the Officers (including myself) were lined up at the Main Gate to greet the Admiral. "Will the Chaplain kindly remove his dog from the Main Gate before the Admiral arrives." The Admiral and our dog, Bimbo, passed each other while I stood fast.

Commander Randle Kettle was the 'best dressed officer on the Station'. On one occasion I saw his dog coming out of the Wardroom galley with a whole joint in his mouth.

I said, "Look, Randle, he's got a whole joint."

"So he has," said Randle, "but it's only a stale one. Your Bimbo comes out with fresh ones."

It was for Commander Jack Carter's Squadron that I took the Commissioning Service. I also baptised his two boys, who were, in Prayer Book language, of riper years. Commander Jim Mackonochie was a stanchion in our church life as well as being such a good neighbour and mess mate, and I must mention his dear wife, Betty. They became good friends of ours and still are. Their younger son, Charles, often slept in our spare bedroom if his parents were going out. On one occasion, when I don't think we even knew he was coming, we passed him on the stairs and he just said, "I'm turning in!"

There was Pete Reynolds, the Commanding Officer of 766 Squadron. He was the leader of 'Fred's Five', Yeovilton's aerobatic display team; because of this he became our younger son, Stephen's, hero.

One Sunday at church I had preached on 'Sunday' and said that it would appear that the majority of Officers in the Ilchester Married Quarters spent Sunday forenoon cleaning their cars instead of worshipping the Lord. Pete Reynolds was in the congregation, and was heard to say, as he left the chapel, "I am thankful that I did not clean my car this morning; I usually do."

Commander Tony Shaw was the Commanding Officer of our first Divisional Service, when his 700 Squadron was paying off. We really started something that Sunday.

Commander Mike Hayward, for whom nothing was too much trouble, was another fine leader. He always led the Engineers' Sunday, and received massive support from his ratings. They would do anything for him.

The Supply Officer, Commander Graham Chambers led the church choir, and when our civilian organist, Mr Rowe, commonly called 'Ginger', was unable to be present, Graham Chambers took over. These two between them persuaded Admiralty to purchase a new organ for the Station. And, of course, there were numerous Ratings who went out of their way to help me and our Church.

The following 'Fact and Faith' films were shown and often those who watched wanted to see them more than once. They included *The God of the Atom; The Prior Claim; The God of Creation; The Voice of the Deep; Time and Eternity; Hidden Treasures; Dust or Destiny; The Three Clocks* . . . and many others.

Evangelistic films included *Oiltown USA,* a film based on Billy Graham's Mission to Houston; *Souls in Conflict,* based on Billy Graham's Harringay, London, Mission in 1954; *The Shield of Faith* based on the South Wales air disaster. Others included the *Life of John Wesley; Life of Simon Peter.*

A meeting of the Heron Church Fellowship was held weekly and usually consisted of hymn singing, prayers and a talk. We often had guest speakers. The addresses were varied; devotional, teaching and we also had question time. These meetings were held in the YMCA, a place which provided a canteen and various quiet rooms, in contrast to the Heron Club which was noisy. The Manager throughout my time was Mr Spurling, who made a valuable contribution to the life of the church and the Station.

Two Vixen Squadrons had their home at Yeovilton. When the Carriers commissioned, 892 Squadron joined, HMS *Eagle* and 893 Squadron joined HMS *Ark Royal.* Both these Squadrons sailed for the Far East and, some weeks after their departure, I received letters from the two Chaplains, Will Sandey of *Eagle* and Kenneth Evans of *Ark Royal.* They both said that they had been approached by the Commanding Officers of these two

Squadrons, offering to lead the Sunday Morning service and would I give them some advice on the matter. In my reply I stated what had happened at Yeovilton. The result was that these two Squadrons were both involved with leading the Church services in their carriers.

It seemed to us at Yeovilton most remarkable that these two HM Ships, which were visiting most of the countries in the Far East were, in fact, fulfilling the words which we so often said in prayers for all those serving in the carriers. 'In all their ways, enable them truly and godly to serve Thee, and by their Christian example to set forth Thy Glory throughout the world.'

At Hounsden Camp, at Yeovil, Army Personnel were trained as Drivers for cars, trucks and lorries by the Royal Army Service Corps. One evening in 1961, the Commander of Yeovilton, Michael Blake and five Station Officers, were invited to dinner by his opposite number at Hounsden Camp, Major Joe Mills, and his Officers.

During the course of the evening, Major Mills said to Michael Blake that there was one Naval Chaplain he wished to locate; the one who took his wedding service in Malta in 1948. His name was the Rev. Lovell Pocock.

Our Commander said, "Come to church at Yeovilton next Sunday and you will meet him. He is our Station Chaplain."

The service started, I gave out the first hymn and then a little later, I happened to glance down the Chapel and saw, with a broad grin across his face, Joe Mills, his wife Sheila, their five children and Commander Michael Blake. Later in the service, I was able to welcome an 'old ship' and his wife whom I had truly married in Malta, and their five children, saying what a pleasure it was for us at *Heron* to have the CO and his family from Hounsden with us for church. I was also able to mention that most of the roads in the district were clogged, practically day and night, with literally scores of L Drivers in all manner of transport with Hounsden printed on them!

After the Service, we had the usual coffee party in the *Heron* Club. Joe Mills told me what a thrill it was to be worshipping with the Royal Navy again. He added that he would like to come every Sunday, but that as he was the only Army Officer to attend their Camp Service at Hounsden, he had to set a Christian example to the few who did come. The few included one Non-Commissioned Officer and a few men under training. His confession seemed to me to be a wonderful testimony to the witness of the Church in the Royal Navy.

During 1962, I gathered a number of Officers, Ratings and WRNS for Confirmation. I took them all to Wedmore Parish Church one evening, to be confirmed by Dr Henderson, the Bishop of Bath and Wells. After the Confirmation we all went to the Town Hall with scores of other candidates from the surrounding villages. The Bishop, much to the dismay of all these other people, spent nearly all his time with my naval party. In fact, I did tell him that we were only a few of his flock, but he didn't leave us. The result of this visit was that he came to Yeovilton Trafalgar Night Dinner as my Guest and the following year, he came as the chief guest and speaker. He had been a Naval Chaplain during the war. As a result of this contact with Yeovilton, he occasionally travelled in *Heron* helicopters on his journeys around the Diocese. We had another Confirmation at Wedmore in 1963, which this time was taken by the Rt Rev. T. Parsons, Bishop of Taunton.

During the year, we had a weekend visit from the Rt Rev. Stanley Betts, the Bishop to the Forces, and he stayed with the Captain, who kindly had a supper party for him on the Saturday. On the Sunday, he celebrated Communion. He then preached at the Morning service which was led by 899 Squadron and, after the Coffee Party in the *Heron* Club, they laid on a party for him in the Wardroom. We had him to lunch after allowing him time to rest and then he met a number of the *Heron* Church Fellowship in our Quarter for a meeting and supper.

On Monday, after Morning Prayer in the Chapel, he spent the whole forenoon with the Squadrons without me. I then took him to the Chiefs' POs' and WRNS' Messes before lunch in the Wardroom.

In the afternoon, he addressed a gathering of wives at Ilchester Married Quarters and had tea with them.

After supper he addressed a large number of Officers and wives in the Wardroom. It was a very moving occasion which showed considerable support for the work of the church on the Station. At the end of his address, he invited questions. I remember one in particular!

"What is a Suffragan Bishop?" someone asked.

"Someone who votes for the Boss!" he replied to laughter from the audience.

On Tuesday morning, we had Morning Prayer and then he left us, having made a tremendous impact and another forward step for the Gospel in the Fleet Air Arm.

One of the most faithful of our supporters, in all activities at the Station Chapel, was Lieutenant Commander Bill Mitford. He had helped us to the limit of his power and was a splendid advertisement and force for the Christian Gospel on the Station. He left us and the Royal Navy to train for Ordination in the Ministry of the Church of England. *He is now, in 1984, a Vicar and Chaplain to HM Prison at Shepton Mallet in Somerset.*

On the Saturday of the Air Division's Sunday the WRNS Metereological Officers were in the chapel arranging the flowers for their Sunday service. They were really doing things on an elaborate scale and I remarked on the expense involved. They said that money was no object. They had plenty and there was plenty over for the collection on the Sunday morning.

"You see," they said, "some of the Air Division won't be there and so this is their Conscience Money."

During the week before the Supply Unit's Sunday Service, I happened to go into their main office and read their Notice Board. Under the heading, 'Our Sunday at the Station Church', I read 'The Supply Officer suggests that all in the Unit contribute the sum of three pence towards the flowers for the Chapel. Those unwilling to do this should see the Supply Officer and it will cost them six pence!'

Once a term, thanks to the help, co-operaton and encouragement of the Commander, I was able to have a Chaplain's At Home in the Wardroom for the benefit of the Officers.

On these evenings I had either a special speaker or a good Christian film. These occasions were very well attended and kept the Christian faith before the Officers, the leaders of the Station, and the Fleet Air Arm.

There was a young Naval Airman on the Station whom I was instrumental in winning for the Christian Faith and who, after several weeks of careful tending, suddenly disappeared. Then, one day two or three months after his disappearance from Chapel life, I was coming out of the Chapel with Bernard Briggs at mid-day when I saw him.

I called out, "Hey! Where have you been all these weeks?"

He said, "I've joined the Pentecostals."

I didn't speak for a few seconds.

He asked, "You believe in Pentecost, don't you?"

"Yes," I replied, "And I believe in Good Friday and Easter Day too."

The lad moved on and Bernard said to me, "If you go into many Parish churches at 11 o'clock on a Sunday morning, you wouldn't know that there had been any Pentecost."

While I was at *Daedalus*, before coming to *Heron*, I had managed to get a Lectern with an Eagle instead of the usual one which was rather like a Commander's Table. My successor at *Daedalus* didn't need the Eagle so I offered to relieve him of it for *Heron*. This I did and again it took the place of the wooden one.

The Hymn Board at *Heron* would only take three numbers and so, if we had four hymns in the Service, only three could be put up. I visited the Dockyard Store at Portsmouth and found a very fine one of oak. I signed for it and discovered it had come from the Battleship, HMS *King George V.* We had a small brass plaque added to the board stating where it came from.

Our daughter, Susan, joined the Hospital for Sick Children in January 1963, the bad winter. Soon after her arrival, she posted a parcel to us from the Post Office in Southampton Row, London.

The Post Master looked at the address and said, "Yeovilton! I've never heard of the place before but on the radio this morning the announcer said that it was the coldest place in England!"

During the following summer of 1963, I realised that my own time was running out at HMS *Heron* at Yeovilton. The Captain informed me that my relief had been appointed. He was the Rev. Chandos Morgan who would follow me, when I left the Station in September for the nearby Hampshire Parish of Martin and civilian life within the Church of England.

On Thursdays, I often went to HMS *Osprey* at Portland with Major Brian Tatchell (R.A.Rtd) where we took out a naval dinghy and sailed in the Channel. On one occasion, when we had returned to Yeovilton, we had tea in our Married Quarter garden. This quarter was the last in the row and the garden was surrounded by a high wire fence. Brian Tatchell remarked, "It is quite like the old days." He had been a P.O.W. in Germany.

So, I prepared to leave behind my life in the Church within the Royal Navy and all the friends I had made over what seemed like a lifetime since I first joined the Service at Devonport in January 1936.

On September 6th 1963, the Wardroom Officers of HMS *Heron* entertained me at a farewell dinner. At the end of the meal the President, the Commander, invited me to tell the 120 Officers present what sort of a place I was going to.

"I am going to a village called Martin, of about 500 inhabitants; Martin is called Winterbourne Bishop in W. H. Hudson's Book *A Shepherd's Life,*" I said. "It is 12 miles south-west of Salisbury and about 40 miles from Yeovilton. There has been no Vicar for five years. No one would go. They can't get anyone and very few folk attend the church, about a dozen I am told. There are six fine bells but they are never rung or used. There is a Church School less than a hundred yards from the Church but not one child attends the Church. There is no Sunday School. The Church is dirty with but few old books and the heating system is broken. The Churchyard is overgrown and the walls broken down, while many of the tombstones are loose and dangerous. The Vicarage has been sold and the new one is only partly built. That's about all, but we are going!"

There was dead silence.

Then someone called out, "What do you intend to do?"

As they all looked at me for an answer, I said, "I don't know what I am going to do but this I do know. 'I shall not cease from mental fight; nor shall my sword, my Bible, sleep in my hand, Till we have built Jerusalem, God's home,

In England's green and pleasant land', in this case Martin."

Whether it was the way I spoke or what I said, I don't know, but to my astonishment and surprise my words were greeted with loud cheering and clapping.

The Commander said that the Chaplain leaves for his small village with the best wishes of the whole Station and of the whole Navy.

Then, turning to me he said, "Have you a last message for us all?"

I said, "Yes; Captain Hawkins's Command to his ship's company. 'Serve God daily'. Say your prayers daily."

And I left them.

311

So ended my years of Service at Yeovilton and in the Royal Navy. It was a great loss to me personally and to our whole family, not only to be leaving Yeovilton but this wonderful Service with its rich friendships, its great charity, its disciplined approach to life, its gaiety, its tremendous sense of purpose and devotion to duty. And finally, above all, its sterling Christian example and practice.

We moved over to the partly built Vicarage at Martin on September 18th 1963; where I was instituted as the Vicar a few days later.

Since our marriage in 1942, we had had over 30 homes, which included Married Quarters, houses, furnished and unfurnished, flats, furnished and unfurnished, apartments, rooms and hotels.

We had stuck together as a family and we wouldn't have had it otherwise. To use the words of Scripture, 'Here we have no continuing city,' probably sums up our experience and pilgrimage.

Our very last night at Yeovilton, when we were all packed up and ready to move, we heard a tremendous screech of brakes on the A303, about a hundred yards away. This was the main road that ran right through the Station. A few minutes later, someone arrived carrying our dog, Bimbo, who had been hit a glancing blow by a passing car. He was bruised but quite lively. At that moment, Captain Carver came in to bid us farewell. He saw Bimbo.

I said, "How very unlucky to be hit on his last night at Yeovilton."

Captain Carver said, "Unlucky? You mean lucky. He has been crossing that road now for three years and this is the first time he has been hit!"

Bimbo survived and spent many happy years on the Martin Downs, on and around the Norfolk Broads, and at Ringwould before he went to his happy hunting ground at a ripe old age!

# CHAPTER XV

## Conclusion

*I had been over to Martin earlier in the summer.*
*I heard one farmer say to another, "Well, what do you think?" The other*
*replied, after looking me up and down, "Let's give him a try!"*

For my Induction at Martin, about a dozen friends came over from Yeovilton to support me on this non-naval occasion. I was being launched into the cold world outside the Service. The team included two Chaplains, the late Rev. Bill Sandey and the faithful Bernard Briggs. Captain Rodney Carver, the Captain of Yeovilton, had hoped to be present, but was prevented from coming.

After the service, I introduced Bernard Briggs to the Bishop of Salisbury, the late Joe Fison and Bernard told him that he would like to come to his Diocese.

The Bishop said, "I have plenty of clergymen and have no place for you."

About six weeks after my own Induction I was at a cocktail party in Martin. There I met a Colonel who was one of the Churchwardens of the parishes of Teffont and Dinton.

He said to me, "We can't get a Rector. The Bishop of Salisbury can't get one. The Bishop of Sherborne can't get one. Nobody can get one for us."

I said, "I can get a first class Rector for you any time you like. Tomorrow if you wish."

The wheels began to turn and I put him in touch with Bernard Briggs.

Sometime in the Spring of 1964 I attended Bernard's Induction by the Bishop of Salisbury at Teffont on a very wet night. No one knew either Bernard or myself and we felt we were breaking into a closed shop!

At the proper moment, the Bishop mounted the steps to the pulpit and gave out his text. 'The Lord is my Light and my Salvation.' As he said the word 'Salvation' all the lights went out and the Church was plunged into darkness.

The Bishop roared out, "Churchwarden, light the candles on the altar."

The poor chap had only just put them out, but striking a series of matches, he stumbled back to the altar and lit two candles.

Again, the Bishop called, "Leave one there and bring the other one to the pulpit and hold it for me so that I can read my sermon."

Just as the Bishop finished his exhortation all the lights came on again!

About 15 months later, I passed the Bishop in the street in Salisbury.

He called out, "Lovell, I can never thank you enough for bringing Bernard

Briggs to this Diocese. He has performed wonders in his two villages."

When I returned to Martin, I rang Bernard and said, "Keep it up. You are doing a good job and I am basking in your glory."

In fact Bernard's work at Teffont and Dinton reminded me of John Whitfield's Journal which I was reading.

In 1738 he wrote, 'preached to a large congregation in Upper Deal and all Deal seems to be in a holy flame'.

Instead of Deal it was Teffont and Dinton, and it seemed that Bernard Briggs was doing the same in his villages. The whole place was catching fire.

In the summer of 1965, I attended the Air Day at HMS *Heron*, RNAS, Yeovilton. While walking round, I thought I recognised a man I had served with in HMS *Ceres* in the years 1939/40. Not wishing to embarrass him, I turned away. Later that afternoon, I was tapped on the shoulder from behind, and a man said to me, "Does HMS *Ceres* mean anything to you? My name is Bill May and you invited me to your bungalow in Singapore after you had left the *Ceres*." . . . We still keep in touch.

While I was Vicar of Martin, I was appointed Officiating Minister of RAF Old Sarum, thanks to the good offices of Major General Billy Barton and with the approval of the Bishop of Salisbury, Dr Joe Fison.

In our village there lived a retired Air Chief Marshall. One day he said to me, "The CO of Old Sarum was always an RAF Officer. For some reason, Officers from the Royal Navy and the Army are included, this means that the RAF only come in every third time. Now there is a Major General from the Royal Marines. Whatever next?"

In the summer of 1966 I went to see the Bishop and told him that Martin needed another Vicar as it was time for me to go.

He said, "You have only just come."

I said, "I am only used to staying in a place for about three years. I have finished."

He offered me two villages about 25 miles away from Martin.

I said, "No thank you. We love Martin and I should always be running back. We have all learnt so much from these wonderful village folk and so I must go far away."

Shortly after this I was offered the living of Ringwould, a village overlooking the Goodwin Sands near Deal, which I accepted.

My last Sunday was January 1st 1967. The Bishop, his wife and four children, all came unexpectedly to Matins and sat in a pew. In fact it was his fourth visit to Martin during our three years there. As we said Goodbye afterwards he handed me a little note in which he said, that months ago, his family had all decided that they would attend my last service at Martin. He added that something remarkable had been going on there and he wanted to be in on it, even at the end. I can't speak for the people of Martin but our years there were an education and a heart-warming experience for us.

I cannot close this particular journal without a mention of 'The Brethren', my brother Chaplains serving in the Royal Navy.

We really saw very little of each other but, in spite of differences of Churchmanship, there was an invisible bond which bound us together in a most remarkable way. Naturally, we saw more of each other in peace time than during the war. I personally was away from the United Kingdom for nearly five years of the war, at sea or overseas, and hardly met any of the four to five hundred RNVR Chaplains recruited for the duration.

The only time we saw some members of our Branch for a few days was at the annual Chaplains' Conference, when about 15 to 20 of us assembled at either Dowdeswell Court, Cheltenham or Amport Houses, Andover.

Because every individual is a different personality, each one's approach to the job, the role, of the Naval Chaplain, will be different and will have a distinct emphasis.

Nevertheless, whatever the Churchmanship, there are two inescapables; Duty to God – Praying, Duty to Man – Visiting, with the overriding purpose, as I have stated earlier, of planting the Message and the Way of the Cross in the heart of every Sailor, every Royal Marine, every Naval Airman, Aviator, every Royal Marine Bandsman and every member of the WRNS.

Several of my brother Chaplains and other men of God have said things to me which have become indelibly stamped on my mind.

A senior Chaplain, who called on me soon after I joined my first ship, said, as he left me, "Remember, young man, that the most important time for you in the week, after you've said your prayers, is when you address the men at Sunday Morning service."

A chaplain, who died during the war, said to me quite casually one day, "If I'm not reading Evening Prayer in the Ship's Chapel at 6 or 6.30 pm, I always have to say it at about half past five. If I leave it any later, my prayers and my meditation are second class because I am either too tired or too busy."

A Clergyman who once wrote to me ended his letter by saying, "I am giving you a sentence from one of Bishop Stephen Neill's books. Include it in your daily routine. 'Two hours on your knees praying and four hours on your feet visiting'."

On being introduced to the Captain by the Commander when I joined my first ship, the Captain said to me, "You are very young and very green aren't you?"

I replied, "Yes Sir."

He went on, "Besides being your Captain, I am also your Churchwarden. Don't make too many mistakes because you must always be right. That will be all Commander."

As I left the Captain's cabin, I determined firstly to do my best as

315

Chaplain and, secondly, not to let my Captain and Churchwarden down.

Chaplains of the Royal Navy come and go. Generations of seamen rise and fall. The ships whether driven by the wind, or steam, or nuclear power, pass in the night.

The world-wide church is a great multitude which no man can number. The Church of the Royal Navy is but a microcosm of the whole. And it is to the whole that the Eternal Gospel is committed, preaching that Christ died for our sins and rose again; that his love and presence are with us until the Kingdom of this world becomes the Kingdom of our Lord and Saviour, Jesus Christ. Amen.